英语教师职业技能

Professional Skills of English Teachers

主　编　曾小珊
副主编　卢秋萍　汪　丽
审　校　鲁绪峰　邱洪杰

西安交通大学出版社
XI'AN JIAOTONG UNIVERSITY PRESS

图书在版编目（CIP）数据

英语教师职业技能 / 曾小珊主编；卢秋萍，汪丽副主编. --西安：西安交通大学出版社，2024.12.
ISBN 978-7-5693-3915-4

Ⅰ. H319.3
中国国家版本馆CIP数据核字第2024197FJ5号

英语教师职业技能
Professional Skills of English Teachers

主　　编　曾小珊
责任编辑　蔡乐芊
责任校对　高海梦
装帧设计　任加盟

出版发行　西安交通大学出版社
（西安市兴庆南路1号　邮政编码710048）
网　　址　http://www.xjtupress.com
电　　话　（029）82668357　82667874（市场营销中心）
（029）82668315（总编办）
传　　真　（029）82668280
印　　刷　西安五星印刷有限公司

开　　本　889 mm×1194 mm　1/16　**印张**　24.75　**字数**　748千字
版次印次　2024年12月第1版　2024年12月第1次印刷
书　　号　ISBN 978-7-5693-3915-4
定　　价　68.00元

如发现印装质量问题，请与本社市场营销中心联系。
订购热线：（029）82665248　（029）82667874
投稿热线：（029）82665371

前　言
Preface

百年大计，教育为本；教育大计，教师为本。教师是立教之本、兴教之源。习近平总书记强调，强教必先强师。要把加强教师队伍建设作为建设教育强国最重要的基础工作来抓，健全中国特色教师教育体系，大力培养造就一支师德高尚、业务精湛、结构合理、充满活力的高素质专业化教师队伍。新征程上，教师教育要坚持以习近平新时代中国特色社会主义思想为指导，以教育家精神为引领，加快构建高质量的教师培养体系，创新拓展教师教育发展路径，不断为教育强国提供更多更高素质的优秀教师。

师范教育是培养教师、服务教育现代化的重要力量。本教材从省级一流课程、英语师范专业核心课程——“英语教师职业技能”的教学过程中积累而来，主要体现以下几个特点：

第一，以立德树人为根本，将课程思政内容融入教材。本教材将“四有”好老师内容选入其中，并结合基础教育教学特点，将思政元素归类为道德品德素养、文化意识和教育情怀三个主要方面，并融入教学过程当中，引导未来的英语基础教育工作者牢记习近平总书记嘱托，练好本领，践行“四有”好老师标准，为国家基础教育贡献力量。

第二，坚持以学生为中心，以问题为导向。在教材编写的过程中，在章节中设置任务活动，便于实施课堂互动，改变教师“一言堂”现象，凸显学生主体性，引导学生树立问题意识，启发学生思维；在每章节结尾处设计讨论问题和实践活动，引发学生课堂内外讨论和思考，培养学生的小组合作意识、团队精神，特别是批判性思维能力，加强、巩固对课文内容的学习和理解。

第三，坚持教学理论与实践相结合，突出实践原则，体现教材的实用性和技能性。突出“学中做”和“做中学”，设置案例分析、任务、讨论、实践等活动，并在任务和实践活动中设置一些与国家教师资格考试相关的试题和案例，进一步强化学生对教学技能的实践和应用，提高实践活动的质量。

第四，坚持与时俱进，将与人工智能时代的技术变革相关的内容编入教材，为学生提供最前沿的人工智能知识、技能培训和实施案例，使其在教学中会用、用好数智技术，提升数字素养和人工智能素养，保障智慧教育的质量。

第五，高校教师与中学教师合作编审，凸显教材的时代性和实用性。在校（高校）–校（中学）融合、协同育人环境下，依托“英语教师职业技能”省级一流课程成果，与中学合作，借鉴中学英语教师的实践经验，持续改进教材。

本教材主要面向在校师范生和即将走上教学岗位的新任教师，同时也希望为一线教师提供一定的参考，为教师提升英语教学水平提供启示。

因水平有限，在编写过程中难免有疏漏之处，敬请批评指正！

编者

2024 年 8 月

目 录
Contents

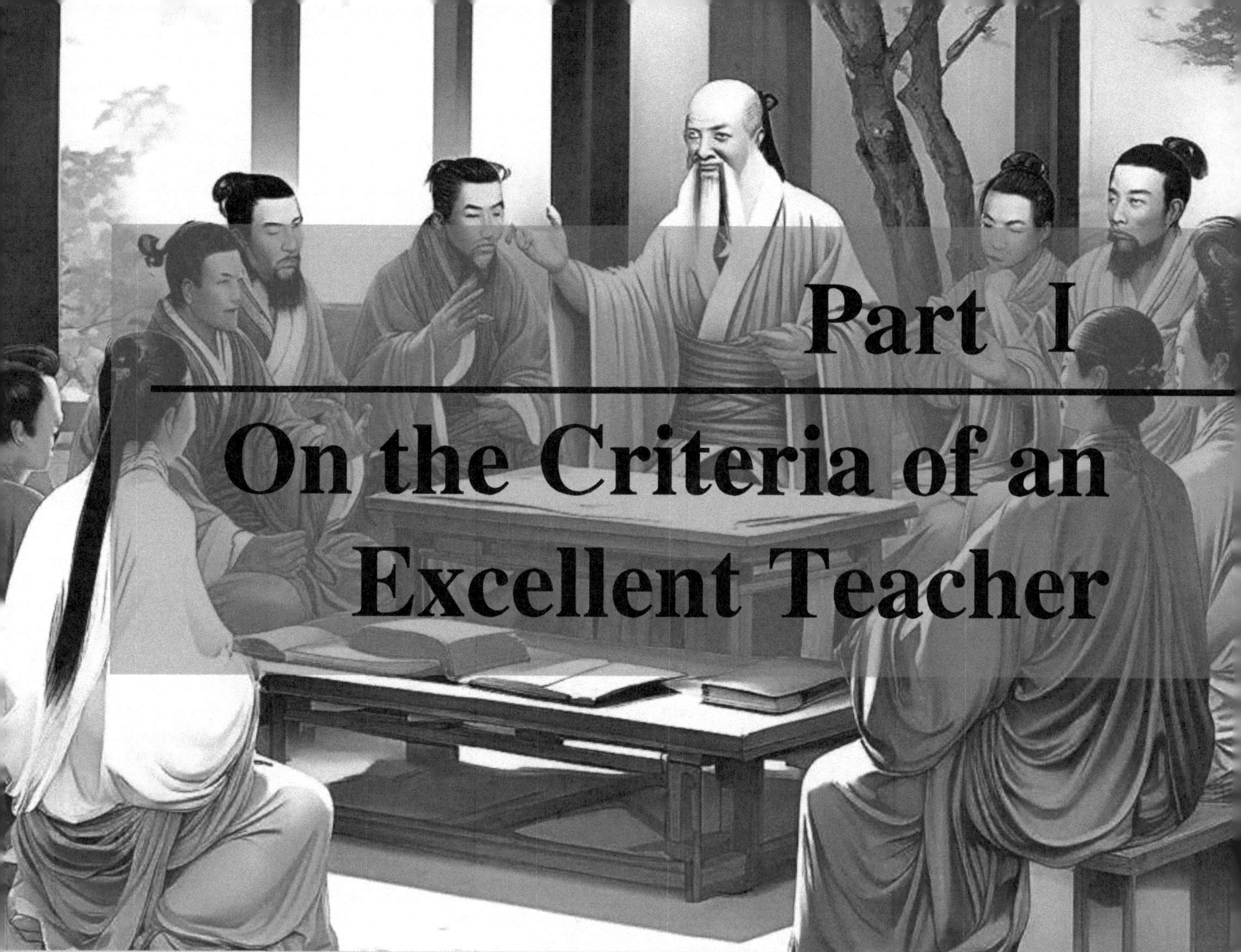

Part I

On the Criteria of an Excellent Teacher

When the ruler himself is upright, his commands are obeyed without being given. But when he is not upright, they are not obeyed, even though orders are given.

—Confucius

Confucius, a Chinese philosopher, educator, and political thinker, lived during the Spring and Autumn period (551–479 BCE). He is widely regarded as the founder of Confucianism, a philosophical and ethical system that has had a profound influence on Chinese culture and society for over two millennia. Confucius's educational philosophy remains highly relevant and influential to this day.

Chapter 1

How to Be a Good Teacher

Objectives

Upon completion of this chapter, you should be able to:

- Understand Xi Jinping's views about qualified teachers
- Appreciate Chinese and foreign views about good teachers

Discussion Questions

If asked to give four words about your understanding of a good teacher, what are they? And why?

Do you want to be a middle school English teacher in the future? Why or why not?

1.1 Xi Jinping's Four Criteria for Teachers

The cause of the CPC and the nation calls for a sizable pool of good teachers. Every teacher should improve his or her performance. On the eve of Teachers' Day in 2014, Xi Jinping proposed four criteria for teachers to the teachers and students of Beijing Normal University. That is, they should have ideals and beliefs, moral integrity, knowledge, and compassion. He reiterated these criteria at a meeting with teachers and students of Peking University in 2018 and again, at the National Education Conference. These criteria have defined the new expectations and requirements for teachers in the new era (Compilation team, 2022).

1.1.1 Ideals and Beliefs

Being true to the long-term goal of communism and the shared ideal of socialism with the Chinese characteristics is the foremost quality of a good teacher.

> ***Quote from Xi Jinping***
>
> *Lofty ideals and beliefs guide teachers in cultivating students as seeds for the future.*
>
> *—Speech at the meeting with teachers and students of Beijing Normal University, September 9, 2014*

A good teacher not only teaches knowledge but also cultivates ideals. Han Yu said, "A teacher communicates beliefs, imparts knowledge, and clears confusion." It is the foremost mission of a teacher to cultivate ideals, and those who only impart knowledge and answer questions are not good enough. Good teachers are expected to take the cultivation of ideals as their most important responsibility. Teachers are guardians of civilization and the guides of students. A teacher with ideals can sow the seeds of dreams in students. In an era with increasingly diversified values, teachers should lead students forward with great ambitions, pure souls, and noble sentiments on the basis of lofty ideals and convictions.

Today, a good teacher should stand with the Communist Party Of China and the people, study Xi Jinping Thought on Socialism with Chinese Characteristics for a New Era, stay true to socialism with Chinese characteristics, enhance his or her confidence in China's socialist path, theory, system, and culture, and guide his or her students in loving the nation, the people, and the Party. If a teacher chooses a career of cultivating talent for national development and rejuvenation and takes pleasure in doing so, then his or her life will be endowed with eternal values, and this career will take on great significance.

1.1.2 Moral Integrity

"A teacher should teach students not only skills but also ethical values." Xi Jinping emphasizes that teachers must be people of moral integrity. "Those who cannot tell good from evil, right from wrong, justice from injustice, or gain from loss, are not good teachers."

> ***Quote from Xi Jinping***
>
> *Apart from their knowledge and ability, teachers also influence their students through personal conduct and the values they hold toward the country, the people, the public, and the private.*
>
> *—Speech at the meeting with teachers and students of Beijing Normal University, September 9, 2014*

Moral integrity is an important standard that teachers should meet in performing their duties. Xi Jinping has noted that the professional nature of teachers determines that they should be models of moral integrity. Good teachers should set a good example by teaching and behaving ethically. They are a mirror of moral conduct to students. As the saying goes, "Teachers are models of good conduct." What they say and do are taken as norms and emulated by their students. If teachers transgress the moral line, they will mislead the students and adversely affect the formation of their beliefs. The *Analects* also states, "A man commands with his integrity." Students not only listen to what teachers say but also observe what they do. As teachers are models in the eyes of their students, they need to aim high and keep improving their moral conduct to equal the virtuous, thus becoming master teachers who may mold the students' character, behavior, and taste.

A teacher's moral conduct needs to be improved through self-cultivation. As Xi Jinping has emphasized, "A teacher's moral conduct should be improved through education and, more importantly, through self-cultivation. Teachers must constantly strive to be noble-minded and resist vulgar interests. They should be selfless and devote their heart and soul to teaching. They should adhere to their ideals and be morally incorruptible. They should take the lead in promoting socialist ethics and traditional Chinese virtues and be models for students." Teachers' moral integrity reflects their intellectual accomplishments and cultural taste. As the saying goes, "A refined character comes from extensive reading." Teachers need to read good books to cultivate noble character. They also need to practice what they preach. They should set strict standards for themselves and demonstrate through action their proper understanding of the relationship between the self, the state, and the people.

They need to, as Confucius put it in the *Analects*, "reflect on themselves three times a day" and constantly strive to equal the virtuous. Only in this way can they appreciate and demonstrate the appeal of noble character and become moral paragons for students.

Good teachers love their careers. As is often said, you should love whatever job you take up. A good teacher should not take teaching just as a means to raise the family. As Xi Jinping has pointed out, only those who are engaged in education as a cause can do it well. Those who are physically at school but aim to climb the social ladder or make monetary profits may ultimately surrender their nobility to money and/or fame. These people cannot make good teachers. A dedicated person devotes wholly and earnestly to his or her purpose. Only those who are dedicated to education will love their students, be strict with themselves, be rigorous in research, and be tireless in teaching, thus becoming role models for their students. Only such teachers will engage in lifelong learning, pursue constant progress, and lead themselves and their students to success. Xi Jinping has stressed, "The greatest success for a teacher is to bring out the best in their students. Consider how reassured and proud the teachers are when they see their students grow to be learned, well mannered, well established, and happy." In the new era, many outstanding teachers have come to the fore. They are dedicated to their career, live a simple life, and never flinch in the face of difficulties. With devotion and passion, they help their students realize their dreams. They are indeed models of all other teachers, who should resist material temptations, always put their students first, and take imparting knowledge and cultivating moral character as their lifelong pursuit.

1.1.3 Knowledge

Teachers have been acclaimed as "sages" since ancient times. Good teachers should have solid knowledge because "shallow water cannot lift a big ship." They are expected to be knowledgeable, competent, diligent, and good at teaching.

Good teachers are well-grounded in knowledge and have broad horizons and vision. Otherwise, they will feel stretched and never be able to accomplish the job with ease. In-depth knowledge of specific areas and pedagogy is the prerequisite and foundation for teaching. Teachers are expected to draw on their knowledge in teaching, know their students' potential well, be effective in their teaching approaches, and help their students learn faster and better. In the information era, they should know much more than what is needed for teaching. They should have solid domain knowledge, a wide range of general knowledge, and a broad mind and vision. They should have the wisdom to learn, to get on with others, to live a meaningful life, and to educate. They not only give fish but also teach how to fish, and they should guide and help students in all respects.

Quote from Xi Jinping

In the past, we believed that teachers should have a bucket of water before they can give students a bowl of water. This is not enough today, as they should have a pond of water before they can give students a bowl of water.

—Speech at the meeting with teachers and students of Beijing Normal University, September 9, 2014

A good teacher should pursue lifelong learning. With the rapid progression of information technology and economic globalization, people are expected to have greater flexibility, adaptability, initiative, team spirit, and innovative skills, and this places higher demands on teachers. Therefore, they should keep learning, acquire frontier knowledge, work hard, and constantly improve and enrich themselves. Teachers should advance with the times, pursue excellence, and meet new challenges proactively. Only in this way can they both continuously improve themselves and prepare students for the future.

Good teachers should have a strong innovative mindset. Xi Jinping has noted that education aims to equip students with practical skills and innovative spirit. Teachers in China should be creative in developing a first-class and modern education system with Chinese characteristics. Teachers' awareness and ability to innovation are of great significance to talent cultivation and educational development. Innovation-minded teachers are self-motivated to build their capabilities for better delivery quality. Their teaching is informed by new knowledge on education and cutting-edge research outcomes, and profits from scientific and efficient teaching approaches. They are capable of guiding their students in making critical inquiries to turn them into pillars of the nation with extensive knowledge, a broad vision, moral integrity, and professional competence.

1.1.4 Compassion

Xi Jinping has pointed out that good teachers emanate compassion. Teachers may teach in different ways, but they should have something in common: love for their students.

> ***Quote from Xi Jinping***
>
> *Education is a profession founded on love and compassion. Love is the soul of education, without which, there would be no education.*
>
> *—Speech at the meeting with teachers and students of Beijing Normal University, September 9, 2014*

Good teachers are loving and trustful. They care about all students, boost their confidence through appreciation, and build up their dignity through trust. They know when to be strict and when to be lenient. They reason with students and move students with affection so that students trust them and believe in what they say. Love is the gate to knowledge and enlightenment. Love nurtures beautiful hearts. Being loving, truthful, and sincere, good teachers foster, inspire, and spread love, forge emotional bonds with students, and become their close friends.

Compassion begets responsibility. Good teachers know that when choosing this career, they shoulder important responsibilities, that is, imparting knowledge, educating students, and fostering their moral integrity. They are expected to perform these responsibilities in their everyday work. Teachers' sense of responsibility determines their achievements. It is their love for education and students that sustains their lifelong dedication to their careers and gives them the courage to stand up when their students are in danger and the determination to make breakthroughs in their studies.

A good teacher respects and understands students. As Xi Jinping has put it, without respect, understanding, and compassion, there will be no education to speak of. Good teachers fill students with confidence and teach them to respect others by showing respect for them. A teacher should, as Confucius said, "continue study without respite and instruct others without growing weary" and no one should be denied education. Just as we cannot find two tree leaves the same in the world, students have different characters, habits, temperaments, interests, family backgrounds, and abilities. Teachers should adopt approaches suited to their students' abilities and conditions, and they should never show indifference or play favorites. Moreover, they must not label students as "good" or "bad" ones. They should try even harder to understand and help low achievers or problem students with care and compassion. Good teachers should treat their students as equals, respect them, understand their sentiments, find out their strengths, and tolerate their shortcomings, so as to bring out their full potential.

Activity 1　How to fulfill President Xi's Four Criteria for a qualified teacher? Discuss in groups some typical details for each criterion and fill in the table.

Typical evidence for the four criteria			
Ideals and beliefs	Moral integrity	Knowledge	Compassion

1.2　Teacher Portraits from Foreign Perspectives

Foreign researchers have studied good teachers, effective teachers, and different kinds of teachers from different perspectives.

1.2.1　What Makes a Good Teacher?

In an attempt to find out what people think about teachers and teaching, Harmer (1994) asked a variety of people the question "What makes a good teacher?" He was especially interested to see what their instant response would be since that might throw some light upon deeply-held beliefs about this fundamental part of human experience.

Some of the respondents were teacher trainers and methodologists. Last but by no means least, he interviewed students of different nationalities studying at private language schools in England, and secondary school students studying at a Cambridge comprehensive school.

The following answers are representative of the many that were given.

(1) They should make their lessons interesting so you don't fall asleep in them.

This was said by an adult student at a private language school in England.

(2) A teacher must love his/her job. If he/she enjoys her job that'll make the lessons more interesting.

This was also said by an adult student in England. Teachers who look fed up or unhappy with what they are doing tend to have a negative effect on their students. When you observe good teachers you will notice that even when/if they are feeling terrible (outside the classroom), they put on a good "teacher's face" when they enter the classroom.

(3) I like the teacher who has/her his own personality and doesn't hide it from the students so that he/she is not only a teacher but a person as well, and it comes through the lessons.

Students tend to be interested in their teachers, at least at first. The ones who share their personality with their classes often have better results than those who don't.

(4) I like a teacher who has lots of knowledge not only of his/her subject.

The preoccupation with the teacher's personality is reflected here too: Teachers should not be afraid to bring their own interests and lives into the classroom (within reason, of course).

(5) A good teacher is an entertainer and I mean that in a positive sense, not a negative sense.

Students enjoy being entertained and amused. However, a balance has to be struck between entertainment (which often gives teachers enjoyable feedback) and teaching/learning. Sometimes, the former can overwhelm the latter.

Although, as we can see, the character and personality of the teacher is crucial in the classroom, by far the greatest number of responses to the question "What makes a good teacher?" were not so much about teachers themselves, but rather about the relationship between the teacher and the students. This is borne out in the following responses.

(6) It is important that you can talk to the teacher when you have problems and you don't get along with the subject.

These are the words of an adult student. Teachers must be approachable.

(7) A good teacher is somebody who has an affinity with the students that they're teaching.

Successful teachers are those people who can identify with the hopes, aspirations, and difficulties of their students while they are teaching them.

(8) A good teacher should try and draw out the quiet ones and control the more talkative ones.

Experienced teachers can tell you of classes which are dominated by bright, witty, loud, extrovert students. It's easy to be captivated by such students. As this EFL teacher implies, it takes more effort to ensure that the quiet, shyer students also get a chance. One of the secondary students questioned said, "A good teacher is someone who asks the people who don't always put their hands up."

(9) He should be able to correct people without offending them.

Explaining to students that they have made a mistake is one of the most perilous encounters in the classroom. It has to be done with tact. The teacher has to measure what is appropriate for a particular student in a particular situation.

(10) A good teacher is someone who helps rather than shouts.

Said by a secondary school student, this was one of the many comments about discipline. The people who resent bad behavior most are not teachers, but other students who feel their time is being wasted. Learning how to manage students and how to control boisterous classes is one of the fundamental skills of teaching.

(11) A good teacher is someone who knows our names.

Class management—the ability to control and inspire a class—is one of the fundamental skills of teaching. Teachers find it much easier if their students believe that they are genuinely interested in them and available for them.

In a book of research called *Making Sense of Teaching*, the authors Sally Brown and Donald McIntyre (1993) selected a group of good teachers, chosen by their pupils. They wanted to find out how these "good teachers" did their job so they asked them about their teaching. This is what they found out.

(12) The most obvious common feature of the different teachers' accounts was that in response to our question about their teaching, they almost always talked about what their pupils were doing.

A simple answer to the question "What makes a good teacher?" therefore, is that good teachers care more about their students' learning than they do about their teaching.

Teachers can never be quite sure what their students think of them, however. The least predictable things can affect their pupils' perception. One 13-year-old girl was adamant that "The teacher needs to have dress sense-not always the same old boring suits and ties!"

1.2.2 Common Characteristics of Successful Teachers

Successful teachers and the institutions where they teach may differ in many ways. For example, teaching is different in the teachers' experience, training, and level of English, or the size of classes, hours of class per week, and the methodology and materials used. However, successful teachers tend to have certain things in common. They usually:

(1) have a practical command of English, not just a knowledge of grammar rules.

(2) use English most of the time in every class, including beginners' classes.

(3) think mostly in terms of learner practice, not teacher explanations.

(4) find time for really communicative activities, not just the practice of language forms.

(5) focus their teaching on learners' needs, not just on finishing' the syllabus or coursebook.

Activity 2 **From the above five points in Section 1.2.2, what can you infer? Please fill in the blanks with proper words or phrases.**

As far as point 1 is concerned, a teacher's development of a command of English should be a __________ hobby as well as a __________ obligation. Of course, a knowledge of the rules and terminology of English grammar and vocabulary is also useful. But teaching, especially language teaching, is much more than just the transfer of __________. If teachers follow point 2, this means that their learners constantly experience the real __________ use of English. It increases their exposure to the language through __________ comprehension and gives them opportunities to speak English. Point 3 relates to two general observations about teaching and learning languages. First, explanations often become long, complicated discussions in the learners' __________ (often referred to as their L1), which may leave little time for the practice and use of English. Second, most people seem to learn much more from the use of a language than from __________ about it. Point 4 again recognizes that language learning is essentially about __________. And point 5 puts the __________ at the centre of teaching. Your success as a teacher is based entirely on their success as learners.

1.2.3 Three Kinds of Teachers

There are many ways of teaching, and part of the enjoyment of being a student in a good classroom is sharing the unique personal identity, style, skills, and techniques that a teacher brings to a lesson.

It sometimes gives things a clearer perspective if we simplify rather than complicate. Scrivener (2020) suggested that there may be three broad categories of teaching styles.

1.2.3.1 The explainer

Many teachers know their subject matter very well but have limited knowledge of teaching methodology. This kind of teacher relies mainly on "explaining or lecturing" as a way of conveying information to the students. Done with style or enthusiasm or wit or imagination, this teacher's lessons can be very entertaining, interesting, and informative. The students are listening, perhaps occasionally answering questions and perhaps making notes, but are mostly not being personally involved or challenged. The learners often get practice by doing individual exercises after one phase of the lecture has finished.

1.2.3.2 The involver

This teacher also knows the subject matter that is being dealt with. (In our case this is essentially the English language and how it works.) However, she is also familiar with teaching methodology; she is able to use appropriate teaching and organizational procedures and techniques to help her students learn about the subject matter.

"Teacher explanations" may be one of these techniques, but in her case, it is only one option among many that she has at her disposal. This teacher is trying to involve the students actively and puts a great deal of effort into finding appropriate and interesting activities that will do this, while still retaining clear control over the classroom and what happens in it.

1.2.3.3 The enabler

Essentially teaching is about working with other human beings. This teacher knows about the subject matter and methodology but also has an awareness of how individuals and groups are thinking and feeling within her class. She actively responds to this in her planning and working methods and in building effective working relationships and a good classroom atmosphere. Her personality and attitude are an active encouragement to learning.

This kind of teacher is confident enough to share control with the learners, or to hand it over entirely to them. Decisions made in her classroom may often be shared or negotiated. In many cases she takes her lead from the students; seeing herself as someone whose job is to create the conditions that enable the students to learn for themselves. Sometimes this will involve her in less traditional "teaching"; she may become a "guide" or a "counsellor" or a "resource of information when needed". Sometimes, when the class is working well under its own steam when a lot of autonomous learning is going on, she may be hardly visible (see Table 1.1).

Table 1.1 Three kinds of teacher

Types	Subject matter	Methodology	People
Explainer	√		
Involver	√	√	
Enabler	√	√	√

These three descriptions of teachers are, of course, very broadly painted. There is no way to categorize all teaching under three headings; many teachers will find elements of each category that are true for them, or that they move between categories depending on the day, the class, and the aims of a lesson. However, this simple categorization may help you to reflect on what kind of teaching you have mostly experienced in your life so far and may also help you to clarify what kind of teacher you see yourself as being now or in the future.

In teacher training courses many participants' initial internal image of a teacher is based on the "explainer", but they are keen to move to become an "involver". Finally, they will keep in mind the important skills, qualities, values, and techniques associated with the "enabling" teacher and get guidance and information that may influence their role and relationships in the classroom.

Scrivener (2020) said that when he thought back on his own experiences of being taught, it was the teaching techniques that he remembered least. He certainly remembered teachers who made subject matter come alive, through their great knowledge and enthusiasm. But the teacher he recalled with the most pleasure and respect was the one who listened to him, who encouraged him, who respected his views and decisions. Curiously this teacher who helped him most was the one who did the least "teaching" of the subject matter and was, seemingly, technique-free, being himself in class. His memories of the teacher's lessons are of what he did, rather than what the teacher did, of his learning rather than the teacher's teaching.

Activity 3 **Think of some teachers you have been taught by in the past. Which of the three descriptions above best suit each one?**

____

____

____

____

____

____

____

____

1.2.4 What Are Effective Teachers?

Effective teaching requires at its baseline individuals who are academically able, who have command of the subjects they are required to teach, and who care about the well-being of children and youth. It also requires individuals who can produce results, mainly those of student academic and social learning. These characteristics are prerequisites for teaching, but they are insufficient without five higher-level attributes (Walker, 2008).

(1) Effective teachers have personal qualities that allow them to develop authentic and caring human relationships with their students, parents, and colleagues.

(2) Effective teachers can create classrooms that model social justice for children and adolescents in a democratic society.

(3) Effective teachers have positive dispositions toward knowledge. They have command of at least three, broad knowledge bases that deal with subject matter, human development and learning, and pedagogy. They use this knowledge to guide the science and art of their teaching practice.

(4) Effective teachers command a repertoire of effective teaching practices known to stimulate student

motivation, enhance student achievement of basic skills, develop higher-level thinking, and produce self-regulated learners.

(5) Effective teachers are personally disposed toward reflection and problem solving. They consider learning to teach a lifelong process, and they can diagnose situations and adapt and use their professional knowledge appropriately to enhance student learning and improve schools.

In the following list, a number of factors are noted in a teacher that might positively affect the learning atmosphere in a classroom.

The effective teacher:

- listens to his/her students;
- shows respect;
- gives clear, positive feedback;
- has a good sense of humor;
- is patient;
- knows his/her subject;
- inspires confidence;
- trusts people;
- empathizes with students' problems;
- is well-organized;
- paces lessons well;
- does not complicate things unnecessarily;
- is enthusiastic and inspires enthusiasm;
- can be authoritative without being distant;
- is honest;
- is approachable.

1.2.5 Teacher–Learner Relationship—A Positive Learning Atmosphere

Some features may be important in creating a positive relationship and a positive learning atmosphere. They will influence the whole teaching and learning in class. Some are mentioned and addressed here.

1.2.5.1 The Importance of rapport

There is an interesting phenomenon Scrivener (2020) noticed. When he recalled his teachers at school, he found it quite hard to recall the details of any specific individual lessons, but he could recall quite strongly the way that the teacher related to the class and how he felt in this teacher's presence. He thought of some whose lessons were bright and enjoyable, some whose lessons were frightening and tense, some who seemed to bring out the best in him, and some who closed him up. The way the teacher related to the learners and consequently how learners related to each other was significant in different classrooms.

What creates this distinctive atmosphere in each teacher's class? What makes the difference between a room where people are defensive and anxious, and a room where people feel able to be honest and take risks? Teachers and trainers often comment on the importance of "rapport" between teachers and students. The problem is that, whereas it is important, it is also notoriously difficult to define or quantify. Sometimes people equate it with "being generally friendly to your students". While this is a reasonable starting point, a wider definition needs to be found, involving many more aspects to do with the quality of how teachers and learners relate.

This does raise a problem, though. If a significant part of a class's success is down to how well the teacher and students relate, does that suggest that successful teachers are born, and if they don't naturally relate well to people, then they are a write-off? Is your "rapport" 100% natural or is it something that can be worked on and improved? It often seems to be the magical ingredient that makes a teacher or not. Rapport has to do with the personal atmosphere a teacher creates in the classroom.

1.2.5.2 Respect, empathy, and authenticity

Carl Rogers, an American psychologist, suggested that there are three core teacher characteristics that help to create an effective learning environment (1961). These are **respect** (a positive and non-judgmental regard for another person), **empathy** (being able to see things from the other person's perspective, as if looking through their eyes), and **authenticity** (being oneself without hiding behind job titles, roles, or masks).

When a teacher has these three qualities, the relationships within the classroom are likely to be stronger and deeper, and communication between people is much more open and honest. The educational climate becomes positive, forward-looking, and supportive. The learners are able to work with less fear of taking risks or facing challenges. In doing this they increase their self-esteem and self-understanding, gradually taking more and more responsibility for their learning rather than assuming that it is someone else's job.

Rogers and Frelberg (1994) considered that, out of these three teacher characteristics, authenticity was the most important. To be yourself. Not to play the role of a teacher but to take the risk of being vulnerable, human, and honest. Gaie Houston (1995) has written that "The foundation of rapport is to learn yourself enough that you know what style you have and when you are being truthful to yourself."

Although there are some practical techniques you can learn to improve communication with others, real rapport is something more substantial than a technique that you can mimic. It is not something you do to other people. It is you and your moment-by-moment relationship with other human beings. Similarly, "respect", "empathy", or "authenticity" are not clothes to put on as you walk into the classroom, not temporary characteristics that you take on for the duration of your lesson. You cannot role-play "respect" or any of the other qualities. On the contrary, they are rooted at the level of your genuine intentions.

In order to improve the quality of our interpersonal relationships in the classroom we do not need to learn new techniques; we need to look closely at what we really want for our students, and how we really feel about them. It is our attitude and intentions rather than our methodology that we may need to work on.

Activity 4 The following are some features that may affect the classroom atmosphere. Decide which items are inborn and which could be worked on and improved. Put a tick (√) in the table.

Features	Inborn	Could be improved
shows respect		
listens to his /her students		
is fair		
has a good sense of humour		
gives clear and positive feedback		
inspires confidence		
is by and large, authentically himself /herself		
is patient		
empathizes with students' problems		
trusts people		
is non-judgemental		
does not complicate things unnecessarily		
is honest		
is well organized		
is approachable		
is enthusiastic and inspires enthusiasm		
can be authoritative without being distant		

Thinking and Doing

A. Questions for discussion

What are the four criteria for teachers by Xi Jinping? As a teacher in the future, What will you do now to fulfill the criteria?

B. Practice

The following are some quotes from some famous foreign experts. Try to translate them into Chinese, and analyze their implications.

a. A good teacher can inspire hope, ignite the imagination, and instill a love of learning. —Brad Henry

b. The mediocre teacher tells, the good teacher explains, the superior teacher demonstrates, the great teacher inspires. —William Arthur Ward

c. Education is not filling a pail, but the lighting of a fire. —W.B.Yeats

d. A teacher affects eternity; he can never tell where his influence stops. —Adam Henry

Checklist

Mark the questions with a check (√) if your answer is yes.

□ Have I understood a teacher's responsibilities and tasks for the nation?

□ Have I understood Xi Jinping's four criteria for a qualified teacher?

□ Have I mastered the principles that can make a good teacher?

□ Have I grasped the features that can affect teaching and learning and how to improve them?

Reflective Journal

Please write down your reflections on what you have / have not learned in this chapter.

◇ The four criteria for a qualified teacher I need to assimilate deeply:

____

____

____

____

____

◇ The diversified roles I need to play in English teaching:

____

____

____

____

____

References

Brown, S., & McIntyre, D. (1993). *Making sense of teaching*. Open University Press.

Compliation team. (2022). *Understanding Xi Jinping's educational philosophy* (Translation team, Trans.). Foreign Language Teaching and Research Press & Higher Education Press.

Harmer, J. (1994). *The practice of English language teaching* (New ed.). Longman Publishing.

Houston, G. (1995). *Supervision and counselling* (Rev. ed.). Karnac Books.

Rogers, C. (2004). *On becoming a person: A therapist's view of psychotherapy* (Y. Guangxue, N. You, & F. Pan, Trans.). China Renmin University Press. (Original work published 1961).

Rogers, C. R., & Freiberg, H. J. (1994). *Freedom to learn* (3rd ed.). Prentice Hall.

Scrivener, J. (2020). *Learning teaching: The guide to English language teaching*. Foreign Language Teaching and Research Press.

Walker, R. J. (2008). Twelve characteristics of an effective teacher: A longitudinal, qualitative, quasi-research study of in-service and pre-service teachers' opinions. *Educational Horizons*, *87*(1), 61–68.

Part Ⅱ

English Teaching Preparation Skills

The art of teaching lies not in imparting knowledge, but in inspiring, awakening, and encouraging.

—Adolf Diesterweg

Adolf Diesterweg (1790–1866) was a prominent German educator and reformer who made significant contributions to modern pedagogy. He advocated for teacher training, student-centered education, and equal access to learning opportunities. His ideas emphasized the importance of inspiring students and fostering critical thinking, which remain influential in educational theory today. Diesterweg is often regarded as a pioneer in progressive education, and his works continue to inspire educators worldwide.

Chapter 2

Lesson Planning and Lesson Plan Presentation

Objectives

Upon completion of this chapter, you should be able to:

- Appreciate what a good lesson contains
- Understand the function and principles of lesson planning
- Know the procedures of lesson planning
- Make a lesson plan for a course and implement it in teaching
- Grasp the principles and steps of lesson plan presentation
- Write a lesson plan presentation and deliver it successfully

Discussion Questions

Do you think a lesson plan is most like ...?

an instruction	leaflet	a photograph
a story	a road map	a computer programme
a series of road signs	a written summary	something else

2.1 Purpose of Planning

Certain individuals believe that there are various pros and cons to having future-oriented plans for instruction, and they argue that it does not solely refer to the meticulous documentation that one might initially associate with such planning.

2.1.1 Why Do We Need to Plan Courses And Lessons?

Several factors contribute to the necessity of organizing our classes and instructional sessions, among which are the following:

(1) Preparing carefully prior to instruction can alleviate doubts or anxiety, replacing them with a sense of assurance and understanding.

(2) It can foster a sense of direction, advancement, and unity in students, which boosts their self-assurance.

(3) It aids in comprehending the necessary research that one should undertake.

(4) It prompts you to gather resources in advance, facilitating your ability to coordinate the schedule and sequence of activities within lessons.

(5) When students are involved in at least part of the planning process, they can also take time to prepare their ideas prior to class.

(6) Utilizing frameworks during lessons can effectively initiate discussions, aid in recalling information, and assist in addressing inquiries from learners.

(7) Engaging in the process of planning both during and after lessons allows for a diverse blend of various materials, subject matter, and forms of interaction to be delivered throughout the course.

(8) The process of designing courses and organizing lessons allows educators to cultivate their unique teaching methods by evaluating all available information, resources, and philosophies, condensing them into a focused approach tailored for a specific audience, timing, and setting. This summary, in conjunction with the dynamics observed in the classroom, showcases a snapshot of your current level of expertise!

2.1.2 What Are the Reasons Against Structuring Courses or Lessons?

While planning is generally advantageous, it does come with certain disadvantages, including the following:

(1) Overly detailed and long-term consideration of lessons and courses can be problematic. This may be a waste of time. This occurs due to the fact that the dynamics can shift once individuals become accustomed to a particular course. What was once planned may no longer align or be appropriate.

(2) Overly meticulous planning can lead to a lack of flexibility within a program, hampering the instructor's capacity to adapt to the needs of their students. This can result in a mindset of, "I've done all the prep work,

and now I'm just going to deliver it no matter what!"

(3) When lesson planning is crafted for an observer or evaluator with preconceived notions about the content and method of delivery, rather than taking into account the needs of the language learners or the growth of the educator, it results in a presentation-oriented lesson accompanied by documentation instead of a meaningful learning experience driven by a practical planning tool. In such instances, the preparation and documentation of lesson plans are essentially aimed at external parties rather than the actual students.

Activity 1 Read the following excerpt carefully and answer the question.

Planning for teaching has both advantages and disadvantages. Some educators believe that planning does not necessarily mean a detailed writing exercise. Below are some of the key reasons why teachers might want to plan their courses and lessons, as well as some drawbacks of planning.

◆ **Advantages of planning**

It reduces feelings of uncertainty and panic, giving teachers a sense of confidence and clarity.

It inspires students with a sense of purpose, progression, and coherence.

It helps teachers identify research needs.

It reminds teachers to organize materials and time efficiently.

Shared planning helps students gather their thoughts before class.

Plans can facilitate class start-up, prompt memory, and help answer student questions.

Post-lesson planning ensures a balanced mixture of materials, content, and interaction types.

Planning develops a teacher's teaching style.

◆ **Drawbacks of planning**

Planning too far ahead or in too much detail can be time-consuming and lead to irrelevance or unsuitability.

Detailed planning can cause inflexibility and limit the teacher's ability to respond to students.

If planning is done for the satisfaction of external observers rather than for the benefit of learners, it becomes more of a display than a useful working document.

Question:

Which of the following statements best represents a drawback of planning for teaching?

A. Planning reduces feelings of uncertainty and panic.

B. Shared planning helps students gather their thoughts before class.

C. Planning too far ahead can lead to irrelevance or unsuitability.

D. Planning helps teachers identify research needs.

Your answer:

____

____

____

2.2 What Constitutes an Effective Course or Lesson?

Effective lesson design empowers educators to tailor their teaching strategies according to the diverse needs and skill levels of their students. By incorporating a variety of activities and methods of evaluation, educators can address different learning preferences, promoting an inclusive environment that facilitates success for every learner.

Prior to embarking on the design of a lesson or course, it is essential to consider the inquiry: What truly constitutes an effective lesson or course?

Establishing strong, individual standards for what constitutes quality work is essential, as each person must navigate their unique circumstances: This is my environment, my design challenge, and this is the approach I will take to address it. I will strive to perform to the best of my abilities, and that is precisely what I will define as "quality!" It's true that we often inherit external standards of what constitutes "quality" from various sources, including our training, influential educators, colleagues, authors, or presenters that we admire. However, it is crucial to reflect on our interpretations of what "quality" means, ensuring they are practical and conducive to achieving our objectives.

Consequently, the parameters that define an effective language course or lesson could vary from person to person, yet they may also encompass commonalities, as a successful lesson or course is characterized by ample language acquisition, alongside the active involvement of both students and the instructor in the process.

(1) Experience comfort in their physical, social, and emotional environments.

(2) Through these experiences, our understanding of each other deepens.

(3) Have a sense of various lessons available to explore.

(4) Recognize some of the knowledge we have acquired.

(5) Possess an understanding of the most effective ways to acquire knowledge.

(6) Recognize that language comprises various elements (including intuition, physical skill, systems, cultural representations, and music, and serves both as a medium for ideas and as the ideas themselves) that are continually evolving, necessitating diverse methods for its teaching and learning.

(7) Know why we are doing the activities we are doing.

(8) Engage in activities during lessons that hold intrinsic value and acquire knowledge that is meaningful beyond the confines of the language learning environment.

(9) Enhance their ability to take charge, assess situations, and determine what holds value and relevance.

(10) Establish beneficial routines that we will carry forward even after parting ways.

(11) Adhere to the established course and lesson frameworks or diverge from them when needed to achieve the aforementioned objectives.

Activity 2 Match each statement with the corresponding criteria listed below. Write the number of the criterion in the front of each statement.

☐ The teacher and students feel relaxed and engaged in the learning environment.

☐ The activities and materials used in the lesson are relevant and applicable to real-life situations.

☐ The students are aware of the goals and objectives of each lesson.

☐ The teacher adjusts the lesson plan when necessary to cater to the students' needs and interests.

☐ The students develop a sense of responsibility and initiative in their learning.

☐ The lesson involves multiple learning strategies and modalities to promote language acquisition.

☐ The teacher and students gain a deeper understanding of each other through interactions in the classroom.

☐ The students recognize the value of language learning beyond the classroom.

Criteria:

(1) We feel comfortable physically, socially, and psychologically.

(2) We are aware of some of the things we have learned.

(3) We know why we are doing the activities we are doing.

(4) We follow our course and lesson plans or depart from them when necessary.

(5) We become more capable of taking the initiative, making decisions.

(6) We accept that language is a mixture of things and needs to be taught in a variety of ways.

(7) We know each other better through the experience.

(8) We do things in class that would be worth doing and learn things that are worth learning for their own sake.

2.3 Lesson Planning

The process of lesson planning is a deliberate and organized approach to defining the subject matter, activities, teaching strategies, and evaluation tools that will be applied during a particular session in the classroom. This process encompasses careful lesson design to facilitate students' active engagement with the material, enabling them to expand their understanding and move toward achieving the overall educational goals (Marshall, 2012).

Various instructors hold distinct viewpoints regarding the process of lesson creation. According to Smith (2015), the process of planning for teaching should be viewed as iterative, requiring ongoing assessment and modifications that respond to the evolving needs and advancements of students. He highlights the need for planning to be flexible and responsive in order to accommodate the evolving demands of both teaching and learning. Morrison and Lowther (2013) highlight the significance of integrating technology into the planning phase of instruction, suggesting that educators should utilize digital resources and tools to enrich the planning experience and create captivating learning opportunities for students. Bruner (1996) conceptualizes the planning of instruction as a mental activity wherein educators interpret the subject matter, organizing it into an accessible and relevant format for learners. He supports employing discovery learning and inductive reasoning methods to foster active participation and a comprehensive grasp of the material.

The process of planning for teaching encompasses various dimensions, including evaluating learners, establishing objectives, choosing materials, crafting instructional strategies, and measuring outcomes.This process is essential for instructors to develop meaningful and stimulating educational experiences tailored to their learners. By integrating various viewpoints and methods, teachers can improve their lesson planning quality and contribute to student achievement.

A structured outline of the teaching process is what most educators develop in order to steer their instructional activities. It functions as a directional guide for the learning environment. This document outlines the educator's plan detailing the topics to be covered, the methods of instruction to be utilized, and the methods for evaluating student learning during a particular class session. This outline establishes an organized approach to the instructional process, guaranteeing that the lesson is oriented toward the fulfillment of the specified educational goals.

2.3.1 The Function of Lesson Planning

Effective lesson planning is essential for educators, as it entails a thoughtful arrangement and structuring of instructional materials, activities, assessments, and more, all aimed at improving the student learning process. It serves as a framework that directs teachers during their teaching journey, making certain that each class is meaningful, stimulating, and in harmony with learning objectives. The following highlights several important roles that lesson planning serves:

2.3.1.1 Defining educational goals

The process of creating lesson plans starts with establishing precise and quantifiable educational goals. These goals serve as a guide throughout the lesson, specifying what learners are expected to know, comprehend, or achieve by the conclusion of the teaching period. Defining clear goals ensures that educators concentrate on essential knowledge and skill development.

According to Guskey (2002), clearly defining the learning targets in lesson plans is essential. He contends that when educators outline the specific outcomes expected from learners, they can concentrate their teaching efforts more effectively and offer tailored assistance to each student.

2.3.1.2 Aligning teaching methods with student requirements

A detailed instructional plan considers the educational requirements of students. It specifies the foundational knowledge and abilities necessary for the session, and designing corresponding activities. By gaining insight into the abilities, challenges, and preferences of the learners, the educator can customize the instruction to optimize its impact and student participation.

According to Smith and Ragan (2005), effective lesson planning should prioritize the student's perspective. They emphasize the importance of recognizing and addressing the unique requirements of learners, be careful, as well as their existing knowledge, plays a vital role in developing lessons that are both engaging and pertinent. When lesson plans are thoughtfully developed, clearly defined learning goals are essential. This enables students to grasp the intended outcomes and understand what the lesson aims to achieve. Awareness of the target allows learners to maintain their attention and enthusiasm throughout the instruction.

2.3.1.3 Organizational content

Well-structured teaching plans arrange information in a coherent and progressive way, advancing from basic concepts to advanced competencies. Dividing the material into smaller, digestible segments allows educators to confirm that students are well-equipped for advanced learning. Moreover, structuring the material enables educators to spot deficiencies in student understanding and devise methods to fill those gaps. The educational materials are thoughtfully chosen and structured to meet the learning goals and support the requirements of learners (Smith & Ragan, 2005).

2.3.1.4 Encouraging engaged learning

Active learning methods are integrated into lesson designs to engage students and promote their critical thinking skills. By utilizing interactive exercises and collaborative discussions, educators strive to enhance the learning experience beyond conventional lecture methods. Employing experiential learning techniques allows learners to better remember information, enhance their critical thinking abilities, and relate academic lessons to practical scenarios in the world. Tasks and activities are crafted to involve learners in experiential learning and enhance their grasp of the material (Bransford, Brown, & Cocking, 2000). The authors Bransford, Brown, and Cocking support the incorporation of dynamic learning strategies within lesson designs. They highlight the necessity of incorporating tasks that prompt learners to interact with the material, develop their understanding, and put their knowledge into practice.

2.3.1.5 Tailoring instruction

Lesson designs are tailored to meet the varied preferences and capabilities of students. Educators can implement several techniques and activities aimed at engaging different types of learners, creating chances for every student to thrive. This may involve adjusting the challenge level, offering extra assistance, or providing stimulating tasks for those who excel, ensuring that individualized teaching allows meaningful educational experiences for all.

Planning lessons enables educators to tailor their instruction according to the unique requirements and capabilities of their students. By incorporating diverse activities and evaluations, educators can address various learning preferences and skill levels, thereby fostering an inclusive environment that supports the achievement of every learner.

2.3.1.6 Evaluating students' comprehension

Instructional strategies draw upon both formative and summative evaluations to assess how well students comprehend the material and their overall development. Ongoing evaluations, such as quizzes conducted in class or direct observations, equip educators with timely insights that help tailor their teaching approaches. Final evaluations, which may include tests at the conclusion of a unit or various project submissions, measure how well students have grasped the educational goals. These evaluations allow educators to pinpoint specific areas where students may benefit from extra help or reinforcement. Assessment techniques are integrated into the instructional framework to evaluate the advancement and comprehension of students (Scriven, 1967).

2.3.1.7 Strategies for advancement and enrichment

Well-structured instructional plans recognize the necessity of accommodating students with supplementary learning opportunities and include provisions for enrichment tasks. By suggesting self-directed reading, providing optional seminars, or motivating students to delve into associated subjects, educators can create avenues for learners to enhance their comprehension and cultivate new passions.

2.3.1.8 Promoting interaction and teamwork

A teaching outline acts as a medium for communication among educators and various associated parties, including parents, school leaders, and fellow teachers. It provides details about the lesson's goals, topics, and the activities planned, enabling others to grasp the intended path and significance of the lesson. This exchange fosters teamwork and mutual comprehension, potentially enhancing student performance.

To sum up, effective lesson planning is essential in the educational process as it establishes clear goals, organizes material thoughtfully, encourages active participation, allows for tailored instruction, evaluates comprehension, and considers opportunities for further exploration. With well-thought-out lesson plans, educators are better equipped to cultivate a stimulating and interactive learning atmosphere that supports the advancement and development of their students.

Activity 3 **Choose the correct answer for each question.**

1. Which of the following is NOT a key function of lesson planning?
   A. Clarifying learning objectives B. Ignoring student needs
   C. Organizing content D. Facilitating active learning

2. Lesson plans provide a structured framework for the teaching process, ensuring that the lesson remains focused on achieving ________.
   A. classroom discipline B. student engagement
   C. desired learning objectives D. lesson length

3. Guskey argues that by clarifying what students are expected to learn, teachers can better ________ their instruction and provide targeted support to students.
   A. modify B. monitor C. focus D. vary

4. According to Smith & Ragan, lesson planning should be centered around ________.
   A. the teacher B. the curriculum
   C. the student D. the school policy

5. Active learning strategies help students retain information better, develop problem-solving skills, and make connections between classroom content and ________.
   A. homework assignments B. assessments
   C. real-world applications D. textbooks

2.3.2 Pre-Planning

It is essential to take into account several important variables before developing a lesson plan, including the proficiency level of the learners, their academic and cultural contexts, anticipated motivation levels, as well as their diverse learning preferences. Certainly, the insights we gain about a group become much more apparent after spending time with them compared to our initial interactions at the course's outset. Initially, when one is not acquainted with the dynamics of a particular group, it is essential to strive for a deeper insight into their characteristics before making any decisions regarding what to teach.

It is also essential to be familiar with the structure and subject matter of the curriculum we are utilizing, along with the criteria for any assessments that the students are preparing for. With a solid understanding of both the students and the curriculum in place, it is now time to explore the four primary components of planning.

2.3.2.1 Activities

Considering the activities planned for the students in the classroom is crucial during the preparation stage. It is essential to think about how they will be organized, whether they will navigate the classroom if they'll collaborate quietly side-by-side while researching online, or if they will participate in an active group-writing session.

Decisions regarding the choice of activities should largely be made without being overly concerned about the specific language or skills that need to be taught. When considering lesson planning, it is crucial to focus on identifying the most suitable activities for a specific group of learners at a certain moment in a class or on a given day. Considering the nature of activities provided to students allows for an opportunity to create a more balanced lesson structure, ultimately enhancing the likelihood of engaging and motivating the entire class.

The most effective lessons incorporate a range of activities throughout the duration of the class. Pupils might engage in partner work for five minutes, collaborating while upright, before settling back into their seats for some independent work. At the conclusion of the lesson, the entire class might engage in a discussion, or they could pair up to create dialogues that allow them to practice specific language functions or grammatical concepts.

Activity 4 Choose the best option to complete each sentence based on the information provided in the passage.

1. When planning a classroom activity, the first consideration should be ____________.
   A. the language or skills to be taught
   B. the way students will be grouped
   C. whether students will be moving around the class
   D. the type of activity that will best engage the students

2. According to the passage, which of the following is NOT a factor to consider when planning classroom activities?
   A. The level of noise during the activity.

B. The seating arrangement of the students.

C. The specific language points to be covered.

D. The amount of time for each activity.

3. Which activity described in the passage involves students working quietly side-by-side?

A. A whole-class discussion.　　B. Pairs writing dialogues.

C. Standing up and working together.　　D. Researching on the Internet.

4. The best classroom lessons usually offer ____________.

A. one main activity for the entire lesson

B. a variety of activities throughout the lesson

C. only individual work for the students

D. only group work for the students

5. When deciding on classroom activities, teachers should ____________.

A. focus only on language skills

B. prioritize quiet activities

C. base decisions on what students enjoy

D. balance the activities to engage and motivate students

2.3.2.2 Skills

When there is a teaching plan. It is essential to ascertain the language capabilities that educators aim to enhance in their students. These capabilities, which are often categorized as auditory comprehension, Speech, read, and writing serve as the essential components of verbal interaction. Nevertheless, determining which competencies to prioritize can often be complex. This choice can often be influenced by the stipulations of the syllabus or the direction provided by the textbook. Nonetheless, as an educator, intentional choices must be made regarding the enhancement of these competencies.

Determining the necessary competencies and their related components. It is essential to determine the particular language skills along with their respective sub-skills that students should enhance. As an illustration, when considering speaking abilities, one might opt to emphasize aspects such as fluency, articulation, vocabulary utilization, and grammatical application. In a similar vein, one might examine reading abilities by concentrating on understanding, vocabulary development, and the skill of drawing conclusions.

Content integration. The selection of skills and their subdivisions is closely connected to the lesson's subject matter. The subjects, concepts, and resources selected must correspond with the skills intended for enhancement. For example, selecting engaging and challenging reading materials that also allow students to practice their comprehension abilities would be essential if the goal is to improve their reading understanding.

Design work. The tasks designed for learners play a crucial role in fostering their language development. Opportunities must be created to allow students to engage in practice and achieve proficiency in the targeted skills. Examples of engaging activities include role-playing scenarios, simulations, and structured debates, all of which significantly enhance verbal communication and auditory comprehension abilities. In addition, engaging in activities like reading journals, creating summaries, and writing response papers can enhance one's abilities in reading and composition.

Factors to consider during the planning phase. It is crucial to consider the requirements, capacities, and preferred learning styles of the students when determining which language skills and sub-skills to focus on. For instance, should learners have difficulties with enunciation, it may be beneficial to dedicate additional time and resources towards practices concentrated on that specific area. Furthermore, it is essential to design activities that not only target specific skills but also captivate and inspire students.

Activity 5 **Identify the key language skills and sub-skills you would like to develop in a lesson you are planning. Match the appropriate skills and sub-skills with the content and activities you would design.**

Content: You are planning a lesson focused on environmental issues, specifically the impact of climate change. You will use an article from a scientific journal discussing the causes and consequences of climate change.

Activities:

1. Group discussion on the key causes of climate change.
2. Reading comprehension exercise involving finding details from the article.
3. Role-play scenario where students debate solutions to climate change.
4. Writing assignment asking students to write a letter to a local politician about the urgency of climate action.

Fill in the table below with the language skills and sub-skills you would focus on for each activity. Explain briefly why you chose those skills and sub-skills.

Activity	Language Skills & Sub-skills	Explanation
1. Group discussion		
2. Reading comprehension exercise		
3. Role-play scenario		
4. Writing assignment		

After completing the activity, reflect on how the choice of language skills and sub-skills is aligned with the content and activities. Discuss any challenges you faced in identifying the most appropriate skills and sub-skills for each activity.

Your reflection:

____

____

____

____

2.3.2.3 Language

A key element in the process of developing lesson plans involves identifying the language elements that should be introduced and that students are expected to engage with. Nonetheless, this choice should be approached thoughtfully and should not dominate the overall planning effort. The selection of a language serves as just one element within a wider context that demands thorough planning and thoughtful evaluation (Harmer, 2015).

A common mistake in crafting lessons occurs when the focus on language takes precedence, causing educators to make it their primary and sole consideration. In these scenarios, after deciding to focus on a particular grammatical form, such as the present continuous tense, there is a strong inclination to resort to a teaching method that relies heavily on repetition. While this method may offer efficiency in certain aspects, it often lacks diversity and might not be the most effective means of reaching the desired educational results.

Before determining which language to teach, it is essential to take into account the educational standards and the skill levels of the students. It is important that the selected language addresses the abilities, interests, and requirements of the learners. Moreover, it is crucial to ensure that the language utilized corresponds with the goals of the lesson and the broader educational objectives.

In addition to merely choosing a language, one must evaluate the most effective ways to introduce and instruct the selected grammatical elements. While drills and repetitive exercises can be beneficial to a degree, they should not be the exclusive methods of instruction. Rather, it is essential to integrate diverse activities and approaches that actively involve learners and promote hands-on engagement.

In addition, it is essential to teach language within the framework of significant and applicable communication. This indicates that attention should be given not just to grammatical structures, but also to the practical applications and roles of language in everyday interactions. Integrating language exercises within meaningful activities allows learners to enhance their communication abilities in a more genuine and fluid way.

Activity 6 **Based on the information provided in this part, choose the most appropriate answer for each question.**

1. When planning a lesson, which of the following should NOT be the sole focal point in deciding what language to introduce?
   A. Curriculum requirements.
   B. Teacher's preference for a specific linguistic structure.
   C. Students' proficiency level.
   D. Lesson objectives.

2. What is a potential pitfall in lesson planning when language becomes the overriding factor?
   A. Overly relying on drill-based teaching.
   B. Ensuring alignment with the curriculum.
   C. Considering student interests and needs.
   D. Using a variety of teaching methods.

3. Why should teachers avoid relying solely on drills and rote memorization when teaching linguistic structures?
   A. They are not efficient in any way.
   B. They may not achieve the intended learning outcomes.
   C. They do not align with the curriculum requirements.
   D. They are not relevant to students' needs and interests.

4. Which of the following best describes how language should be taught in the context of meaningful communication?
   A. Focusing solely on linguistic forms.
   B. Ignoring the functions and uses of language.
   C. Embedding language practice in contextualized activities.
   D. Teaching language structures separately from communication.

5. Which statement best summarizes the main idea of the passage?
   A. Teachers should always teach the present continuous tense.
   B. Deciding what language to introduce is the most important step in lesson planning.
   C. Curriculum requirements and student needs should be the sole consideration in deciding what language to introduce.
   D. Deciding what language to introduce should be part of a broader lesson planning process, considering curriculum, student needs, and teaching strategies.

2.3.2.4 Content

Instructors must choose material that is likely to capture the attention of their students and encourage active participation, and their familiarity with their learners places them in a strong position to make suitable choices.

Even when the selection of themes and materials is influenced by a textbook, it remains possible to determine the appropriateness of the topics provided, along with the possibility of substituting them for alternative subjects. One can anticipate, to a certain degree, which themes are likely to resonate well and which are expected to fall flat.

Nonetheless, even the most captivating subjects can appear tedious if the associated activities and exercises lack creativity. In a similar vein, even topics that might seem dull can be transformed into engaging experiences if conscientious educators devote effort to devising the most effective ways for learners to interact with them.

In considering the components we have examined earlier, it is essential to recognize both our understanding of the learners and our commitment to establishing a suitable equilibrium between diversity and consistency. Considering all these characteristics, it becomes essential to transpose our reflections into the realm of practical application. This involves integrating our understanding of the classroom environment, available resources, time constraints, and the institutional atmosphere, which collectively direct our planning toward actionable steps. As Figure 2.1 shows, we are in a position to move from pre-planning to the plan itself. Consequently, the transition from initial considerations to the actual planning phase can now take place.

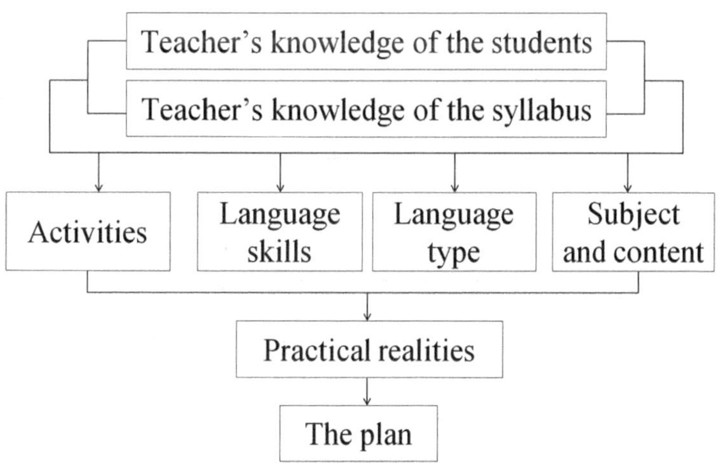

Figure 2.1 From pre-planning to the plan (Harmer, 2015)

Activity 7 **Imagine you are going to teach a lesson on "Environmental Protection" to a group of high school students. Your students are generally interested in current affairs and are eager to learn about topics that have real-world implications. Use the information provided in the document and your creativity to answer the following questions:**

1. Select two topics related to "Environmental Protection" that you think would inspire curiosity and engagement in your students. Please elaborate on your selections and the rationale behind choosing them.
2. Evaluate the resources and tools available in your classroom environment. What strategies might you employ to enhance student engagement during your lesson focused on environmental conservation?
3. Propose an activity or task that could be incorporated into the lesson, ensuring that it incorporates both diversity and a sense of unity. Elaborate on how this activity would correspond with the selected subject areas and capture the students' interest.
4. Imagine facing a scenario with restricted time available for instruction. What strategies would be implemented to effectively manage and select the topics and exercises included in a lesson plan for optimal effectiveness?
5. Consider the importance of the educator's function in creating an effective lesson plan. In what ways can you ascertain that the selected materials and tasks align with the specific needs and preferences of your students?

Your answer:

____

____

____

____

____

____

____

2.3.3 The Plan

After engaging in some initial planning and determining the type of lesson intended for delivery, it becomes possible to construct the lesson framework. The format this takes can vary widely, influenced by the specific details of the lesson as well as one's overall perspective on the planning process.

2.3.3.1 The planning continuum

Teachers' approaches to lesson planning are influenced by the specific context of the lesson and the teacher's level of expertise. Some educators might engage in all the preliminary thought processes in their minds, making decisions about lesson content as they rush through the halls to their classroom. Those who are seasoned in their teaching can sometimes rely on this method due to their familiarity with established practices.

A similar situation arises at the other end of the spectrum when educators rely heavily on a textbook, adhering closely to its instructions, which ultimately allows the authors of the course material to dictate the teaching strategy. This approach can be particularly appealing for educators facing significant time constraints; however, neglecting to reflect on how to implement the coursebook tasks and their implications may lead to challenges down the road. The effective utilization of coursebooks involves a greater level of complexity.

At the far end of the instructional planning spectrum lies a lesson style likened to a meandering path through a jungle, where educators enter the classroom without a clear plan of action, often prompting the question, "What did you do over the weekend?" and use the students' responses as a basis for the lesson. They could also inquire about the activities the learners wish to engage in for that particular day or initiate an activity at the beginning of the session without a clear direction of the outcomes it may yield for themselves and their learners. This method is considered preferable as it allows for more spontaneous discovery rather than adhering rigidly to a predetermined schedule, an educator ought to approach their role similarly to how a physician does, tailoring instructions based on precise assessments. Each classroom and each group of learners possesses unique characteristics, therefore, determining in advance what learning objectives to pursue on a particular day (especially if this decision is made days prior) restricts their ability to engage fully with their immediate educational experiences and the unique individuals present in the classroom.

It is quite possible that seasoned educators can conduct productive classes in such a manner, even in the absence of structured preparation. While these lessons can be highly gratifying when they succeed, they frequently risk becoming confusing and lacking direction. A significant concern exists when educators lack a defined purpose for their lessons, and equally important, when students are unable or unwilling to contribute to the structure of the lesson, potentially leading to an absence of any valuable outcomes.

While some learners might relish the thrill of navigating the jungle trail, most will gain significant advantages both in language development and mental well-being from the careful planning that the educator has put into the lesson.

On the opposite side of the spectrum, some educators create detailed formal outlines for their lessons, explaining both their intended actions and the reasoning behind them. This may occur due to impending observations or mandates from an overseeing body.

Most course plans may occur between these two extremes. Some educators might jot down brief notes in their planners, occasionally recording just the title of a book or an activity's name. Other educators might document more intricate details. They might jot down essential vocabulary or formulate inquiries they intend to pose. They might compile a compilation of online resources that they want their students to explore, along with the details they need to search for on the web.

The specific appearance of a plan holds less significance than the consideration invested in its creation; The primary consideration is to establish clear objectives for what students are expected to accomplish in the classroom, and this awareness should influence the strategies employed to achieve those goals. Nevertheless, instructional documents, whether they are basic outlines or thoroughly developed plans, serve important roles in the teaching process. They also serve an additional role by documenting previous events, and assisting educators during the lesson by recalling their predetermined decisions, the necessary resources, and the allocated time for specific tasks.

We can represent this planning continuum diagrammatically as shown in Figure 2.2:

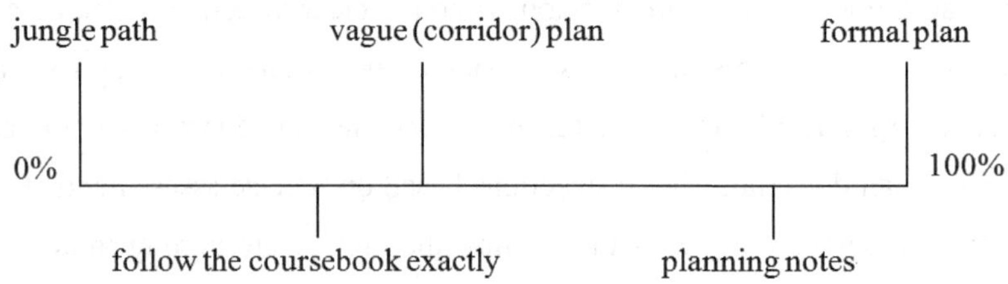

Figure 2.2 The planning continuum (Ur, 2017)

2.3.3.2 Foundational issues for clarifying learning objectives

Clarifying learning objectives is a crucial step toward ensuring the effectiveness of teaching and learning processes. Learning objectives provide a clear roadmap for students, outlining what they are expected to know, understand, and be able to do by the end of a lesson, unit, or course. This document aims to discuss the importance of clarifying learning objectives and offer strategies for effectively formulating and implementing them.

1. The importance of clarifying learning objectives

The importance of defining educational goals is evident in their role as a central point of reference for both educators and learners. For educators, establishing clear learning aims is crucial for informing the creation of curricula, planning lessons, and designing assessments. They establish a structural approach for choosing pertinent and engaging material, allowing educators to organize content logically and progressively. For learners, the objectives of a lesson act as a guideline for assessing their understanding and progress. These objectives assist learners in grasping the particular standards set for the lesson or course, enabling them to evaluate their advancement toward fulfilling these aims. Well-defined educational targets also boost learners' enthusiasm and involvement, as they offer a distinct aim and guidance for their academic pursuits.

2. The strategies for effectively formulating learning objectives

There are several strategies that teachers can employ to formulate clear and effective learning objectives.

Firstly, learning objectives should be specific and measurable. They should state explicitly what students are expected to learn, and how their learning will be assessed. Objectives should be written in student-friendly language so that students understand what they are expected to learn and achieve. Clarifying learning objectives helps teachers focus the lesson content and activities to meet the needs of the learners. For example, a learning objective might be stated as: "By the end of this lesson, students will be able to identify three key causes of climate change and explain their significance."

Secondly, learning objectives should be aligned with the overall goals and objectives of the curriculum. They should build upon previous knowledge and skills, and prepare students for future learning. By ensuring that learning objectives are aligned with the curriculum, teachers can help students develop a coherent and comprehensive understanding of the subject matter.

Thirdly, learning objectives should be student-centered. They should focus on what students will do and what they will learn, rather than on what teachers will teach. This shifts the emphasis from the teacher to the student and encourages a more active and engaged learning process.

3. Two models for establishing efficient learning objectives

• Objectives should be SMART

Several methodologies for formulating educational aims have emerged, with SMART criteria standing out for their distinctiveness and ability to be measured effectively (Doran, 1981; Mager, 1997; Marzano & Kendall, 2007).

The term SMART for learning objectives represents the qualities of being specific, measurable, achievable, relevant, and time-bound. This structure guarantees that educational goals are explicitly outlined, easily monitored, attainable for learners, pertinent to the curriculum, and established within a defined timeline.

Specific: SMART goals should be clear, well-defined, and unambiguous. This enables educators to avoid vague language, focus on what needs to be accomplished, why it matters, and who is involved.

Measurable: SMART goals must have clear criteria for measuring success. This enables educators to evaluate the advancement of their students and offer appropriate feedback.

Achievable: The objectives ought to be established at a degree that presents a suitable challenge without causing excessive strain for learners. Goals should inspire students to put in the effort while ensuring that they remain within achievable limits.

Relevant: SMART objectives must be relevant to the course content and student life. They ought to relate to practical situations in the real world and offer tangible benefits.

Time-bound: Each goal must have a clear deadline or time frame for completion. This approach ensures that attention and progression are consistently upheld during the learning experience.

SMART learning objectives play an important role in improving the efficiency of the learning process. They outline a structured path for learners, assisting them in grasping what knowledge is necessary and how they can advance. These tools allow educators to monitor the advancements of their pupils and offer prompt evaluations, pinpointing the specific areas where extra assistance may be beneficial. Setting specific, measurable targets empowers learners to take charge of their educational journey, inspiring them to strive for the defined objectives. By relating to practical scenarios, the application of SMART objectives increases the significance and usefulness of the educational experience.

Below are various approaches to successfully apply SMART learning targets within the educational environment:

Begin with a broader perspective: It is essential to recognize the primary aims and objectives of the course or unit. These goals will establish the basis for formulating more precise SMART objectives.

Decompose the goals: Segregate the primary aims into smaller, more feasible targets. Every SMART goal should emphasize a particular skill or idea.

Establish measurable criteria: It is essential that every SMART goal includes a way to quantify progress. This could entail the use of evaluation criteria, scoring metrics, or various assessment methods.

Encourage growth while maintaining a sense of control: Establish targets that are sufficiently demanding yet still within reach. It is important to strike a balance by avoiding goals that are excessively simplistic or overly ambitious, as such extremes may result in disinterest or disappointment.

Linking the goals to tangible situations helps to enhance their significance by demonstrating real-life applications and scenarios. This will enable learners to recognize the tangible benefits of their studies.

Establish a schedule: Determine a clear time period for reaching each specific and measurable objective. This approach will maintain student engagement and ensure they remain on course.

Continuously evaluate and modify: Keep track of students' advancement toward the set goals and implement necessary changes when required. This could include offering extra assistance, altering the goals, or prolonging the schedule.

Activity 8 **Set a SMART goal for improving your students' English speaking and listening skills. Remember to include all the elements of SMART.**

Your answer:

____

____

____

____

____

____

____

____

- **Objectives can be expressed by ABCD Principle**

The ABCD Principle can be utilized to articulate learning objectives (Armstrong & Savage, 1983). In educational settings, well-defined learning targets form the foundation of any teaching strategy. The ABCD method is a strategy that offers a systematic way to formulate educational goals that are precise, focused, and centered around the students' needs.

The concept of ABCD encompasses four key elements: Audience, Behavior, Condition, and Degree. This model guarantees that learning goals are customized to align with the distinct requirements and skills of the intended audience. The components of the ABCD model are essential in crafting precise and impactful learning objectives.

Audience (A): The initial phase of the ABCD framework involves determining the specific group of individuals targeted for the educational aim. This involves detailing the specific learners or individuals who will pursue the established objective. It is crucial to comprehend the traits, requirements, and capabilities of the intended audience for crafting objectives that are applicable and fitting.

Behavior (B): The subsequent stage involves articulating the particular actions or skills that learners are anticipated to exhibit. This step entails articulating the actions or tasks that learners will be capable of executing upon reaching the objective. The actions must be distinctly outlined and capable of being quantified.

Condition (C): The condition component outlines the specific scenarios or situations in which learners are expected to exhibit the targeted behavior. This encompasses any resources, materials, or situational factors that may be essential for learners to effectively exhibit the behavior. Gaining insights into the circumstances that students will face in practical environments is essential for ensuring the learning goals are both applicable and meaningful.

Degree (D): Ultimately, the proficiency level indicated by the degree component outlines what standards or benchmarks learners need to reach when exhibiting the specified behavior. This may encompass measurable standards such as the tempo, precision, or regularity of the execution. The expectations should be well-defined and achievable for students, taking into consideration their existing competencies and talents.

In the process of crafting learning goals using the ABCD framework, careful consideration of each component is essential. An illustration of the application of the ABCD principle in crafting a significant learning goal is provided here:

Audience (A): Elementary school students.

Behavior (B): Correctly identify shapes and name them (circles, triangles, rectangles).

Condition (C): Provide a collection of images depicting various shapes and an accompanying reference sheet containing the titles and visuals of each shape.

Degree (D): Accuracy of 80%.

The aim of the learning objective is: "Students in elementary education will be able to accurately recognize and label geometric shapes (circle, triangle, rectangle) when presented with various images of these shapes along with a supportive visual guide, achieving a minimum accuracy of 80%."

This aim is well-defined, precise, and suited to the requirements of the intended audience. It outlines the actions (recognizing and labeling geometric forms), the context (utilizing images and a guide sheet), and the level of accuracy required (achieving 80% correctness).

There are several benefits to using the ABCD principle when setting learning goals.

Clarity: The ABCD principle ensures that learning objectives are clear and easy to understand. This creates a mutual comprehension of the anticipated results for both educators and students.

Specificity: The ABCD principle promotes the specificity of learning objectives by specifying behaviors, conditions, and degrees. This allows learners to concentrate on developing the targeted skills or knowledge more effectively.

Measurability: The ABCD framework aids in tracking the advancement of students. The specific criteria for behaviors and levels set the foundation for evaluation and constructive feedback.

Relevance: The ABCD principle helps ensure the relevance and practicality of learning objectives by considering the target audience and real-world conditions. This fosters greater enthusiasm and participation among learners.

Activity 9 **Apply the ABCD principle in designing learning objectives for middle school English language learners.**

Audience A: ____________________

Behavior B: ____________________

Condition C: ____________________

Degree D: ____________________

The resulting learning objective is:

____

____

____

____

____

4. The application of action verbs in expressing learning objectives

Action verbs play a crucial role in setting accurate and measurable learning goals. They clarify the behaviors anticipated from students, enabling educators to create customized teaching methods and evaluations. Choosing the right action words is crucial to accurately represent the desired levels of cognitive challenge and student involvement (Krathwohl, 2002).

Bloom's Taxonomy serves as a framework for categorizing educational objectives related to cognitive skills (Anderson & Krathwohl, 2001). This framework encompasses six distinct levels, progressing from the simple recall of information to higher-order thinking skills such as critical analysis and creative thought. Employing specific action-oriented verbs at each tier of the taxonomy is essential for crafting precise and quantifiable educational objectives (see Table 2.1).

Table 2.1 Six levels of cognitive goals and their action verbs

Levels and action verbs	Explanations and examples
Remember	Students retrieve relevant knowledge from long-term memory.
recite, recall, list, recognize name, define. describe, identify, label, outline, select, state, etc.	e.g.:Students will recall the key steps of the scientific method.
Understand	Students will demonstrate comprehension and interpretation of information.
explain, interpret, describe, infer, summarize, classify, talk about, distinguish, exchange, substitute, etc.	e.g.:Students will explain the meaning of a poem using textual evidence.

Continued

Levels and action verbs	Explanations and examples
Apply	Students apply knowledge in a new context.
apply, utilize, solve, implement execute, retell, demonstrate, predict, prepare, show, read aloud, spell, say, use, etc.	e.g.:Students will apply the principles of physics to solve a real-world problem.
Analyze	Students analyze and break down information into its component parts.
analyze, categorize, compare contrast, identify, differentiate	e.g.:Students will analyze the causes and effects of the Industrial Revolution.
Evaluate	Student judge the value, worth, or quality of ideas, materials, or methods.
Evaluate, judge, criticize, assess, rate, prioritize	e.g.:Students will evaluate the credibility of sources for a research project.
Create	Students generates new ideas, products, or ways of thinking.
Create, design, compose, develop, invent	e.g.:Students will create a multimedia presentation that synthesizes information from different subjects.

Establishing instructional goals that adhere to Bloom's Taxonomy necessitates the careful selection of precise and suitable action words. By thoughtfully choosing verbs that align with the various levels of cognitive difficulty, educators can guarantee that objectives remain understandable, quantifiable, and sufficiently stimulating for learners.

Activity 10 **Choose an appropriate the action verb to fill in each blank.**

1. Students will be able to ___________ the key historical events of the 20th century.
2. After studying the poem, the students should be able to ___________ its central theme.
3. The students are expected to ___________ the newly learned mathematical formula to solve complex problems.
4. Students will be able to _________ the main causes and consequences of climate change and discuss their roles in mitigating its impact.
5. Students will be asked to ___________ the performance of the main actors in the movie based on their acting skills, emotional depth, and overall impact on the story.

5. Ways to apply the learning objectives in the classroom setting

One approach involves presenting the learning goals to students, ensuring they are both understandable and accessible. This could involve documenting them on the whiteboard, showcasing them through a presentation slide, or providing them in printed form for students. When the aims are prominently displayed, learners can consult them throughout the session, using them to direct their educational journey.

A further approach involves embedding the learning goals within the activities and evaluation methods used in the lessons. For instance, educators might create tasks and tests that focus specifically on these goals, allowing students to showcase their comprehension and abilities. By embedding these objectives within the lessons, educators can facilitate active student participation toward meeting them.

Ultimately, educators ought to keep track of and evaluate the progress of their students in relation to the defined learning goals. This evaluation can be conducted through consistent assessments, observations within the classroom, and opportunities for self-evaluation by students. By keeping an eye on student achievements, educators can pinpoint specific challenges and offer immediate feedback and assistance. This practice facilitates focused strategies and additional support to help students reach the established learning targets.

2.3.3.3 Get to know our students

Understanding the individual characteristics of students is essential in the realm of education. Recognizing their previous knowledge, skills, preferences, and learning modalities is a core principle that is crucial for designing effective instructional plans. This concept acknowledges the uniqueness of each student and highlights the necessity of considering these specific traits to create a customized and stimulating educational experience.

Prior knowledge. Understanding students' prior knowledge is crucial for determining the appropriate starting point for a course. By understanding students' prior knowledge, instructors can pinpoint specific subjects where additional practice or advanced work is necessary. For example, should a student not have a foundational grasp of algebra, the educator may offer supplementary lessons or tutorials to address these deficiencies (Brown & Lee, 2020). If learners have already established a strong base in a specific subject, knowledge can be expanded upon, allowing for the introduction of higher-level concepts. On the other hand, should students not possess the necessary foundational understanding, it is essential to offer additional basic information to help them grasp and engage with the lesson material.

Ability. Understanding students' abilities is also important. Some students can achieve outstanding results in specific fields, while others may require more support. We offer tailored training programs that understand each student's strengths and weaknesses, providing them with the necessary challenges and support. This helps ensure that every student can fully unleash their potential and make progress in their studies.

Interest. Understanding the interests of students serves as an effective strategy to foster their engagement in educational activities. When individuals are enthusiastic about a subject, they tend to exhibit higher levels of motivation and take a more active role in classroom discussions. Consequently, it is crucial to take steps to discover the hobbies, preferences, and passions of the students. This valuable insight can then be utilized to develop lessons that resonate with their interests, thereby increasing both their motivation and enjoyment in the learning journey.

Learning style. Every learner possesses a distinct approach to acquiring knowledge, which influences how they engage with and interpret new information. Certain individuals may lean towards the use of graphics and charts, whereas others might lean towards auditory or hands-on approaches. Gaining insight into the various learning preferences of students, varied instructional strategies and activities can be integrated into lesson plans to accommodate diverse learning preferences. This approach promotes an inclusive environment where every student has the chance to engage with content in a manner that aligns with their strengths and learning capabilities.

Activity 11　Choose the right answers for the following questions.

1. In order to plan effective lessons, teachers should first ____________.
   A. determine the curriculum standards
   B. focus on their teaching methods
   C. understand their students' prior knowledge and abilities
   D. ignore individual differences among students

2. Which of the following is NOT a factor that teachers should consider when getting to know their students?
   A. Students' interests and hobbies.
   B. Students' learning styles and preferences.
   C. Students' age and height.
   D. Students' home environments and cultural backgrounds.

3. A teacher notices that a student often has difficulties in grasping new concepts. What should the teacher do to help the student?
   A. Ignore the student's problems.
   B. Blame the student for not trying hard enough.
   C. Understand the student's learning style and provide tailored support.
   D. Only provide additional worksheets and homework to the student.

4. Why is it important for teachers to know their students' prior knowledge?
   A. To assess students' academic performance.
   B. To compare students' abilities with each other.
   C. To build on what students already know and fill in knowledge gaps.
   D. To determine who the brightest student in the class is.

5. Which of the following strategies helps teachers better understand their students?
   A. Focusing only on the most gifted students in the class.
   B. Ignoring students who are struggling academically.

C. Using standardized tests to assess all students' abilities.

D. Conducting regular conversations and assessments to learn about students' individual needs and backgrounds.

2.3.3.4 Choose suitable material

The choice of educational content is crucial for crafting a learning experience that is both impactful and productive. In the context of curriculum development or educational programming, the selection of material is crucial for influencing how students engage with their learning experiences. Selecting material that is pertinent, captivating, and consistent with the established learning goals is essential.

Relevance. The significance of choosing appropriate material cannot be overstated. Materials should be intimately connected to the experiences, interests, and existing knowledge of the students. Engaging material captivates learners' interest and encourages them to participate actively in their educational journey. Additionally, it enables learners to link newly acquired knowledge with their existing experiences, which enhances the retention and practical use of the information (Tomlinson, 2017).

Engagement. Captivating educational materials plays a vital role in sustaining learners' engagement and enthusiasm. Materials that lack excitement can result in a loss of interest among students, which undermines the overall learning experience. As a result, it is crucial to integrate engaging, experiential learning tasks and practical illustrations that spark students' interest and motivate them to investigate and learn about new ideas (Davis, 2009).

Consistency with the learning objectives. By choosing material that corresponds with the established educational targets, the program can maintain its clarity and efficiency. The material selected must effectively support the goals, equipping learners with the essential skills and knowledge needed to achieve the desired results. Establishing a coherent connection between the material and the goals facilitates a more organized and intentional learning experience (Smith & Ragan, 2005).

Balancing challenge and excess complexity. Selected material should be sufficiently stimulating to enhance students' thinking skills and encourage analytical reasoning. However, it is vital that the content does not become so intricate that it causes frustration, as this can deter learners from actively participating. Achieving the right degree of difficulty in alignment with students' intellectual capacities is key to sustaining their enthusiasm and nurturing a mindset geared toward growth (Jones & Clark, 2019).

Enhancing understanding through existing knowledge. When educational material is connected to what learners already know and have experienced, it tends to be remembered better and utilized effectively in everyday contexts. By drawing on students' prior comprehension, new information can seamlessly fit into their mental frameworks, promoting significant learning and the transfer of knowledge (Anderson & Krathwohl, 2001).

Developing new skills. Ultimately, the material should create avenues for learners to cultivate new abilities and proficiencies. This encompasses not just academic abilities but also essential interpersonal skills, including collaboration, critical analysis, and problem-solving. Educational content that encourages the acquisition of different skills equips learners to face upcoming challenges and seize new opportunities (National Research Council, 2012).

2.3.3.5 Creating interactive learning experiences

Well-structured lesson plans incorporate a variety of stimulating activities that encourage students to engage actively in their learning process. These pursuits not only enhance involvement but also facilitate teamwork, enabling students to leverage the knowledge and skills they have gained in real-world and relevant scenarios. The formulation of these pursuits is crucial for meeting the expected educational objectives and should be customized to fit the students' capabilities and preferences.

The use of engaging activities is crucial for fostering a rich learning experience. By utilizing a variety of techniques such as collaborative discussions, simulations, practical experiments, and role-playing scenarios, educators can stimulate students' senses and cognitive skills. This strategy not only promotes student agency in their educational journey but also plays a vital role in cultivating a thorough comprehension and long-term retention of knowledge.

Activities ought to be tailored to promote teamwork among learners. Engaging in collaborative tasks and facilitated discussions allows attendees to exchange perspectives, gain insights from one another, and enhance their analytical abilities. By participating in these dynamic interactions, learners can leverage each other's expertise and skills, resulting in a more enriched and vibrant educational atmosphere.

Activities that captivate students should be specifically designed to correspond with the lesson's learning goals. It is essential for educators to recognize the fundamental ideas and competencies that need to be acquired and create exercises that correspond with these goals. The designed activities must cater to the varying abilities and interests of the students, considering their unique backgrounds and life experiences. Such an approach allows educators to provide challenges that are stimulating and engaging for learners, motivating them to participate actively in their educational journey.

Activity 12 Choose an appropriate answer to each question.

1. Which of the following is NOT an engaging activity that fosters active learning?

   A. Group discussions　　B. Lectures without student participation

   C. Role-playing　　D. Hands-on experiments

2. Engaging activities are designed to achieve which of the following?

   A. Passive learning　　B. Lack of student participation

   C. Desired learning outcomes　　D. Unnecessary challenges

3. Which of the following statements is true about engaging in activities?
   A. They do not promote collaboration among students.
   B. They should be designed to align with the teacher's interests only.
   C. They allow students to apply their knowledge in practical contexts.
   D. They do not encourage students to take ownership of their learning.

4. Why are engaging activities tailored to match the learning objectives?
   A. To make them easier for students.
   B. To ensure they are challenging but not overwhelming.
   C. To allow teachers to show their creativity.
   D. To ensure they meet the school's requirements.

5. Which of the following activities encourages students to share ideas and learn from each other?
   A. Solo reading　　B. Watching videos
   C. Pair-share discussions　　D. Silent practice

2.3.3.6 Comprehensive evaluation

Evaluation plays a crucial role in the development of lesson plans, providing essential information regarding student advancement and the achievement of educational goals. An effective evaluation strategy integrates both ongoing and conclusive assessments, facilitating a thorough and equitable appraisal of student achievement.

The emphasis of formative evaluation lies in monitoring student development throughout the lesson while offering prompt responses for both educators and learners. This form of assessment is continuing in nature and can be carried out through multiple approaches, such as observing student interactions in the classroom, testing, and interactive discussions. Observing students in the classroom allows educators to assess their level of engagement directly, and understand as well as assess students' grasp and utilization of information. Assessments like quizzes, conversely, provide a brief overview of students' grasp of specific subjects or ideas. These techniques yield crucial insights that can be utilized to modify teaching practices to better align with students' individual requirements and preferred learning approaches. Formative evaluation serves to enhance the experience for both educators and learners. By obtaining prompt evaluations, learners can pinpoint specific aspects where enhancement is necessary and refine their study approaches accordingly. This ongoing cycle of evaluation and feedback cultivates an environment of perpetual growth and learning within the classroom (Black & Wiliam, 1998).

At the conclusion of a lesson or unit, assessments known as summative evaluations measure how well students have achieved the learning goals. This type of evaluation is generally conducted through various methods such as tests, examinations, projects, or presentations. These assessments capture a moment in time that reflects students' understanding of the material and their proficiency in applying the acquired knowledge and skills. Furthermore, summative evaluations play a crucial role in determining students' grades and tracking their advancement toward fulfilling educational objectives.

Utilizing both formative and summative evaluations provides a holistic perspective on students' academic performance. Ongoing assessments give continuous feedback and assist learners throughout their educational journey, whereas concluding assessments provide a comprehensive measure of student success. Both forms of evaluation are vital to monitor student progress towards their educational objectives and to assess the effectiveness of instructional methods (Shepard, 2000).

Integrating both types of assessments, formative and summative, into lesson plans allows educators to better comprehend the progress and requirements of their students. This knowledge can subsequently inform adjustments to instructional methods, offer tailored assistance, and guarantee that every learner is positioned to realize their utmost capabilities.

Activity 13 **Fill in the blanks with appropriate words.**

1. Formative assessment provides timely feedback to ____________ and teachers, focusing on the student's progress during the lesson.
2. Classroom observations enable teachers to directly observe students' ____________, comprehension, and application of knowledge.
3. Quizzes offer a quick snapshot of students' understanding of a ____________ topic or concept.
4. Summative assessment evaluates students' achievement at the end of a lesson or a ____________ of study.
5. The combination of formative and summative assessments offers a ____________ view of student performance.

2.3.3.7 Flexible planning

A key feature of effective lesson planning is its inherent adaptability. Educators need to create their lesson frameworks with the awareness that the classroom setting can change rapidly and may not always follow a set course. Therefore, these plans must incorporate a level of adaptability that allows for alterations in response to unforeseen events or developments that may arise throughout the instructional period.

The ability to adapt lesson plans allows educators to adjust their strategies in response to the reactions of their students. Every learner possesses distinct characteristics, as well as their specific requirements, be careful, and their skills differ. Consequently, instructors ought to be adaptable and willing to modify their strategies based on the responses they obtain from learners. For example, when students demonstrate enthusiasm and curiosity about a specific subject, the educator might choose to elaborate on the subject, introducing supplementary materials or engaging tasks. On the other hand, should learners seem uncertain or lack interest, the educator has the option to adjust the instruction to enhance its relevance and captivate the learners (Stipek, 2002).

The speed at which the lesson unfolds is also an important element that may necessitate adaptability. At times, a lesson may unfold at a faster rate than expected, resulting in additional time remaining toward the conclusion. In such instances, educators might make the most of the remaining time by facilitating a related task, engaging in a brief dialogue, or conducting a rapid summary. Conversely, when a lesson extends beyond the anticipated timeframe, educators need to be flexible and are encouraged to abbreviate specific sections or tasks to guarantee coverage of the key learning goals (Bransford, Brown, Cocking, 2002).

Various unforeseen circumstances may emerge that necessitate adjustments in instructional strategies, such as technical difficulties, sudden student absences, or crises. It is essential for educators to be prepared to manage these scenarios effectively and modify their lessons as needed. Such adaptability guarantees that the educational process is not disrupted, ensuring the continuity of student learning (Fullan, 2007).

In preparation for effective lesson execution, it is essential to consider potential disruptions that might require adjustments to instructional strategies. These could be attributed to issues with technology, sudden student absenteeism, or unforeseen crises. Educators ought to be prepared to manage these circumstances effectively and modify their lesson outlines as needed. By maintaining this adaptability, they can ensure a continuous and effective learning experience for their students.

2.3.3.8 The procedures of lesson planning

1. Evaluation of learner context

It is essential to assess the current English language skills, interests, and preferred learning approaches of the students prior to starting the lesson. This evaluation will aid in customizing the lesson to suit their needs and increase their involvement. In discussing 'The Procedures of Lesson Planning', it is presumed that the individuals participating are future educators or those aiming to refine their teaching abilities.

2. Examination of instructional resources

The instructional resources will emphasize the essential phases involved in devising lesson plans. Topics that will be addressed include determining educational goals, selecting suitable instructional strategies, developing teaching resources, and assessing how effectively the lesson achieved its intended outcomes. The selected resources will be tailored to maintain relevance, precision, and engagement for the intended audience.

3. Objectives of teaching and learning

In crafting educational goals for a specific course or lesson, it is essential to take into account various aspects to facilitate a well-rounded and thorough growth of learners.A range of aspects should be taken into account when designing educational goals, emphasizing both the conventional three-dimensional framework (knowledge, skills, values/attitudes) and the updated four-dimensional model (linguistic proficiency, cultural insight, cognitive skills, and learning capabilities).

• Conventional three-dimension model

Knowledge level: Students will master the necessary facts, principles, concepts, and theories related to the topic.Students will show their comprehension of the subject through spoken or written forms of expression.

Ability level: Students will develop the ability to apply knowledge to solve problems and make wise decisions. Students will improve their capabilities in evaluation, integration, and analytical reasoning.

Dimension of Quality/Attitude: Learners will cultivate an eagerness for knowledge and foster traits such as curiosity, determination, and tenacity in their educational journeys. Students will demonstrate a commitment to ethical principles and social responsibility in both their academic endeavors and personal lives.

• Four-dimension model

Language Skills: Learners will cultivate their abilities in understanding, conversing, reading, and writing within the designated language. Learners will improve their command over vocabulary and grammatical structures to achieve effective communication.

Cultural Understanding: Learners will develop a greater understanding and appreciation for various cultures, including their own. Learners will explore how culture influences communication and the use of language.

Thinking quality: Cultivate students' logical, analytical, and creative thinking abilities to process information and generate ideas. Learners will be encouraged to explore, form theories, and draw conclusions based on the information available.

Learning Skills: Pupils will gain methods and approaches to study autonomously and effectively. Students will cultivate a passion for knowledge and embark on a lifelong journey of personal and intellectual development.

4. Teaching focus and difficulties

- Focus: Highlighting the importance of a structured methodology in lesson preparation and its contribution to improving student outcomes.
- Difficulty: Help students identify relevant learning goals and overcome the initial challenge of choosing appropriate teaching methods.

5. Teaching methods

Students will be actively involved in the lesson through a mix of presentations, dialogues, and hands-on activities. Theoretical insights will be presented through lectures, while collaborative discussions will encourage the exchange of ideas and solutions. Engaging in hands-on activities will enable learners to implement the theories discussed in practical situations.

6. School supplies

- Utilizing a combination of PowerPoint presentations and a blackboard to effectively convey the essential ideas and procedures of the main topics.
- Illustrations to showcase optimal methods.
- Engaging methods like group discussions and role-playing exercises can facilitate deeper understanding.

7. Teaching process

- Introduction: Engage students' interest, inspire their enthusiasm, and create a link between what has been previously learned and the forthcoming material.
- Presentation: Present the new information in a manner that is most conducive to initial comprehension.
- Conversation: Inspire learners to express their thoughts and personal experiences pertaining to the subject matter.
- Task: Organize the students into small teams and have them engage in activities related to a specific subject.
- Suggestions: Offer insights regarding students' engagements and identify potential areas for enhancement.
- Conclusion: Summarize the key points and encourage students to continue developing their learning.

8. Designing a traditional or virtual whiteboard

In educational settings, the material presented on the chalkboard may differ based on various factors such as the subject matter, learning goals, and individual teaching style. Nonetheless, typical instances of what could be displayed on the chalkboard include:

- Course title or topic: The main title or topic of the course is usually outlined at the top of the blackboard, outlining the content to be included.
- Essential terminology: Instructors might document significant terms associated with the topic and provide definitions for their students. This practice aids learners in becoming acquainted with the specific language utilized in the session.

- Core principles or concepts: Essential themes, guidelines, or ideas that are being covered in the lesson can be inscribed on the chalkboard to facilitate students' comprehension and retention of the primary points.
- Visual resources such as diagrams and illustrations: In accordance with the topic being discussed, educators may utilize the blackboard to create graphs, sketches, or other visual aids that enhance the written explanations.
- Creating lists and outlines can enhance students' ability to follow and structure their thoughts while detailing the essential steps of a procedure, process, or essay.

In class discussions, educators often jot down questions or topics on the board to encourage critical thought and facilitate dialogue.

- In subjects like mathematics or sciences that involve formulas or practical examples, instructors often illustrate solutions and provide clarifications on the board for the students to easily comprehend.
- Details of the assignment: At the conclusion of each lesson, educators frequently note down the homework tasks, deadlines, and any significant information associated with evaluations or forthcoming lessons.

9. Teaching reflection

Following the lesson, reflecting on the instructional methods is crucial to pinpoint aspects that could be enhanced. This assessment will concentrate on analyzing the teaching strategies implemented, gauging the involvement of students, and recognizing any obstacles faced during the process. The understanding developed through this reflection will contribute to the improvement of upcoming lesson strategies and educational approaches.

Activity 14 **You are going to attend a teaching contest and design a 45-minute lesson plan before delivering your teaching. Choose a unit from the high school English textbooks, design a lesson plan, and discuss it in your group, and improve it.**

____

____

____

____

____

____

2.3.3.9 Implement the teaching plan

No matter how meticulously a plan is devised, or what shape it takes, its eventual application in the classroom will be essential, as well as its role in documenting learning for future reference.

1. Action and response

Preparing a lesson involves more than just writing a script for it. Regardless of how our strategies align along the spectrum of planning, what is brought into the lesson exemplifies an approach aimed at actionable outcomes, instead of being a strict guide to adhere to without question. The suggested course of action, implemented within the classroom setting, is sure to generate a response from students (Thomas & Stephens, 1993). We must then evaluate how to address that response and determine whether. Therefore, we should proceed with our original strategy or if adjustments will be necessary as we move forward.

Several factors might compel us to adjust our action plan while a lesson is ongoing.

• Magical moment

In language classes, some of the most impactful experiences arise during unanticipated discussions or when a subject ignites an unexpected interest among learners. These spontaneous instances are crucial for fostering and maintaining the collective enthusiasm of the group. It is essential to acknowledge such moments when they appear and thoughtfully decide whether to nurture their growth, rather than stifling them simply because they deviate from the established curriculum.

• Reasonable classifications

A further reason for straying from our initial strategy arises when unforeseen events occur that cannot be overlooked, such as an unexpected reaction from a student regarding a reading assignment or the sudden news of a wedding announcement. In instances of seizing the moment for instruction, educators utilize unexpected opportunities to teach newly arisen language concepts. In a similar vein, we may suddenly find ourselves inspired by a topic or a connection in language that we feel compelled to explore right away.

• Unexpected issues

No matter how meticulously everything is arranged, unexpected challenges can still arise. Certain learners might perceive an activity we deemed engaging as surprisingly dull. The duration of an activity might diverge from our expectations, either taking longer or shorter than anticipated. It is conceivable that a task we assumed would be straightforward for the students might actually prove to be quite challenging (or the other way around). There may have been an expectation of a certain number of attendees for the planned activity, but it becomes clear that some students are not present. Sometimes, it occurs that students are already familiar with the subjects or materials we intend to discuss in class, and logically, it is clear that proceeding might not be the best choice.

No matter how meticulously we strategize, our strategy remains merely a proposal for what might occur during the lesson. The actual implementation of it hinges entirely on the reactions and interactions of the students. As stated by Jim Scrivener, it is essential to prepare in depth. Yet, in the classroom, the focus should be on educating the students—not adhering rigidly to the strategy.

2. Plans as documentation and analytical resources

A written plan is not just a suggestion for future actions; it also serves as documentation of events that have occurred.When engaged in a continuous series of lessons, one can reflect on past activities to determine the next steps to take.

To effectively adapt lessons based on student feedback, it is essential to maintain a detailed log of the effectiveness of various activities to support our recollection. Keeping a detailed account of the lessons can be beneficial for fellow educators who may need to step in during our absence.

Thus, the initial plans that were documented will need to be adjusted based on the actual experiences from the classes conducted. This may simply involve removing the initial activity title or the page number from the coursebook and substituting it with what was employed during the lessons. If there is an opportunity to document the experiences of both the teacher and the learners during the lesson, carefully evaluating which activities were effective and which were not, this reflection will not only facilitate adjustments for future implementations of the same activities but also prompt consideration of teaching methodologies and possible revisions in both tasks and strategies. Approaching lesson preparation in this manner enables individuals to function as their evaluators, contributing to their professional growth.

2.4 Lesson Plan Presentation

A presentation of a lesson plan involves verbally articulating the educational framework and fundamental principles associated with a particular subject to peers or evaluators, aimed at fostering discussion and enhancement of the instructional design. Presentations of lesson plans play an essential role in the realm of education, not only highlighting educators' teaching capabilities but also fostering ongoing development and cooperation among members of the educational community.

2.4.1 Categories of Lesson Plan Presentations

Different forms of lesson plan presentations exist, each designed to serve specific objectives and offer distinct advantages.

Predictive demonstration. It acts as a practice session prior to the commencement of actual instructional activities. This form of presentation allows educators to assess their lesson outlines, evaluate the progression of their concepts, and detect any possible flaws or sections that require improvement. It provides a chance to recreate the classroom scenario, assess the effectiveness of instructional methods, and facilitate a cohesive and interactive lesson experience. By anticipating possible obstacles and resolving them in advance, educators can approach the classroom with enhanced assurance and readiness.

Reflective demonstration. This is a retrospective analysis conducted after class. Through this demonstration, teachers can evaluate the impact of the training program and consider the successful aspects and those that were less effective. It provides an opportunity to analyze how students reacted, assess how effectively the teaching strategies were implemented, and gain perspectives that will inform upcoming teaching sessions. Engaging in reflective presentations fosters a sense of self-awareness and contributes to professional development, as educators continuously strive to enhance their instructional methods informed by data-driven insights.

Competitive presentation. Teachers showcase their teaching plans during competitions or events. This environment promotes a spirit of teamwork and constructive rivalry among teachers, fostering both innovation and creative thinking. When educators deliver presentations to their colleagues or evaluators, they have the opportunity to obtain valuable insights, assess their performance relative to others, and aim for higher standards in their teaching methodologies. Engaging in competitive presentations allows for the exchange of effective strategies and sparks innovative concepts.

Illustrative demonstration. This refers to a presentation that exemplifies an ideal framework or outstanding lesson outline. In this case, a teacher shares a thoroughly developed and effectively implemented lesson plan, which serves as an exemplary model for colleagues to follow. This approach emphasizes exemplary practices, creative instructional techniques, and successful evaluation methods. For educators who are either new to the field or aim to refine their instructional techniques, practical demonstrations serve as a crucial resource by showcasing effective lesson planning in a concrete manner.

Topical presentation. It centers around a particular topic or problem, encouraging an in-depth exploration and comprehension of an educational dilemma or idea. Such presentations can be designed to tackle current issues in education, new teaching methodologies, or niche topics. Presentations on various topics prompt educators to think critically about their profession, keep up with recent findings, and engage in the wider educational conversation.

Activity 15 Read the following scenarios carefully and for each one, identify the type of lesson plan presentation it represents. Then, briefly describe how the scenario aligns with the characteristics of that presentation type. Have a discussion in your group.

Scenario 1: Ms. Li is preparing for her upcoming lesson titled "How Different Are People's Daily Routines" in Unit 6—A Day in the Life. She has designed a detailed lesson plan, including interactive activities and multimedia resources. Before the class, she conducts a "dry run" with a colleague, simulating the classroom environment to ensure her ideas flow smoothly and identify any potential issues.

Type of Presentation: ________________________________

Description: ________________________________

____

____

____

Scenario 2: After delivering a lesson on "How Different Are People's Daily Routines" in Unit 6—A Day in the Life, Mr. Zhang gathers feedback from his students and reflects on the lesson plan's effectiveness. He notes which activities engaged students most and which concepts they struggled with. He plans to use this information to improve his future lessons.

Type of Presentation: ________________________________

Description: ________________________________

____

____

____

Scenario 3: At an annual teachers' conference, a group of educators participate in a lesson plan competition. Each teacher showcases their unique approach to teaching a common topic, receiving feedback from a panel of judges and their peers.

Type of Presentation: ________________________________

Description: ________________________________

____

____

____

The scenario depicts a competitive presentation where teachers engage in a contest, showcasing their lesson plans and creativity. The format fosters healthy competition, encourages innovation, and provides a platform for constructive feedback and benchmarking against others.

Scenario 4: At a new teacher induction program, an experienced teacher presents a model lesson plan on how to teach reading comprehension effectively. The presentation includes a step-by-step guide, practical tips, and examples of successful assessment strategies.

Type of Presentation: ________________________________

Description: ____

____

____

____

Scenario 5: During a professional development workshop, a panel of educators discuss the impact of technology on modern classrooms. They present research-based arguments, share case studies, and engage in a lively debate about the benefits and challenges of integrating technology into lesson planning.

Type of Presentation: ____

Description: ____

____

____

____

2.4.2 Guidelines for Delivering a Lesson Plan Presentation

As one begins the path toward becoming an outstanding educator, gaining proficiency in delivering effective lesson plans, or what is commonly referred to as the skills involved in presenting lesson plans. This represents an essential achievement. It not only reflects one's grasp of the topic but also highlights the capability to organize, and convey ideas with clarity. The key elements of preparing an engaging lesson plan presentation are as follows.

2.4.2.1 Comprehend the intent

To begin with, it is essential to understand that the aim of presenting a lesson plan is to effectively share one's approach to instructional design, teaching strategies, and anticipated outcomes in a manner that is both clear and captivating. This is a chance to showcase one's understanding of teaching strategies, originality, and dedication to enhancing student learning experiences (influenced by various references on educator preparation and instructional frameworks).

2.4.2.2 Understand your audience

Customize your presentation according to the audience's needs. Think about the individuals who will be present: whether they are industry specialists, educators, administrators from the school, evaluators in a competition, or possibly a combination of these groups. Familiarize yourself with the anticipations they might hold and the standards they could apply in assessing your lesson plan, informed by standard practices within educational contexts and professional growth initiatives.

2.4.2.3 Organize your presentation

An effectively organized presentation is essential. In general, a presentation focused on a lesson plan should encompass elements derived from established guidelines and frameworks for lesson plan creation and presentation.

Overview: Provide a concise overview of the subject matter, appropriate grade level, and overall goals pertaining to the lesson.

Contextual details: Offer relevant information that frames your lesson, enabling your audience to grasp its importance.

Learning objectives: Clearly explain to students specific, measurable, achievable, relevant, and long-term (SMART) learning goals.

Teaching approaches: Elaborate on the instructional techniques, engagements, and materials that will be implemented to meet the desired educational outcomes. Discuss the rationale behind selecting these approaches and how they will capture and maintain students' interest.

Evaluation and response: Describe the methods that will be utilized to evaluate student comprehension and ensure that feedback is provided promptly. Establish the benchmarks for achievement and describe the structure of the evaluations.

Reflections and conclusions: Provide a recap of the lesson plan, emphasizing its merits along with possible areas for enhancement. Commitment to continual professional growth and enhancement is essential.

2.4.2.4 Use intelligent visual assistance

The use of visual elements like slideshows, films, or physical items can significantly improve the effectiveness of a presentation by increasing its engagement and memorability, as demonstrated by studies in multimedia education and presentation strategy. It is important to utilize these tools thoughtfully and selectively, ensuring they support your spoken message rather than detracting from it. Make certain that the visuals employed are polished, unambiguous, and intricately aligned with the objectives of your lesson plan.

2.4.2.5 Practice and exercise

Rehearsing your presentation several times is essential, as highlighted in the studies of performance psychology and training in effective communication skills. This practice will assist in enhancing the substance, rhythm, and presentation style. If feasible, capturing a video of yourself can be beneficial, as reviewing the recording will highlight areas that may require enhancement. It is important to consider aspects such as posture, vocal inflection, and gaze to effectively convey self-assurance and excitement.

2.4.2.6 Anticipate possible inquiries

Consider potential inquiries from your audience and formulate clear, insightful responses grounded in effective practices for presenting and advocating educational concepts. This reflects a deep understanding of the topic and showcases the ability to respond quickly and effectively. Keep in mind that inquiries from your audience frequently indicate their interest and involvement.

2.4.2.7 Accept suggestions

Embrace feedback that is aimed at improving performance, a principle widely recognized in the realms of professional growth and educational psychology. Consider it a chance for personal growth and enhancement. Utilize the evaluations you obtain to enhance your presentation abilities regarding lesson planning and to improve your teaching methodologies.

Activity 16 **Choose the best answer to each question.**

1. The primary goal of a lesson plan presentation is to ____________.
   A. entertain the audience with funny anecdotes
   B. showcase the teacher's artistic abilities
   C. demonstrate the teacher's understanding of the subject and teaching skills
   D. convince the audience to adopt a specific teaching method
2. When tailoring your lesson plan presentation to your audience, what is the most important factor to consider?
   A. The number of slides in your PowerPoint.
   B. The level of technical detail in your explanation.
   C. The audience's expectations and evaluation criteria.
   D. The amount of time you have to present.
3. SMART learning objectives in a lesson plan are ____________.
   A. Simple, Measurable, Advanced, Relevant, and Time-bound
   B. Specific, Meaningful, Achievable, Realistic, and Time-bound
   C. Specific, Measurable, Achievable, Relevant, and Time-bound
   D. Strategic, Memorable, Actionable, Realistic, and Targeted
4. In a well-structured lesson plan presentation, what typically comes after the "Introduction" section?
   A. Instructional methods B. Assessment and feedback
   C. Background information D. Conclusion and reflection
5. Visual aids in a lesson plan presentation should be used ____________.
   A. as the primary means of communication
   B. excessively to impress the audience

C. sparingly and strategically to enhance the presentation

D. only if the audience is visually inclined

6. Which of the following is NOT a benefit of practicing and rehearsing your lesson plan presentation multiple times?

A. It helps refine the content and pacing.

B. It improves the delivery and confidence.

C. It ensures that no questions will be asked during the actual presentation.

D. It allows for self-reflection and improvement.

7. When preparing for a lesson plan presentation, anticipating questions and preparing answers demonstrates ____________.

A. a lack of preparation for the unexpected

B. the teacher's lack of knowledge in the subject area

C. the teacher's ability to think critically and respond to challenges

D. an unwillingness to engage with the audience

8. The conclusion and reflection section of a lesson plan presentation should ____________.

A. focus solely on the successes of the lesson plan

B. ignore any areas for improvement

C. summarize the plan and highlight both strengths and areas for improvement

D. only discuss potential issues and challenges

9. In terms of effective communication during a lesson plan presentation, what is crucial to project confidence and enthusiasm?

A. Using complex terminology to demonstrate expertise.

B. Maintaining a neutral tone of voice throughout.

C. Paying attention to body language, tone of voice, and eye contact.

D. Focusing solely on the content and ignoring nonverbal cues.

10. Embracing feedback after a lesson plan presentation is important because it ____________.

A. means the teacher does not have to make any changes

B. proves that the teacher is perfect and does not need to improve

C. offers an opportunity for growth and refinement of teaching skills

D. shows that the teacher is open to criticism but will not make any changes

2.4.3 Components of a Lesson Plan Presentation

A lesson plan presentation usually consists of the following nine steps, which have been mentioned in the previous part.

(1) Analysis of the teaching materials: the textbook and supplementary materials;

(2) Analysis of the students: the characteristics of the learner;

(3) Teaching/learning objectives: expected learning outcomes;

(4) Focal and difficult points;

(5) Teaching methods: approaches of teaching;

(6) Teaching aids;

(7) Teaching procedures: steps of the teaching;

(8) Blackboard writing design;

2.4.4 Sample of a Lesson Plan Presentation

The following is a model case of a lesson plan presentation.

1. Analysis of the reading material

This passage is an exposition, which introduces the Longji Rice Terraces in Longsheng County in Guangxi Zhuang Autonomous Region. It describes the spectacular view of Longji Rice Terraces in different seasons, the background of Longji Rice Terraces, the reasons why local people build rice terraces, the working principle of Longji Rice Terraces, and its value nowadays. Through learning, students can understand the main idea, genre, and detailed information in this passage. Besides, they can apply the reading strategy to daily reading comprehension tasks. Most importantly, they can recognize the harmonious relationship between man and nature, explore the significance of protecting agricultural heritages, and develop cultural confidence.

2. Analysis of students

The students in this class have a relatively good English level and a high enthusiasm for English learning. They could find out the main idea and topic sentences easily. They are capable of understanding the main idea of the passage and finding out the detailed information in this passage. However, they may have difficulty in expressing their ideas in English logically and fluently and their thinking quality should also be developed through some meaningful activities.

3. Learning objectives

By the end of the period, students are expected to

(1) have a good understanding of the passage;

(2) learn to use the reading strategy in their daily reading comprehension;

(3) explain how the terraces work;

(4) learn the relationships betweens humans and nature and form the right values;

(5) explore the significance of protecting agricultural heritages;

(6) develop cultural confidence.

4. Learning key and difficult points

(1) Learning key points

Figure out the type of the passage and the author's purpose by finding topic sentences and geting the detailed information in this passage.

Learn to use the reading strategy in the reading task.

Retell the working principle of Longji Rice Terraces.

(2) Learning difficult points

Recognize the harmonious relationship between man and nature.

Explore the significance of protecting agricultural heritages and develop cultural confidence.

5. Teaching Methods

Task-based language teaching & situational language teaching method.

6. Teaching aids

PPT slides, video, chalks, and blackboard.

7. Teaching procedures

(1) Lead in

Activity 1: Let students enjoy a video about Longji Rice Terraces.

Activity 2: Let students learn something about the description of beauty.

(Activity 1 enables students to get closer to Longji Rice Terraces and appreciate their beauty. Activity 2 helps students learn some advanced words to describe something beautiful.)

(2) Pre-reading

Activity 3: Let students answer the question: Do you think Longji Rice Terraces are a wonder of nature or a creation of humans?

(Activity 3 puts forward a question that students can think about during the whole reading process and lays a foundation for their subsequent understanding of the relationship between man and nature.)

(3) While-reading

Fast reading:

Activity 4 & Activity 5: Ask students to find out the genre and the writing purpose of this passage.

(To help students figure out the type and the writing purpose of this passage.)

Detailed reading:

Activity 6: Let students find out the topic sentence of each paragraph and match the main idea with each paragraph.

Activity 7: Let students apply the reading strategy to the exercise in the college entrance examination.

Activity 8: Let students read paragraph 1 and answer the question: What colors are these terraces in different seasons?

Activity 9: Let students read paragraph 2 & 3 and complete the form. (Who, Where, How long, Why)

Activity 10: Let students read paragraph four and find out four verbs or verb phrases to fill in the blanks.

Activity 11: Let students retell the working principle by themselves and then students retell the working principle together.

Activity 12: Let students read paragraph 5 and answer the question: Why do the local people still maintain the terraces?

(To help students figure out the type and writing purpose of this passage, get some detailed information and retell the working principle of Longji Rice Terraces by themselves.)

(4) Post-reading

Actitity 13: Let students perform the task: Suppose you are going to introduce Longji Rice Terraces to foreign tourists as a guide, prepare the tour guide presentation.

Activity 14: Let students think about the question: What is the significance of protecting agricultural heritages?

(Activity 13 lets students become more familiar with the passage and gives students the opportunity to show themselves. Activity 14 lets students explore the significance of protecting agricultural heritages and enhances their cultural confidence.)

8. Blackboard design

The blackboard design shown in Figure 2.3 embodies the structure and main idea of the text.

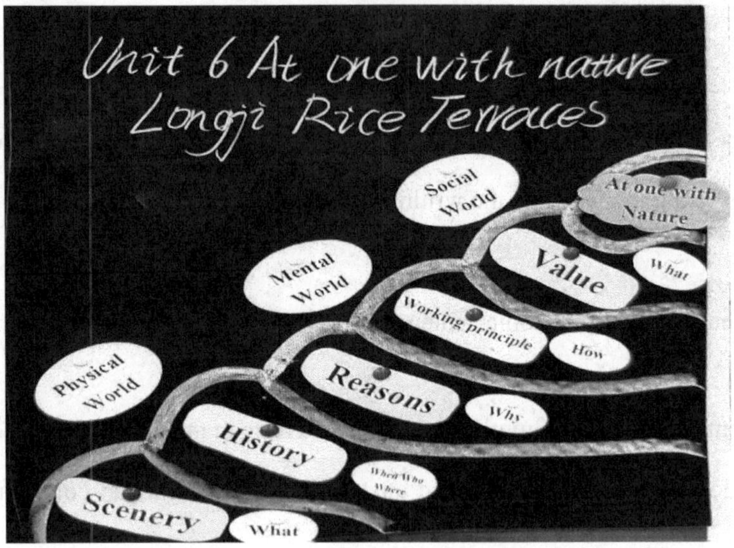

Figure 2.3 Blackboaird design of the text

9. Reflections

(1) Highlights

- The teacher's demeanor transitioned naturally and smoothly, with an aesthetically pleasing blackboard design.
- Reading techniques were learned and immediately applied, with timely connections to college entrance exam questions.
- Students had sufficient and effective practice time in class, and the post-reading activities were thoughtfully designed with depth.
- Emphasis was placed on enhancing students' knowledge, abilities, and overall qualities.

(2) Reflections

- If certain paragraph details are simple to comprehend, the allocated time can be appropriately reduced.
- Consider adding flexibility to the tour guide commentary section.
- Focus on the completeness of teaching activities; no homework was assigned.
- Design corresponding questions for the introduction part to encourage students to view the video with a sense of purpose.

(3) Improvements

- Allocate time more reasonably based on task difficulty to provide more time for student presentations.

- Increase the flexibility of tasks to allow students room for self-expression.
- Reserve time to present homework assignments.
- Pay attention to the design of questions to encourage students to view videos with a problem-solving mindset, making the learning more targeted.

Thinking and Doing

A. Discussion questions

(1) List what you consider to be the characteristics of good students and good teachers. How will this affect your lesson planning?

(2) How much detail do you feel is necessary in writing your lesson plans? Would this change if a supervisor wanted copies of your lesson plans?

(2) As a novice teacher, what aspects of lesson planning are the most daunting? How will you go about getting assistance in planning your lessons?

B. Practice

1. Design a 10-minute oral English teaching plan according to the given information and language material, which should at least contain the following points:

- learning objectives
- teaching contents
- key and difficult points
- major steps and time allocation
- activities and justifications

The following are the given materials:

About the students: The students are in grade 2 from a rural senior high school, with 40 members in one class. Most of the students have achieved Academic Quality Level 1 of the High School Curriculum Standards.

Language material

We've been told since we were toddlers that "It's good to share". Parents and teachers keep reminding us to share toys, snacks, books, happy memories, and sometimes even sorrows with others. When we grow up, we share photos, life stories, and opinions with people around us and with those we don't know via social media. Taking it as an object of study, psychologists have published various papers stating that the behaviour of sharing is beneficial to set up positive emotional bonding.

Today, the action of sharing takes on extra meaning. It's not just about sharing sweets or frustration; it has expanded to almost every aspect of our lives—the whole world seems to be into sharing. We are using technology to reduce the money that we spend on goods and services, or to make money out of those that we don't use ourselves all of the time. These vary from car shares to home shares, and even to pet shares. The sharing economy is taking off in all sorts of areas. It is creating new ways of thinking and providing services to people when and where they want them.

Notes: The language material is excerpted from Unit 4 Everyday Economics of Optional Compulsory 4 from 2019 FLTRP.

2. Choose a unit from a junior high school English textbook, discuss how to write a 10-minute lesson plan presentation draft for a 45-minute English class in your group, and each group will give a lesson plan presentation in class by a representative.

C. Exercises for instructional skills

1. Which of the following should a teacher avoid when his/her focus is on developing students' ability to use words appropriately?
   A. Teaching both the spoken and written form.
   B. Teaching words in context and giving examples.
   C. Presenting the form, meaning, and use of a word.
   D. Asking students to memorize bilingual word lists.

2. If a teacher asks students to make their learning plans, he/she is trying to develop their __________.
   A. cognitive strategy B. affective strategy
   C. communicative strategy D. meta-cognitive strategy

3. Which of the following tasks fails to encourage active language use?
   A. Reciting a text. B. Bargaining in a shop.
   C. Writing an application letter. D. Reading to get a message.

4. Which of the following tasks fails to develop students' skill of recognizing discourse patterns?
   A. Analyzing the structure of difficult sentences.
   B. Checking the logic of the author's arguments.
   C. Getting the scrambled sentences into a paragraph.
   D. Marking out common openers to stories and jokes.

5. Which of the following does NOT belong to the contents of a lesson plan?

A. The objective of the lesson.
B. Teaching aids that are required.
C. Teaching procedures.
D. Students' answers to teachers' questions.

6. Which of the following activities does NOT belong to teaching activities?

A. Survey and interview.
B. Planning text structure.
C. Impromptu speaking and discussion.
D. Cooperative learning.

7. Objectives should be SMART, which means that the teaching objectives should be specific, measurable, attainable, relevant, and ____________.

A. true
B. time-bound
C. tidy
D. thick

8. In the designing of teaching objectives, there is an ABCD rule. Which one is NOT included in the following?

A. audience
B. behavior
C. consideration
D. degree

9. Which of the following statements about task design is INCORRECT?

A. Activities must have clear and attainable objectives.
B. Activities should be confined to the classroom context.
C. Activities must be relevant to students' life experiences.
D. Activities should help develop students' language ability.

10. There are five principles for a good lesson plan. Which of the following is NOT included in the five principles?

A. clear aims
B. variety
C. focus
D. learnability

Checklist

Mark the questions with a check (√) if your answer is yes.

- ☐ Have I understood the functions and principles of lesson planning?
- ☐ Have I made certain the procedures of lesson planning?
- ☐ Am I clear about how to write a lesson plan and implement it in teaching practice?
- ☐ Have I grasped the principles and steps of lesson plan presentation?
- ☐ Can I write a lesson plan presentation and deliver it successfully in front of the audience?

Reflective Journal

Please write down your reflections on what you have / have not learned in this chapter.

◇ The essential skills I need to possess and develop for lesson planning and lesson plan presentation:

____

____

____

____

____

◇ Anything I wish to further explore (i.e., puzzles and difficulties):

____

____

____

____

____

References

Anderson, L. W., Krathwohl, D. R., Airasian, P. W., et al. (2001). *A taxonomy for learning, teaching, and assessing: A revision of Bloom's taxonomy of educational objectives*. Pearson Education, Inc.

Armstrong, S. A., & Savage, T. L. (1983). Mastering the techniques of teaching. Jossey-Bass.

Black, P., & Wiliam, D. (1998). Assessment and classroom learning. *Assessment in Education: Principles, Policy & Practice*, *5*(1), 7–74. https://doi.org/10.1080/0969595980050102

Bransford, J. D., Brown, A. L., & Cocking, R. R. (2002). *How people learn: Brain, mind, experience, and school*. National Academy Press.

Brown, A., & Lee, C. (2020). Bridging gaps in student knowledge: A case study. *Teaching and Teacher Education*, *36*(1), 67–83. https://doi.org/10.1016/j.tate.2020.103124

Bruner, J. S. (1996). *The culture of education*. Harvard University Press.

Davis, B. G. (2009). *Tools for teaching* (2nd ed.). Jossey-Bass.

Doran, J. M. (1981). There's a SMART way to write management's goals and objectives. *Management Review, 70*(11), 35–36.

Fullan, M. (2007). The new meaning of educational change (4th ed.). Teachers College Press.

Guskey, T. R. (2002). *Professional development and teacher change.* Teachers College Press.

Harmer, J. (2015). *The practice of English language teaching* (5th ed.). Longman.

Jones, E., & Clark, R. C. (2019). Balancing challenge and complexity in instructional design: A cognitive load perspective. *Educational Psychology Review, 31*(4), 789–812. https://doi.org/10.1007/s10648-019-09478-0

Krathwohl, D. R. (2002). A revision of Bloom's taxonomy: An overview. *Theory into Practice, 41*(4), 212–218. https://doi.org/10.1207/s15430421tip4104_2

Mager, R. F. (1997). *Goal analysis and development: A guide for managers and trainers* (2nd ed.). Addison-Wesley.

Marshall, S. P. (2012). Effective lesson planning: A research-based guide for teachers and teacher educators. Routledge.

Marzano, R. J., & Kendall, J. S. (2007). *The art and science of teaching: A comprehensive framework for helping teachers translate theory into practice* (2nd ed.). ASCD.

Morrison, G. R., & Lowther, D. L. (2013). Integrating computer technology into the classroom: Yesterday, today, and tomorrow. *American Educational Research Journal, 50*(2), 195–204. https://doi.org/10.3102/0002831212469737

National Research Council. (2012). *Education for life and work: Developing transferable knowledge and skills in the 21st century.* The National Academies Press. https://doi.org/10.17226/13398

Scriven, M. (1967). The methodology of evaluation. In R. W. Tyler, R. M. Gagne, & M. Scriven (Eds.), *Perspectives of curriculum evaluation* (pp. 39–83). Rand McNally & Company.

Shepard, L. A. (2000). The role of assessment in a learning culture. *Educational Researcher, 29*(7), 4–14. https://doi.org/10.3102/0013189X029007004

Smith, P. L. (2015). *Teaching planning and preparation: Reflective practice and classroom management.* Routledge.

Smith, P. L., & Ragan, T. J. (2005). *Instructional design* (3rd ed.). Wiley.

Smith, T., & Ragan, S. J. (2005). *Effective teaching: Strategies and practices for mainstream K-12 classrooms.* Pearson Education.

Stipek, D. J. (2002). *Adapting instruction to student needs. In Motivation to learn: Integrating theory and practice* (4th ed., pp. 123–150). Allyn & Bacon.

Thomas, R. M., & Stephens, S. D. (1993). *Curriculum development: A guide to practice*. Pearson.

Tomlinson, C. A. (2017). *How to differentiate instruction in academically diverse classrooms* (3rd ed.). ASCD.

Ur, P. (2017). *A course in language teaching: Practice and theory* (6th ed.). Pearson Education Limited.

Chapter 3

Skills for Employing Instructional Methods

Objectives

Upon completion of this chapter, you should be able to:

- Understand the concept of each instructional model
- Know the main procedures of each instructional model
- Utilize the instructional models correctly in the lesson plan and teaching practice with the authentic teaching material

Discussion Questions

Do you know the PPP approach and the communicative approach? If you are asked to compare these two approaches, from which perspectives will you compare them?

Pedagogical strategies are defined as enduring frameworks and regulated activities designed according to particular educational theories or philosophies. These methodologies serve as a detailed outline for structuring and executing educational activities, highlighting the interconnectedness and roles of different elements in the teaching and learning sphere. This chapter discusses a dozen significant pedagogical methods and presents techniques for their incorporation into the design of English language instruction. Such practices enable teachers to develop vibrant and stimulating educational settings that promote effective language learning. Gaining insight into the core elements, their underlying principles, and the execution process is essential for improving the effectiveness of both instructional design and teaching practices in the classroom.

3.1 The Role of Various Pedagogical Methods in Education

Central to the advancement of education is the understanding that selecting a suitable instructional method that aligns with the individual needs, capabilities, and learning preferences of students is crucial for improving educational results. Various strategies such as the constructivist method, inquiry-driven approaches, problem-based learning, or hybrid learning models establish guidelines for teachers to develop engaging, impactful, and student-focused educational experiences.

3.1.1 Design Effect

The methods of instruction play a crucial role in shaping the planning phase by offering a distinct goal and focus for constructing lessons. Utilizing a particular framework allows educators to effectively synchronize their objectives, subject matter, and classroom activities with the intended learning achievements. This organized method guarantees that teaching resources are pertinent, stimulating, and effective in enhancing student achievement.

3.1.2 Supporting Execution

Methods of instruction not only shape the design framework but also enhance effective execution within the educational setting. They provide a framework for teachers, guiding them through the different phases of teaching, from the initial presentation to the final wrap-up. This framework minimizes uncertainty and enhances uniformity in educational approaches, facilitating educators in tailoring their techniques to better meet the diverse needs of their students.

3.1.3 Improving Educational Outcomes

The fundamental aim of developing and executing educational strategies is to improve the effectiveness of learning. Educational strategies are crucial in facilitating this by creating settings that promote involvement, analytical thinking, and innovative problem-solving. Research indicates that models focused on collaborative learning can enhance student performance and foster greater engagement.

3.1.4 Agility and Responsiveness

Teaching methodologies inherently possess a level of flexibility and responsiveness, which empowers instructors to customize their teaching strategies according to the distinct requirements of their learners. This could involve altering the speed of teaching, changing activities, or integrating innovative technologies. Such methodologies offer a structure that can evolve and be refined over time.

3.1.5 Evaluation and Response

Assessment and feedback play essential roles in the framework of instructional design. Strategies for teaching provide insight into how to effectively implement both formative and summative evaluations that are in harmony with educational goals and yield meaningful feedback on student development. As a result, this allows teachers to modify their teaching strategies and offer tailored assistance to individual learners.

3.1.6 Fostering Teamwork

Instructors frequently highlight the necessity of teamwork, encouraging interactions not only among learners but also between teachers. For instance, participatory learning frameworks promote teamwork among learners, enabling them to address challenges collectively, exchange perspectives, and assist each other in their educational journeys. In a similar fashion, educators may work together to exchange effective strategies, materials, and perspectives, cultivating an environment that encourages ongoing enhancement and growth in their profession.

3.2 Teaching Design and Practice with the 5E Approach

The instructional model known as 5E, which encompasses the phases of Engagement, Exploration, Explanation, Elaboration/Extension, and Evaluation, serves as a popular and effective method for crafting educational experiences. Introduced in 1989 by the Biological Sciences Curriculum Study (BSCS), this framework emphasizes the importance of experiential learning, higher-order reasoning, and a profound comprehension of topics (Bybee, 1997). This paper will examine the implementation of the 5E model within the context of teaching English, focusing on its various phases and possible applications.

3.2.1 Teaching Philosophy

The 5E teaching model focuses on learner-oriented experiences, encouraging individuals to build knowledge through exploration and inquiry. It underscores the significance of intellectual involvement, creating a learning atmosphere driven by curiosity. The approach prioritizes the combination of interactive tasks with analytical reasoning and conversation, promoting a comprehensive grasp of ideas.

The learner-centered approach of the 5E model prioritizes the involvement and responsibility of students in their educational journey. Learners are prompted to immerse themselves in the material, conduct observations, pose inquiries, and develop their theories.

The theory of constructivism asserts that individuals create their understanding through active interaction with their environment. This foundational idea is enhanced by the 5E instructional model, which encourages learners to develop new insights built upon their existing knowledge and experiences.

The foundational element of the 5E instructional model is inquiry, which plays a vital role during both the

Exploration and Explanation stages. Learners participate in research-oriented tasks, gather information, and evaluate findings to develop interpretations of the phenomena they observe.

The 5E framework unfolds in a systematic sequence that guides learners from their first involvement to a profound grasp and utilization of concepts. Learning progresses as each stage builds on the one before it, promoting an additive and orderly development of knowledge.

The 5E framework emphasizes the significance of catering to the various facets of learner development. Students participate in experiential tasks, engage in dialogue, and contemplate their learning, thereby fostering growth in cognitive, emotional, and physical skills.

In the context of the 5E instructional model, the Evaluation stage places significant emphasis on both formative and summative assessments, serving to guide teaching practices and offer constructive feedback to learners. This continuous evaluation method guarantees that educational progress is maintained while also highlighting areas for additional growth.

3.2.2 Main Procedures

The instructional framework consists of five different yet linked phases: Engagement, Exploration, Explanation, Elaboration/Extension, and Evaluation. Each of these stages plays a unique role in the teaching and learning process, collectively facilitating the students' active acquisition of knowledge (Bybee, 2006) (see Figure 3.1).

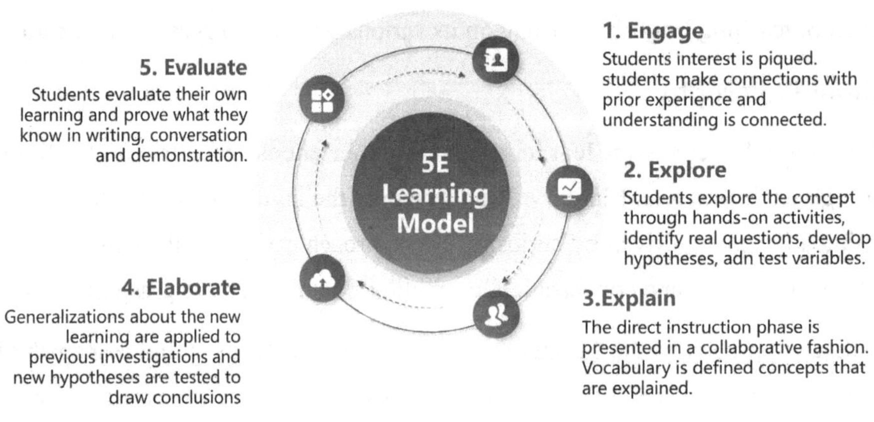

Figure 3.1 5E Learning Model

Engagement (E1): The first step of the 5E framework is designed to kindle students' intrigue and wonder by fostering relevant and captivating educational situations. This is accomplished through the presentation of authentic challenges, demonstrations, or stimulating inquiries that relate to the learners' existing knowledge and experiences.

Exploration (E2): In this key stage, learners participate in interactive tasks or inquiries to investigate various phenomena, collect information, and develop preliminary interpretations. They engage in solitary or collaborative efforts, identifying trends, making connections, and questioning their findings. In this context, educators support students by offering essential materials and direction, empowering them to take charge of their educational journey.

Explanation (E3): The phase of explanation emphasizes reinforcing students' comprehension through facilitated discussions and the clarification of concepts. Educators guide learners in examining their collected data, connecting it with existing knowledge, and formulating scientifically sound interpretations. This stage entails articulating phenomena with the support of evidence and employing suitable terminology.

Elaboration/Extension (E4): The elaboration stage promotes the application of newly acquired knowledge to novel or analogous scenarios, which leads to enhanced understanding and knowledge transfer. Activities in this phase may include designing experiments, participating in thoughtful discussions, or tackling intricate problems. The objective is to cultivate and refine the students' conceptual frameworks while facilitating connections among diverse concepts and contexts.

Evaluation (E5): The concluding stage focuses on evaluating the learning outcomes of students and delivering constructive feedback. This evaluation encompasses various dimensions, comprising ongoing assessments, conclusive evaluations, reflections by the learners themselves, and reviews conducted by peers. The emphasis lies in recognizing the advancements students have made in their educational journey and pinpointing areas where they can grow further.

3.2.3 Implementation of Teaching Design and Application

The 5E instructional model emerges as a guiding light within contemporary teaching methodologies, designed to cultivate a profound, evidence-based, and learner-focused educational experience. This methodology offers a well-organized framework that can be tailored by educators to suit various subjects and educational levels. Its application, nonetheless, does not lend itself to a universal solution; it necessitates a deep comprehension, adaptability, and readiness to cater to the varied learning preferences of students. Below are some suggestions for effectively implementing this methodology within educational design.

1. Engage

Objective: Generating enthusiasm. The Engage stage marks the beginning of the educational journey by intriguing learners and arousing their interest in the subject matter. This stage establishes a foundation for exploration and fosters a context that is both meaningful and captivating for the students.

Strategies

- Incorporating a variety of resources, such as digital media, tangible objects, or genuine materials, to foster an engaging educational atmosphere, and maintain student engagement.

Facilitating students in sharing their relevant experiences and insights regarding the subject matter.

- Engaging students' curiosity through practical illustrations, relevant case studies, or stimulating inquiries.

Example: In a class centered on environmental phenomena, an instructor might start by recounting a personal anecdote about a significant meteorological occurrence, inviting pupils to share their own stories, and subsequently posing the inquiry, "What might take place if the Earth were to pause for a brief period?" "What kinds of calamities could arise?"

Teachers' role: The teacher commences the lesson by presenting an interesting and pertinent scenario or inquiry that ignites curiosity and creates links to previously acquired knowledge.

2. Explore

Objective: Facilitated exploration. During the Exploration stage, learners delve into the subject matter by engaging in experiential tasks and employing analytical reasoning.

Strategies

- Enabling a chance for experiential learning: Learners can collaborate in pairs or small teams to investigate the linguistic frameworks, terminology, and cultural elements pertinent to the subject matter.
- Promoting inquiry and predictive thinking among students: This fosters their curiosity along with enhancing their cognitive abilities.

Example: Participants engage with a passage from a narrative that describes an earthquake, such as "The Night the Earth Didn't Sleep," where they pinpoint significant occurrences and the emotions illustrated within the story. Subsequently, they collaborate in smaller groups to develop a chronological sequence of these incidents and examine the application of metaphorical expressions.

Teachers' role: The educator plays a crucial part by offering direction and assistance as learners participate in practical tasks, and investigations, or engage in reading and discourse that allow them to delve into the subject matter.

3. Explain

Objective: Clarification of ideas. In the Explain phase, the instructor delivers explicit guidance and elucidates concepts, or assists learners in analyzing and interpreting their findings, resulting in a comprehensive grasp of the fundamental ideas.

Strategies

- Enhancing students' comprehension of the desired language by providing both illustrative examples and counterexamples.
- Fostering engagement among students, educators might encourage learners to articulate the guidelines and share relevant examples.
- Employing images, comparisons, and straightforward teaching methods to enhance comprehension and address misunderstandings.
- Promoting an environment where learners feel empowered to express their thoughts and pose inquiries.

Example: Following the examination of the text, a class discussion is facilitated by the teacher, focusing on the reasons behind earthquakes and their subsequent impacts, supported by visual aids and diagrams to improve understanding. Learners are invited to express their thoughts and pose inquiries.

Teachers' role: In the teacher's capacity, they guide conversations and offer clarifications that enhance what students have previously investigated, aiding them in linking newfound knowledge with what they already understand.

4. Elaborate

Objective: Utilization and developmental growth. The process of elaboration focuses on utilizing and broadening the recently attained insights by applying them to unfamiliar contexts and challenges. This deepens comprehension and encourages analytical thinking.

Strategies

- Students can participate in various activities such as simulations, group discussions, and written exercises to practice the target language effectively.
- Educators can promote advanced cognitive abilities by prompting learners to dissect, integrate, and critically assess data.

Example: Students collaborate in teams to produce a public awareness message regarding preparedness for earthquakes, applying the language and tactics acquired from the reading material. They share their presentations with the class, gathering input from both classmates and the instructor.

Teachers' role: An educator's responsibility involves creating opportunities for learners to deepen their comprehension by implementing concepts in ways that hold significance.

5. Evaluate

Objective: Evaluation and feedback. The stage of evaluation is dedicated to examining student understanding and delivering prompt and significant responses. This involves the utilization of both types of assessments that gauge progress and outcomes.

Strategies

- Employing a range of evaluative techniques, which encompass both ongoing and final assessments, such as direct observations, tests, creative projects, verbal presentations, written tasks, and assessments by oneself or peers, to compile a thorough overview of student comprehension.
- Offering targeted and actionable observations, which encompass both self-reflection and assessments from peers, to gauge the development of learners and inform subsequent educational pursuits.
- Motivating learners to consider their educational journey and share constructive criticism with their classmates.

Example: Students complete a written reflection on their learning experience, discussing what they have learned about earthquakes, how they applied this knowledge in their public service announcement, and what they still find challenging. Additionally, they engage in peer evaluation of their group's presentation, focusing on communication skills and the effectiveness of the message.

Teachers' role: The teacher evaluates students' understanding through a variety of methods, including quizzes, projects, and self- and peer-assessments.

Activity 1 The following are 7 connection-based questions related to the 5E Instructional Model, each with a focus on the 5E stages and their characteristics or applications in teaching and learning.

1. Match the 5E Stage with its purpose.

Engage	A. Deepening understanding through application
Explore	B. Assessing learning and providing feedback
Explain	C. Capturing students' attention and motivating learning
Elaborate	D. Guiding students to make sense of their experiences
Evaluate	E. Allowing students to investigate and experiment

2. Pair the 5E Stage with a teacher action.

Engage	A. Leading a class discussion to clarify misconceptions
Explore	B. Assigning a research project on the topic
Explain	C. Presenting a real-world scenario to spark curiosity
Elaborate	D. Observing and providing formative feedback
Evaluate	E. Designing a lab activity for students to investigate

3. Connect the 5E Stage to a student activity.

Engage	A. Collaborating on a group project
Explore	B. Making observations and recording data
Explain	C. Reflecting on their learning through journaling
Elaborate	D. Participating in a role-play to demonstrate understanding
Evaluate	E. Completing a multiple-choice quiz

4. Match the Evaluation strategy to the 5E Stage.

Engage	A. Pre-test to assess prior knowledge
Explore	B. Exit ticket to gauge understanding during the lesson
Explain	C. Peer review of worksheets
Elaborate	D. Rubric-based project evaluation
Evaluate	E. Reflective writing on learning outcomes

5. Pair the 5E Stage with a learning objective.

Engage	A. Understanding the relevance of the topic to real-world issues
Explore	B. Demonstrating the ability to conduct scientific investigations
Explain	C. Identifying key concepts and vocabulary related to the topic
Elaborate	D. Applying knowledge to solve complex problems
Evaluate	E. Reflecting on personal growth and learning throughout the process

6. Connect the 5E Stage to a classroom resource.

Engage	A. Facilitator of discussions and activities
Explore	B. Guide and observer of student experimentation
Explain	C. Clarifier of concepts and misconceptions
Elaborate	D. Coach and encourager of deeper learning
Evaluate	E. Assessor and provider of feedback

7. Match the teacher role in the 5E Stages.

Engage	A. A video showcasing the topic's applications
Explore	B. A set of laboratory materials for experimentation
Explain	C. A visual aid (e.g., diagram, model) to clarify concepts
Elaborate	D. A collaborative worksheet with extension questions
Evaluate	E. A rubric for evaluating a final project or presentation

8. Connect the key features of the 5E Model to their impact on learning.

Engage	A. Stimulates curiosity and motivates learners
Explore	B. Encourages hands-on investigation and discovery
Explain	C. Provides clarity and connections between concepts
Elaborat	D. Enhances understanding through application and extension
Evaluate	E. Ensures learning outcomes are achieved and addressed

3.3 Teaching Design and Practice with the PPP Framework

The PPP teaching method, which encompasses the stages of Presentation, Practice, and manufacturing has functioned as a fundamental strategy in numerous English language teaching environments. This teaching method has been well-established within the realm of language education, especially in classrooms focused on English. It offers an organized and methodical framework for presenting new language concepts, enabling learners to evolve from basic familiarity to advanced proficiency. The PPP methodology focuses on creating an effective mix of teacher-led guidance and activities tailored to students, cultivating a setting that enhances the learning of a new language.

3.3.1 Teaching Philosophy

The PPP methodology, as outlined by Richards and Rodgers (2001), is prominently utilized in the field of English teaching, especially for the instruction of grammatical structures, vocabulary acquisition, and practical language use. Its foundation lies in behaviorist theories of learning, advocating for a systematic methodology for introducing new linguistic concepts. Highlighting well-organized demonstration, focused practice, and purposeful output, this method offers an effective and systematic framework for teaching the English language. By segmenting the educational journey into distinct phases, this method guarantees that learners receive guidance throughout, which ultimately enhances their language proficiency and self-assurance in English usage. This method provides an organized framework for helping learners navigate through the language learning journey, ensuring they achieve both comprehension and skillfulness.

3.3.2 Main Procedures

Presentation (P1): The initial stage, Presentation, is essential because it allows students to explore new linguistic ideas, whether related to lexicon, grammar structure, or practical phrases. At this phase, in this phase, the educator commonly presents the target language within a context that resonates with the learners. This is frequently accomplished through methods like narrative techniques, dialogues, or through visual representations. The main aim of this stage is to help students understand the essential elements of the content, placing significant emphasis on understanding and appropriate application. For instance, assuming the discussion revolves around the use of the past simple tense, the instructor could recount a tale that illustrates a series of events which took place earlier, emphasizing actions that occurred in prior instances,

Presentation (P2): After establishing a solid foundation during the initial Presentation phase, the instructor then transitions to the Practice stage, which involves a variety of guided activities which aim to strengthen comprehension of the language concepts that were just presented. Tasks like fill-in-the-blank exercises, reordering sentences, or practice with replacement drills are frequently utilized. This phase primarily emphasizes precision. Learners are motivated to consistently utilize the target language, facilitating the assimilation of structures and principles. The instructor's role continues to be central, offering timely corrections and constructive feedback to avoid the establishment of persistent mistakes. For example, after presenting the past simple tense, the instructor may share sentences that have verbs removed, encouraging learners to insert the accurate past tense forms.

Presentation (P3): The concluding stage, Production, signifies a transformation in classroom interactions. During this phase, students take on greater ownership of their use of language. During this phase, the activities become less structured, focusing on enhancing fluency. Individuals are motivated to express themselves in the target language with increased freedom and creativity, implementing it in practical situations. This may include engaging in simulated interactions, discussions, or tasks that involve students creating their sentences or conversations utilizing the language patterns they have acquired. The instructor adopts a more supportive position, overseeing the tasks and offering guidance when appropriate while granting students more freedom to explore. For instance, learners may be prompted to compose a brief narrative describing their weekend experiences. They often reminisced about their recent activities during the weekend.

A notable advantage of the PPP methodology is its distinct organization, which facilitates an efficient and clear lesson-planning process. It offers a consistent model, which helps educators and learners grasp the lesson's development. Nevertheless, there are some critiques regarding its application. Some believe that the framework may lack flexibility, which can restrict the opportunity for unplanned language practice or for accommodating unforeseen educational demands that surface during instruction. Opponents of the approach argue that an excessive focus on precision during the practice stage may restrict fluidity and the ability to communicate effectively, as learners might become overly tentative and apprehensive about making errors (Pratista, 2023).

In spite of the criticisms leveled against it, a significant number of educators consider the PPP method to be a valuable resource, especially for learners at the beginner or intermediate stages who gain from its organized framework. In more advanced settings, instructors may modify the framework to include greater communicative and task-oriented strategies, thereby addressing the varied requirements of their students.

3.3.3 Implementation and Design Applications in Instruction

1. Purpose

The objective of implementing the PPP methodology in teaching English is to provide a structured and effective framework for language acquisition. This method seeks to establish a robust understanding of grammar and terminology while fostering the ability to communicate effectively through relevant and contextual language practice.

2. Strategies

- Differentiation: Adapt the level of difficulty in each phase to cater to the diverse needs and abilities of students.
- Authentic materials: Incorporate authentic texts, images, and videos to enhance context and relevance.
- Interactive techniques: Encourage pair and group work to foster collaboration and peer support.
- Feedback: Provide specific and timely feedback throughout the practice and production phases to guide student learning.

3. Teachers' role

- Facilitator: Guide students through the presentation phase and facilitate their practice and production.
- Assessor: Evaluate student progress and provide constructive feedback to inform future learning.
- Resource provider: Supply appropriate materials and activities to support student learning.

- Motivator: Create a positive and encouraging learning environment that inspires student engagement and participation.

4. Case Study

The topic of the lesson: Present Perfect Tense

Presentation stage: The instructor elucidates the structure and significance of the present perfect tense by utilizing a timeline and straightforward sentences. Illustrative examples are provided based on recent events, such as, "They have traveled to the Great Wall."

Practice phase: Participants take part in an activity that involves substituting important terms in given statements with references to their personal experiences. Next, there is an activity where learners fill in the blanks by providing the appropriate present perfect tense forms to complete the sentences.

Production stage: Working in pairs, students conduct interviews with each other regarding their recent experiences, documenting their dialogues by employing the present perfect tense. A concluding reflection session takes place, in which learners present the discussions they had and obtain insights from their instructor and fellow students.

Activity 2 Decide whether the following statements are True or False.

1. The Presentation stage of the PPP model solely focuses on teaching vocabulary.
2. During the Practice stage, students should be provided with opportunities to make errors without immediate correction.
3. The Production stage marks the end of language learning, where students are fully proficient.
4. The PPP model discourages the use of authentic materials and real-life situations in language teaching.
5. All three stages of the PPP model are equally important in promoting language acquisition.

3.4 Teaching Design and Practice with the 5Ps Framework

The 5Ps instructional framework, also referred to as the PPPPP model, offers a structured methodology aimed at improving teaching strategies for educators in diverse learning environments. This teaching model encompasses five essential elements: preparation, presentation, practice, production and progress with each element playing a distinct role in fostering a well-rounded educational experience (Larsen-Freeman & Anderson, 2011).

3.4.1 Teaching Philosophy

The PPPPP teaching model represents a comprehensive strategy in the realm of language education that emphasizes the importance of active participation, profound comprehension, and the successful application of knowledge in real-world scenarios. By incorporating supplementary stages into the conventional PPP structure, the method seeks to improve learners' proficiency in language abilities, encourages advanced language competence and innovative thinking, and enhances their capacity for effective communication.

3.4.2 Main Procedures

Preparation: The stage of planning is essential as it allows educators to define and arrange the goals and resources needed for the instructional session. Thorough planning necessitates a comprehensive grasp of the topic at hand, which includes recognizing essential principles and desired educational results. Additionally, it requires the establishment of a stimulating educational atmosphere that accommodates various learner preferences and styles. This stage requires careful consideration, as the foundation established during this time has a considerable impact on the later phases of teaching. In this context, educators compile various multimedia tools, such as visual presentations, sound recordings, and engaging activities, to effectively introduce the past simple tense. Learners are encouraged to think of previous situations they can share as illustrations during the forthcoming session.

Presentation: After the initial groundwork has been laid during the Preparation phase, attention now turns to the Presentation stage. This phase focuses on presenting the material in an engaging way that enhances students' understanding and interest. Educators utilize a range of teaching strategies, including presentations, practical examples, and digital tools, to communicate information effectively. The delivery of the material ought to be clear, well-organized, and captivating, emphasizing key points while encouraging analytical thinking. Moreover, encouraging inquiries and gathering responses at this point can assess comprehension and enhance a more participatory educational experience. To illustrate the application of the past simple tense while recounting historical events, the educator employs a timeline as a visual aid. Learners engage by taking notes and inquiring about the lesson.

Practice: After the presentation, this phase provides learners an opportunity to engage with and solidify the knowledge they have just gained. The activities for practice are crafted to be repetitive while also increasing in difficulty, thus allowing learners to strengthen their grasp and enhance their skills. Such activities may involve various forms of exercises, tasks, and teamwork that encourage active involvement and a more profound connection with the subject matter. The effectiveness of practice relies on timely feedback that allows learners to pinpoint and rectify mistakes, which is essential for the mastery of skills and concepts. For instance, pairs of students collaborate to practice constructing sentences in the past simple tense utilizing provided verbs and sentence starters.

Production: In the Production stage, learners are motivated to apply their understanding in a thoughtful and self-sufficient manner. This phase promotes advanced cognitive involvement by prompting learners to amalgamate information and create unique outputs. In this phase, students may participate in various activities such as collaborative projects, engaging presentations, and tackling practical problems that necessitate the application of their knowledge in fresh and innovative ways. This stage not only reinforces comprehension but also nurtures analytical thinking, innovation, and assurance in students. As an illustration, learners can craft a narrative or deliver a speech utilizing the past simple tense, drawing upon their own experiences or creatively envisioned situations.

Progress: The final evaluation stage focuses on measuring and appraising the learning results exhibited by students. This stage is crucial for determining how well the educational goals have been met, which includes both ongoing and concluding evaluations. Ongoing evaluations, which are carried out during the teaching process, offer ongoing feedback regarding student development and guide necessary changes in teaching strategies. Concluding evaluations conversely assess the cumulative learning outcomes upon the conclusion of a teaching period. Furthermore, the phase of advancement focuses on personal evaluation and contemplation, motivating learners to engage actively in their educational experience by identifying their strengths and areas that need development. For instance, learners share their narratives for peer evaluation, with the instructor offering personalized insights regarding language usage, vocabulary, as well as the overall effectiveness of communication. To evaluate their grasp of the past simple tense, a concluding quiz is administered to the students.

3.4.3 Implementation and Application in Educational Design

1. Purpose

The PPPPP framework seeks to tackle the difficulties encountered in conventional language teaching approaches by creating a more engaging and learner-focused environment. The main objectives of implementing this framework in the teaching of English are as follows:

The PPPPP framework promotes active participation among students at every phase, ensuring their sustained interest and enthusiasm throughout the educational journey.

The focus of the model is on engaged practice and active usage, resulting in improved abilities in speaking, listening, reading, and writing.

Continuous evaluation and monitoring of progress facilitate the addressing of individual student requirements, allowing for timely interventions to fill knowledge gaps.

2. Strategies

- Before the class begins, educators need to ascertain the goals for learning, select appropriate resources, and create captivating exercises.
- The introduction of new language elements through effective visual aids and practical examples enhances the students' understanding of the material.

- Through engaging in structured and purposeful practice exercises, learners can reinforce what they have learned and gained proficiency.
- Facilitate opportunities for learners to utilize their newly acquired language abilities in real-world or practice scenarios, such as interactive simulations or group discussions.
- Regular evaluations, both formative and summative, ought to be performed to track advancement and modify teaching methods as needed.

3. Teachers' role

Educators cultivate a supportive learning atmosphere by promoting engagement, offering constructive input, and nurturing a feeling of belonging among students.

In both the presentation and practice phases, instructors lead learners through unfamiliar linguistic elements, making certain they grasp and utilize them effectively.

Continuously evaluating enables educators to discern the unique strengths and challenges of each student, allowing them to customize their teaching approaches to effectively address learners' requirements.

4. Case study

Lesson Subject: "Exploring the World"

To facilitate the lessons, a variety of travel-themed visual materials, including videos, images, and vocabulary flashcards, are assembled by the educator. The objectives for learning include recognizing various nations, articulating travel experiences, and stating individual preferences.

The instructor utilizes a multimedia approach to present new terminologies that are associated with travel. Learners participate in quizzes and engage in interactive discussions.

Pairs of students engage in dialogues, focused on inquiring and responding about their travel adventures while incorporating the recent terminology. The instructor moves around the room, offering support and constructive criticism.

Students work collaboratively in groups to design a theoretical itinerary for a country they select. They share their itineraries, detailing the locations they intend to visit, activities planned, and their motivations for selecting that particular nation.

The concluding evaluation consists of a reflective writing piece focused on the lesson, emphasizing the vocabulary acquired, individual travel experiences, and identifying aspects that need enhancement.

Activity 3 **Choose the best answer to each question.**

1. What is the main focus of the preparation phase in the PPPPP instructional approach?
   A. Delivering engaging content to students
   B. Evaluating student learning outcomes
   C. Planning learning objectives and materials
   D. Providing opportunities for student practice

2. Which phase of the PPPPP approach emphasizes the importance of repetitive and challenging activities to reinforce learning?
   A. Presentation B. Practice C. Production D. Progress

3. In the PPPPP approach, which phase encourages students to use their knowledge in novel situations and produce original work?
   A. Preparation B. Presentation C. Practice D. Production

4. What is the primary purpose of the progress phase in the PPPPP approach?
   A. To adjust the instructional approach based on student feedback
   B. To create an engaging learning environment
   C. To deliver the content using various teaching methods
   D. To evaluate and assess student learning

5. Which phase of the PPPPP approach involves the use of different teaching techniques, such as lectures and multimedia resources, to effectively convey information?
   A. Preparation B. Presentation C. Practice D. Production

6. In the PPPPP approach, which phase emphasizes the provision of immediate feedback to help students correct their mistakes?
   A. Preparation B. Presentation C. Practice D. Progress

7. What is the main goal of the PPPPP instructional approach?
   A. To create a structured framework for teaching and learning
   B. To accommodate diverse learning styles
   C. To promote comprehensive understanding and application of knowledge
   D. All of the above

3.5 Teaching Design and Practice with the ESA Approach

The Engage, Study, and Activate model, a contemporary instructional framework focuses on adaptable strategies for teachers seeking to boost both learner involvement and educational effectiveness. Originating from the work of Jeremy Harmer (1998), this methodology is particularly relevant to language education but is also applicable across a range of educational fields. The emphasis lies in establishing an environment that prioritizes students, encouraging engagement and participation, thus enriching the classroom experience with greater interactivity and energy.

3.5.1 Teaching Philosophy

The educational framework proposed by ESA is founded on several key tenets:

Learner-focused: This method highlights the significance of students' engagement and independence throughout their educational journey.

Communicative teaching: The communicative approach emphasizes enhancing students' ability to communicate effectively through engaging and purposeful activities.

Integrated learning: This method combines a range of competencies (listening, speaking, reading, and writing) along with different language components (vocabulary, grammar, and pronunciation) to foster an all-encompassing development in language proficiency.

3.5.2 Main Procedures

Engage: The aim of the Engagement stage is to draw students into the learning experience from the very beginning. This may include exploring what learners already know, awakening interest through challenging inquiries, or incorporating various multimedia formats like videos and imagery. The aim is to engage students on an emotional level and prepare their minds for the upcoming learning experience. Methods such as narrative techniques, games, interactive activities, and participatory conversations are frequently utilized in this stage. For example, in short, an engaging video that pertains to the day's subject can serve as a fantastic way to initiate conversation, encouraging greater openness and willingness among students to explore the subject matter.

Study: The focus of the Study stage is on the primary material that needs to be addressed. This phase is where the fundamental processes of education and learning happen. At this phase, learners are presented with and engage in activities related to novel concepts, which may include aspects such as grammatical structures, word usage, or targeted language competencies that align with the lesson's objectives. Techniques such as direct instruction, collaborative exploration, and working in pairs or individually tend to yield the best results in this phase. During this phase, it is important for educators to motivate pupils to express their inquiries and resolve uncertainties, which creates an opportunity for a more profound comprehension of the topic at hand. Achieving a proper equilibrium between teaching and hands-on activities is essential; therefore, the range of activities could include anything from practice sheets and tasks to engaging quizzes and group projects.

Activate: The Activate stage motivates learners to apply their acquired knowledge in a way that is both interactive and significant. The purpose is to enable learners to engage with language through practical situations, thereby enhancing their self-assurance and reinforcing their comprehension. Activities such as simulations, discussions, or presentations may serve as effective methods for learners to engage with and utilize their acquired knowledge. As an illustration, once students have mastered terms related to travel, they may be tasked with enacting a dialogue in a travel agency scenario, where they engage in making a reservation or requesting information.

A notable benefit of the ESA method is its flexibility. Instructors have the freedom to deviate from a rigid sequence of steps. They have the flexibility to adjust the order of activities based on the requirements of their students. For instance, an instructional session could begin with a quick engaging exercise, transition into an in-depth study phase, return to engagement activities, and then proceed to activation tasks. This adaptability allows educational sessions to be lively and effectively address the diverse learning preferences present in a classroom.

Additionally, the ESA emphasizes the significance of engaging in self-evaluation. Instructors are urged to assess the impact of their teaching techniques and implement any required modifications. This continuous self-examination contributes to the enhancement of teaching techniques and promotes a higher standard of education. Key components of this reflective approach include teacher collaboration, input from learners, and personal evaluations.

3.5.3 Implementation and Design in Teaching

1. Purpose

The intent behind implementing the ESA method in teaching English is to boost learner participation, encourage experiential learning, facilitate personalized instruction, improve linguistic skills, and nurture self-assessment in students. Employing this framework in educational practices allows educators to design vibrant and impactful learning environments that address the varied requirements of their students, ultimately facilitating enduring language mastery.

2. Strategies

The implementation of the ESA method in English language classrooms can be achieved through a variety of techniques aimed at improving educational results. Here are the techniques corresponding to each stage of the framework:

Engage phase strategies

Tailoring lessons to students' individual experiences and passions can enhance the relevance and engagement regarding the subject matter. For instance, an instructor might kick off a session on the past tense by inviting learners to recount a significant moment from their histories.

Utilize visuals such as photographs, videos, and tangible objects to enhance the accessibility and engagement of the material. As an illustration, educators might display visuals pertinent to a subject and encourage learners to engage in dialogue about their observations.

Utilizing engaging games or brief activities is an effective approach to fostering a lively and positive environment. One example could be a word association game that aligns with the theme of the lesson.

Implement inquisitive approaches by posing open-ended inquiries to encourage reflection and dialogue. As an illustration: Inquire, "What advantages do you perceive in mastering an additional language?"

Study phase strategies

Offer a straightforward and brief overview of new linguistic concepts. For instance, a slide deck can be utilized to present fresh vocabulary alongside definitions and illustrative examples.

Present fresh concepts in a well-organized and gradual fashion. For instanc, begin with uncomplicated sentences and progressively advance to more intricate forms.

Involve students in working together in pairs or small groups to practice and refine their use of new language structures. For instance, students might work collaboratively on a fill-in-the-blank task to reinforce their understanding of new terms.

Provide timely and helpful responses to assist learners in enhancing their precision. For example, use a traffic light system (green for correct, yellow for almost correct, red for incorrect) to provide feedback on written work.

Activate phase strategies

Design activities that replicate real-world contexts, allowing learners to employ the target language effectively. For instance, arrange a situation where learners perform a skit based on a job interview.

Design tasks that challenge learners to utilize the language in innovative and significant ways. As an illustration, students might be tasked with producing a brief video or designing a poster centered around a subject they find intriguing.

Motivate learners to take control of their educational journey by establishing individual targets. One suggestion is to have learners maintain a journal for reflecting on their progress in language acquisition.

Involving students in sessions where they evaluate each other's work can significantly improve their teamwork and communication abilities. For instance, after students showcase their projects, they can give suggestions and insights to their peers.

3. Teachers' role

In the Engage phase, the educator cultivates an enriching and encouraging educational atmosphere, motivates engagement, and nurtures a strong sense of belonging among students.

During the Study phase, instructors are responsible for offering explicit information, support, and evaluation to assist students in gaining new knowledge and abilities.

During the Activate phase, the educator observes the students' activities, provides support as necessary, and offers words of encouragement and commendation.

4. Case study

Lesson Subject: Perfect Tense Usage

Initiate by presenting a collection of images or clips that capture moments from the past, yet continue to hold significane e.g. visiting various nations. Encourage pupils to speculate on the activities the presenter has participated in, utilizing the simple present tense, before introducing the present perfect tense to discuss past experiences that have current relevance.

Conduct a session to define the present perfect tense's structure and regulations, incorporating illustrative examples and engaging activities. Enhance comprehension through practice drills and fill-in-the-blank tasks.

Engage students by organizing them into pairs or small groups and tasking them with interviewing one another regarding their travel experiences, utilizing the present perfect tense. They should be encouraged to present their narratives to the class, allowing for the practice of fluent and precise usage of the language structure.

5. Course plan template

Lesson Focus: Exploring New Locations

Level: Intermediate

Objectives

Upon completion of this lesson or unit, learners will possess the necessary skills to achieve the following outcomes:

(1) To accurately recall and utilize a minimum of 20 vocabulary terms associated with travel, encompassing various destinations, transportation methods, and travel-related activities through the use of visual materials, engaging games, and concrete examples from real life.

(2) Participants will create a minimum of five statements employing the present perfect tense to convey their travel experiences. Each statement will reflect correct grammar and express clarity, encompassing locations explored, activities participated in, and emotions felt regarding those adventures. This will be achieved through collaborative discussions, role-playing activities, and written tasks derived from travel stories.

(3) To engage proactively in oral and auditory tasks centered on travel situations, illustrating enhanced fluency and understanding through mock travel dialogues, comprehension activities, and sessions of constructive feedback among peers in response to travel-themed audio materials, complemented by encouraging evaluations from classmates and instructors.

Materials

Images featuring renowned sites of interest; materials containing vocabulary and example sentences; tourist guide; a recording capturing the essence of a journey.

Procedures

1) Engage phase

Warm-up activities: Present images of well-known monuments and invite learners to identify their locations. Pairs of students engage in discussions about which famous sites they are eager to explore and their reasons for choosing them.

Lead-in: Listen to a brief audio recording where an individual recounts their adventure while traveling.

Learners are engaged in listening exercises and are required to respond to inquiries related to the audio material.

2) Study phase

Presentation of Vocabulary: Introduce fresh terminology associated with travel through the use of a PowerPoint presentation. Pupils are instructed to jot down notes and echo the teacher's words.

Grammar Focus: Explain the present perfect tense while illustrating its application in discussing travel experiences.

Learners engage in a fill-in-the-blank activity to enhance their understanding of the present perfect tense.

3) Activate phase

Oral practice: Groups of students collaborate to develop a brief conversation regarding their imagined travel adventures, utilizing the present perfect tense. Every group presents their conversation in front of the class.

Role-play: The learners engage in a scenario where they assume the roles of travel agents and customers, utilizing travel pamphlets to suggest various travel locations.

Individuals seeking travel advice inquire about various locations, while representatives in the travel industry offer details using the language and grammar outlined in the lesson.

6. Evaluation and feedback

Offer insights regarding the students' application of vocabulary and grammatical structures during their speaking exercises.

Evaluate the learners' comprehension and their capability to use the present perfect tense appropriately in relevant situations.

Activity 4 Design a lesson plan for an intermediate English class that focuses on the theme of "Travel." Your lesson plan should incorporate the ESA teaching model. Below is a template to guide you in creating your lesson plan.

Lesson Plan Template

Lesson title: Discovering Destinations

Level: Intermediate

Teaching objectives: By the end of this lesson/unit, students will be able:

(1) to recall and use accurately at least 20 travel-related vocabulary words related to travel, including destinations, modes of transportation, and travel activities in a conversation through a combination of visual aids, interactive games, and real-life examples.

(2) to construct at least five sentences using the present perfect tense to describe their travel experiences, each sentence demonstrating proper grammar and clarity, including places visited, activities engaged in, and feelings associated with those experiences, by means of group discussions, role-plays, and written exercises based on travel narratives.

(3) to participate actively in speaking and listening activities focused on travel scenarios, demonstrating improved fluency and comprehension through simulated travel conversations, listening comprehension exercises, and peer feedback sessions by responding to travel-related audio clips, and positive feedback from peers and the teacher.

Materials

Pictures of famous landmarks; handouts with vocabulary and sentences; travel brochures; audio recording of a travel experience

Procedure

1) Engage phase

Warm-up Activity:

Activity: Show pictures of famous landmarks and ask students to guess where they are.

Task: Students discuss in pairs which landmarks they would like to visit and why.

Lead-in:

Activity: Play a short audio recording of someone sharing their travel experience.

Task: Students listen and answer questions about the recording.

2) Study Phase

Vocabulary Presentation:

Activity: Present new vocabulary related to travel using a PowerPoint presentation.

Task: Students take notes and repeat the words after the teacher.

Grammar Focus:

Activity: Introduce the present perfect tense and provide examples of how it is used to talk about travel experiences.

Task: Students complete a gap-fill exercise to practice the present perfect tense.

3) Activate Phase

Speaking Practice:

Activity: Students work in groups to create a short dialogue about their hypothetical travel experiences using the present perfect tense.

Task: Each group performs their dialogue for the class.

Role-play:

Activity: Students role-play as travel agents and clients, using the travel brochures to recommend destinations.

Task: The "clients" ask questions about destinations, and the "travel agents" provide information using the vocabulary and grammar from the lesson.

Feedback and assessment

Provide feedback on the students' use of vocabulary and grammar during the speaking activities.

Assess the students' understanding and ability to apply the present perfect tense in context.

Homework

Write a short paragraph about a dream vacation using the present perfect tense and at least five new vocabulary words from the lesson. Remember to include clear instructions, timing for each activity, and any necessary follow-up questions or tasks to ensure a smooth transition between the Engage, Study, and Activate phases.

____

____

____

____

____

____

____

3.6 Teaching Design and Practice with the BOPPPS Model

The BOPPPS approach, an acronym standing for Bridge-in, Objective, Pre-assessment, Participatory Learning, Post-assessment, and Summary, has gained significant traction in recent years as an effective pedagogical approach for enhancing student engagement and learning outcomes. Originating from the field of engineering education, its adaptability and efficacy have been recognized across various disciplines, including English language teaching (ELT). This approach promotes a structured yet flexible learning environment that aligns well with the principles of active and student-centered learning (Gagnon & Collay, 2020). The approach has been found to be particularly effective in improving student engagement and comprehension (Ismail, Ngadi, & Yunus, 2010).

3.6.1 Teaching Philosophy

The constructivist learning theory serves as the foundation for the BOPPPS method, which highlights the significance of learners' existing knowledge and experiences throughout the educational journey. This perspective suggests that learners achieve optimal understanding when they engage actively in their educational journey and relate novel concepts to their existing framework of knowledge. The BOPPPS model offers a structured method for educators to foster a setting that promotes engagement and aids learners in grasping new ideas.

3.6.2 Main Procedures

The following are the main procedures of the BOPPPS model (Mu & Li, 2015):

Bridge-in: The process of establishing a link between the lesson or subject that has just been covered and the current topic is crucial. This process encourages learners to tap into their existing understanding, stimulating their interest in the upcoming subject. A practical approach would be initiating a discussion where learners share memorable experiences from their early years, especially when introducing a lesson on past tense.

Objectives: Clearly define the expected outcomes for the lesson. This enables learners to grasp the achievements they should accomplish by the conclusion of the session. For example, "At the end of this lesson, students will have the ability to accurately utilize the past tense in their sentences."

Pre-assessment: Initially evaluating students' existing knowledge and comprehension of the subject matter is essential before commencing the lesson. This evaluation can be carried out through various methods such as quizzes, discussions, or other strategies aimed at formative assessment. For instance, educators might encourage learners to jot down all their understanding related to the past tense prior to delving into new concepts.

Participatory learning: Foster an environment where students can deeply involve themselves in their education through collaborative tasks, debates, dramatizations, or other hands-on experiences. This process assists learners in utilizing their understanding and enhances their ability to think critically. One way to facilitate this is by splitting the class into smaller groups and assigning them the task of crafting conversations in the past tense.

Post-assessment: Determine how well students comprehend and have grasped the subject matter once the lesson concludes. This evaluation can take shape as a quiz, examination, or other final assessment approach. For instance, an option could be assigning students a brief essay task requiring them to correctly apply the past tense.

Summary: In conclusion, it is essential to encapsulate the main elements of the lesson while bringing closure to the subject matter. This serves to strengthen the students' comprehension and memory of the discussed topics. For instance, a recap of the conventions associated with the past tense could be beneficial, along with highlighting frequent mistakes to steer clear of.

3.6.3 Implementation and Application in Educational Design

1. Purpose

The BOPPPS framework aims to enhance the involvement, understanding, and retention of language skills among students during English instruction. Implementing this organized framework enables educators to cultivate a more engaging and learner-focused classroom setting that encourages participatory learning and enhances the grasp of the English language.

2. Strategies

- Bridge-in: Use a video clip related to the target vocabulary or grammar, a thought-provoking question, or a personal travel experience to engage students.

- Objective: Clearly outline the language goals (e.g., mastering a specific tense, expanding vocabulary on a theme).
- Pre-assessment: Quick quizzes or self-reflection activities to gauge students' familiarity with the topic.
- Participatory Learning: Group discussions on travel experiences using the present perfect tense. Role-plays simulating real-life scenarios that require the use of new vocabulary or grammar structures. Collaborative writing tasks where students contribute to a class travelogue.
- Post-assessment: Formative feedback through peer reviews, language proficiency tests, or oral presentations.
- Summary: A review of key vocabulary, grammar rules, and a reflection on how students can apply these in their daily lives.

3. Teachers' role

Within the BOPPPS framework, the educator assumes the role of a guide instead of that of a traditional lecturer. The main duty of the educator is to facilitate the students' learning journey, offer constructive feedback and assistance, and foster environments where learners can engage with and utilize their newly gained knowledge and capabilities.

4. Case study

An instructional example utilizing the BOPPPS framework within a lesson plan derived from a reading selection in a secondary school English textbook. The passage discusses the significance of preserving the environment and highlights the initiatives undertaken by various organizations to safeguard threatened wildlife. An outline of a comprehensive lesson plan is presented as follows:

Lesson Topic: Investigating the Hydrological Cycle through Literary Works

Students typically in grades 7 to 9 are considered to be at a middle school level.

Outline for a BOPPPS Lesson Plan

Bridge (5 minutes)

Activity: Start with an engaging time-lapse presentation that showcases the various phases of the water cycle, including stages such as evaporation, condensation, precipitation, and collection.

Once the video has concluded, encourage students to pair up and discuss one unexpected piece of information they discovered that was previously unknown to them.

The aim is to engage learners and forge a link between the environment and the forthcoming exploration of literature.

Objectives (2 minutes)

- By the completion of this lesson, learners will gain the ability to:

  Utilize textual references from a brief narrative to identify and elucidate the essential phases of the hydrological cycle.

- Examine how a character's feelings or decisions are shaped by the environmental patterns of water throughout the narrative.

- Imagine a different scenario in the tale, where the behavior of the hydrological cycle alters the course of events.

Pre-assessment (5 minutes)

Activity: Organize a brief true/false quiz featuring statements about fundamental ideas connected to the water cycle (e.g.The process of evaporation takes place when water changes into vapor.). Gather information to assess students' existing knowledge.

The goal is to pinpoint strengths and highlight areas that may benefit from additional explanation or guidance.

Participatory learning (25 minutes)

Activity 1 (10 minutes): Read aloud a short story (e.g., "The Cloud-Seeker: by a fictional author) that incorporates the water cycle as a central theme. Afterward, students work in small groups to identify and label the stages of the water cycle mentioned in the story.

Activity 2 (15 minutes): Groups then discuss how the water cycle impacts the plot and character development. Each group presents their findings to the class, supported by textual evidence.

Post-assessment (10 minutes)

Activity: Provide students with a graphic organizer featuring the stages of the water cycle. They must complete the organizer by filling in how each stage is represented in the story and how it affects the characters.

Objective: To assess students' understanding of the key stages of the water cycle and their ability to apply this knowledge to literary analysis.

Summary (8 minutes)

Teacher-Led: Recap the main points covered during the lesson, emphasizing the connection between the water cycle and its portrayal in literature.

Student Reflection: Have students reflect in their journals on what they found most interesting about the water cycle's role in the story and how it might inspire them to appreciate nature differently.

Closing Thought: End with a thought-provoking question, such as "How do stories like these help us understand our relationship with the natural world?"

Activity 5 Read the following scenario and complete the tasks that follow.

Scenario: You are an English language teacher preparing to teach a lesson on the use of articles ("a," "an," and "the") to a group of intermediate-level students.

Tasks	Task description	Your answer
Bridge-in (10 points)	Design an activity that connects the concept of articles to your students' prior knowledge or experiences. Explain how this activity will engage students and prepare them for the lesson on articles.	
Objective (10 points)	Write a clear and concise learning objective for the lesson on articles. Ensure that it is specific, measurable, achievable, relevant, and time-bound (SMART).	
Pre-assessment (10 points)	Create a pre-assessment activity to determine students' existing knowledge of articles. This could be a short quiz, a question-and-answer session, or a writing prompt.	
Participatory learning (30 points)	Develop two interactive activities that will encourage students to actively engage with the material in the articles. One activity should be a group work exercise, and the other should be an individual task. Explain how each activity promotes understanding and application of articles.	
Post-assessment (20 points)	Outline a post-assessment method to evaluate students' mastery of the use of articles after the lesson. This could include an in-class test, a writing assignment, or a peer-editing session.	
Summary (10 points)	Write a summary of the lesson on articles that includes key points, common mistakes to avoid, and suggestions for further practice. Ensure that the summary provides closure and reinforces learning.	
Reflective Question (10 points)	Reflect on the teacher's role in facilitating the BOPPPS model. How does this approach differ from traditional lecture-based teaching, and what benefits might it offer to students learning English as a second language?	

3.7 Teaching Design and Practice with the ADDIE Approach

The ADDIE approach (Dick, Carey & Carey, 2005) , an acronym for Analysis, Design, Development, Implementation, and Evaluation, is a structured approach to instructional design. Developed in collaboration between the University of Florida and the United States Army in 1975, this model has been widely adopted in various educational settings to ensure effective and efficient learning outcomes. ADDIE offers a systematic framework that guides educators through the complex process of instructional design, allowing for flexibility and continuous improvement.

3.7.1 Teaching Philosophy

The ADDIE model represents a comprehensive and cyclical technique for instructional design. It stresses the importance of conducting a detailed evaluation of the requirements of learners, a well-defined articulation of learning goals and teaching methods, the successful creation of educational resources, and execution of scheduled activities, alongside ongoing assessment of educational results. This method creates an environment focused on the learner, encouraging students to take an active part in their own education, ultimately improving their competencies and understanding.

3.7.2 Main Procedures

The ADDIE model consists of five interrelated phases, each essential to achieving effective instructional design (Branch, 2009).

During the Analysis phase, educators need to evaluate students' foundational details, their initial competencies, as well as their motivations and preferred learning approaches. Teachers may collect information regarding students' proficiency in English and their course expectations through various means such as questionnaires and discussions. Evaluating the learning environment is also vital, which includes reviewing the available resources and the condition of classroom facilities.

The Design phase, informed by the analysis outcomes, aims to establish precise educational goals, choose suitable instructional approaches, and create engaging learning experiences. This may involve formulating a curriculum that highlights essential learning outcomes and establishing engaging exercises that improve students' oral communication skills. The planning phase ought to encompass the creation of evaluation instruments to guarantee that students can be accurately assessed throughout their learning journey.

The Development stage focuses on the creation and organization of educational materials and resources for learning, which may include textbooks, digital presentations, and online learning platforms. In this stage, educators must choose or develop appropriate materials aligned with the established curriculum to enhance various learning dimensions and cater to diverse learning preferences.

In the Implementation phase, the established strategy is enacted. Instructors follow the curriculum and apply a variety of instructional techniques to captivate their learners. It is important to highlight interactions in the classroom to foster student involvement and solicit their perspectives. Adjustments are continuously made throughout the teaching process to enhance the effectiveness of instruction.

The Evaluation phase consists of both formative and summative evaluations. Formative assessments are integrated throughout the process to offer real-time feedback and facilitate necessary modifications. In contrast, summative assessments take place at the conclusion of the process to evaluate the learners' overall success in meeting the educational objectives, as well as to provide valuable information for enhancing future instructional methods.

3.7.3 Application in Teaching Design and Implementation

The ADDIE model serves as an effective guide for teaching languages, especially in the context of English instruction. This approach guarantees that learners of the language experience carefully organized, stimulating, and pertinent instruction that aligns with their objectives and requirements. By implementing the ADDIE framework, teachers can effectively create lesson plans that enhance learners' abilities in language usage, cultural insights, and communication techniques.

1. Purpose

The implementation of the ADDIE model in the context of teaching English aims to methodically address educational challenges, enhance the instructional process, and elevate students' proficiency in the language. By employing a structured framework for creation and assessment, educators can verify that each phase is aligned with the intended learning goals.

2. Strategies

- Conduct a thorough needs analysis to identify learners' language proficiency levels and learning preferences.
- Design lessons that incorporate various teaching methods, such as task-based language teaching (TBLT) and communicative language teaching (CLT).
- Develop engaging and interactive multimedia materials to enhance learning.
- Implement the lessons, ensuring that learners have ample opportunities for practice and feedback.
- Continuously evaluate the effectiveness of the instruction and make necessary adjustments.

3. Teachers' role

In the framework of ADDIE, educators assume various responsibilities:

- Conducting thorough analyses of learners, content, and environment.
- Creating instructional plans and selecting appropriate strategies and materials.
- Developing engaging and effective teaching materials and resources.
- Guiding learners through the learning process, promoting collaboration and critical thinking.
- Assessing student learning and using evaluation data to improve future instruction.

4. Case study

Setting: A teacher is designing an English language course for intermediate-level learners, focusing on improving their listening and speaking skills.

Analysis: The teacher surveys students to understand their language proficiency, learning preferences, and motivations. They also review the curriculum requirements and assess the availability of resources.

Design:

Based on the analysis, the teacher designs a course with the following key features:

Learning objectives: To improve students' ability to understand spoken English in various contexts and to communicate confidently in spoken English on everyday topics.

Instructional strategies: The teacher decides to incorporate a blend of interactive listening activities, role-plays, and group discussions. Authentic audio and video materials from news broadcasts, TED Talks, and interviews will be used to expose students to real-life language.

Assessments: Formative assessments, such as peer and self-evaluations during group activities, will be conducted regularly. A summative speaking test and a listening comprehension quiz will be administered at the end of the course to measure learning outcomes.

Development: The teacher develops the following materials and resources:

Lesson plans: Detailed lesson plans outlining the sequence of activities, time allocations, and learning objectives for each class.

Multimedia materials: A curated collection of authentic audio and video clips, with accompanying comprehension questions and discussion prompts.

Assessment tools: A rubric for evaluating speaking performance, a listening comprehension quiz, and peer/self-evaluation forms.

Implementation: During class, the teacher follows the lesson plans, engaging students in interactive listening activities, role-plays, and discussions. They use multimedia materials to facilitate language input and encourage students to apply their listening and speaking skills in practical contexts. The teacher circulates the classroom, providing individual and group feedback to guide students' progress.

Evaluation: At the end of the course, the teacher administers the summative assessments and collects student feedback through surveys and interviews. Based on the results, the teacher identifies areas where students excelled and where further improvement is needed. This evaluation informs the teacher's planning for future iterations of the course, focusing on refining instructional strategies, enhancing multimedia resources, and adjusting learning objectives as necessary.

Activity 6 **Match the following stages with their descriptions.**

A. Analysis
B. Design
C. Development
D. Implementation
E. Evaluation

1. ________ comprises understanding the learners' basic information and learning environment.
2. ________ includes preparing teaching materials such as textbooks and multimedia presentations.
3. ________ involves creating specific teaching objectives and designing learning activities.
4. ________ is when the designed plan is put into practice through teaching classes.
5. ________ encompasses both formative and summative evaluations to assess learning outcomes.

3.8 Teaching Design and Practice with the Five-Star Model

The Five-Star instructional model, also known as the First Principles of Instruction, is a contemporary teaching framework proposed by renowned educational technologist and psychologist, Professor M. David Merrill (Merrill, 2012). This approach aims to improve the effectiveness of online, multimedia, and E-learning environments by addressing the common issue of prioritizing information presentation over instructional quality.

3.8.1 Teaching Philosophy

Central to the Five-Star instructional approach lies the concept of focusing on problem-solving. It emphasizes placing specific learning tasks (facts, concepts, procedures, or principles) within a progressively challenging context of real-world problem-solving scenarios. The approach revolves around a recurring cycle of "activate prior knowledge," "demonstrate new knowledge," "apply new knowledge," and "integrate knowledge." This approach fosters deep learning, aligning with cognitive and constructivist theories of education.

3.8.2 Main Procedures

The following are the five stages of the Five-Star teaching model (Wei, 2012).

Focus on problem solving: Introduce a specific, complex, and authentic task to represent what learners will achieve by the end of the instruction.

Activate prior knowledge: Encourage learners to recall, explain, or demonstrate relevant previous knowledge and experiences.

Demonstrate new knowledge: Present and argue the new knowledge, linking it to the problem-solving task.

Apply new knowledge: Provide opportunities for learners to apply and practice the newly acquired knowledge through varied exercises.

Integrate knowledge: Facilitate learners to apply their knowledge in real-life situations, reflecting on their progress and creating personalized applications.

3.8.3 Application in Teaching Design and Implementation

1. Purpose

The Five-Star instructional model increases the efficacy of teaching English by promoting a focus on learners and encouraging a problem-based learning strategy. This approach guarantees that students not only gain language skills but also cultivate the capacity to utilize these skills in relevant situations.

2. Strategies

Start by introducing a practical communication exercise, like drafting an email or engaging in a simulated dialogue.

Encourage learners to reflect on their previous experiences and language skills that are relevant to the task through discussions or engaging activities.

Incorporate illustrations, video materials, or engaging simulations to highlight the new language attributes and techniques pertinent to the assignment.

Integrate a range of activities such as fill-in-the-blank tasks, simulations, or structured discussions that encourage participants to utilize the recently acquired information across various situations.

Stimulate learners to evaluate their advancement, share their insights, and develop tailored uses for the acquired knowledge, such as delivering a presentation or producing a multimedia project.

3. Teachers' role

- Leading participants through the process of addressing issues, while offering assistance and constructive criticism.
- Guiding students to effectively use and enhance their acquired knowledge through organized tasks.
- Monitoring the advancement of the students, offering supportive comments along with necessary guidance for improvement.

- Inspiring students to think critically about their educational journey and enhance their abilities to solve problems autonomously.

4. Case study

Lesson topic: Teaching English Writing Skills

Task: Write a persuasive essay on the topic "The Importance of Environmental Conservation."

Step 1: Focus on Problem Solving

Introduce the task and motivate learners by discussing the relevance of environmental conservation and the impact of their writing.

Step 2: Activate Prior Knowledge

Ask learners to brainstorm previous knowledge on persuasive writing techniques and environmental issues.

Step 3: Demonstrate New Knowledge

Use a model essay to demonstrate the structure and language features of a persuasive essay, highlighting techniques such as thesis statements, evidence, and counterarguments.

Step 4: Apply New Knowledge

Provide learners with a range of activities, including outlining, drafting, peer-reviewing, and revising their essays.

Step 5: Integrate Knowledge

Encourage learners to reflect on their writing process and present their final essays to the class, followed by a class discussion on the effectiveness of the arguments.

Activity 7 Choose the best answer to each question.

1. Who is the primary proponent of the Five-Star instructional approach, also known as the First Principles of Instruction?

A. Benjamin Bloom B. M. David Merrill

C. John Dewey D. Lev Vygotsky

2. What is the central teaching philosophy of the Five-Star Instructional Model?

A. Memorization of facts B. Focusing on information presentation

C. Recitation of textbook material D. Problem-solving in authentic contexts

3. Which of the following steps in the Five-Star Instructional Model comes before "Apply New Knowledge"?

A. Focus on Problem Solving B. Activate Prior Knowledge

C. Demonstrate New Knowledge D. Integrate Knowledge

4. During the "Activate Prior Knowledge" phase, what do teachers encourage learners to do?
   A. Learn new vocabulary words
   B. Recall relevant past experiences and knowledge
   C. Complete grammar exercises
   D. Watch educational videos

5. What type of activity would best fit the "Demonstrate New Knowledge" phase of the Five-Star Model?
   A. A debate on a historical event
   B. A teacher reading a textbook passage
   C. A student writing a persuasive essay
   D. Using a video to show new linguistic features

6. In the context of English language teaching, which of the following could be considered a "real-world communication task" for the "Focus on Problem Solving" phase?
   A. Completing a crossword puzzle B. Memorizing grammar rules
   C. Participating in a simulated job interview D. Reciting poetry

7. What is the primary role of the teacher during the "Apply New Knowledge" phase?
   A. To present new material
   B. To assess learners' progress
   C. To provide varied opportunities for practice
   D. To reflect on the instructional process

8. Which of the following is NOT a valid teacher role in the Five-Star Instructional Model?
   A. Facilitator B. Evaluator C. Lecturer D. Mentor

3.9 Teaching Design and Practice with the POA

The Production-oriented Approach (POA) is a Chinese local teaching methodology created by Wen Qiufang (2015, 2017). It is developed specifically for Chinese university students to enhance their English proficiency, especially in communication skills. It integrates the strengths of Western instructional approaches with Chinese contextual features.

Over the last ten years, the POA has been created to tackle the shortcomings found in conventional English language teaching within China's higher education framework. In contrast to traditional methods that prioritize texts and input, this approach focuses on enhancing productive skills like speaking, writing, translation, and interpretation. It seeks to merge the processes of learning and practical application of language through three fundamental elements: pedagogical principles, theoretical assumptions, and instructional strategies mediated by educators.

3.9.1 Teaching Philosophy

The foundation of the POA is built upon three fundamental teaching doctrines alongside three supporting theories, which collectively establish the conceptual basis for this method.

1. Teaching principles

The research conducted by Xu and Long presents their conclusions regarding the instructional principles of POA in the following areas (Xu & Long, 2021):

Learning-centered principle: This principle asserts that teaching in a classroom must maximize educational achievements within a constrained timeframe. It prioritizes the activation of the learning experience rather than simply centering on the participant. This approach questions the traditional view of "learner-centered approaches" by highlighting the necessity for classroom activities to be structured, purposeful, and guided by professional standards. Consequently, it introduces the idea of "focusing on learning".

Learning-using integration principle: This approach promotes a fluid combination of acquiring language skills and actively employing them. It stresses the importance of promptly utilizing newly acquired linguistic features in productive tasks following input experiences. This guideline seeks to address the limitations present in traditional text-focused, input-oriented English instruction while tackling the inadequacies in language expansion found in Western strategies that are task-driven or project-based.

Whole-person education principle: It posits that teaching English should address not only practical objectives, such as enhancing students' ability to communicate in English, but also broader humanistic aims, including the development of critical thinking skills, the ability to learn independently, and the capacity for intercultural communication. This principle highlights the necessity of thoughtfully choosing educational resources and crafting learning activities that support the overall development of students.

2. Hypotheses

Output-driven hypothesis: This hypothesis suggests that when the process of language output serves as the primary catalyst, the results in language acquisition are enhanced, coming before the input phase. This approach alters the conventional sequence of input followed by output, positioning the creation of language as both the initial and concluding focus of the learning process.

Input-enabling hypothesis: The hypothesis posits that providing relevant materials can enhance educational results when paired with learning activities focused on output. It is essential for these resources to align well with the tasks being executed.

Selective learning hypothesis: The hypothesis supports the idea of prioritizing specific input resources according to their significance to productive activities, thereby enhancing the efficacy of the learning process. (Xu & Long, 2021)

3.9.2 Main Procedures

Motivating phase

- Describe relevant communicative scenarios with high value.
- Have students try out productive tasks to identify gaps in their knowledge and skills.
- Set clear communicative and linguistic objectives for the lesson.

Enabling phase

- Guide students through a series of carefully designed steps to expand their knowledge and skills.
- Divide large productive tasks into mini-tasks and provide enabling materials.
- Have students selectively learn from the input materials to accomplish mini-productive tasks.

Assessing phase

- Establish assessment criteria jointly with students.
- Collect and evaluate students' productive work collaboratively in and out of class.
- Maintain portfolios of students' work for formative and summative assessment.

3.9.3 Application in Teaching Design and Implementation

1. Purpose

The POA aims to overcome the focus on input over output in Chinese English teaching, develop students' English productive skills for genuine communicative activities, enhance learning efficiency and student engagement, and cultivate students' autonomous learning, intercultural competence, and humanistic qualities.

2. Strategies

- Learning through practical scenarios: Engage learners by presenting authentic communication situations.
- Curated input: Offer materials that are pertinent and supportive for designated productive activities.
- Collaborative assessment: Engaging students in the evaluation process can significantly improve their educational achievements.

3. Teachers' role

Facilitator: Guide students in productive activities and selective learning.

Designer: Design appropriate teaching activities and assessment methods.

Supporter: Provide necessary support and assistance to students.

Assessor: Collaboratively assess students' productive outcomes.

4. Case study

Theme designation: The Intersection of Art and Nature

Motivating phase

The instructor describes two scenarios: discussing art in China and the West, and preparing a presentation on similarities and differences between Chinese and Western paintings.

Students attempt to discuss the topics, realizing their gaps in knowledge and expression.

The teacher sets communicative and linguistic objectives for the unit.

Enabling phase

The teacher explains how to accomplish the productive tasks and provides enabling materials (Text A on Mona Lisa and Text B on classical Chinese paintings).

The large productive task (comparing Western and Chinese paintings) is divided into mini-tasks.

The assignments are turned in by learners, and several examples are assessed together during the class.

Students practice mini-productive tasks, such as describing features of specific paintings.

Assessing phase

Assessment criteria for written comparisons and oral presentations are developed by both the instructor and the students.

The assignments are turned in by learners, and several examples are assessed together during the class.

Once a class has concluded, the leftover assignments are evaluated, and records are kept to provide grades and constructive critiques.

Activity 8 Imagine you are a teacher implementing the POA in your classroom. Describe a lesson plan for a unit on "Technology and Society", and include the following elements.

The specific productive task you would assign to your students.

The enabling input materials you would provide.

The assessment criteria you would use to evaluate student performance.

Your answer:

____

____

3.10 Teaching Design and Practice with the LBE

Learning by Extension (LBE), also known as Xu Theory—a local English teaching theory proposed by Wang Chuming (2005, 2005, 2012, 2016, 2018), suggests that the language skills of learners can be considerably improved through tasks that focus on extending existing dialogues or materials. Through a structured instructional process that emphasizes authentic input, creative Xu tasks, and supportive feedback, learners are empowered to take control of their language learning journey, enhancing their fluency, accuracy, and complexity in language output (Wang & Wang, 2015) (see Table 3.1).

Table 3.1 Categories of Xu tasks

Speaking continuation	Writing continuation	Translating continuation
the listening-speaking integrated continuation task	the reading-writing integrated continuation task	the reading-translating integrated continuation task
the watching-listening-speaking integrated continuation task	the listening-reading-writing integrated continuation task	
the reading-speaking integrated continuation task	the picture-discourse-writing integrated continuation task	
the contrasting-speaking integrated continuation task	the contrasting-writing integrated continuation task	

3.10.1 Teaching Philosophy

At the core of Learning by Extension lies the belief that language acquisition is an interactive and dynamic process that involves both comprehension and production. This educational approach highlights the significance of utilizing input materials rich in context that push learners beyond their current linguistic capabilities, motivating individuals to broaden their use of the language in significant and genuine contexts. By engaging in follow-up tasks, learners are motivated to progress beyond simple imitation or rote learning and participate in innovative, independent exploration of language.

3.10.2 Main Procedures

The teaching process centered on Learning by Extension typically consists of the following key steps.

Preparation: Choose materials that are appealing, authentic, and slightly above the learners' proficiency. These resources must generate a keen interest in extending further.

Presentation: Introduce the materials to learners through either reading or listening or a blend of both. Provide opportunities for learners to comprehend the content and language features.

Extension task: Assign an extension task that requires learners to extend the input material, either in writing, speaking, or both. Encourage learners to use their new language knowledge creatively.

Collaboration & feedback: Facilitate peer or group discussions to share and receive feedback on the continuation tasks. Teachers also provide constructive feedback, focusing on both content and language use.

Reflection & revision: Encourage learners to reflect on their learning process and revise their extension tasks based on the feedback received.

3.10.3 Application in Teaching Design and Implementation

1. Purpose

Xu Theory in ELT aims to promote systematic language development by bridging the gap between language comprehension and production. It tries to foster creativity, critical thinking, and self-directed learning skills while improving learners' language accuracy, fluency, and complexity.

2. Strategies

- Diverse resources: Choose a wide range of teaching materials, including short stories, news articles, podcast excerpts, and video clips, to cater to different learning styles and interests.
- Extension tasks: Design extension tasks that progressively rise in difficulty, challenging learners to expand their language skills.
- Authentic evaluation: Integrate genuine assessment methods within the ongoing tasks, assessing students' capabilities of using language innovatively and effectively within context.

3. Teachers' role

Facilitator: Create a supportive and inclusive learning environment that encourages risk-taking and experimentation in language use.

Coach: Provide individualized guidance to learners, addressing their specific language requirements and goals.

Assessor: Evaluate learners' Xu tasks using criteria, emphasizing both language accuracy and communication.

Model: Demonstrate effective language use and Xu strategies through modeling and shared activities.

4. Case study

In a high school English class, a teacher assigns a read-to-write extension task. Students are asked to read a story, analyze the characters and plot, and then write a Xu story with a narrative style and tone.

The teacher facilitates peer feedback sessions and provides individualized guidance on language use and plot development. As a result, students not only improve their writing skills but also have a deeper understanding of the story and its themes.

Activity 9 **阅读下面材料，根据其内容和所给段落开头语续写两段，使之构成一篇完整的短文。(25 分)**

Jayce began noticing when he was in kindergarten that he looked different from his classmates.They had two hands while he had one.Due to their young age Jayce was encouraged that he was just like an angel with one wing folded to prepare for something.

It started when one boy laughed at him.From that day, 5-year-old Jayce turned sad.He returned home with questions. "Why am I different? Why me?Why?" He cried to ask his mother, Lewis. Seeing Jayce was mad at God for making him that way, the poor mother felt it was a huge dagger to her heart.What made her more sorrowful was that she didn't know what to do at that point and how to provide answers to her son's questions which she could never find out herself, The white lie burst just like bubbles that day.

A few weeks later, Lewis turned on the TV to a news story, where she was shocked to find out the answer. It was Trashaun, an eighth grader, who displayed positive energy from his head to his toe. The 14-year-old sunny boy performed his slam dunks (大灌篮) on the TV, who had been a hit on the Internet. However, like Jaycc, he had missed most of his left arm since his childhood! Lewis called her son Jayce in. The poor little boy got spellbound, watching dunk after dunk.

At the time, it seemed that watching Trashaun would simply be an inspiring moment for Jayce. He saw Trashaun as a tough role model who had a seemingly similar disability but led a brilliant life. And had it stayed just that, Lewis would have been happy. But little did she know that a family friend had already reached out to Trashaun, asking him to help set up a meeting with Jayce to rebuild his confidence.

注意：1. 续写词数应为 150 左右；2. 请按如下格式在答题卡的相应位置作答。

The day was not spent drowning in self-pity but for fun. ______________________________

____

____

____

____

____

Staring at the shirt, he sent Jayce, Trashaun began to talk about their left arms. ______________________________

____

3.11 Teaching Design and Practice with the ABELA

The activity-based English learning approach (ABELA) offers a lively and interactive strategy, aiming to enhance learners' fundamental skills in mastering and utilizing the language. It advocates an integrated, relevant, and practical method of learning, where students engage in a variety of activities to improve their language proficiency, culture, and analytical thinking abilities.

3.11.1 Teaching Philosophy

The ABELA is based on the understanding that students achieve optimal learning outcomes when they participate in relevant and interactive experiences. It aligns with the English Curriculum Standards (2022, 2017), which emphasize the cultivation of students' core competencies, including language skills, cultural awareness, thinking qualities, and learning skills. By integrating engaging tasks, teachers create a comprehensive teaching environment that incorporates language, culture, and thinking, enabling students to understand, interpret, and evaluate texts and express their opinions, emotions, and attitudes in the right way (Zhang Cewen, 2019).

3.11.2 Main Procedures

The ABEL follows a structured process that progresses from basic understanding to advanced application and creation. The three main steps are:

Learning and understanding: This stage aims to introduce students to new language and cultural concepts through text-based activities. Teachers create thematic contexts, activate students' existing knowledge, and provide necessary language and cultural background information. Activities focus on perceiving, noticing, retrieving, summarizing, generalizing, and synthesizing information to build a foundational understanding of the text theme.

Applying and practicing: Students engage in deeper text-learning activities. These activities include describing, interpreting, analyzing, judging, and internalizing the language to consolidate knowledge and promote the automation of language use. Teachers guide students to participate actively in these activities, helping them apply and practice their newly acquired language and cultural knowledge.

Transferring and creating: Students use their language and cultural knowledge in new contexts, engaging in critical thinking and creative expression. Activities include reasoning, arguing, criticizing, evaluating, imaging, and creating beyond the material. Students use their language skills to analyze and solve problems, express their personal opinions, emotions, and attitudes in unfamiliar situations, and achieve deep learning (Ji & Dai, 2018; Yao & Wang, 2023).

3.11.3 Application in Teaching Design and Implementation

1. Purpose

The purpose of applying the ABELA is to foster an environment where students engage actively in language learning, develop their core competencies, and achieve deeper understanding and proficiency in English. It encourages students to learn by doing, cultivating a lifelong love for language learning and use.

2. Strategies

- Design contextualized activities: Activities should be designed around thematic contexts that are relevant, engaging, and meaningful to students' lives and interests. This enhances students' motivation and promotes a deeper connection to the learning material.
- Apply multimodal texts: Make use of oral and written multimodal materials to promote comprehension and expression. This multimodal approach supports students' language development and cultural awareness.
- Progressive learning: Activities should be structured progressively, moving from basic understanding to advanced application and creation. This gradual progression helps students build a solid foundation and progress toward higher levels of proficiency.
- Teacher guidance: Teachers should actively guide students throughout the learning process, providing scaffolding and support as needed. This guidance ensures that students stay focused, engaged, and productive in their learning activities.

3. Teachers' role

In the ABELA, teachers play a multifaceted role as facilitators, guides, and assessors. They construct learning opportunities, activate students' prior knowledge, and help their progress through effective guidance and scaffolding. Teachers encourage students to participate actively in learning activities, guide them to think critically, and provide feedback that promotes continuous improvement.

4. Case study

Lesson title: Exploring Cultural Differences through Short Stories

Objective: To develop students' ability to understand and compare cultural similarities and differences.

Teaching Steps:

Learning and understanding: Teachers introduce a short story with cultural elements from a different country. Students read the story, identify cultural references, and summarize the main ideas.

Applying and practicing: In pairs or groups, students compare the cultural aspects of the story with their own cultural experiences. They analyze the differences and similarities, using language skills to interpret and express their findings.

Transferring and creating: Students create their own short stories incorporating cultural elements from a third country. They present their stories to the class, engaging in discussions about the cultural differences and similarities highlighted in their work.

Activity 10 Match the following activity descriptions to their corresponding stages in the activity-based learning approach.

Activity description	Corresponding stage
Establishing connections between new and old information through sorting and integrating.	
Comparing cultural similarities and differences using language skills.	
Guiding students to express personal opinions, emotions, and attitudes creatively in new contexts.	
Creating situations around themes and activating students' prior knowledge.	
Engaging students in describing and interpreting texts based on the theme and their new knowledge structure.	

3.12 Teaching Design and Practice with TBLT

The Task-Based Language Teaching (TBLT) methodology prioritizes the incorporation of real-world tasks as a fundamental aspect of the learning process (Ellis, 2003). This instructional method seeks to involve students in significant tasks that enhance their ability to communicate and learn the language. The implementation of Task-Based Language Teaching has become increasingly favored in the teaching of English, primarily because it emphasizes authentic situations and prioritizes the needs of students.

3.12.1 Teaching Philosophy

TBLT prioritizes a learner-focused methodology that highlights the importance of genuine language application and significant interaction. Instead of dictating language patterns in advance, learners are encouraged to uncover and master the language as they engage in intentional tasks. This approach emphasizes blending language usage with its practical application, creating a setting where individuals tackle challenges, make choices, and collaborate to meet authentic communication objectives.

3.12.2 Main Procedures

TBLT consists of three core phases: the Pre-Task, Task Cycle, and Language Focus (Hismanoglu & Hismanoglu., 2011).

Pre-task phase

This stage involves introducing the theme, familiarizing students with relevant vocabulary, and textual or auditory input, and priming them with task-specific words and phrases. The teacher then outlines the task, setting the stage for engagement.

Task cycle

Activity: Pupils collaborate in pairs or small teams, utilizing their language skills to complete the assigned task while the instructor observes and fosters their development.

Preparation: Groups compile a concise oral or written summary to communicate their results or insights to the class. Throughout this rehearsal, the educator serves as a support resource, responding to inquiries and resolving any issues.

Presentation: The students present their findings, while the instructor gives immediate critiques, emphasizing substance over structure.

Language focus

Examination: Engaging in discussions or evaluations of the language characteristics found within the task reports or input materials enhances comprehension of how language functions.

Practice: Drawing insights from the observations made during the Task Cycle, the instructor crafts specific tasks aimed at strengthening the acquisition of new vocabulary, expressions, and grammatical structures, thereby solidifying the students' learning experience.

3.12.3 Application in Teaching Design and Implementation

1. Purpose

The objective of TBLT is to connect educational settings with practical communication by offering students the chance to engage with language through meaningful activities that reflect real-life situations. This approach emphasizes comprehensive language acquisition by seamlessly combining the skills of listening, speaking, reading, and writing, while also fostering abilities in critical analysis, effective problem resolution, and relationship-building.

2. Strategies

- Task Design: Incorporate a range of task formats, such as information gap, reasoning gap, and opinion gap tasks, to meet varied learning needs and actively involve learners at different levels of proficiency.

- Scaffolding: It is essential to offer sufficient assistance and a structured approach for students, especially those who are new to the material or have lower skill levels, to facilitate their effective engagement in activities.
- Customization: Create assignments that are inherently adaptable to support the diverse skills, interests, and approaches to learning seen among students.
- Realism: Strive to make assignments as realistic as possible, reflecting actual scenarios to foster significant linguistic application.

3. Teachers' role

Facilitator: Guide learners toward independent language discovery and encourage autonomous learning.

Partner: Collaborate with students during tasks, fostering a sense of camaraderie and encouraging open communication.

Supporter and feedback provider: Offer ongoing support throughout the task cycle and provide constructive feedback that helps learners refine their language use.

4. Case study

Consider a "Restaurant Reservation Task" where students, working in pairs, must reserve a table for a hypothetical dinner event, including specifying the date, time, number of guests, and any special requests.

Before the task, students are exposed to a sample conversation and relevant vocabulary. During the Task Cycle, they engage in role-play, making reservations with each other. In the Language Focus phase, the teacher guides a discussion on the linguistic features used, such as politeness markers and phrase structures, and then designs practice activities to reinforce these concepts. This task not only reinforces language skills but also fosters interpersonal communication and decision-making abilities.

Activity 11 **Choose the best answer to each question.**

1. What is the central component of Task-Based Language Teaching (TBLT)?

   A. Grammar rules　　B. Authentic tasks

   C. Vocabulary lists　　D. Reading comprehensions

2. In TBLT, which phase involves students working in pairs or groups to accomplish a task?

   A. Pre-Task phase　　B. Task Cycle phase

   C. Language Focus phase　　D. Post-Task Analysis phase

3. During the Task Cycle phase, what role does the teacher typically assume?

   A. Direct instructor　　B. Resource and monitor

   C. Task evaluator　　D. Content expert

4. What is one of the strategies for implementing TBLT effectively?
   A. Relying solely on written exercises
   B. Ensuring tasks are as authentic as possible
   C. Avoiding any interaction among students
   D. Focusing on language form over function

5. In the provided case study, what task do students engage in?
   A. Writing an essay about dining etiquette.
   B. Making a restaurant reservation for a hypothetical event.
   C. Reading a menu and translating it into another language.
   D. Cooking a meal following a recipe in English.

3.13 Teaching Design and Practice with CLT

Communicative Language Teaching (CLT) is founded on the notion that communication is the core function of language. This approach focuses on enhancing learners' proficiency in applying language in practical, everyday contexts. In contrast to conventional methods that prioritize grammatical rules and translation, the approach prioritizes interaction as a crucial element of the educational experience, encouraging the development of language skills through relevant exchanges and genuine use of the language.

3.13.1 Teaching Philosophy

The core philosophy of CLT is rooted in the belief that language learning should be driven by real-life contexts and focused on the learners' needs (Canale & Swain, 1980). This approach emphasizes:

Authenticity: Materials and activities should mimic real-life situations to enhance the transferability of language skills.

Interaction: Learners are encouraged to engage in meaningful conversations and negotiations for meaning.

Fluency over accuracy: While accuracy is important, CLT prioritizes fluency and the ability to communicate effectively, even with imperfections.

Learner autonomy: Students are encouraged to take an active role in their learning process, making decisions and taking responsibility for their progress.

Functional language: The focus is on teaching language that is functional and used for specific communicative purposes.

3.13.2 Main Procedures

The following are the main procedures of CLT (Jacobs & Farrell, 2003).

Needs analysis: This process entails recognizing the language requirements of learners, their objectives for learning, and the situations where the language will be utilized. By gaining insight into the learners' aspirations and necessities, educators can customize the curriculum and instructional activities to more effectively address those needs.

Situation setting: The subsequent action involves formulating or choosing genuine scenarios that replicate authentic communication environments. These contexts act as the environment for language acquisition, offering a significant framework where learners can enhance and utilize their linguistic abilities.

Language input: Teachers provide learners with comprehensible input that is slightly above their current proficiency level ("i+1" principle). This input can appear in various forms, such as texts, videos, audio recordings, or live demonstrations, and is designed to engage learners and expose them to new vocabulary, grammar structures, and discourse patterns.

Interactive communication: Students engage in pair work, group discussions, role-plays, and other interactive activities that propel them to use the language for meaningful communication. These activities enhance language production, negotiation of meaning, and the development of communication strategies.

Skills integration: CLT strengthens that language skills are interconnected and should be integrated into learning activities. Teachers create activities that necessitate the simultaneous use of various language competencies, fostering a comprehensive method of language acquisition.

Feedback and adjustment: Teachers offer both constructive and affirmative evaluations on students' use of language, aiding students in recognizing areas for enhancement and on the other hand helping themselves adjust their instructional strategies or the difficulty level of tasks to better suit learners' needs.

Autonomous learning: Teachers provide students with opportunities for self-assessment, goal-setting, and independent research. This fosters a sense of ownership over the learning process and prepares learners for lifelong learning.

Cultural awareness: Teachers integrate cultural elements into their courses, helping students understand the social and cultural contexts in which the language is used. This not only improves students' communicative competence but also promotes their cultural sensitivity.

3.13.3 Application in Teaching Design and Implementation

1. Purpose

- Enhance learners' ability to communicate effectively in English.
- Develop learners' confidence in using English in various social contexts.
- Encourage the development of both linguistic and sociolinguistic competence.

2. Strategies

- Design tasks that mirror real-life situations, motivating students to utilize language for particular communication goals.
- Implement extended assignments that involve students in investigation, teamwork, and English presentation.
- Assign long-term projects that require learners to research, collaborate, and present in English.
- Engage learners with various formats such as videos, podcasts, news articles, and other authentic materials to expose students to native speakers and diverse linguistic expressions.

3. Teachers' role

Facilitators: Guiding learners through tasks and encouraging autonomous learning.

Collaborators: Participating in group discussions and providing support when needed.

Assessors: Providing ongoing formative feedback and evaluating learners' communicative competence.

Resource providers: Introducing authentic materials and fostering connections to real-world language use.

4. Case study

This comprehensive case study aims at promoting students' ability to communicate effectively in English. The lesson focuses on shopping for clothing, addressing both linguistic and pragmatic aspects of communication.

Learning objectives

- Upon the completion of this lesson, learners will possess the ability to:
- describe clothing items by using proper vocabulary;
- be skilled in using language structures for expressing preferences, sizes, and fitting;
- demonstrate effective communicative skills when bargaining prices and making purchases;
- develop cultural awareness regarding clothing preferences and shopping etiquette in different contexts.

Target learners

The students are intermediate-level English language learners, aged 14–16, from diverse cultural backgrounds.

Course contents

The materials are centered on the concept of "Clothing Shopping." This involves vocabulary associated with various styles of clothing, including aspects like colors, sizes, and fabrics, alongside communicative functions for articulating choices, contrasting products, and making inquiries.

Teaching methods

Practical task engagement: Students are assigned activities that replicate authentic experiences found in shopping contexts.

Pair and group work: Students engage with one another to enhance their conversational skills while also providing constructive feedback.

Authentic materials: Utilizing genuine resources such as actual clothing brochures, e-commerce platforms, and interactive role-play activities.

Digital whiteboard: Showcasing vocabulary and language structures visually.

Feedback and correction: Ongoing, constructive feedback to facilitate improvement and enhance the learning process.

Evaluation plan

Formative assessment: Observation during tasks and group work, peer feedback, and teacher-student conferences.

Summative assessment: An ultimate role-playing exercise that showcases students' proficiency in utilizing their language abilities within a retail environment. Additionally, a questionnaire for self-evaluation is provided.

Lesson plan sample

Stage 1: Warm-up (10 minutes)

Brainstorming session: Students work in pairs to list different types of clothing.

Stage 2: Presentation & Practice (20 minutes)

The teacher introduces new vocabulary and language structures using an interactive whiteboard.

Students practice the new language in pairs, role-playing customers and sales assistants.

Stage 3: Guided Tasks (25 minutes)

Group work: Students are given a clothing catalogue and asked to prepare a shopping list based on preferences.

Role-play: Students engage in a shopping scenario, negotiating prices, sizes, and fitting.

Stage 4: Feedback & Reflection (15 minutes)

Peer feedback on role-plays.

The teacher provides summary feedback and highlights key language points.

Students reflect on their learning in a journal.

Materials and resources

Clothing catalog

Screenshots from an online retail platform

Software for interactive whiteboards

Cards designed for role-playing that include various situations and cues.

Questionnaire for personal evaluation

Implementation tips

Encourage students to use their creative ideas in the role-plays.

Provide clear guidelines for peer feedback to guarantee that it remains supportive and courteous.

Differentiate tasks based on students' language proficiency to guarantee that each learner is suitably engaged and challenged.

Incorporate technological elements whenever feasible to make the learning more engaging and relevant.

Conclusion and reflection

The lesson focused on clothing shopping within CLT successfully improved learners' abilities in communication and their understanding of cultural nuances.

Incorporating real-world materials and activities, along with approaches that prioritize student engagement, fostered a dynamic and impactful educational experience. Nonetheless, it is essential to consistently evaluate how effective the lesson has been, the teacher needs to adjust the materials and methods, and adjust activities as necessary to address the varied requirements of the learners. Upcoming sessions might delve into more intricate purchasing situations or incorporate further cultural dimensions to expand students' linguistic abilities and cultural awareness.

Activity 12 **Fill in the blanks with proper words or phrases.**

CLT is an instructional approach that has revolutionized language education. Originating from the belief that language is primarily a tool for communication, CLT emphasizes the development of learners' ability to use language effectively in real-life situations. Unlike traditional grammar-translation methods, CLT places (1) __________ at the center of the learning process, fostering linguistic competence through meaningful interactions and authentic language use.

The underlying philosophy of CLT includes the following principles:

Authenticity: Materials and activities should (2) __________ real-life situations to enhance the transferability of language skills.

Interaction: Learners are encouraged to engage in (3) __________ conversations and negotiations for meaning.

Fluency over accuracy: While accuracy is important, CLT prioritizes (4) __________ and the ability to communicate effectively, even with imperfections.

Learner autonomy: Students are encouraged to take an active role in their learning process, making decisions and taking responsibility for their (5) __________.

Functional language: Focus is on teaching language that is (6) __________ and used for specific communicative purposes.

In CLT, the first step is to conduct a (7) __________ analysis, identifying the learners' linguistic needs and the contexts in which they will use the language. Teachers provide learners with (8) __________ input that is slightly above their current level of proficiency. The heart of CLT lies in (9) __________ communication, where learners engage in interactive activities that encourage them to use the language for meaningful purposes. Ongoing (10) __________ is essential in CLT, helping learners identify areas for improvement and reinforcing successful communication strategies.

Thinking and Doing

A. Questions for discussion

1. What are the key aspects to consider for utilizing the various teaching approaches in classroom teaching?
2. Which of the teaching approaches do you prefer to use in your teaching practice? And why?

B. Practice

1. Go through all the teaching approaches deeply and try to construct a mind map of each teaching approach.
2. Try to design two lesson plans for the same teaching material but with two different teaching approaches. Compare and analyze in detail the teaching steps and teaching activities in each lesson plan.

C. Exercises for instructional skills

1. When teaching pronunciation, a teacher should put phoneme, stress, intonation, and __________ in the syllabus.
   A. consonant B. vowel C. rhythm D. speech

2. What is being practiced if a teacher asks students to read words like "cot, hot" and "dog, log"?
   A. Spelling and structure. B. Stress and sound.
   C. Minimal pairs D. Phonetic symbols.

3. A student finds it difficult to learn the English sounds [θ] and [ð]. If you are an English teacher, which of the following statements can be used?
   A. Explain how to make the sounds. B. Use tongue twisters.
   C. Write them on the blackboard. D. Make up sentences.

4. When a teacher asks students to read words like "bid, bad", he/she intends to draw students' attention to the __________.
   A. minimal pair B. intonation C. stress D. spelling

5. There are __________ syllabuses in the word "tomorrow".
   A. two B. three C. four D. five

6. The most distinguishable linguistic feature of a regional dialect is its __________.
   A. accent B. use of words C. morphemes D. use of structures

7. Which of the following practices aims at pronunciation-skill training?
   A. Odd one out. B. Reading aloud.
   C. Context practice. D. Reciting.

8. __________ is speech variation according to the particular area where a speaker comes from.
   A. Regional variation B. Language variation
   C. Social variation D. Register variation

9. The open syllable refers to the syllable that has no __________.
   A. coda B. onset C. nucleus D. rhyme

10. In which of the following can be used in stress and intonation practice?
    A. The teacher can indicate the stress and intonation by clapping hands.
    B. The teacher can raise the voice to indicate the stress and intonation.
    C. The teacher can highlight the stress and intonation on the blackboard by underlining them.
    D. All of the above.

Checklist

Mark the questions with a check (√) if your answer is yes.

- ☐ Have I understood the main procedures of the teaching approaches?
- ☐ Have I grasped the concepts of the teaching approaches?
- ☐ Am I clear about teachers' different roles in different approaches?
- ☐ Can I design a lesson plan or teach a lesson successfully by using a specific teaching approach?

Reflective Journal

Please write down your reflections on what you have / have not learned in this chapter.

◇ The essential skills I need to possess and develop for the instructional approaches I have learned in this chapter:

____

____

____

____

____

____

____

◇ Anything I wish to further explore (i.e., puzzles and difficulties):

____

____

____

____

____

____

References

Branch, R. M. (2009). *Instructional design: The ADDIE approach*. Springer, NY.

Bybee, R. W. (1997). The 5E instructional model: A teaching strategy for science education. *Science Education*, *81*(5), 624-632.

Bybee, R. W. (2006). The cognitive principles of learning underlying the 5E model of instruction. *International Journal of STEM Education*, *1*(1), 1-12.

Canale, M., & Swain, M. (1980). Theoretical bases of communicative approaches to second language teaching and testing. *Applied Linguistics*, *1*(1), 1–47.

Dick, W., Carey, L., & Carey, J. O. (2005). *The systematic design of instruction* (6th ed.). Longman.

Ellis, R. (2003). *Task-based language teaching and learning*. Oxford University Press.

Gagnon, S., & Collay, J. (2020). Effective pedagogical strategies for engineering education. *Journal of Engineering Education*, *102*(4), 345-360.

Harmer, J. (1998). *How to teach English*. Pearson Education Limited.

Hismanoglu, M., & Hismanoglu, S. (2011). Task-based language teaching: What every EFL teacher should do. *Procedia-Social and Behavioral Sciences,* 15, 46–52. https://doi.org/10.1016/j.sbspro.2011.03.049

Ismail, M., Ngadi, A., & Yunus, Z. (2010). Enhancing student engagement through the BOPPPS model in English language teaching. *Journal of English for Academic Purposes*, *9*(3), 207-221.

Jacobs, G. M., & Farrell, T. S. C. (2003). Understanding and implementing the CLT (communicative language teaching) paradigm. *RELC Journal*, *34*(1), 5–30.

Ji, X. T., & Dai, J. H. (2018). "六要素"整合下的英语学习活动观及其实践 [The English Learning Activity View under the integration of the "Six Elements" and its practice]. *Teaching and Management,* (19), 64–66.

Larsen-Freeman, D., & Anderson, M. (2011). *Techniques and principles in language teaching*. Oxford University Press.

Liu, L., & Wang, C. M. (2018). "续论"与对外汉语动结式的学习 [The "Continuation Theory" and the acquisition of Chinese verb-resultative compounds in CSL]. *Journal of Guangdong University of Foreign Studies*, *29*(3), 21–28.

Merrill, M. D. (2001). First principles of instruction. *Journal of Structural Learning and Intelligent Systems*, *14*(4), 459-466.

Ministry of Education of the People's Republic of China. (2017). 普通高中英语课程标准 [*English curriculum standards for senior high schools*]. People's Education Press.

Ministry of Education of the People's Republic of China. (2022). 义务教育课程标准 [*Compulsory education curriculum standards*]. People's Education Press.

Mu, H., & Li, C. (2015). BOPPPS 模型及其在研究型教学中的应用探究 [*Exploring the application of BOPPPS model in research-oriented teaching*]. Shaanxi Education (Higher Education), (10), 27–30.

Pratista, G. Y. (2023). *Presentation practice production vs task-based language teaching: A comparison of two teaching templates*. Jurnal Edupedia, Universitas Muhammadiyah Ponorogo.

Richards, J. C., & Rodgers, T. S. (2001). *Approaches and methods in language teaching* (2nd ed.). Cambridge University Press.

Wang, C. M. (2005). 外语写长法 [The Length Approach in foreign language writing]. *China Foreign Language*, (1), 45–49.

Wang, C. M. (2005). 以写促学中的词汇学习 [Vocabulary learning through writing in the Length Approach]. *Foreign Language and Literature Research*, (1), 1–5, 20.

Wang, C. M. (2012). 读后续写：提高外语学习效率的一种有效方法 [Continuation task: An effective method to enhance foreign language learning efficiency]. *Foreign Languages*, (5), 2–7.

Wang, C. M. (2016). 以"续"促学 [Promoting learning through continuation: A theoretical perspective]. *Modern Foreign Languages*, *39*(6), 784–793, 873.

Wang, C. M., & Wang, M. (2015). Effect of alignment on L2 written production. *Applied Linguistics*, 36(5), 503–526. https://doi.org/10.1093/applin/amt051

Wei, G. (2012). 五星教学四十年：追求效率、效果与魅力之路 [Forty years of the Five-Star Teaching Model: Pursuing efficiency, effectiveness, and engagement]. *Open Education Research*, *18*(6), 61–69.

Wen, Q. F. (2015). 构建"产出导向法"理论体系 [Constructing the theoretical system of the Production-Oriented Approach]. *Foreign Language Teaching and Research*, (4), 547–558.

Wen, Q. F. (2017). "产出导向法"的中国特色 [The Chinese characteristics of the Production-Oriented Approach]. *Modern Foreign Languages*, *40*(3), 348–358, 438.

Xu, J. F., & Long, Z. B. (2021). 英语教学新发展研究 [*New developments in English language teaching*]. Tsinghua University Press.

Yao, C. H., & Wang, S. R. (2023). 素养本位的基础教育英语课程教学 [Competency-oriented English curriculum and teaching in basic education]. *Foreign Language Teaching and Research & Practice*, (6), 42–50, 98.

Zhang, C. W. (2019). 英语学习活动观的内涵、特点与价值 [The connotation, characteristics, and value of the English Learning Activity View]. *Teaching and Management*, (19), 47–50.

Chapter 4

Information Technology Skills in English Teaching

Objectives

Upon completion of this chapter, you will be able to:

- Understand the concept and functions of information technology
- Grasp the concept and contents of TPACK
- Know the functions and uses of hardware and software tools
- Integrate information technology into English teaching properly
- Use traditional and modern information technology tools to organize proper activities in classroom teaching

Discussion Questions

Do you know what TPACK stands for? Could you name several AI software abroad and in China? Share your experience with some educational technology media in your life or study.

The advancement of information technology has undergone significant development from traditional media such as textbooks, chalkboards, and audio recordings to digital technology and various online resources, interactive visual displays, and digital education platforms. In the present day, this advancement involves the adept integration of artificial intelligence into educational information technology. Instructors are required to skillfully create adaptive learning experiences and engaging materials while utilizing artificial intelligence to interpret and leverage students' performance data, refine instructional strategies, and create a setting that effectively accommodates the diverse requirements and advancements of each student. This chapter highlights the ongoing necessity for teachers to enhance their technical skills in information systems, capitalizing on a wide range of developments to catalyze creativity and improve educational standards.

4.1 Overview of Information Technology in English Teaching

4.1.1 Definition of Information Technology in Education

The application of contemporary technological and scientific innovations in education involves equipping, documenting, archiving, transmitting, and managing educational data. It includes a variety of tools, both hardware and software, that enhance the teaching and learning experience, allowing traditional classrooms to evolve into engaging and interactive spaces.

4.1.2 Why Is Information Technology Essential for Educators?

In an era dominated by technology and characterized by rapid advancements, the significance of digital tools in the teaching of the English language has become crucial. Teachers are now called to go beyond the conventional methods of instruction, integrating modern technologies and resources that foster better educational experiences and address the varied learning preferences of their students.

Enhanced learning experience

A significant factor that underscores the importance of mastering digital tools is their capability to turn traditional learning into a dynamic and interactive experience. By utilizing diverse media elements such as films, audio recordings, and hands-on simulations, educators can cultivate rich environments that ignite students' interest and enhance their comprehension of linguistic elements.

Personalized instruction

Customizing educational experiences to cater to the individual capabilities, challenges, and preferred learning methodologies of each student serves as a fundamental element of contemporary teaching. Advancements in technology allow educators to utilize analytical tools to monitor student development, detect areas needing improvement, and tailor teaching methods appropriately. Utilizing these resources, educators can tailor feedback and support for individual students, promoting personalized advancement for each learner.

Accessibility and inclusivity

Technology can serve as a vital link for learners who have unique requirements, those who study from a distance, or individuals encountering difficulties with language. Various digital tools and personalized educational programs can support diverse learning preferences, like auditory, visual, or tactile approaches, thereby fostering a more inclusive and fair educational environment.

Professional development

The realm of information technology offers a plethora of digital materials, online seminars, and teamwork platforms that support educators' professional growth. Educators have the opportunity to take flexible learning courses, attend online seminars, and connect with colleagues around the globe, improving their instructional methods and remaining updated in their profession.

In an increasingly interconnected global landscape, effective communication and collaboration beyond national boundaries are essential. Digital tools empower educators to link their classrooms with peers worldwide, promoting an understanding of different cultures while improving language skills. Utilizing tools such as video calls, virtual exchange initiatives, and joint projects, learners are provided with genuine linguistic interactions that enrich their understanding of various cultures and viewpoints.

Efficiency and time management

The advancement of information technology simplifies administrative functions and boosts the overall effectiveness of the classroom. Educators can leverage electronic resources for functions such as assessment, organization of student information, planning schedules, and developing lesson outlines, which allows them to dedicate more time to teaching and engaging with students. Moreover, tools that facilitate automated evaluations and monitor progress assist educators in promptly recognizing topics that need focus, which enables more precise interventions and optimizes classroom engagement.

Incorporating digital technologies into the teaching of English is a significant shift that demands educators embrace a culture of creativity and teamwork. It calls for educators to embrace experimentation, engage in reflective practices, and remain flexible while navigating this age of technology. This approach enables them to transcend traditional teaching roles, positioning themselves as guides in the learning process, cultivators of analytical skills, and champions for fair and accessible educational experiences.

4.1.3 Functions and Benefits of Education Technology Media

Educational technology media offers a wealth of advantages that contribute positively to educational effectiveness. Its primary roles are the following:

Educational content can be generated without limitations related to time, geographic location, or the scale of distribution, thus ensuring that learning resources are available at all times and in all places.

- It combines different types of media, including visuals, voice, and written content, to create a rich, immersive learning environment.

- Facilitates active learning experiences, promoting participation and teamwork among students.
- Grants access to an extensive array of media resources and digital materials, thereby enriching educational experiences.
- Emulation of real-world situations through immersive digital environments supports enriched practical education.

4.2 TPACK

As education continues to transform, the importance of seamlessly incorporating technology into teaching methodologies is increasingly recognized. A significant framework that has come to the forefront to support this integration is known as Technological Pedagogical Content Knowledge (TPACK).

4.2.1 Theoretical Roots

The foundational concepts of TPACK originate from the research conducted by Lee Shulman, especially highlighted in his influential paper titled "Those who understand: Knowledge growth in teaching." In this work, Shulman proposed the idea of Pedagogical Content Knowledge (PCK), emphasizing that effective teaching entails more than simply possessing knowledge of the subject matter; it involves a comprehension of how to effectively impart that knowledge to learners. This idea of merging instructional strategies with subject knowledge served as a foundation for the evolution of TPACK (Shulman, 1986) (see Figure 4.1).

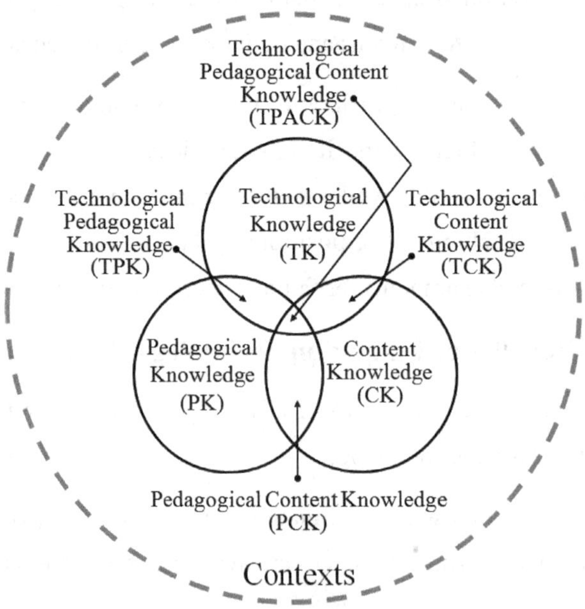

Figure 4.1 TPACK framework

4.2.2 Concept

Informed by Shulman's contributions, In the early 21st century, TPACK was envisioned by Mishra P. and Koehler M. (2006). They acknowledged the necessity of enhancing the PCK framework to incorporate technological aspects, emphasizing that educators should also acquire the expertise and capabilities necessary for weaving technological resources into their teaching methodologies. Thus, the TPACK framework emerged, which integrates Technological Knowledge (TK), Pedagogical Knowledge (PK), and Content Knowledge (CK), along with their overlaps—TPK, PCK, TCK—and the fundamental area encompassed by TPACK itself.

4.2.3 Development Process

The TPACK framework was developed through a process characterized by continuous collaboration and iteration among a diverse group of educators and scholars from multiple fields. Through a series of investigations, case analyses, and collaborative workshops, Mishra and Koehler, along with their collaborators, further refined and expanded upon the initial TPACK framework. This journey led to an enriched comprehension of the intricate factors associated with integrating technology and underscored how contextual elements play a crucial role in the evolution of TPACK.

4.2.4 Main Components

This model acknowledges that successful incorporation of technology necessitates a comprehensive comprehension of both the tools and the subject matter being delivered, as well as the teaching methods that are most effective in promoting learning within a tech-immersive setting.

4.2.4.1 The core elements of TPACK

Central to the TPACK framework are three overlapping domains:

The concept of Technological Knowledge (TK) pertains to educators' comprehension of diverse technological instruments, resources, and the functionalities they offer. This includes a variety of devices such as physical equipment (e.g. devices such as desktop computers, mobile tablets, and various applications as well as operating systems and programs, digital learning tools and interactive e-learning environments).

Pedagogical knowledge (PK) encompasses the instructional techniques, theoretical frameworks, and approaches utilized by educators to enhance the learning process. This encompasses elements such as managing a classroom, evaluating student performance, and designing educational programs.

Content Knowledge (CK) encompasses the thorough understanding that educators possess regarding their disciplines, which includes their grasp of essential facts, core concepts, and fundamental principles.

The convergence of these three areas gives rise to TPACK, reflecting the skill to seamlessly incorporate technology into discipline-specific instruction in a relevant and impactful way.

4.2.4.2 Composite components

The TPACK framework also identifies numerous interconnected elements that arise from the convergence of its fundamental areas:

Pedagogical Content Knowledge (PCK) refers to the amalgamation of teaching strategies and the understanding of specific subject matter, empowering educators to customize their instructional methods for distinct academic disciplines.

Technological Pedagogical Knowledge (TPK) encompasses the skill to effectively integrate technology within diverse instructional approaches and methodologies.

Technological Content Knowledge (TCK) emphasizes the role of technology in improving both the presentation and comprehension of specific academic subjects.

The various components play a significant role in the overall enhancement of TPACK, which supports educators in crafting and executing lessons that incorporate technology effectively.

4.2.5 The Five Characteristics of TPACK

The TPACK framework highlights the necessity for adapting technology integration methods to suit particular environments, taking into account the needs of learners, the available resources in schools, and the requirements of the curriculum.

As advancements in technology continue, so does the enhancement of educators' TPACK, highlighting the need for continuous professional growth and flexibility.

TPACK fosters teamwork among educators with diverse specialties, enabling the exchange of effective methods and creative concepts related to the incorporation of technology.

This approach prioritizes the students' needs and preferences, leveraging technological tools to boost interest, drive, and personalized educational journeys.

4.2.6 Influence and Acceptance

Since its introduction, the TPACK framework has profoundly influenced the practices of teaching and the education of teachers. Its incorporation into educator training programs has led to the creation of a variety of tools and curricula designed to bolster educators' understanding of how to effectively combine technology, pedagogy, and content knowledge. In addition, the TPACK framework has fostered a dynamic research landscape that delves into various dimensions of integrating technology, particularly its influence on student outcomes, educators' perceptions, and the interactions within classrooms.

Activity 1 **Choose the best answer to each question.**

1. TPACK stands for ____________.
   A. Technological Pedagogical and Cultural Knowledge
   B. Technological Personal and Content Knowledge
   C. Technological Pedagogical and Content Knowledge
   D. Teaching Practices and Content Knowledge

2. What is the central idea behind TPACK?
   A. Teachers should focus solely on content knowledge.
   B. Technology should replace traditional teaching methods.
   C. Teachers must possess a unique blend of technological, pedagogical, and content knowledge.
   D. Pedagogical knowledge is more important than technological knowledge.

3. Technological Knowledge in TPACK refers to ____________.
   A. the ability to design innovative lesson plans
   B. the use of digital tools and resources for instructional purposes
   C. understanding classroom management strategies
   D. having a deep understanding of the subject matter

4. Which of the following is NOT a component of Pedagogical Knowledge?
   A. Classroom management　　B. Instructional methods
   C. Subject matter expertise　　D. Assessment techniques

5. Which of the following does TPACK emphasize the importance of?
   A. Ignoring the role of technology in teaching
   B. Isolating technological, pedagogical, and content knowledge
   C. The interconnectedness of technology, teaching strategies, and subject matter
   D. Teaching the same way regardless of technological advancements

6. How does TPACK encourage teachers to improve their practices?
   A. By reflecting on practices, evaluating technology use, and adapting strategies.
   B. By avoiding reflection and continuous learning.
   C. By discouraging the use of technology.
   D. By focusing solely on content knowledge.

7. Effective teachers with strong TPACK skills can leverage digital tools to ____________.
   A. ignore student engagement
   B. distract students from learning
   C. enhance student engagement and motivation

D. replace traditional teaching methods entirely

8. Which of the following is NOT true about TPACK?
   A. It recognizes technology as a means to transform learning experiences.
   B. It emphasizes the importance of context in teachers' knowledge and practices.
   C. It involves a continuous cycle of learning and improvement.
   D. It suggests that teachers should ignore technological advancements.

9. Professional development programs that enhance TPACK often include ____________.
   A. avoiding technology in the classroom
   B. hands-on experiences with various hardware and software
   C. focusing solely on content knowledge
   D. ignoring pedagogical knowledge

10. In the TPACK framework, which of the following are teachers better equipped to address?
    A. Only the learning needs of traditional students.
    B. Only the technological demands of the classroom.
    C. The diverse learning needs of students, including those with special educational requirements.
    D. None of the above.

4.3 The Evolution of Information Technology in Education

Throughout the years, there has been a fundamental transformation in the methods of instruction and learning due to advancements in technology. What was once viewed merely as an enhancement to conventional teaching approaches has now transitioned into a vital component of the educational domain. The incorporation of technology in teaching English has significantly improved the overall learning experience while also boosting student participation and results.

The potential of integrating technology into educational settings has until very recently, not been realized to a significant extent. Computers were frequently regarded as additional resources primarily for recreation or as infrequent support for teaching. Yet, until recently, there has been a considerable transformation, with educational technology gaining broader accessibility, cost-effectiveness, and true practicality in both academic settings and domestic environments.

The advancement of technology has led to significant changes in teaching methods, especially in the realm of English language education. Currently, teachers are equipped with an extensive selection of digital resources that can enrich language instruction, making it more interactive, captivating, and effective.

4.3.1 Essential Technologies in Teaching English

Presented here is an extensive compilation of essential technologies that have played a significant role in the ongoing development of English language education.

- Smartboards: Smartboards have increasingly come to play a vital role in numerous English classrooms, providing opportunities for educators to showcase multimedia materials, engage with learners, and develop interactive and engaging lessons.
- Online resources for language acquisition: A vast array of tools is available for those learning English on the web, which encompasses educational websites, glossaries, digital articles from news outlets, and audio programs. Various research instruments, such as search engines and databases, make it simple to locate and utilize these valuable materials.
- Presentation tools: Applications such as PowerPoint, Prezi, Canva, and Google Slides provide enhanced and interactive features for collaborative presentations. These resources empower educators to craft visually engaging and informative slides that enhance their lectures and captivate students' interest.
- Affordable or no-cost educational tools: The increase in readily available low-cost or free educational applications, like Grammarly for grammar correction and Edpuzzle for lessons featuring videos, has enabled access to technology for both educators and learners.
- Mobile devices (e.g., Tablets, Smartphones): With the rise of mobile learning, students can access educational apps, online resources, and interactive quizzes on their devices, promoting flexibility and personalized learning.
- Social media and shared learning platforms: Platforms like wikis, blogs, Twitter, and Facebook abroad and Baidu Baike, WeChat, Weibo, Zhihu, and Xueersi can facilitate collaborative learning and encourage students to engage in authentic language use.
- Virtual Learning Environments (VLEs): Virtual learning environments like Moodle, TianxueNet, Baicizan, LiulishuoEnglish, ShanbeiSpeaking EFeducation, 51Talk, China University MOOC provide a secure online space for students to access course materials, participate in discussions, and submit assignments.
- Artificial intelligence and machine learning: Recent advancements in AI and machine learning have led to the development of language learning apps that offer personalized feedback, speech recognition, and adaptive learning paths, as well as paving the way for teachers' teaching. The following are some of the large-scale AI models: GPT-3/4, BERT, Transformer, RoBERTa, ALBERT, Electra, Tongyiqianwen, Xunfeixinghuo, Wenxinyiyan, Doubao, Zhipuqingyan, Pangu, Baichuan, and Hunyuan.

4.3.2 Digital Natives, Immigrants, and Newtech Honeymoons

In the 21st century, many students have grown up with digital technology as an integral part of their lives, earning them the title of "digital natives." Conversely, some teachers may feel like "digital immigrants," striving to catch up and understand this new technology. However, it is important to recognize that familiarity with technology doesn not necessarily equate to proficiency in its educational applications. Teachers must take the time to learn and become proficient in the technology that benefits their students.

It is essential to utilize technology for genuine educational purposes. A computer will not provide instruction to learners any more effectively than a chalkboard or an audio tape player does. The effectiveness relies on how one utilizes these resources. However, it is quite common to become enamored with a novel technological device solely for its novelty. Teachers may find it takes considerable time to master the operation of a new gadget or program and to gain confidence using it. The risk is that the majority of one's effort may be directed at mastering that technology, leaving little time to contemplate its practical application in the classroom. Consequently, initial lessons using a new device might become overly centered on the technology itself, demonstrating the impressive features of the latest technological innovations, instead of being solely goal-oriented. It is important to move beyond the initial excitement and achieve a level of comfort with the technology that enables deeper analysis of how to truly leverage it, rather than merely utilizing it.

Activity 2 **Decide whether the following statements are True or False.**

1. Technology has become a minor part of the educational landscape.
2. Computers were once viewed as supplementary tools for entertainment and occasional aids to instruction.
3. The integration of technology in English language teaching has decreased student engagement and outcomes.
4. Interactive Whiteboards (IWBs) are no longer used in English classrooms.
5. The internet provides limited resources for English learners.
6. Presentation software like PowerPoint and Google Slides has made presentations less dynamic and collaborative.
7. Mobile devices such as tablets and smartphones promote flexibility and personalized learning.
8. Virtual Learning Environments (VLEs) do not provide a secure online space for students.
9. Artificial intelligence (AI) and machine learning have hindered the development of personalized feedback and adaptive learning paths.
10. Familiarity with technology always equates to proficiency in its educational applications.

4.4 Using Technology Media in English Teaching

The following are some of the specific examples of how to use some of the previous technology media in English teaching and learning.

4.4.1 Interactive Whiteboard (IWB)

4.4.1.1 Introduction to IWB

A digital whiteboard is a versatile, interactive surface that responds to touch, typically connected to a computer along with a sound system. A data projector casts an image onto the board.

An interactive whiteboard generally allows users to:

- Utilize a unique pen (or your finger) to write or sketch, similar to how one would on a conventional board; the difference is that the resulting image is digitally generated and displayed;
- Keep a record of your work for future access;
- Modify or eliminate what has been recorded or initiate a fresh document;
- Display files, images, and various materials present on the device, such as those created with word processing software.
- Utilize presentations, audio recordings, music files, or various sound tracks.
- Review and enhance documents that were previously formatted in a word processing application.
- Utilize the board as an oversized screen to view videos and images.
- Connect to the Internet (if the display board is linked through a cable or wireless network) to project the image across the entire classroom.
- Take the opportunity to access previously saved digital boards or pages from the lesson and create printed copies for distribution.

For the sake of your students

- Automate the display and execution of content. Numerous pre-designed templates are available for crafting engaging automated tasks and exercises, such as quizzes, puzzles, and assessments.
- Utilize interactive whiteboard resources that are commercially available. A variety of textbooks include versions designed for IWBs featuring engaging animations and participatory tasks.

4.4.1.2 Characteristics of IWB

IWB can generally be categorized into two primary varieties:

Fixed IWB. It is affixed to the wall, typically replacing the traditional blackboard. Typically mounted on the ceiling, there is a device for projecting images, along with a computer and its accessories located in an easily accessible area.

Portable IWB. It is a small box that can be positioned at the base of a conventional non-interactive whiteboard (e.g. using suction cups) to enhance engagement. A different compact option could involve utilizing a tablet device (e.g. a compact digital device that enables users to write directly on its display with a stylus, which can then be shown on a suitable whiteboard or wall.Naturally, both of these approaches still necessitate the use of a data projection device, which can also be compact, although its bulbs are often delicate and can be quite costly.

On a fixed IWB, most functions can be activated by tapping a pen on an icon menu located along one edge of the display. Different companies provide various software for interactive whiteboards, yet many core features tend to be consistent across them.

Design a notepad or a flip chart. This represents the digital archive of every page you create.

Add a blank page. This provides you with a surface to either write or sketch, or it can serve as an additional page or two as you continue your work.

Select pen type. This enables the choice of various colors and the thickness of the pen tip.

Highlighter. It functions similarly to a conventional highlighter, enabling the user to apply a vivid background hue to their text.

Conceal or disclose an object or a page. At times, one can employ a cover to conceal portions of text or design forms that obscure elements below. These tools enable the unveiling of responses to inquiries, obscured aspects of visuals, fragments of written content, and similar elements.

Adjusting the calibration or utilizing keystone correction. Adjusting the calibration ensures that the position of the writing tool corresponds accurately with the marks it creates. When the calibration of the board is inaccurate, it becomes a frustrating tool: One begins to write; however, the text may end up shifted five centimeters towards the upper-right corner. The dimensions and form of the projected rectangle can be modified using keystone adjustment.

4.4.1.3 Approaches for instruction with IWB?

Teach as you typically would. The interactive whiteboard offers an excellent opportunity for regular teaching methods. When there is a need for a board, utilize it just like any traditional board. Begin by mastering the basic tools effectively, such as various colored markers, displaying and uncovering information. Implement improvements as needed, for instance, referring back to the board you utilized yesterday to remind learners of particular information, or checking the Internet in real time during the lesson to verify a word's meaning, or locating an image of a subject you have been discussing.

Interacting with written materials. While reading extensive passages from the board may not be the most effective approach, it serves as an excellent means to draw focus on linguistic nuances. For instance, once learners have reviewed a narrative and addressed comprehension queries related to their textbook, the text can be displayed on the board. Teachers can then analyze it, add remarks, highlight key points, extract specific excerpts for deeper examination, and engage in activities such as collaboratively completing charts and templates.

Showcasing students' accomplishments. A display board serves as an effective platform to highlight learners' achievements. It provides an opportunity to exhibit exemplary work, revisit graded assignments, engage in group discussions on drafts, and collaboratively improve those drafts. Additionally, students can create and deliver presentations, taking the lead in sharing their insights.

Incorporate online resources into the teaching process. An entirely fresh array of resources is available for innovative use: collections of visuals (accessible through search engines), news website magazines, YouTube videos, engaging talks and showcases (for instance, found on the TED platform), discussion platforms covering nearly every conceivable subject. The interactive whiteboard allows educators to effortlessly divert from the current lesson to access online resources (such as a brief video segment) before returning to their instructional material. This creates an opportunity for endless information to be accessed in the classroom, fulfilling a teacher's aspirations. However, it is critical to bear in mind that effective integration of these tools is essential; viewing a 20-minute clip on an interactive whiteboard can be just as monotonous as watching it on a conventional television unless it is utilized effectively.

Run automated exercises (e.g. drag and drop). Both teachers and students might discover a fondness for engaging with automated exercises. These activities can possess an engaging quality similar to video games, encouraging individuals to participate in grammar drills that they might otherwise avoid in traditional book formats.

Activity 3 Discuss the following questions in groups.

1. Can you provide specific examples of how IWBs can be used to make lessons more interactive and effective?

2. What are some potential challenges teachers might face when integrating Interactive Whiteboards (IWBs) into their English teaching practices?

4.4.2 Software for Presentations

4.4.2.1 An overview of presentation tools

The software commonly used for presentations is likely best identified through its brand names, such as Powerpoint.

Various presentation tools available today include Microsoft, Apple's Keynote, the complimentary Impress from OpenOffice, and a variety of online choices—some free, some paid—such as Prezi and Presentations via Google Docs.

For many teachers, the utilization of presentation tools has emerged as a vital method for structuring, managing, and displaying educational materials. The fundamental idea resembles a slideshow format. Each slide can incorporate visuals, message, and audio, including various combinations of video segments. This material can be creatively organized on the slide and programmed for sequential or animated displays. It frequently serves as an integral part of foundational explanatory material, supplying visuals and written information to reinforce the instructor's dialogue. A simple way to create a handout is by printing smaller versions of the slides. At first, mastering presentation tools can appear intimidating, though a brief introduction of 10 minutes can make it much easier, and shouldn't present a significantly greater difficulty than operating a text editing program.

4.4.2.2 The role of presentation applications

Use concise text in presentations. Limit the amount of written content on slides and focus on essential phrases. Highlight titles, crucial terms, and significant concepts. These elements can serve as focal points around which discussions can revolve, involving elicitation, narration, and inquiry. Incorporate relevant examples and illustrations, without delving into detailed explanations.

Set high standards for your visual elements. Many presentations feature stock illustrations and images. When selecting an artwork, invest time in finding exceptional visuals that stimulate thought and motivate. There is plenty of quality stock material available. It is beneficial to extend your search duration instead of simply including a clichéd cartoon character that fails to impress your audience.

Create a presentation that features solely images. An excellent method for teaching vocabulary. Gather a diverse collection of effective visuals, animations, or video clips. Leverage these materials effectively to enhance the learning experience. Resist the temptation to overcrowd the slides with excessive text, words, and detailed explanations!

Animation grammar. Explore innovative perspectives on the structure of sentences concerning various tenses and grammatical concepts. Utilize the options available for animations to reposition text, enabling a new conclusion to connect with a verb or illustrate a word's changing location.

Drills. Introduce words, images, or various prompts individually to conduct exercises in a structured, imaginative, and original manner.

Download shows. There are lots of shared, read-made, copyright-free accessible online resources, which can serve as excellent sources of inspiration. Additionally, they can always be customized to better fit the specific requirements of your students, starting from an existing template.

Ask yourself. Would the students gain the same level of understanding if they simply brought the show home without engaging in any classroom activities? It is essential to enhance the material presented on screen. If the lesson serves as the performance, then why not simply present it and leave?

4.4.2.3 Considerations when utilizing presentation tools

Software like PowerPoint can be excellent resources, however, they also carry the risk of hindering the teaching process. Some considerations should be noted.

The inflexibility of presentation. A slideshow is organized prior to the instruction. Once set, the facilitator is confined to the predetermined sequence. This significantly lessens the adaptability that an educator requires to navigate and address spontaneous inquiries from students, allowing for various directions of the lesson to unfold. It is beneficial to embrace the idea of rearranging on the fly: pausing the presentation, locating the necessary slides, and then continuing from a new point.

PowerPoint—interaction between teacher and IWB. Much inexperienced teaching with presentation software shows that as soon as teachers stare using it, the interaction patterns in class change. Instead of interacting with the students, the teacher interacts mainly with her own words and activities on screen.

PowerPoint death. There are too many slides. Too many words. No interaction. The teacher merely vocalizes the text displayed on the slides. Presenting information through slides alone does not constitute effective teaching. Effective design compels teachers to impart knowledge while encouraging learners to engage actively.

Dead lessons. Teachers have consistently developed new instructional content upon the foundations of previous lessons; however, with the rise of presentations, there exists a stronger allure to let established materials remain untouched, perceiving the presentation as finalized and allowing it to solidify over time. Be cautious of lessons that have become stagnant! Find methods to compel oneself to innovate and make changes. Establish a personal guideline that mandates reviewing any PowerPoint presentation before reusing it.

Activity 4 Create a small courseware on present continuous tense by using PPT in your group, and display it in class. Explain the reasons for your design and comment on it.

____

____

____

____

____

____

____

4.4.3 Teaching and Learning Online

4.4.3.1 Virtual Learning Environments

A Virtual Learning Environment (VLE), also known as a Learning Management System (LMS), is a website that integrates various resources for managing a course. In China, some common VLE platforms include China University MOOC, Rain Classroom, and Smart Tree. To operate a VLE, you need a server, which is essentially a host computer that remains constantly online and accessible by other computers.

Common VLE features include:

- Forums: Where students and teachers can send and read messages.
- Attachment capabilities: Allowing the addition of text documents, videos, audios, presentations, etc., which students can download.
- Assignment submission and assessment: Students can submit assignments, teachers can grade them, and the marks can be compiled in a grade book.
- Automated exercises, activities, and tests: These can be created to help students reinforce their knowledge.
- Additional features: Such as wikis (for example, enabling online collaborative creation of encyclopedias) and blogs (for instance, for class diaries).

Teachers are granted authoring or editing rights, allowing them to create content, while learners have user access to read, download content, and post messages on forums.

Applications of VLEs:

- Independent distance programs: Where the entire course, including all interactions and content, is managed on the VLE.
- Blended learning: As a supplement to face-to-face instruction. For example, teachers can use the VLE to complement their lessons by posting handouts, whiteboard images, internet links, or additional reading materials and tasks online.

4.4.3.2 Networks for personal learning

An online community dedicated to personal education, known as a Personal Learning Network (PLN), consists of individuals with whom one interacts to engage in discussions about academic topics and related matters. This network can be intentionally established, or it may develop organically as a collection of individuals who engage with and reply to your posts. A professional learning network may include classmates as well as connections from various educational institutions locally or globally. Educators also benefit from personal learning networks as a way to stay informed about contemporary concepts.

A personal learning network can be nurtured through various online tools that promote interaction, such as WeChat groups, QQ groups, Zhihu, and Weibo. For example, Weibo functions as a system for distributing messages. After registering on Weibo, users have the option to "follow" particular individuals. Whenever a message is sent by one of them, all individuals who have chosen to follow that individual will get the message. Each communication may include hyperlinks within their content, enabling a Weibo post to connect you to an informative site, including various types of online posts. One compelling advantage of Weibo is that its concise format and straightforward access allow users to view and communicate via messages at any moment and in any place (e.g., utilizing your cellphone during a brief tram ride back home).

A valuable tip for Weibo users pertains to the use of tags (specifically, words that start with the "#" sign). These tags serve as an effective means of categorizing your posts under specific topics. For instance, if one shares a post regarding teaching English, incorporating a tag such as #EnglishTeaching or #TEFL could be beneficial. This way, individuals interested in such subjects can easily search for the tag #EnglishTeaching and access all the posts that include that particular label.

Activity 5 Choose the best answer to each question.

1. What is another term for a Virtual Learning Environment (VLE)?
   A. Learning Management System (LMS) B. Online Assessment Tool (OAT)
   C. Digital Classroom (DC) D. E-Learning Platform (ELP)

2. Which of the following is a common feature of VLEs?
   A. In-person tutoring B. Forums for communication
   C. Physical textbooks D. Live sports events

3. What capability does a VLE provide for the addition of various types of documents and media?
   A. Automated grading B. Assignment submission
   C. Attachment capabilities D. Wiki creation

4. In the context of VLEs, what can automated exercises and activities help students with?
   A. Socializing with classmates B. Reinforcing their knowledge
   C. Purchasing textbooks D. Finding job opportunities

5. What rights are teachers typically granted in a VLE?
   A. Only reading access B. User access to post messages
   C. Authoring or editing rights D. Limited to assignment submission

6. Which of the following is an application of VLEs for independent distance programs?
   A. Supplementing face-to-face instruction B. Managing the entire course online
   C. Facilitating in-person discussions D. Organizing school events

7. What is a Personal Learning Network (PLN)?
   A. An online course catalog
   B. A network of online stores
   C. An online group for educational discussions
   D. A system for online gaming

8. Which platform is mentioned as particularly useful for maintaining a PLN?
   A. WeChat
   B. Weibo
   C. Zhihu
   D. QQ

9. What is the purpose of using hashtags on Weibo?
   A. To increase the character limit of messages
   B. To mark messages on a certain subject
   C. To prevent others from seeing the message
   D. To create a private group chat

10. How can the brevity of Weibo messages benefit users?
   A. By allowing complex discussions
   B. By enabling quick and easy message checking and sending
   C. By providing in-depth articles
   D. By requiring less mobile data usage

4.4.4 Teachers' AI Literacy

4.4.4.1 Concepts related to teachers' AI literacy

Informatization, digitalization, and intelligentization are three important stages in the development of technology, along with the early computer technology at the very beginning. At the same time, the evolution from information literacy to digital literacy, and then to AI literacy, reflects the evolution of the educational field's requirements for technology application and skills. In this process, the role and literacy of teachers also need to continuously change and upgrade (Xue, et al., 2024).

Ala believes that literacy should be seen as a continuum from instrumental skills to productive competence and efficiency (Ala-Mutka K., 2011). In the technological development process from informatization and digitalization to intelligentization, people's understanding of "literacy" is constantly evolving. Before the 1990s, people mainly focused on "computer literacy," emphasizing the ability to use computer software and hardware, which led to overly simplified tool-oriented teaching. By the end of the 1990s, the concept shifted to "information literacy," emphasizing the identification, location, use, and evaluation of information. UNESCO describes information literacy as covering five elements: "identifying information needs, evaluating information quality, retrieving and storing information, ethically using information, applying information to create and communicate knowledge. (Catts R., Lau J., 2008)" Entering the 21st century, the concept of "digital literacy" began to emerge (UNESCO, 2021). As early as 1997, Gilster defined it as the ability to understand and use information from various sources and in various formats presented through computers (Gilster P., 1997). Martin and Grudziecki (2006) supplemented it, considering the ability to use digital tools and resources in specific contexts, adding contextual and digital tool elements. The definition given by UNESCO is more comprehensive: "It refers to the ability to use digital technologies, communication tools or networks to find, evaluate, use, and create information, as well as the ability to understand and use information from multiple sources, in various forms, presented through computers, or the ability of individuals to effectively perform tasks in a digital environment (UNESCO, 2018)." With the development of artificial intelligence and big data, scholars have begun to propose concepts such as "digital intelligence literacy" and "AI literacy." Long and Magerko (2020) pointed out that with artificial intelligence literacy (AI competencies), people can critically evaluate AI technology, effectively communicate and cooperate with AI, and use AI as a tool in networks, homes, and workplaces. The evolution of concepts from information literacy and digital literacy to AI literacy can be summarized in Table 4.1.

Table 4.1 Evolution of literacy: From information to AI

Content	Literacy			
	Computer Literacy	Information Literacy	Digital Literacy	AI Literacy
Timeline	Early 20th Century	Late 1990s	Early 21st Century	2020s
Definition	The ability to use computers and related technologies efficiently, encompassing skills from basic operation to advanced problem-solving (Luehrmann, 1981).	The capacity to identify, locate, evaluate, and effectively use information for decision-making or problem-solving (American Library Association [ALA], 2000).	the competence to critically engage with digital tools and platforms, integrating technical skills with cognitive and ethical discernment in digital environments (Gilster, 1997).	the understanding of artificial intelligence concepts, applications, and ethical implications, enabling individuals to interact with, evaluate, and design AI-driven systems responsibly (Long & Magerko, 2020).
Tool Usage	Basic computer hardware and software usage	Tools for information identification, location, use, and evaluation	Use of digital tools and resources in specific contexts	Critical assessment and effective communication with AI technologies
Scope of Usage	Limited to basic computer operations	Broadened to include information retrieval and ethical use	Expanded to include digital tools and multi-format information	Encompasses AI technology evaluation, communication, and integration into various environments
Ethical Consideration	Minimal focus on ethics	Ethical use of information becomes a component	Ethical considerations expanded with digital tools	Ethical implications of AI and responsibility for AI outcomes are central
Skills and Competency	Technical skills focused	Critical thinking and information evaluation skills	Contextual application and digital tool proficiency	AI technology understanding, communication, and ethical responsibility

These four types of literacy are interconnected and build upon each other, forming a progressive skill set necessary for navigating today's technology-driven world. Each layer adds complexity, moving from basic operation (computer) to critical use (information), holistic digital engagement (digital), and AI-specific competencies (AI). Digital literacy encompasses aspects of computer and information literacy, while AI literacy relies on all three. For example, a computer-literate person can use a search engine, an information-literate person can assess the credibility of search results, a digitally literate person understands algorithms shaping those results and creates content responsibly, and an AI-literate person recognizes AI-generated content, adjusts prompts for better outputs, and questions biases in AI models.

4.4.4.2 Teachers' digital literacy

The report of the 20th National Congress explicitly proposes to "advance the digitalization of education." Teachers are the main force in improving educational standards, and it is necessary to continuously enhance their capabilities and literacy. Therefore, the Ministry of Education (2022) has developed the "Standards for Teacher Digital Literacy" for training and evaluating teacher digital literacy to solidly promote the national strategy for educational digitalization, improve the standard system for educational informatization, and enhance teachers' awareness, ability, and responsibility to optimize, innovate, and transform educational and teaching activities using digital technology. Teacher digital literacy refers to the awareness, ability, and responsibility that teachers possess to appropriately use digital technology to acquire, process, utilize, manage, and evaluate digital information and resources. It involves identifying, analyzing, and solving educational and teaching problems, as well as optimizing, innovating, and transforming educational and teaching activities.

The "Teacher Digital Literacy" standards include five dimensions: digital awareness, digital technology knowledge and skills, digital application, digital social responsibility, and professional development. Under each primary dimension, there are several secondary dimensions, tertiary dimensions, and specific descriptions (see Figure 4.2 and Appendix 1).

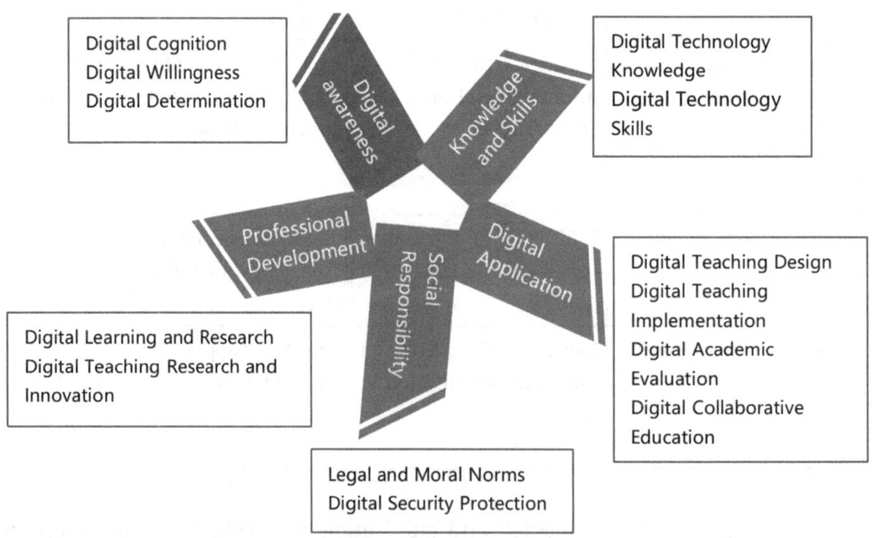

Figure 4.2 Teacher digital literacy framework

Teachers should actively and thoroughly study the "Teacher Digital Literacy" standards, enhance their awareness, ability, and responsibility to use digital technology to optimize, innovate, and transform educational and teaching activities, continuously improve teaching methods, and enhance the quality of education and teaching.

4.4.4.3 AI literacy

With the in-depth development of information technology, the degree of government information disclosure and data openness has been continuously improved. Various market-oriented online information media and digital tools have rapidly become widespread. Consequently, technical literacy concepts such as computer literacy, information literacy, media and information literacy, digital literacy, data literacy, and algorithmic literacy have emerged one after another, and now it has come to the AI literacy era (Yin, 2023). According to Yin Kaiguo' s research, AI literacy includes five elements, they are AI awareness, AI cognition, AI skills, AI thinking, and AI Ethics (see Figure 4.3).

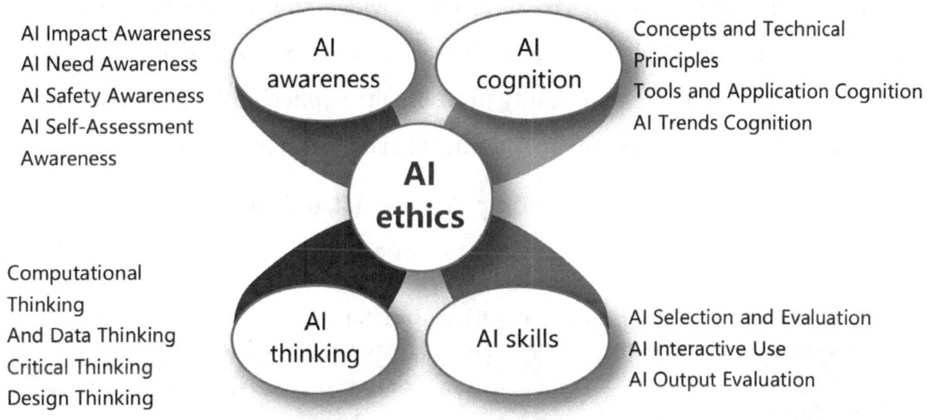

Figure 4.3 AI literacy framework

AI awareness refers to the sensitivity towards AI development and the basic perception and understanding of the existence, application, and social impact of AI technology.

AI cognition is a core component of AI literacy, involving an understanding of basic AI concepts, technical principles, application scenarios, and insight into the development trends of AI technology.

The cultivation of **AI skills** focuses on the practical operation level, requiring individuals to apply theoretical knowledge to identify, evaluate, apply, and integrate AI technology, tools, and resources to achieve specific goals, solve practical problems in digital life, learning, work, and social scenarios, enhance personal efficiency, optimize decision-making processes, and become active participants in the AI world.

AI thinking primarily refers to the modes of thought and methodologies that individuals should possess when using AI technology and adapting to the AI social environment.

AI ethics focuses on the moral use of AI concepts and applications, closely related to legal, cultural, ethical, and social value issues in an intelligent society. Its complexity lies in balancing technological development with human values.

Therefore, as English teachers in the new era, we must embrace new technologies, face new challenges, and master new skills. We should not be ostriches burying our heads in the sand but rather pioneers who bravely confront new challenges and harness AI.

4.4.4.4 Teachers' AI literacy

The rapid rise of artificial intelligence (AI) systems is having profound implications for teaching and learning, particularly regarding the role of teachers and the competencies they require to navigate the ever-evolving technological landscape. The use of AI in education is raising fundamental questions about teacher agency and their capacity to determine how and when to make judicious use of this technology.

According to Xue Shumin (2024), no scholars have yet provided an accurate definition of AI literacy for teachers. In her opinion, teachers' AI literacy refers to "teachers' understanding of the basic principles of AI technology in an educational context, their ability to assess the applicability of AI tools, and their capacity to creatively and ethically use AI technology in the teaching and learning process."

In September 2023, UNESCO released a draft for public consultation on the "AI Competency Framework for Teachers" (abbreviated as AI CFT), the main contents of which can be summarized in Table 4.2.

Table 4.2 The AI competency framework for teachers by UNESCO

Aspects	Progression		
	Acquire	Deepen	Create
Human-centered mindset	Human agency	Human accountability	Social responsibility
Ethics of AI	Ethical principles	Safe and responsibility	Co-creating ethical rules
AI foundations and applications	Basic AI techniques and applications	Application skills	Creating with AI
AI pedagogy	AI-assisted teaching	AI pedagogy integration	AI-enhanced pedagogical transformation
AI for professional development	AI enabling lifelong professional learning	AI to enhance organizational learning	AI to support professional transformation

The AI CFT is presented in a two-dimensional matrix: five aspects of competency which evolve across three progression levels, forming fifteen blocks. The first dimension comprises the five aspects of AI competency: human-centred mindset, ethics of AI, AI foundations and applications, AI pedagogy, and AI for professional development. While each aspect represents a unique constituent element of AI competency, the aspects are related to each other as they are complementary, interdependent, and synergistic. Their relatedness contributes to the cohesive growth of AI competence. The Human-centred mindset aspect defines the values and attitudinal orientation towards human AI interactions that teachers need to nurture. The Ethics of AI aspect delineates essential ethical principles, regulations, institutional laws, and practical ethical rules that teachers need to understand, apply, and help adapt. The AI foundations and applications aspect specifies conceptual knowledge and transferable skills teachers need to understand and apply in selecting, applying and creatively customizing AI tools to serve student-centred, AI-assisted teaching and learning environments. The AI pedagogy aspect proposes a set of competencies required for purposeful and effective AI pedagogy integration. This covers the ability to validate and select proper AI tools and to integrate them into pedagogical strategies to support course preparation, teaching, learning, socialization, social caring, and learning assessment. The AI for professional development aspect outlines competencies teachers need to develop in order to use AI properly in driving their lifelong professional learning, supporting collaborative professional development, and exploring professional transformation.

The AI CFT's second dimension is the scaffolded progression of competency development. Progression levels represent the levels teachers could possibly develop over time in all five competency aspects as part and parcel of AI competency. The framework recognizes that competence development is a complex, context-dependent process that is neither hierarchical nor linear. However, the framework serves as a reference pathway for teacher progression, emphasizing and outlining desired outcomes at each level per aspect rather than setting out rigid, prescribed steps that teachers must go through. The three progression levels are: "Acquire", which defines the essential set of AI competencies all teachers need in order to evaluate, select, and use AI tools appropriately in education; "Deepen", which specifies intermediate competencies that are needed to design meaningful pedagogical strategies that integrate AI; and "Create", which sets out advanced competencies required for the creative configuration of AI systems and innovative use of AI in education. By crossing these three levels with the five aspects of competency, the AI CFT defines fifteen competency blocks. These competency blocks are designed to support all teachers, from those with no knowledge at all about AI to those with a higher degree of competency and experience in AI. The AI CFT proposes a set of competencies around which teachers need to be prepared to make proper use of AI in education. However, the effective and ethical use of AI in education depends on various factors including, but not limited to, access to digital infrastructure, and the internet in particular; availability of AI resources; regulations on data security and privacy; policy guidance and incentives; and professional development opportunities. It is also contingent on the trustworthiness and performance features of the AI tools that are adopted at scale and their implications for teachers' workloads. All of these, and potentially other factors, would likewise affect the extent to which teachers' AI competency can be practised, observed, and advanced.

Following the AI CFT in 2023, UNESCO released the Student AI Literacy Competency Framework

(Abbreviated as AI CFS) in 2024. The AI CFS specifies twelve competency blocks based on a matrix of two dimensions. The first dimension comprises four interlinked aspects of AI competencies, while the second dimension includes three levels of progression or mastery that students are expected to engage with iteratively. While the AI CFS anchors the definition of AI competency on three pillars that frame wider core competencies for students—namely, knowledge, skills, and values—it also aims to encourage an ethical understanding of human-led methods underlying AI systems. Based on this conceptualization, the framework defines four essential constituent elements of students' AI competency: a human-centred mindset, ethics of AI, AI techniques and applications, and AI system design. These elements focus on fundamental values, social responsibilities to uphold ethical principles, foundational knowledge and skills, and higher-order thinking skills for system design. While different elements can be developed through domain-specific learning and pedagogical methodologies, AI competencies are ultimately a set of interdisciplinary, general abilities and value orientations that extend beyond particular AI domains or tools (see Table 4.3).

Table 4.3 AI competency framework for students

Competency aspects	Progression levels		
	Understand	Apply	Create
Human-centered mindset	Human agency	Human accountability	Citizenship in the era of AI
Ethics of AI	Embodied ethics	Safe and responsible use	Ethics by design
AI techniques and applications	AI foundations	Application skills	Creating AI tools
AI system design	Problems scoping	Architecture design	Iteration and feedback loops

4.4.5 Becoming a Wise Teacher Using Generative AI

How can teachers utilize AI successfully in their teaching? Wei Fei summarizes the following aspect:

Generative AI is a model and technology that generates content based on user intent, which can be regarded as a tool for content creation. It is capable of generating new texts, images, music, and even videos based on the user's perspective. Nowadays, a large number of creative intelligent tools are springing up like mushrooms after rain, and their widespread application has given rise to new lifestyles and work methods, with the impact of social transformation gradually becoming apparent.

In the field of education, the integration of generative AI can not only enrich teaching content and methods but also innovate educational and teaching models, bringing about revolutionary changes to education. Against the background of the country's vigorous promotion of digital transformation, understanding, comprehending, and learning about generative AI has become the core content for teachers to enhance their digital literacy and implement the reform of core literacy.

However, how secure is generative AI? How can we use it properly? This section will explain four aspects:

recognizing risks, understanding scenarios, acquiring skills, and innovating applications, to help teachers better meet new challenges and requirements, and become wise teachers in the AI era (Wei, 2024).

4.4.5.1 Understanding risks

Generative AI generates content that meets user needs by learning from and deeply analyzing large-scale datasets, imitating human language and behavior patterns. Its strength lies in the diversity and creativity of the generated content. However, it also harbors numerous risks and challenges.

The risk of value orientation. During training, generative AI systems may absorb and amplify biases present in their training data, leading to content with misleading directions. Algorithmic bias and the filter bubble effect are two related and non-negligible issues. If the training data itself contains erroneous ideas, the content generated by AI could negatively impact users' values and judgment.

The risk of data security. The potential hazards regarding data protection. The utilization of generative AI involves significant quantities of information for its instructional and developmental processes, which might encompass confidential and private data, thereby heightening concerns regarding data safeguarding. Inadequate safeguards for the data regarding students could result in an infringement of their privacy rights. In addition, insufficient data governance protocols may cause mishandling and inappropriate utilization of information, which could result in misuse or unauthorized access to data.

The risk of content quality. The essence of content generation by generative AI is pattern prediction, relying on massive amounts of high-quality data for learning and content generation. In the context of ongoing curriculum reforms, if the data used for AI training (including policies, theories, and case studies) is not comprehensive or of poor quality, the generated materials may have significant biases or uncertainties.

For teachers, without sufficient professional competence and experience to reasonably evaluate and judge the content generated by AI, there could be serious misleading risks, adversely affecting students. Therefore, teachers should strengthen their awareness of data ethics and security, actively engage in professional learning, enhance their professional competence, and continuously improve their sensitivity and judgment in the ethical and professional use of generative AI. Ensuring compliance with ethical safety and professional standards is a fundamental prerequisite for educational and teaching applications.

4.4.5.2 Understanding scenarios

Generative AI, trained on large-scale datasets including educational theories and practical cases, teaching methods and strategies, and online literature resources, generates creative suggestions based on educational concepts and best practices. It can effectively assist teachers in routine applications within everyday practice scenarios. The following are typical application scenarios of generative AI in education.

Instructional design. Based on the analysis of teaching objectives and subjects, teachers can use generative AI to assist in designing key elements such as unit big ideas, higher-order questions, authentic contexts, learning scaffolds, and learning activities. This aims to implement core literacy cultivation and achieve high-level education.

Resource development. AI can support the design and creation of presentations, images, videos, etc., enriching resource formats and improving the efficiency of resource development. In constructing inquiry environments, AI can be used to create highly interactive environments based on technologies like virtual reality and the metaverse, as well as spaces for higher-order thinking. This enhances students' abilities in problem analysis, reflective evaluation, and critical thinking.

Student data analysis. AI can be employed for data cleaning of evaluation data, calculation of key indicators, data analysis based on learning analytics models, and generation of visualization charts. This allows more focus on understanding data and analyzing students.

Daily management. Generative AI can help teachers record and analyze classroom data, assist in writing notifications, reports, and other parent-teacher communication emails, reducing the investment in clerical work and enhancing management efficiency;

Research projects. Generative AI can assist in designing and refining research questions, hypotheses, data collection tools, and research outlines. It standardizes report formats and broadens research perspectives.

4.4.5.3 Acquiring skills

Teachers need to master key skills for the operation and use of generative AI.

Mastering prompt engineering and writing effective prompts. Generative AI can only provide appropriate feedback after clearly understanding specific human needs; in other words, high-quality input questions are required to obtain higher-quality responses. The prompt for generative AI should accurately express the human role, work instructions, context, relevant data, and output requirements (including evaluation criteria for expected results). Work instructions are specific tasks that you want the generative AI to perform, such as designing teaching activities based on the 5E Instructional Model. Context includes the task's background or contextual information, such as informing about the activity's target audience, duration, environmental information, etc. It also includes some theoretical models, evaluation standards, reference examples, or learning materials to guide generative AI in better responding to task requirements. Here is an example of ChatGPT prompt.

> *Basic Prompt: Create a character for a story.*
>
> *Elaborated Prompt: Create a character for a sci-fi story. Use the raw material from my notes below to understand what I'm trying to do.*
>
> *I am designing an ad campaign for a government project to raise awareness about solar energy. The sci-fi story I create should help in that. I want my character to have a super power that helps it to do photosynthesis like plants.*

Possessing process thinking, articulating tasks in a language understood by large models. If the instructional task is too complex, the question is unclear, or the requirements are not specific enough, generative AI will struggle to deliver satisfactory answers. When posing questions, it is essential to consciously break down tasks and processes, dividing complex tasks into several specific sub-tasks. For example, regarding the question "How to improve classroom teaching efficiency," one could decompose it from angles like classroom management, teaching methods, teaching content, student assessment, etc., expressing needs through sub-questions like "How to effectively manage student discipline in class," "What teaching methods can enhance student engagement and interaction," "How to design learning content based on students' levels and interests," and "What methods can accurately assess learning outcomes."

Evaluating and judging the generated content. By continuously enhancing their professional competence and judgment, they should meticulously analyze and rationally assess the accuracy of the generative AI's output, its implicit values, and its potential impact on teaching and students.

Faced with possible "hallucinations" and "nonsensical seriousness" from generative AI, teachers should have keen critical awareness. Using professional accumulation, practical experience, and literature resources, they should comprehensively review the output results of generative AI. Through a collaborative mechanism involving "human-in-the-loop," actively participate in the answer generation process, promptly identify and correct errors made by generative AI, and proactively construct an understanding of the problem.

4.4.5.4 Innovative applications

Teachers should explore the deep integration of generative AI with education and teaching.

Teachers should innovate homework and task design to increase cognitive challenge difficulty. As "digital natives," students will naturally use AI to assist learning. The low-threshold, boundless generative function may encourage plagiarism and reliance behaviors among students, which is not conducive to developing problem-solving skills and critical thinking.

To avoid academic inertia or the phenomenon of "achievements without growth," teachers must innovate task design to ensure students have ample opportunities for intellectual training and capacity building. For example, adopting open-ended tasks based on real scenarios and problem-solving to enhance cognitive challenges, guiding students in process evaluation, and reflecting to develop self-awareness and monitoring abilities.

Teachers should research and accumulate technical resources for generative AI, creating spaces for autonomous and inquiry-based learning for students. For instance, establishing virtual laboratories allows students to conduct scientific experiments and exploratory activities in a safe, controllable environment; simulating various real-life scenarios helps students learn in specific contexts, enhancing the practicality and interactivity of learning; constructing data analysis environments enables students to explore complex relationships between data, fostering data analysis skills and critical thinking.

Educators ought to cultivate an awareness of the interdisciplinary potential inherent in generative AI tools, which can significantly improve students' overall literacy. As digital technologies, particularly generative AI, naturally encompass a variety of fields, they serve as key instruments for facilitating multidisciplinary initiatives. By leveraging scenario development, supporting inquiries, and tailoring guidance through generative AI, educators can create and execute projects that span multiple disciplines.

For instance, employing generative AI to craft historical visuals for an engaging, inquiry-focused learning experience. In art education, the application of generative AI can yield innovative artworks that inspire the imagination of learners. These cross-disciplinary initiatives enable students to grasp the fundamental relationships between various knowledge areas while also honing their creative thinking and problem-solving skills.

4.4.5.5 Functions of AI in English teaching

The integration of artificial intelligence in education serves several key roles. It facilitates personalized learning experiences, enhances engagement through interactive content, and aids in the development of language competence. Such technological advancements support educators in creating lesson plans that are more adaptive to individual student needs, ultimately fostering a richer learning environment.

Tailored learning experiences: AI facilitates the creation of customized learning pathways that address the distinct requirements of each student. Through the examination of educational data, AI technologies can suggest suitable resources and activities, allowing learners to progress at their own speed and skill level.

Interactive learning: Conversational agents and AI-driven chatbots facilitate engaging educational experiences, enabling learners to enhance their speaking and listening abilities within a context that mimics real-world interactions. This engagement fosters hands-on learning experiences and improves proficiency in the language.

Automated assessment: Tools powered by AI can evaluate written work, tests, and other assignments, offering rapid responses to learners. This not only lightens the burden on educators but also enables learners to swiftly detect and rectify mistakes.

Ongoing assessment and adaptation: AI technologies actively track the evolution of student performance, modifying educational strategies as needed. Such flexibility guarantees that learners are provided with the most pertinent and impactful educational materials.

4.4.5.6 Pros and cons to consider

Advantages

- Tailored education: Artificial intelligence addresses the unique preferences of learners, improving both the efficiency of the learning process and the quality of the results.

- Engaging language practice: Conversational agents and chatbots offer users the chance to participate in immersive language training experiences.
- Time-saving evaluation: The use of automated systems for grading and delivering feedback benefits both educators and learners by conserving their time.
- Customized learning experience: AI technologies are designed to monitor and adapt to the progress of individual learners, providing a personalized educational journey.

Disadvantages

- Student data protection: Accessing delicate information about students is necessary for AI technologies, which introduces possible risks related to cyber-security.
- Dependence on technological tools: Relying too heavily on artificial intelligence may hinder learners from developing their study skills.
- Expenses: The cost associated with certain AI platforms can be high, making them less accessible to some educational institutions and learners.

4.4.5.7 Various AI software applications and their features

The influence of AI has infiltrated numerous facets of daily life, revolutionizing our approaches to work, education, and creativity. Numerous influential AI software applications are currently driving change across diverse sectors, especially within areas such as brainstorming, content creation support, linguistic improvement, photo manipulation, musical arrangement, and personalized educational experiences.

1. ChatGPT

By utilizing cutting-edge artificial intelligence methodologies, ChatGPT marks a noteworthy advancement in the realm of AI, especially regarding its capacity to participate in fluid, intricate, and frequently perceptive dialogues with individuals.

Essential features and capabilities

- Comprehending natural language: The ability of ChatGPT to understand intricate and subtle aspects of human communication enables it to participate in significant dialogues on a wide array of subjects.
- Interaction flow: It ensures that the dialogue remains logical and contextually relevant over multiple exchanges, resulting in a seamless and instinctive communication experience.
- Innovative production: ChatGPT possesses the ability to create unique textual pieces, poetry, programming code, and even basic software applications, demonstrating its inventive and analytical capabilities.

- Versatile Functionality: In addition to engaging in dialogue, it can carry out various tasks including the summarization of extensive documents, language translation, and delivering verified facts.
- Ongoing Education: Through continuous updates and training efforts, the knowledge repository of ChatGPT grows, thereby improving its performance and accuracy as time progresses.

Applications in education

- Customized Education: ChatGPT is capable of adjusting to the unique requirements of individual learners, offering personalized educational resources and clarifications that align with their comprehension levels.
- Language Learning Companion: Functions as an engaging guide, helping individuals improve their conversational abilities, refining their pronunciation, and boosting overall proficiency in the language.
- Academic Support: Assists learners in locating pertinent materials, condensing study results, and elucidating difficult ideas, thereby enhancing the efficiency of the research undertaking.
- Assistance in Academic Writing: Provides writing ideas, reviews drafts, and offers suggestions for enhancement, thereby improving learners' writing abilities while upholding academic honesty.
- Programming Education: Supports learners with coding challenges, clarifying various concepts, and presenting engaging tasks that make the field of programming more approachable.
- Inclusive Learning: Empowers individuals with disabilities by offering voice-driven interactions and materials designed to be easily accessible.
- Analytical Abilities: Promotes inquiry among students, allowing them to consider various viewpoints while enhancing their skills in logical reasoning and assessment.

2. GitMind AI

GitMind AI emerges as a leading mind-mapping tool that utilizes the capabilities of artificial intelligence to transform how individuals and teams brainstorm and organize their project planning.

Key characteristics and features

- Optimized layout automation: Leverage the power of GitMind AI to enhance your mind maps automatically, ensuring that they are presented in a structured and attractive manner while saving both time and effort.
- Intelligent topic recommendations: When users introduce topics, GitMind AI evaluates the material and proposes related subtopics or associations, encouraging inventive thinking and deepening the complexity of mind maps.

- Synchronous teamwork: Engage in effortless collaboration among colleagues, facilitating the instantaneous sharing, altering, and discussion of concepts, regardless of their physical distance.
- Various export formats: You can seamlessly export your mind maps into different formats such as PDF, PNG, SVG, and others, which makes it simple to share and showcase your work with ease and versatility.

Application for education

GitMind AI revolutionizes the educational sector, enhancing the learning experience for both learners and instructors. Sessions focused on idea generation promote analytical thinking and nurture innovation by offering various subject options and arranging concepts in a coherent manner. When it comes to developing curricula, GitMind AI facilitates a more efficient approach by enabling teachers to design detailed lesson frameworks that are visually appealing and straightforward to navigate. In the context of research coordination, it facilitates the efficiency of compiling, analyzing, and presenting data, thereby improving students' investigative abilities and their capacity for critical assessment.

3. Notion AI

The comprehensive platform known as Notion AI has transformed the landscape of content generation by incorporating sophisticated AI-assisted writing tools into its framework. The writing assistant functionality is a transformative tool, providing exceptional assistance by proposing well-organized sentences, coherent paragraphs, and even complete articles based on user input. This cutting-edge method notably boosts the speed of writing while fostering originality and improving the overall quality, making the process of creating content both effective and captivating.

Essential characteristics and capabilities

- Text generation automation: The sophisticated algorithms utilized by Notion AI evaluate user input to produce meaningful and polished text, allowing users to save time and minimize the necessity for extensive manual writing.
- Grammar and style suggestions: The platform offers features like grammar verification, stylistic advice, and tone modification, which guarantee that the resulting content is sophisticated, professional, and tailored to meet the preferences of the user.
- Effortless integration with Notion's suite of tools: Within the extensive Notion framework, the writing assistant offers a fluid connection to other impactful features like databases, kanban boards, and calendars, enhancing a cohesive and efficient workflow.
- Team collaboration areas: Engage in effective teamwork within specialized areas designed for collaboration, which facilitate instantaneous feedback, cooperative editing, and the collective generation of materials.

Application for educational purposes

Notion AI serves as a formidable resource for both educators and learners, revolutionizing the methods by which educational materials are crafted and utilized. Teachers can leverage the platform to swiftly create captivating instructional materials, evaluation tools, and lesson outlines, thereby allowing them to devote more time to other important responsibilities. Conversely, learners can take advantage of the writing assistant's support in crafting essays, conducting research, and completing creative writing projects, which helps them develop better time management abilities, enhance their inventive writing skills, and elevate their overall proficiency in writing. By leveraging its writing assistant, Notion AI cultivates a more productive, cooperative, and imaginative learning environment.

4. Grammarly

Grammarly, an omnipresent and reliable tool for enhancing writing, employs advanced artificial intelligence to transform the way individuals express themselves in written form. It thoroughly reviews and rectifies issues related to grammar, spelling, and stylistic variations in real time, guaranteeing that each word, phrase, and segment is refined to be excellent. In addition to basic corrections, Grammarly provides a wide range of sophisticated tools designed to enhance the overall quality of your writing.

Key attributes and capabilities

- Comprehensive grammar and spelling evaluations: Its sophisticated algorithms identify even the most subtle grammatical intricacies and delicate spelling mistakes, guaranteeing that your material remains devoid of typographical errors and inaccuracies.
- Suggestions for modifying tone: Acknowledging the significance of tone in effective communication, Grammarly offers recommendations to tailor your writing style according to the specific context, audience, or intended effect.
- Plagiarism prevention: In order to maintain the integrity of academic and professional writing, Grammarly features a comprehensive plagiarism detection tool that meticulously analyzes your work against an extensive repository of online materials, guaranteeing that your content remains entirely unique.
- Compatibility with various platforms: Effortlessly connects with a range of writing tools, web browsers, as well as software like Microsoft Office and Google Docs, making it a user-friendly and adaptable asset for all aspects of writing.

Application for educational purposes

For learners, Grammarly serves as an essential tool throughout their writing process. It not only aids in enhancing writing abilities and building confidence in composing assignments, but it also safeguards academic honesty by mitigating the risk of plagiarism. With the help of Grammarly, learners can concentrate on the core aspects of their work, effectively and impressively articulating their thoughts in examinations, essays, research papers, and other assignments. Ultimately, Grammarly equips students to communicate with precision, every single time.

5. Pixso AI

As a leader in the field of image enhancement, Pixso AI utilizes state-of-the-art algorithms to simplify and automate even the simplest aspects of image adjustments. With the addition of batch processing functionalities, Pixso AI enables users to simultaneously adjust filters, resize, and enhance a whole set of images, greatly minimizing the amount of time dedicated to repetitive activities and allowing for more creative exploration.

Essential characteristics and capabilities

- Image processing in batches: Eliminate the hassle of editing images individually. With Pixso AI's feature for batch modifications, users can achieve consistent changes to numerous images swiftly, thus significantly reducing hours spent on manual adjustments.
- Creative enhancements & artistic filters: With Pixso AI, users can explore an extensive selection of artistic filters and enhancements that open the door to imagination. Whether aiming for delicate modifications or striking visual shifts, individuals can transform their photos, significantly increasing their aesthetic appeal.
- Intelligent color adjustment driven by AI: Utilizing advanced AI innovations, Pixso AI fine-tunes the color balance, contrast, and saturation levels to guarantee that every image is thoroughly optimized for its specific goals.
- Effortless teamwork: Enhance collaboration and increase efficiency with the innovative features of Pixso AI that enable smooth teamwork. Numerous participants can engage in the same project at once, contributing edits and providing feedback in real-time.

Application for education

Pixso AI revolutionizes how teachers and learners craft captivating visual resources, create informative infographics, and assemble interactive multimedia displays. By simplifying the process of editing images, Pixso AI motivates learners to tap into their imagination and boost their digital skills, enabling them to visually communicate their thoughts and knowledge. With the assistance of Pixso AI, learners can direct their attention towards the essence and communication of their artwork, as the application manages the intricate details.

6. Suno AI

AIVA, often referred to as Suno AI, represents a revolutionary advancement in music composition technology. This remarkable creation harnesses artificial intelligence to produce original music that conveys deep emotions, exploring a broad array of musical styles while artfully merging human artistry with the accuracy of automated logic.

Essential characteristics and capabilities

- Original music creation: AIVA goes beyond conventional limits, producing original and enchanting tunes that strike a chord with audiences. The pieces it creates are not simple reproductions but genuine demonstrations of artistic creativity.
- Tailorable compositions and emotions: With unmatched adaptability, AIVA empowers users to modify musical pieces to fit distinct genres and feelings, whether it's calming lullabies or lively rock tracks. This adaptability inspires creativity and individual expression.
- Effortless integration with digital audio workstations: AIVA can be incorporated into various digital audio workflows, boasting high compatibility with widely-used DAWs. This integration enhances the creative journey, fostering smooth collaboration between AI tools and human musicians.
- Music creation through collaboration: AIVA cultivates an environment that encourages interaction among musicians, composers, and educators, allowing them to explore new dimensions in music composition. Participants can exchange concepts, enhance each other's contributions, and collectively craft remarkable works that extend beyond the confines of human creativity.

Application for education

AIVA transforms the landscape of music education by offering a vibrant space for creativity, collaboration, and innovation. Both learners and instructors can leverage artificial intelligence to navigate uncharted musical realms, redefine traditional composing practices, and nurture an environment rich in innovation and creativity. Through their interaction with AIVA, aspiring musicians are equipped to discover their distinct artistic identities, while teachers acquire an effective resource to elevate their instructional approaches and motivate emerging musical talents.

7. ERNIE Bot

ERNIE Bot, part of Baidu's comprehensive AI framework, represents an advanced solution in natural language processing (NLP) that excels in interpreting human linguistic input and generating well-crafted replies, articles, and various forms of content. With its vast repository of knowledge and top-tier generative features, it acts as a vital resource for numerous writing endeavors, enhancing creativity in the process.

Essential attributes and capabilities

- ERNIE Bot excels in comprehending and creating language, allowing it to grasp intricate inquiries and produce responses that are insightful and logically sound.
- Tailored Content Development: Customized to meet the distinct tastes and needs of each individual, ERNIE Bot produces material that connects profoundly with users, guaranteeing that each creation genuinely mirrors the author's intent.
- Interdisciplinary Knowledge Enrichment: With extensive expertise across numerous fields, it serves as a multifunctional aide, enhancing written work with accuracy and substantive detail.
- Smooth Coordination with Baidu Ecosystem: By effectively harmonizing with various Baidu services, ERNIE Bot enhances operational efficiency, fostering better teamwork and increased productivity.

Application for education

Both instructors and learners have the opportunity to utilize ERNIE Bot effectively for academic research, completing assignments, and generating creative content. This tool acts as a crucial asset, not only promoting innovative thinking but also enabling a more profound comprehension of subjects, ultimately driving improved educational results. With the support of ERNIE Bot, learners are able to refine their writing capabilities, while instructors obtain a powerful asset to improve their pedagogical approaches.

8. Tencent AI Lab

While it may not be universally acknowledged as a distinct software offering, the innovations from Tencent AI Lab have been quietly reshaping the creative landscape through their sophisticated AI drawing and design capabilities. These innovative instruments utilize the capabilities of artificial intelligence algorithms to convert user-generated content into breathtaking, high-quality visuals and designs, thereby transforming the creative workflow.

Essential characteristics and capabilities

- Smart visual creation: By comprehensively grasping the concepts and ideas presented by users, these tools produce captivating images that embody the spirit of innovation.
- Style adaptation and personalization: Seamlessly change images into various artistic expressions or customize them to fit particular motifs, allowing individuals to fully explore their imaginative potential without boundaries.
- Collaboration with design applications: Enable smooth cooperation with widely-used design applications, optimizing productivity and fostering effective teamwork between human creatives and AI-powered assistants.

Application for educational programs

These innovative digital art tools present remarkable chances for those studying design and visual arts. Learners can utilize these platforms to unleash their creativity, trial different design ideas, and enhance their abilities with the support of advanced digital mentors. Educators can enhance their teaching by integrating these resources into their lessons, motivating the upcoming generation of innovators.

9. Zhipu Qingyan

Zhipu Qingyan is a multifaceted artificial intelligence solution developed by a team rooted in Tsinghua University, utilizing extensive text datasets along with cutting-edge natural language processing methodologies.

Essential characteristics and capabilities

- Mathematical tasks: Managing a variety of standard mathematical inquiries, such as arithmetic, algebra, and geometry, demonstrating strong capabilities in mathematical processing.
- Assistance in creative writing: Providing support with various writing endeavors such as generating titles, crafting advertising content, and enabling efficient completion of writing projects.
- Coding support: Offering assistance across various programming languages, facilitating auto-complete features, error identification, and boosting overall coding productivity.
- Inquiry and response: Providing information on a wide spectrum of subjects, including the fields of science, technology, culture, and history, addressing various informational requirements.
- Logical reasoning and discussion: Proficient in addressing intricate logical challenges, while engaging in reasoning and debates.
- Character simulation: Able to take on the personas of various individuals, such as notable historical personalities or specialized professionals, thereby creating tailored interactive experiences.
- Facilitating extensive exchanges in conversation and comprehending the context allows for fluid and natural interactions over a series of dialogues.
- Understanding and producing language: Leveraging a vast collection of numerous texts, it demonstrates proficiency in various tasks, including generating text, classifying content, translating languages, and analyzing sentiment.
- Document analysis and programming capabilities: Delivering comprehensive document examination and programming capabilities, ideal for developing models at an industrial level.
- The open-source approach: Encouraging the growth and availability of AI technology, enabling individuals interested in the field to explore and master sophisticated methodologies.

Application for educational purposes

- Tailored educational resources: These are designed to align with individual student requirements and their learning advancements, encouraging individualized learning pathways.
- Improved writing capabilities: Provides support for various writing tasks, expanding learners' lexical resources, grammar, and comprehension of intricate materials.
- Enhancement of accessibility: This tool can function as a text-to-speech application, aiding learners who face challenges with reading, and include captions for individuals with auditory challenges.
- Promoting academic integrity: Implementing systems for detecting instances of plagiarism promotes honesty and encourages students to produce original work.

10. Kimi

Kimi serves as a holistic platform that combines effective administration, smart suggestions, and tailored personalization. Its purpose is to enhance the everyday routines and processes of users through advanced algorithms, providing practical functionalities, including organizing schedules, sending reminders for tasks, and offering tailored content suggestions.

Essential characteristics and capabilities

- Data retrieval: Efficiently accesses pertinent data from extensive sources such as articles, images, journals, and news outlets.
- Document handling: Analyzes, interprets, and manages files across multiple formats, creating overviews, translations, and providing responses based on the contents of the files.
- Code creation: Assists developers by producing programming code in various languages such as Python, Java, C++, SQL statements, and Markdown files.
- Artistic composition: Provides support for crafting poetry, novels, scripts, promotional content, communications, and correspondence, thereby boosting both creativity and productivity in writing.
- Analysis of data: Engages in evaluating sales and financial metrics, assisting users in recognizing patterns and facilitating well-informed decision-making.
- Practical guidance: Offers insights and recommendations for resolving common issues, thereby enhancing skills in effective problem resolution.
- Dialogue and interaction: Participates in discussions, providing companionship, emotional assistance, and collaborative idea generation.

Application for educational opportunities

- Support for academic research: Assisting learners by gathering pertinent data and distilling essential insights, thus conserving time and reducing effort.
- Composition support: Facilitating the writing process by enhancing the clarity, accuracy, and uniqueness of essays, thereby promoting improved writing capabilities.
- Coding instruction: Supporting those who are new to programming as well as experienced individuals through assistance in generating and troubleshooting code, thereby increasing the accessibility of computer programming.
- Educational assistance: Providing round-the-clock support for inquiries, allowing learners to resolve uncertainties whenever needed.

11. iFLYTEK Spark

The iFLYTEK Spark serves as the leading platform for intelligent mobile Internet interactions from iFLYTEK, establishing itself as an innovator and a top contender in the global arena of artificial intelligence and voice recognition advancements. Its purpose is to provide users with digital interactions that are smooth, natural, and tailored to their individual preferences.

Key capabilities and features

Cutting-edge voice recognition technology is central to iFLYTEK Spark, enabling it to convert spoken language into written text swiftly and with remarkable accuracy. Whether it is for sending texts, browsing the Internet, or using your device without hands, iFLYTEK Spark guarantees that your commands are recognized distinctly and effectively.

Conversational AI that thinks: Experience the advanced dialogue capabilities of iFLYTEK Spark's intelligent chat technology, which transcends basic command inputs. This system can process intricate inquiries, retain context throughout exchanges, and facilitate smooth, natural conversations. It evolves based on user interactions, customizing itself to better align with individual preferences and requirements over time, thus delivering an exceptionally tailored experience.

Support for multiple languages: Aimed at a diverse global audience, iFLYTEK Spark provides strong capabilities for multiple languages, accommodating a variety of tongues and dialects. The platform guarantees seamless communication, whether in Putonghua, English, or any of the numerous languages it supports, ensuring that language differences do not hinder interaction.

Effortless compatibility with applications and devices: iFLYTEK Spark offers effortless compatibility with a wide range of well-known applications and devices, allowing users to manage them all using voice commands. Whether it is for your home automation, workplace tools, messaging platforms, or music services, iFLYTEK Spark offers an unparalleled connection to your digital ecosystem.

Tailored content and offerings: By utilizing sophisticated algorithms and cutting-edge machine learning techniques, iFLYTEK Spark examines user engagement patterns and preferences to provide customized content and services that resonate with individual interests. Whether it is keeping up with the latest news or suggesting forms of entertainment, iFLYTEK Spark ensures you stay both informed and engaged.

Transforming the landscape of efficiency and inclusivity, iFLYTEK Spark represents a significant advancement for both professionals and everyday users. This innovation removes the necessity for traditional typing, enabling users to concentrate on their ideas and concepts while their devices manage the input. Moreover, it provides a straightforward and user-friendly means for those with disabilities to engage effectively with their technology.

Application for educational purposes

iFLYTEK Spark functions as an innovative solution that connects conventional educational approaches with contemporary technological advancements. Through the incorporation of sophisticated artificial intelligence into educational practices, iFLYTEK Spark enables teachers, learners, and families to reach unprecedented levels of interaction, efficiency, and availability.

Personalized learning journeys: The intelligent assessment of student data by iFLYTEK Spark, which encompasses academic performance, interests, and preferred learning methods, allows the platform to design educational paths that cater specifically to the individual requirements of each learner. This tailored strategy guarantees that learners encounter lessons that are both stimulating and pertinent, thereby promoting profound comprehension and elevated success rates.

Interactive learning experiences: This platform leverages cutting-edge voice recognition technology and conversational AI to foster engaging and participatory educational experiences. Learners can take part in engaging discussions, engage in simulated scenarios, and refine their linguistic abilities in a dynamic, online atmosphere. Such interactive experiences not only make the learning process enjoyable but also significantly improve understanding and memory retention.

Education for everyone: iFLYTEK Spark tackles the challenges of accessibility that frequently hinder individuals with disabilities from fully engaging in the learning process. The platform features a user-friendly interface that can be operated through voice commands, enabling individuals with varying physical capabilities to engage with premium educational materials and resources.

Maximizing tutoring efficiency: Educators can utilize the sophisticated features of iFLYTEK Spark to enhance the effectiveness of their tutoring sessions. The platform's capabilities for converting spoken language into text, and vice versa, enable seamless interaction and teamwork during sessions. Additionally, its analytical instruments offer valuable data regarding students' development and pinpoint specific areas needing attention. This empowers educators to modify their teaching methods in real-time, ensuring that learners obtain the necessary assistance to thrive.

Integration with digital textbooks and learning materials: iFLYTEK Spark offers smooth integration with online courses, digital textbooks, and various educational resources, enhancing them into engaging and interactive multimedia formats. Through voice commands, learners are able to participate in lectures, jot down notes, and complete quizzes and evaluations, thereby enhancing the overall efficiency and enjoyment of their educational experience.

Parental engagement and monitoring: The iFLYTEK Spark platform provides parents with insights into their child's educational pathway. With this tool, they are able to track their child's advancements, review performance analytics, and participate in online parent-teacher meetings. This increased involvement cultivates a deeper collaboration between the educational environment and home, which in turn aids in enhancing students' academic development and achievements.

To conclude, software powered by artificial intelligence, such as iFLYTEK Spark, Kimi, and Zhipu Qingyan, is revolutionizing the field of education by providing tailored, engaging, and user-friendly learning opportunities. The innovative capabilities these tools possess, including processing natural language as well as recognizing and generating speech, are revolutionizing how learners engage, work together, and evaluate their advancement. As these innovative technologies advance, there is considerable promise for improving the effectiveness and accessibility of educational experiences around the world.

It is essential to recognize that, while these resources provide considerable advantages, they ought to be viewed as enhancements to human knowledge and creativity, rather than substitutions for them. Both educators and students need to approach the digital world with a mindset focused on critical analysis and moral implications, making sure that advancements in AI contribute positively to the educational journey rather than detract from it.

The following are some implications of using AI in English teaching:

- Process over product
- Helping learners learn to learn (with and without AI)
- Improving speaking confidence via speaking (with chatbots vs humans)
- Helping students to determine their learning goals in an ethically situated way
- Teaching nuance (what falls between the black and white of an issue)
- Showing interest, curiosity, and care, inspiring students to learn, modeling, and fostering empathy
- Creating supportive and collaborative learning environments

- Determining the reliability and authenticity of a text
- Reinforcing higher-order thinking skills and showing how they can be applied to the use of AI
- Working with students on exploring the challenges of interpretation, identifying underlying subtext, ideologies, etc.
- Fostering reflection on learning
- Pragmatic awareness
- Reconceptualizing relationships in multimodal communication
- Correcting language and culture and learning to emotions
- Humour!

Activity 6 Which of the following traditional goals of language learning might AI do (better)?

1. vocabulary acquisition
2. normative grammar knowledge and ability to apply that knowledge to writing and speech
3. mastery of mechanics (spelling, punctuation formatting)
4. ability to speak in spontaneous and prepared, dialogic and monologic contexts (e.g. conversations, presentations)
5. ability to read, comprehend, and interpret a wide variety of L2 texts
6. ability to write clear expository, narrative, and argumentative prose
7. knowledge of L2 culture, pragmatics

____

____

____

____

____

____

4.5 Organizing Activities by Means of Media in Teaching

This part will present some tools or media teachers can apply properly to organize activities in classroom teaching.

4.5.1 Flashcards

Flashcards are ELT jargon for pictures (or diagrams, words, etc.) that you can show to students, specially something you can hold up when standing in front of the whole class.They are also useful for handing out as part of various activities.They are a very useful teaching aid, especially in your earlier years of teaching.

4.5.1.1 The collection of flashcards

The easiest way to find good pictures is to do an Internet image search, even nowadays some AI tools can construct the picture for you. Many schools have a library of published flashcards.

If you find a good picture, rather than using it once, keep it and slowly build up your stock of resources. To start collecting, you need to approach the world with a "flashcard" frame of mind! Whenever you look at a magazine, advertising leaflet, etc, keep your eyes open for suitable pictures.When the publication is ready to head for the bin, cut out the pictures you need. Generally, choose larger pictures that will be visible even from the back of the classroom. You will find some subjects are very easy to find (cars, food products, perfumes, etc.) whereas others (people doing specific everyday tasks, faces expressing different moods, etc.) are harder. When you have a number of pictures, you will have to find some way to organize them, maybe in folders sorted by topic. It may also be worth taking the extra time to make cards longer-lasting, by sticking them down on cardboard, keeping them in plastic pockets, or even by laminating them.

4.5.1.2 Uses of the flashcards

Flashcards are a versatile and effective teaching tool that can be utilized in a multiude of ways to enhance hanguage learning. They can be used to:

- to quickly show the meaning of a lexical item, e.g., to iron;
- to illustrate presentations of language, for example by giving a visual image to an imaginary character, e.g. *This is Marilyn. Every day she gets up at six o'clock* ..., etc.;
- to tell a story, providing occasional images to give students something tangible to look at and help their understanding, e.g. *... and then a large green lorry turned around the corner and drove towards them*;
- as prompts to remind them of a specific grammar point or typical error, e.g. a flashcard with the word *past* on it to quickly remind students to make verbs in the past form;
- as seeds for student-based story telling activities, e.g. handing out a small selection of pictures to groups of students and asking them to invent a story that incorporates all those images;
- as prompts for guessing games, definition games, description games, etc. For example, one person in a team has a picture of a person, which they describe. Then the other students are shown a pile of seven pictures (including the original one) and have to work out which picture was described.

4.5.1.3 Picture stories

Pictures and picture stories can be in a book or handout, drawn on the board or OHP, or on flashcards or posters. Traditionally they have been used as a starting point for writing exercises, but they are also very useful for focusing on specific language points or as material for speaking and listening activities. Most picture stories seem inevitably to involve the practice of the past simple and past progressive (see Figure 4.4).

This material could be approached in a variety of ways, for example, to contrast two broadly different approaches: "accuracy to fluency" and "fluency to accuracy".

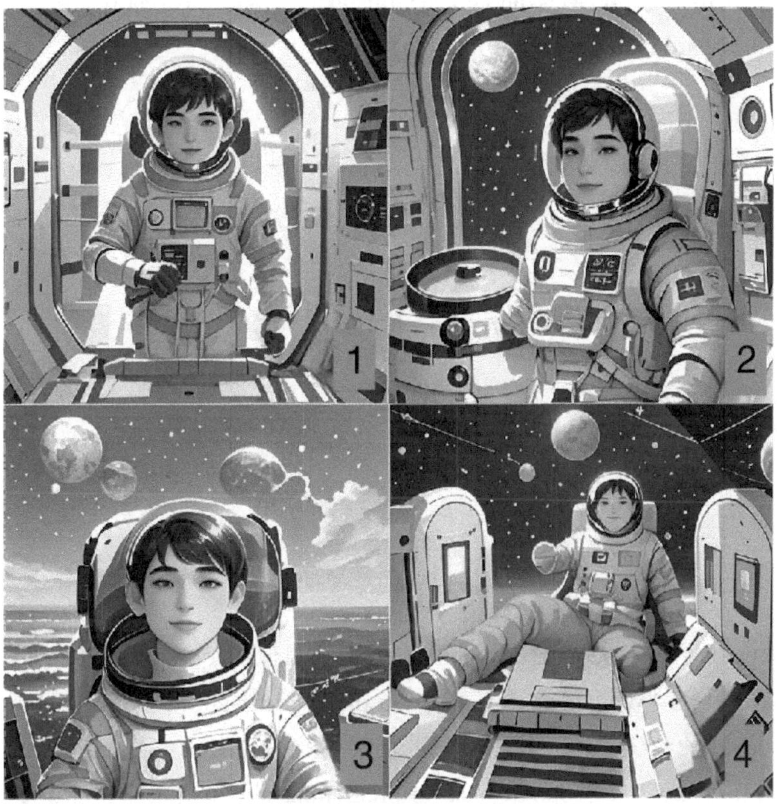

Figure 4.4 Prompts for space story

Accuracy to fluency

This heading suggests that we start by looking at the language involved in the story and getting this understood and correct before we move on to tell the story. The following could be the route:

(1) Introduction of topic / subject

(2) Focus on interesting or essential lexis, grammar, or function

(3) Look at the pictures and discuss; possibly more language focus

(4) Tell the story

(5) Writing exercise

Teaching steps

(1) Ask students: Do you believe in UFOs? or Would you like to travel to another planet? (Students discuss).

(2) Draw a blank UFO-shaped frame on the board, hand out board pens, and invite students to fill the frame with words connected with space and space travel. Students are encouraged to discuss words, check their meanings, look words up in dictionaries, and correct mistakes. You occasionally add words yourself. By the end of the activity, the board may look like Figure 4.5.

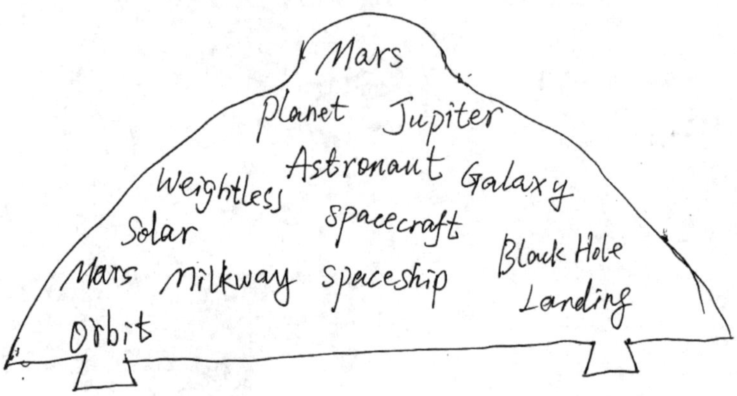

Figure 4.5　Space vocabulary

(3) Reveal the first picture and encourage students to talk by asking questions such as "What's he doing?" to focus on the picture and "Why is he doing it?" to invite ideas about motive, intentions, feelings, etc. Specific language could be focused on (e.g. modal verbs for speculation: he might be..., he could be..., he must be..., etc.). When it seems appropriate, ask for predictions about what is in the next picture, and, after a little discussion, reveal picture 2 and start to work with that.

(4) When students have had enough opportunities to talk through the story, put them into pairs and ask them to tell the complete story to each other.

(5) Ask students to still work in pairs, and write it out.

The focus on accurate use of language in Step 2 and 3 prepares students for an opportunity to use the language more fluently in the speaking activity (Step 4). If writing is the main aim, it still makes sense to start with work such as this because such oral preparation ensures that students are more familiar with the grammar and lexis, and are thus better prepared for the task of writing a good story.

Fluency to accuracy

An alternative lesson procedure could start with a fluency activity and only focus on the accurate use of language at a later stage. The lesson might have this step:

(1) Introduction of topic / subject

(2) Look at the pictures and discuss

(3) Tell the story

(4) Focus on interesting or essential lexis, grammar, or function

(5) Tell the story more accurately

(6) Writing exercise

The following is an example of a fluency activity:

(This activity could be used as a starting point for the lesson. It is an **information gap activity** that uses a **jigsaw technique**, that is to say, some of the students have information that others don't have; in order to piece together a complete description of what is happening, they need to communicate and work out how the separate pieces fit together.)

The students are divided into groups of four. At Step 2, each student hands one picture from the sequence, with the instruction "Keep it secret!" "Don't show it to anyone else!" The task is for each group to work out what order the pictures go in without looking at each other's pictures. This can be done by intelligent questioning, good describing, and a few leaps of imagination.

After they have achieved this task, students will probably find they are able to tell the story in Step 3. Then you might choose to move on to later stages in which students do some accuracy work, as described above.

4.5.1.4 Storytelling

Many teachers use stories as an interesting route into grammar lessons but bear in mind that stories have a great deal of value in their own right. Just tell stories for pleasure; not stories and then comprehension exercises; not stories and then students retell; not stories and then write it up for homework. The aim here is the same as that of the mother reading to her children at bedtime or a group of friends in a bar telling anecdotes—to tell a story for the listener's pleasure. Storytelling is a useful short activity for the end of a lesson, or mid-lesson to provide a change of mood.

Basic technique

(1) Mentally prepare your story beforehand; internalise the mood, the smells, the look, the colours, the key events, and any special words or expressions; make skeleton notes if you wish but don't write it out in too much detail.

(2) Give a clear instruction along the lines of "I'm going to tell you a story. Listen and see if you enjoy it. There will be no comprehension questions afterward, no exercises." This essential instruction sets your audience free; there is often a visible reduction in tension among the students: changes of posture, relaxing of facial expression, etc.

(3) Tell your story. Don't read it—a "told" story is often far more immediate and involving than a "read" one.

(4) When it is finished, ask them to talk about it if they want to (discussion of feelings, interpretations, etc. should be a genuine reaction to what they have heard; don't break the promise you made before the story).

(5) Leave it and go on to something else.

Can we justify this in the ELI classroom? What are the students getting from it?

This exercise is about real listening; not listening because I am going to hound you with questions afterward, but listening because you want to. For that reason, it is all the more focused and involving. There is much academic speculation that students learn language best when they forget about studying grammar and get totally involved in the content itself.

Good seeds for stories are:

- small incidents in your own life (maybe slightly dramatised);
- fairy tales and legends, especially rare or local ones (raid the secondhand bookshops for Chinese, Arab, African tales, etc);
- ghost and mystery stories;
- single incidents from longer biographies and novels;
- versions of stories you read in the newspaper or magazine;
- soap operas or TV shows, etc.

4.5.1.5 Songs and music

Songs on recordings, video/DVD, or perhaps played on a guitar in the classroom are often used as a "filler" activity to change the mood or pace of a lesson.They sometimes tend to get relegated to the "Friday afternoon" slot as a sort of reward for the week's hard work. But do be aware that songs can also be usefully integrated into the main flow of your course.

Many coursebooks nowadays include songs that specifically focus on grammatical or functional items; these may have been selected because of their content or specially written and recorded for students of English. You can also select interesting authentic songs yourself, with the advantage, that they are often more up-to-date.

Activities of using songs in class

- Gapped text. Give students the lyrics with certain words blanked out. Students listen carefully and fill in the missing words. Or using the gaps as a pre-listening exercise, with students predicting what the missing words are.
- Song jumble. Cut the lyrics up into separate lines. In small groups, students try to work out the original order. When ready, they listen and compare their guess with the actual song.
- Matching pictures. Show twenty pictures connected with the song and ask students to listen and put them in the order in which they hear them in the song.
- Reading or listening comprehension. Use the song text as a normal reading or listening text with the bonus of hearing it sung afterward.
- Dictation. Dictate the chorus or the whole song. Compare with the recording.
- Picture dictation. Decide on a representative picture of something that happens in the song. Dictate the information about this picture, a line at a time, to the students who draw (not write) their interpretation. For example, "The sun is shining in the sky, there are a lot of people in the street, there is a dark cloud overhead, it's just starting to rain," etc. By the time you have finished, a lot of the essential lexis and phrases from the song will have been circulating, and the song should be not too difficult to follow.
- Listen and discuss. Get students to listen to the whole song once or twice, or to a shorter section. Discuss what happened, reactions, interpretations, predictions, etc.
- Sing along. The aim is to learn the tune and to get the rhythm well enough to sing along with the original recording.This can be quite challenging and requires some careful preparation work on practising stress and rhythm.
- Compose "Here's the tune—now you write the lyrics." (Again, an activity that is quite challenging on stress and rhythm.)
- Action movements. Listen to one line at a time. For each line, the students invent a mimed action, which they teach each other and then all perform. Regularly replay the song from the beginning for them to recall and do the relevant actions. After they have done one or two verses, hand out the complete lyrics; in small groups, the students find movements for the rest of the song. At the end, all come together to watch a performance of the different versions.

Ideas for using music in class

- to set the mood at the start of the lesson;
- to give you something to talk about with your students at tie start of the lessons;

- as background music while students work on "dull" exercises;
- as background music to set the scene while students do a particular task;
- simply for pleasure or as a break between activities;
- to help students relax;
- for "imaging": students close their eyes and visualize images from their imagination or your words or someone else's;
- to create anonymity in small or quiet classes;
- to close down, conclude, round off the lesson—to say goodbye with.

4.5.1.6 Poetry

Many teachers don't feel confident using poetry because they are not confident about reading it or writing it themselves. Creativity arises out of the act of writing. You start with nothing. The difficulty of writing forces the new ideas to the surface.

Reading poems

Choose a poem with some interesting and accessible metaphors. Before they see the poem, dictate to students the sentences that have similes or metaphors but leave out the actual comparison itself. Ask students to brainstorm their comparisons. They can then compare them with each other and finally with the ones used in the poem itself.

- Tell students the topic of the poem and let them brainstorm as many words as they can that might be in it.
- Alternatively, look at a list of words and decide which words might be in a poem about a certain subject.
- Before the lesson, write out a poem as if it were a newspaper article or mini-story, etc. Students study and understand this easier version before they look at the poem.
- Do a picture dictation: describe the scene in the poem, item by item, and students draw a picture. At the end, they compare pictures and then read the poem, deciding who is closest to the original.

Writing poems

- Finish it. Provide a nearly complete poem with gapped parts to complete.
- Form to poem. Give or elicit specific aspects of a poetic form, e.g. a rhyme scheme (or actual rhymes), a precise rhythm, the precise number of syllables, etc. Students then make a poem following this exact pattern.

- Alterations. Give each student group a different published poem.The groups must copy out the text with a fixed number of altered words. When they see the copied text, the other teams must guess what is not from the original.
- Found poems. Students search for and find potential "poems" within prose texts (or in signs, posters, etc.) by selecting phrases or blocks of normal text, copying them out and adding line breaks.
- Cut-ups. Students are given (or find for themselves) various lines from magazines, brochures, newspapers, etc. They order these to make a poem.
- Facts to metaphor. Students write a list of facts following your instructions; when they've finished, they go back over their list adding a metaphor to each.
- Instant poetry. This is a surprisingly simple activity that often produces outstanding results. Give a series of instructions that ask students to look, listen, and notice what is around them and within them. Each instruction is given, followed by a long pause to allow students to follow the instruction.

4.5.1.7 Drama

Six types of drama activities are commonly found in English language teaching classrooms:

- Role play. Students act out small scenes using their own ideas or from ideas and information on role cards.
- Simulation. This is really a large-scale role play. Role cards are normally used, and there is often other background information as well.
- Drama games. Short games that usually involve movement and imagination.
- Guided improvisation. You improvise a scene and the students join in one by one in character until the whole scene takes on a life of its own.
- Acting play scripts Short written sketches or scenes are acted by the students.
- Prepared improvised drama. Students in small groups invent and rehearse a short scene or story that they then perform for the others.

All of these are good ways to get students to use the language. By bringing the outside world into the classroom like this, you can provide a lot of useful practice that would otherwise be impossible in cafes, shops, banks, businesses, streets, parties, etc. There may also be a freeing from the constraints of culture and expected behaviour. Curiously, it is sometimes the shyest students who are often most able to seize the potential.

Activity 7 **Search for some songs that can be used in classroom teaching of grammar, such as teaching different tenses, and design the teaching activity.**

____

____

____

____

____

____

____

Thinking and Doing

A. Discussion questions

1. What is your idea about the rapid spread and use of AI? How to utilize AI rationally in your daily life and learning?
2. How can you integrate traditional teaching media with modern informational technology, such as AI?

B. Practice

1. Observe an EFL class. What was the objective of the lesson? What aids did the teacher use? Think of additional aids that would have improved the lesson.
2. Choose a unit from middle school English textbooks, design a 45-minute teaching plan, and modify it by using any AI software.

C. Exercises for instructional skills

1. Which of the following is NOT the element in the TPACK?

A. technological B. production C. content D. knowledge

2. Which of the following statements is NOT true?

A. Media may provide a contextualized situation in teaching.

B. Media may reinforce the relation between the language classroom and the outside world.

C. Media may help teachers input multiple sources in language learning.

D. Media may minimize students' use of their prior knowledge.

3. Which of the following is NOT technical media?

   A. whiteboards
   B. radio
   C. overhead projector
   D. self-access center

4. Which of the following about the framework for structuring media lessons is NOT correct?

   A. The framework is illustrated with a typical lesson.
   B. The framework should be put into language teaching without the change of the sequence.
   C. The transfer stage is the most important part of the five stages.
   D. The feedback stage contains teacher-feedback and students-feedback.

5. Which of the following should be discouraged concerning the use of Internet resources?

   A. Teachers depend on Internet resources for teaching materials.
   B. Teachers use Internet resources to supplement their textbooks.
   C. Teachers adapt Internet resources before using them for language input.
   D. Teachers select Internet resources according to their teaching purposes.

Checklist

Mark the questions with a check (√) if your answer is yes.

- ☐ Have I understood deeply have a deep understanding of the TPACK framework?
- ☐ Have I developed proficiency in using various technological tools and platforms?
- ☐ Have I grasped teaching strategies to leverage the unique affordances of technology?
- ☐ Can I integrate technology with the English language content I teach?
- ☐ Can I learn how to analyze student data generated by technology tools?

Reflective Journal

Please write down your reflections on what you have/have not learned in this chapter.

◇ The essential skills I need to possess and develop for English teaching:

____

____

____

____

____

◇ Anything I wish to further explore (i.e., puzzles and difficulties):

____

____

____

____

____

References

Ala-Mutka, K. (2011). *Mapping digital competence: Towards a conceptual understanding* (JRC Technical Reports). Publications Office of the European Union.

American Library Association. (2000). *Information Literacy Competency Standards for Higher Education*. ALA.

Catts, R., & Lau, J. (2008). *Towards information literacy indicators*. UNESCO.

Gilster, P. (1997). *Digital literacy*. Wiley.

Long, D., & Magerko, B. (2020). What is AI literacy? Competencies and design considerations. In Proceedings of the 2020 CHI Conference on Human Factors in Computing Systems (pp. 1–16). ACM. https://doi.org/10.1145/3313831.3376727

Luehrmann, A. (1981). Computer literacy: What schools should be doing about it. *The Computing Teacher*, *8*(8), 21-26.

Martin, A., & Grudziecki, J. (2006). DigEuLit: Concepts and tools for digital literacy development. *Innovations in Teaching and Learning in Information and Computer Sciences*, *5*(4), 246–264.

Ministry of Education of the People's Republic of China. (2022).

关于发布《教师数字素养》教育行业标准的通知 [Notice on the release of the educational industry standard "Digital Literacy for Teachers"]. Retrieved from http://www.moe.gov.cn/srcsite/A16/s3342/202302/t20230214_1044634.html

Mishra, P., & Koehler, M. J. (2006). Technological pedagogical content knowledge: A framework for teacher knowledge. *Teachers College Record, 108*(6), 1017–1054.

Shulman, L. S. (1986). Those who understand: Knowledge growth in teaching. *Educational Researcher*, *15*(2), 4–14.

UNESCO. (2018). UNESCO ICT competency framework for teachers (Version 3). https://unesdoc.unesco.org/ark:/48223/pf0000265721

UNESCO. (2021). Reimagining our futures together: A new social contract for education. https://unesdoc.unesco.org/ark:/48223/pf0000379707

Wei, F. (n.d.). 如何利用生成式 AI 做智慧教师？ [How to use generative AI to become a smart teacher?]. Retrieved October 10, 2023, from https://mp.weixin.qq.com/s/__biz=MzAwNDY0NTEyNg

Xue, S. M., Yan, Y. Y., & Xu, M. J. (2024). 教师 AI 素养：人工智能时代的教师准备——基于 UNESCO “AI CFT”

框架和 7 份政策文本的分析 [Teacher AI literacy: Preparing teachers for the AI era—An analysis based on the UNESCO “AI CFT” framework and seven policy documents]. *Journal of Teacher Education Research*, *36*(4), 105–113.

Yin, K. G. (2024). 人工智能素养：提出背景、概念界定与构成要素 [Artificial intelligence literacy: Background, definition, and components]. *Library and Information*, (3), 60–68.

Part Ⅲ

English Teaching Micro-skills

Education is not the answer to the question. Education is the means to the answer to the question.

—Inspired by B.F. Skinner's educational philosophy

B.F. Skinner (1904–1990) was an influential American psychologist, behaviorist, and educator, best known for his work on operant conditioning and behavior modification. He developed the theory that behavior is shaped by reinforcement and punishment, which has had a profound impact on psychology, education, and even technology. His ideas, such as programmed instruction and the use of positive reinforcement, have significantly influenced modern educational practices.

A teacher is one who transmits the truth, imparts knowledge, and resolves doubts.

—Han Yu

This famous saying is from *On the Teacher* by Han Yu, a literary figure of the Tang Dynasty. Han Yu was a renowned writer, thinker, and philosopher of the Tang Dynasty, hailed as the foremost among the "Eight Great Masters of the Tang and Song." He lived between 768 and 824 AD and was one of the leaders of the Ancient Prose Movement, advocating for a return to the simplicity and unadorned elegance of ancient literature. Han Yu's literary works are extensive, encompassing poetry, prose, essays, and more, with *On the Teacher* being one of his representative works that underscore the significance of the teaching profession and the responsibilities of educators. His achievements were not limited to literature; he also had a profound impact on politics and education.

Chapter 5

Handwriting, Board Writing, and Sketching Skills

Objectives

Upon completion of this chapter, you should be able to:

- Grasp the basic knowledge of English handwriting, board writing, and sketching
- understand the major principles of handwriting, board writing, and sketching
- Improve English handwriting, design blackboard writing properly, and integrate sketching into classroom teaching.

Discussion Questions

Do you know Chinese calligraphy? Can you list some Chinese calligraphic styles?

Do you think your Chinese character writing might affect your English handwriting?

How do you understand the Chinese saying "文如其人"? What is your assessment of your own Chinese and English handwriting?

In English instruction, a teacher's role extends beyond just language instruction. It consists of a wide range of skills that enhance the learning experience and foster a deeper connection with students. Among these skills, English handwriting, board writing, and simple sketching are both beneficial and essential for effective learning and teaching.

5.1 English Handwriting

Handwriting is an essential part of English teaching, as it involves modeling correct letter formation and penmanship techniques to students. Teachers should have clear and consistent handwriting skills so that they can demonstrate and emulate their students.

5.1.1 The Functions of Handwriting

Showing professionalism and credibility

Handwriting is usually the first written impression one leaves on others, and it holds significant weight in professional settings. A teacher's clear and elegant handwriting may set the impression of professionalism and credibility. When a teacher's handwriting is legible, organized, and aesthetically pleasing, it transmits a sense of competence and dedication to the craft. Well-executed handwriting suggests respect for the recipient and reinforces the instructor's reputation as a trusted and reliable professional.

Facilitation of learning

Handwriting with clarity and legibility plays a vital role in enhancing the learning process. When students are presented with clearly handwritten notes, lessons, and instructions, they can focus on the content rather than struggling to decipher illegible characters. It will reduce frustration and creates a more positive learning environment. Additionally, teachers' good handwriting habits will encourage learners to emulate them, fostering better penmanship skills and a deeper engagement with the written word.

Cultural expression

Handwriting is not only a means of communication, it is also a rich form of cultural expression. It is an effective way to immerse oneself in the linguistic and artistic traditions of the global community by understanding and practicing English handwriting. Each letter, each word, and even the overall style of handwriting can tell a story about its writer's cultural background, and personal growth preferences. The practice of calligraphy and other forms of decorative handwriting offers an avenue for innovative self-expression, allowing a person to explore his/her artistic side while simultaneously honing his/her writing skills.

5.1.2 Handwriting Standards

The guidelines of writing standards are as follows:

- Letter writing: When writing a letter in English, pay attention that the capital letters are half the height of the small letters. Be careful of the proportion and position of uppercase and lowercase letters (see Figure 5.1).

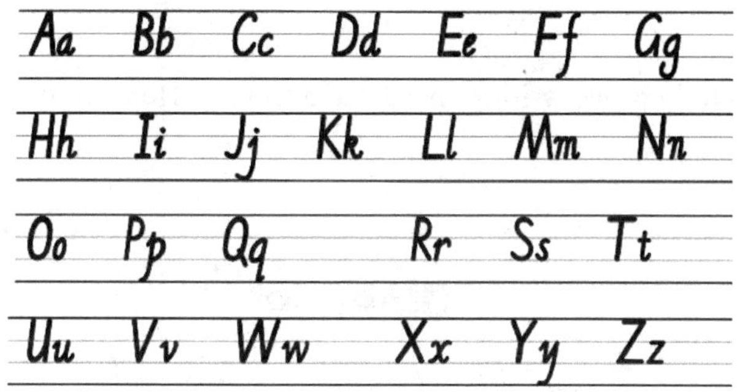

Figure 5.1 Right letter writing

- Letter space: The spacing between two letters should be consistent, that is, not too close, nor too sparse (see Figure 5.2).

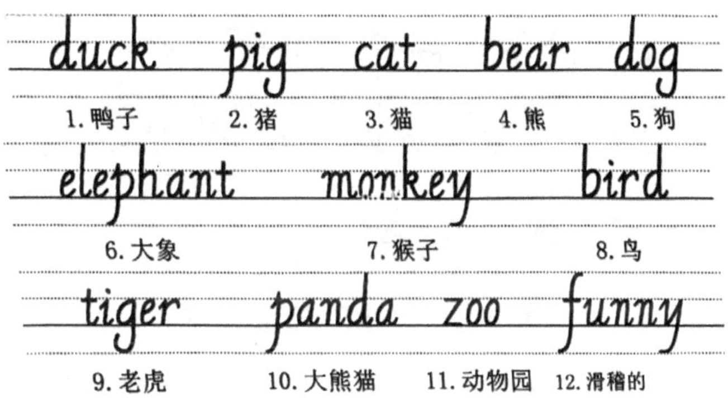

Figure 5.2 Right letter spacing

- Stroke thickness: Remain the regularity of stroke thickness so that the letters will look neat and aesthetically pleasing, such as in the example above.
- Stroke continuity: Don't lift the pen frequently to make the strokes of letters look continuous and smooth (see Figure 5.3).

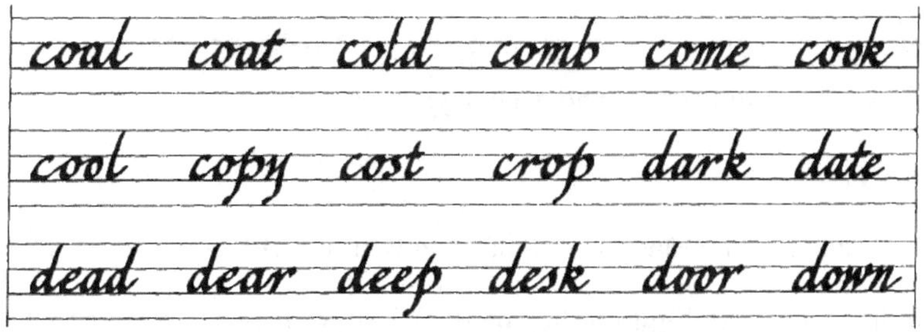

Figure 5.3 Stroke continuity

5.1.3 Stroke Order

Correct stroke order helps to improve writing speed and accuracy. Here are the example of stroke order for the 26 letters (see Figure 5.4).

Figure 5.4 Correct stroke order

5.1.4 Practice Methods

Practice is key to improving English handwriting skills. Here are some suggestions for practice methods:

- Letter practice: Practice writing each letter from A to Z, paying attention to maintaining stroke continuity and writing standards.
- Word practice: Choose common words for writing practice, especially those you often misspell.
- Sentence practice: Gradually transition to writing complete sentences, including simple and complex sentences.
- Combining reading and writing: When reading English articles or stories, you can copy sentences or paragraphs to improve writing speed and accuracy.

5.1.5 Use of Tools

The right writing tools are also important for English handwriting. Here are some suggestions:

- Pens or ballpoint pens: Use high-quality pens or ballpoint pens that write smoothly for English handwriting to improve writing effects.

- Exercise books: Use exercise books specifically for practicing English handwriting, which facilitate error correction and progress recording.

5.1.6 Self-Assessment

Regular self-assessment can help you identify and correct problems in handwriting. Here are some suggestions:

- Check if the letter shapes and sizes are standardized.
- Observe whether the spacing between letters is appropriate.
- Analyze if there are any trembles, broken pens, or other issues.
- Correct spelling and grammatical errors.

5.1.7 Common Mistakes of English Handwriting

Teachers in the teaching process need to understand some of the typical problems that Chinese students have in writing so that teaching can be targeted. The following are some common mistakes made by Chinese English learners in English writing:

Incorrect use or misuse of comma. Generally speaking, in English, commas are only used to connect sentences in the following two situations: (1) when connected by conjunctions; (2) when one sentence acts as a component of another sentence. However, Chinese students, influenced by the use of commas in Chinese, are prone to misuse English commas. The usually use them between two or more complete sentences.

e.g.: *Incorrect: The library is closed on Sundays, it is very quiet.*

Correct: The library is closed on Sundays; it is very quiet.

Using Chinese book title marks in English. There are no book title marks in English. Book titles are generally written in all capital letters or with the first letter of each substantive word capitalized. In print, they are usually represented in italics.

e.g.: *Incorrect: I have finished writing the summary of《Jane Eyre》.*

Correct: I have finished writing the summary of Jane Eyre.

Using the Chinese "dunhao" in English. In English writing, we use commas to separate phrases in a sentence or items in a list.

e.g.: *Incorrect: I liking singing、drawing、playing guitar、and hiking.*

Correct: I like singing, drawing, playing guitar, and hiking.

Using Chinese ellipsis in English. The Chinese ellipsis is "......", whereas the English ellipsis is "...".

e.g.: *Incorrect: I've traveled to many places...... New York, Paris, Tokyo...... each with its unique charm.*

Correct: I've traveled to many places... New York, Paris, Tokyo... each with its unique charm.

Incorrect use of colons in English correspondence. In English correspondence, the salutation generally uses a comma, but many students, influenced by Chinese, will use a colon.

e.g.: *Incorrect: Dear Sir or Madam:*

Correct: Dear Sir or Madam,

Bad habit of dotting after writing a few words. This practice results in a sentence being split into several independent sentences.

e.g.: *Incorrect: He. speaks. very fluent. English.*

Correct: He speaks very fluent English.

The first word after a period in a sentence is not capitalized.

Irregular letter writing. Some students' English letter writing is not standardized, resulting in ambiguous spellings. Common ones include confusing *r* with *v*, *1* with *e*, *o* with *u*, and *t*.

Random line breaks, not adhering to English line break rules.

e.g.: *Incorrect: The little tramp was charming, a social failure with a determin-ation to overcome difficulties and always kind.*

Correct: The little tramp was charming, a social failure with a determina-tion to overcome difficulties and always be kind.

Using Chinese numerals "一、二、三、四..." instead of the Roman numerals " Ⅰ, Ⅱ, Ⅲ, Ⅳ," which are commonly used in English. It is also a common mistake made by Chinese students in writing.

e.g.: *Incorrect: The following is the outline:* 一、*Introduction;* 二、*Main Ideas;* 三、*Examples;* 四、*Conclusion.*

Correct: The following is the outline: I. Introduction; II. Main Ideas; III. Examples; IV. Conclusion.

Teachers should strictly demand students from the beginning, establish a serious and rigorous academic style, correct mistakes as soon as they are found, and thus help students develop good writing habits.

Activity 1 **Write anything you like on the following sheet, such as a poem, a story, etc. to practice your English handwriting.**

5.2 Board Writing

At the core of educational information technology lies the blackboard. Introduced in the early 19th century, the blackboard was a revolutionary tool that transformed classroom dynamics. It allowed teachers to visually present information to a larger audience at once, fostering a more interactive and participatory learning environment. With the simple, moving stroke of chalk, some complex diagrams/figures, equations, and sentences could be illustrated, fostering better comprehension and engagement among students. The blackboard was constructed for basic use, but it laid the foundational principles of direct instruction and collaborative learning that are still revered today.

5.2.1 The Functions of Board Writing

Board writing is a traditional, simple but enduring teaching tool, which remains an important part of language instruction. Its significance lies firstly in its capacity to reinforce learning and secondly in fostering learner's engagement, creativity, and active class participation.

Managing information. Blackboard writing enhances the management of the learning information in a way that is easy for students to follow. It provides a clear outline of the information, highlighting the main ideas and supporting the details, all of which will help comprehension.

Enhancing comprehension and retention. Blackboard writing plays a crucial role in facilitating comprehension and promoting retention of main concepts and vocabulary. By visually presenting main ideas and structures, instructors can provide a tangible reference for students to recall during and after class. This fosters the internalization of knowledge since students are able to relate abstract linguistic concepts to tangible visual representations (Harris & Graham, 2015).

Engaging active learning. Effective English blackboard writing, such as guided outlines and interactive whiteboard exercises, can facilitate active learning. By incorporating questions, fill-in-the-blank activities, or figures onto the board, instructors can encourage students to engage in critical thinking and processing of information.

Improving creativity and personalization. Blackboard writing provides teachers with an opportunity to personalize their teaching and activate their creativity. By incorporating hand-drawn demonstrations, colored markers, or unique layouts, the lessons will become more visually appealing and memorable for students.

Supporting different learning styles. Learns have different learning styles, and blackboard writing can cater to these various needs. Some students may prefer visual aids to textual explanations, while others may benefit from the structured presentation of information on the board. By using blackboard writing effectively, teachers can be certain that all students have access to information that resonates with their personal learning preferences.

Increasing teacher-student interaction. Blackboard writing acts as a medium for ongoing communication between instructors and learns. At the time when teachers write on the board, they can engage in virtual discussions, asking questions, seeking clarification, and adjusting their teaching based on student reactions.

Modeling proper writing skills. Teachers use blackboard writing to model correct spelling, grammar, and punctuation, which is crucial for English language learners. It demonstrates the thought process and structure of writing, serving as a guide for students.

Promoting visual literacy. Effective blackboard writing involves the use of figures, charts, and other visual tools that improve comprehension and promote visual literacy skills, which are vital in today's multimedia-driven world.

5.2.2 The Principles of Board Writing

5.2.2.1 Chalk board writing

- A correct handwriting posture as well as the right ways of holding and using the pen;
- An appropriate size of the letters;
- an evenly applied force, with suitable stroke thickness, strong and powerful;

- Consistently maintained tilt in letters;
- Proper spacing between letters, words, and lines;
- Writing proficiently and smoothly, achieving a certain speed;
- Using colored chalk appropriately according to needs.

5.2.2.2 Classroom board writing

- Purposefulness: Closely related to the teaching content, reflecting the teaching content and objectives;
- Pertinence: Targeting key points and difficulties in teaching, and the actual level of students;
- Summarization: Focusing on key points, keywords, phrases, and sentences, providing a clear outline;
- Logicality: Reflecting the connections and contrasts between knowledge, with clear and distinct clues, neat, clear, and eye-catching;
- Planning: Reasonable layout of blackboard writing, appropriate word spacing and line spacing, avoiding arbitrary actions and filling in gaps;
- Flexibility: Diverse forms and appropriate use of colors;
- Normality: Neat, correct, and standardized writing has a subtle educational effect on developing students' good writing habits and study habits.
- Coordination: Demonstrating and explaining while writing on the blackboard, with coordinated body movements.

5.2.3 Methods and Techniques of Board Writing

5.2.3.1 Planning and preparation

As has been shown in chapter 2, blackboard design is one element in a lesson plan, therefore, teachers should have a preparation for the board writing of a lesson or unit in advance before they enter the classroom. The following are the rules:

Preparing a blackboard layout before the class: Planning the blackboard layout ensures a smooth and efficient lesson flow. Teachers should visualize how they will present each concept, allocate space accordingly, and prepare any necessary visual aids in advance.

Identifying key points and structuring the content: Before writing on the board, teachers should identify the most critical points of the lesson and devise a clear structure for presenting them. This allows them to focus their writing and ensure that students receive a well-organized and coherent message.

The importance of a clear and organized blackboard design: A well-designed blackboard not only facilitates learning but also reflects the teacher's professionalism and attention to detail. It creates a positive first impression and sets the tone for the entire lesson.

5.2.3.2 Chalk writing techniques

Chalk holding

Hold the chalk with the tips of your thumb, index finger, and middle finger about 1cm from the front end, forming a triangle. The ring finger and pinky should naturally curl and press against the middle finger, forming a cohesive grip with the five fingers (see Figure 5.5).

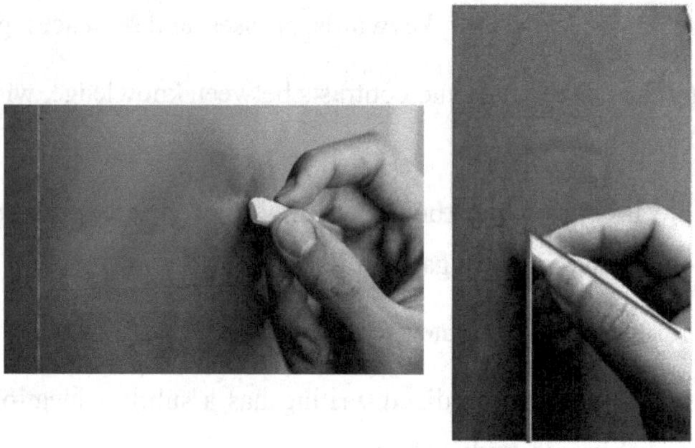

Figure 5.5 Correct chalk holding

Writing technique

The thickness of the stroke depends on the contact area between the chalk and the board, which in turn is determined by the angle of the chalk, the shape of the chalk tip, and the amount of pressure applied. The chalk should be held at an angle to the board, not vertically. Rotate the chalk constantly while writing to maintain even thickness and ensure legible, smooth letters.

Writing posture

Stand upright with your legs apart, right leg slightly forward. Bend your arm and extend it forward, keeping your elbow and wrist slightly raised. The distance between your body and the board should be based on your arm length, ensuring ease of movement. Coordination between your fingers, wrist, and arm is crucial for balanced and fluent writing. Avoid writing too lightly or too thickly, which can result in unclear text or broken chalk.

Controlling letter size

The size of the font in blackboard writing directly affects its effectiveness. If the font is too large, it reduces the efficiency of the board space; if it is too small, students cannot see clearly, which defeats the purpose of using a blackboard. So make sure the letters are large enough to be seen clearly from the back of the classroom and maintain uniformity.

Controlling letter height and slope

Letters should slope slightly to the right at about 5 degrees. The ratio of height to width for letters should be approximately 2:1. Avoid making letters too tall or too short (see Figure 5.6).

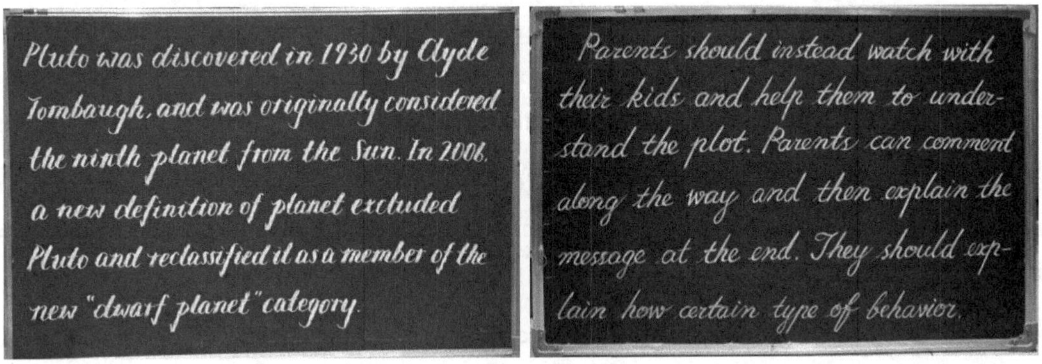

Figure 5.6 Sample board writing

Controlling spacing and line spacing

The space between words should be approximately the width of one letter. The letter spacing and line spacing of the board writing should aim for visual aesthetics. If the content is sparse and the font size is large, the letter spacing and line spacing should be appropriately increased. Conversely, if the content is dense, it should be reduced. The line spacing for uppercase letters can be equal to the height of the letters, while for denser layouts, it can be half the height to maintain clarity. Leave enough space for the ascenders and descenders of letters to prevent them from overlapping with adjacent lines.

Controlling straightness

Board writing should be level and aligned, avoiding slanting, gradual upward or downward slopes. Since there are no lines on the board, it can be challenging to write straight, which is a common issue for beginners. Pay attention to the following aspects during practice:

- Keep your legs moving parallel to the right as you write, maintaining the height of your arm and the distance between your wrist and body.
- When designing the blackboard writing, it is important to determine the allocation of the blackboard, such as dividing it into two or three parts, so that each line does not have to be too long.
- Find a reference for the writing line, such as the top edge of the blackboard, and try to write the first line straight. Then, make sure each subsequent line is as parallel as possible to the first line.

5.2.4 Common Issues of Board Writing in English Teaching

Blackboard writing is an indispensable auxiliary means in classroom teaching, and its success is closely related to the effectiveness of the lesson. However, the importance of blackboard writing is often overlooked in practical teaching, leading to phenomena such as teachers writing casually, not writing on the blackboard at all, or having a single form of blackboard writing, which negatively impacts students' learning enthusiasm. The following are some main issues.

Lack of planning and purpose. Teachers may not have a clear idea of what to write on the board, therefore, they randomly write on the blackboard whatever comes to mind, or write on any random spot on the blackboard, and the position of the writing is messy and disorganized, which results in students' confusion of the learning contents. Disorganized content that does not effectively support the lesson objectives.

Inappropriate quantity of blackboard writing. Some teachers write too much on the board, overwhelming students with information, while others write too little, failing to provide sufficient visual aids.

Monotonous form of blackboard writing. Many teachers stick to a single stereotypical style, most of the time there are only some unchanging outlines to show the progress of the teaching, which can make the lesson dull and unengaging.

Lack of coordination between writing and teaching. Coordination between blackboard writing and verbal explanation is essential for effective teaching and learning. But in reality, some teachers may focus too much on writing, sometimes writing for a long time without a word, neglecting their interaction with students, which results in students' easier distraction of attention from class and a decrease in their interest in the teaching contents.

Lack of complementarity between blackboard content and PPT slides. Teachers may repeat the same information on both the blackboard and PPT, or they rely too much on PPT, writing little on the board, depriving students of valuable visual aids.

5.2.5 Board Writing Contents and Presentation Suggestions

Boardwork is a crucial tool in English teaching, serving as a visual aid to enhance understanding and retention of information.

5.2.5.1 Board writing contents

The content of boardwork can be categorized into four main types, each serving a specific purpose in the learning process.

Permanent or reference material

Some of the information should remain on the board throughout the lesson, providing a constant reference for students. For example:

- New or key vocabulary: Write down new words or key vocabulary related to the lesson, including phonetic spelling, definitions, and examples of usage to reinforce learning.
- Grammar points: Highlight important grammar rules, structures, or patterns. Use figures, charts, or bullet points for clarity.
- Examples: Provide examples of sentences, phrases, or dialogues that illustrate the target language. This helps students understand how to use the language in context.
- Error correction reminders: Write down common mistakes students make and remind them to avoid the mistakes during the lesson. This can help improve accuracy and fluency.

Material for the course development

It refers to some information that fosters the progression of the course and engages students in the learning process. For example:

- Dialogues and role-plays: Write down dialogues or role-plays that students will practice. Highlight key vocabulary and phrases for easy reference.
- Phrases and examples: Write down useful phrases or examples that students can use in their speaking and writing activities.
- Pictures and figures: Use pictures or figures to illustrate concepts or vocabulary. This makes the information more memorable and engaging.
- Simplified grammar rules: Present simplified grammar rules or structures to help students understand complex concepts.

Impromptu work

There is usually some unexpected information arising during the teaching, often in response to student questions or discussions. Examples include:

- Student questions: Write down questions from students and answer them on the spot. It shows that the teacher values students' input and encourages active participation.
- Non-standard answers: Write down non-standard answers given by students and discuss them with the class. It improves critical thinking and comprehension of language nuances.
- Explanations: Write down explanations of certain sentences or words arising during the teaching. It helps clarify any confusion and ensures individual understanding of the content.

Notes and reminders

It refers to some additional information that supports the teaching and learning process, such as:

- Date and time: Write down the date and time at the top of the board in English. It helps students practice reading dates and learn the conventions of English writing.
- Promised questions: Write down questions that the teacher promises to answer later. It shows that the teacher is considerate of students' concerns and encourages them to continue thinking about the topic.
- Reminder notes: Write down any important reminders or instructions for the students. It helps students stay on track of learning and focus on the course objectives.

5.2.6 Presentation Suggestions

Boardwork preparation

It is crucial to plan the allocation of the board. According to the four types of board writing contents, the board surface can be divided into three main areas:

- Key area: This section contains permanent or reference material, which is predictable and should be planned.
- Development area: This section might occupy the largest space and can be placed in the center of the board.
- Impromptu and reminder area: This section should be separate from the other two. After categorizing the content, a reasonable layout of the board should be created.

Timely presentation of boardwork

The vitality of boardwork lies in its dynamic generation. Boardwork should evolve with the progress of the lesson and the learning of the students. Therefore, teachers need to grasp the timing and be flexible when presenting boardwork. Suggestive boardwork can be completed before the lesson, spontaneous boardwork should be presented during the lesson, and conclusive boardwork should be presented at the appropriate time for analysis, summarization, and conclusion. For example, when learning sentence patterns, examples are typically written as they are discussed, while the sentence structure is presented after analysis and induction. This allows for the close coordination of spoken language and the "silent language" of boardwork, enhancing students' perception and impression of the knowledge. Additionally, boardwork that is no longer needed should be erased promptly to avoid distracting students.

Ensuring clear student vision

It seems natural enough to write standing in front of the board. Unfortunately, this blocks the view of what you are writing for the class and they cannot read it till you have finished (see Figure 5.8 (A)). You also cannot talk to them easily. When you get a chance in an empty classroom, practise writing on the board in a way that your body does not block the view for everyone and you can make eye contact with the class (see Figure 5.8 (B)). This requires a slightly sideways position, which will feel odd at first, but it allows you to talk to students, ask questions, and look around, all of which can be very helpful in maintaining a good working atmosphere.

(A) (B)

Figure 5.7 Standing posture for board writing

The teacher can speak while writing on the board. Writing speed should be slightly faster than spoken language, adding density and rhythm to the class. The content of the boardwork should be read out loud word by word and sentence by sentence. After writing on the board, the teacher should step back to avoid blocking the view. A pointer can be used if necessary to lead the reading or explain the content on the board.

Focusing the prominent visual effect

- Use different colors and text sizes: for example, highlighting key vocabulary words in bold or underlining them with a different color to draw attention.

e.g.: *When teaching a lesson on "Household Chores," you could write the following sentence on the board: My mom cleans the house and does the laundry every Saturday. (Emphasize "clean" and "laundry" in different colors to focus on the target vocabulary.)*

- Incorporate graphics and diagrams: for example, using figures or tables to illustrate grammar structures or concepts.

e.g.: *When teaching the past continuous tense, you could draw a timeline with arrows representing the time and actions, making it easier for students to understand the concept.*

- Use white space: for example: Leaving enough space between lines and categories to avoid clutter and make the board easier to read.
- Use icons and symbols: to represent different categories or types of information.

e.g.: *You could use a book icon for reading activities, a microphone icon for speaking activities, and a pen icon for writing activities.*

- Engage students in creating boardwork: for example, Encouraging students to write on the board or contribute their ideas. This promotes active learning and engagement.

e.g.: *When learning new vocabulary, students can come up to the board and write a sentence using the target words.*

- Use technology: for example, using interactive whiteboards or digital tools to create dynamic and engaging boardwork. You can add images, videos, and animations to promote the learning experience.

Grasping the above tips, you may have excellent board writing. See Figure 5.9 as a sample board wrinting with visual effect.

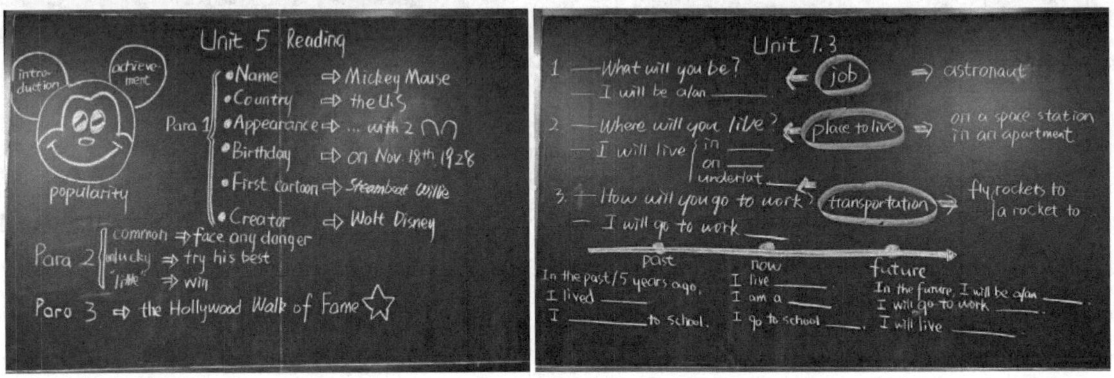

Figure 5.8 Sample board writing with visual effect

Activity 2 **You are going to attend an English teaching contest. Design a blackboard writing for a 15-minute teaching, for either listening, reading, speaking, or writing lessons.**

Your blackboard design:

5.3 Sketching Drawing

Sketching, or simple drawing, as a visual teaching aid, has gained increasing popularity and is being utilized frequently in English teaching due to its unique characteristics and potential benefits. English teachers, especially English majors learning teacher training programs, should learn and grasp the concept and characteristics of sketching,

5.3.1 Concept and Characteristics of Sketching in ELT

As for English teaching, sketching means the use of simple, quickly drawn illustrations to refer to objects, actions, or concepts. It acts as a visual tool to promote language learning and comprehension, making abstract ideas more concrete and memorable. Simple sketching can be used in a variety of teaching settings, such as vocabulary introduction, grammar explanation, storytelling, and classroom interaction.

The following are some characteristics of sketching:

- Easy to learn: Simplified sketching is accessible to people of all ages, especially beginners, as it does not require advanced drawing skills.
- Rapid expression: It allows for quick capturing and conveying the essence of a scene or object.
- Emphasis on form: Sketching reduces the details of the scene or object so that it focuses more on the basic features and structures of the subjects.
- Creativity: The simple lines of the sketching can inspire students' rich imagination and creativity.

5.3.2 The Basic Principles of Sketching

It is important for English majors to understand the fundamental principles of sketching for effective classroom application.

Simplicity and clarity. One of the main principles of sketching in English teaching is to keep the sketching simple and clear. Simple sketching is easier for students to understand and process, allowing them to focus on the language being taught rather than the complexity of the drawing. Teachers should aim for the simplest designs that convey the intended message with no unnecessary details.

Relevance and contextualization. Sketches should be related to the lesson's content and context. They should show a clear purpose, such as illustrating vocabulary, demonstrating grammar points, or facilitating comprehension of a text (Mori, 2014). The language concepts can be reinforced when the sketching is contextually appropriate.

Engagement and interaction. Sketches should be used as a means to attract students' attention and encourage students' interaction. Teachers can involve students in the drawing of sketching, which makes the learning process more dynamic and provides opportunities for practice and reinforcement (Meddings & Thornbury,

2009). Interactive sketching activities can be games, storytelling, and collaborative drawing exercises.

Accessibility and inclusivity. Sketching should be understood by all students, regardless of their artistic competency. Teachers should create an environment where all students feel comfortable participating in sketching activities (Larkin, 2013). This can be achieved by using simple features and lines that anyone can replicate.

Sequential and incremental. It is important to explain concepts sequentially and incrementally when using sketching in English teaching. Teachers should begin with basic shapes and move to more complex sketches while students become more comfortable with the activity (Nakata, 2015). The gradual progress from simple shapes to complex drawings helps to build students' confidence and ensures that students are not overwhelmed.

Feedback and reflection. Teachers should get feedback from students after using sketches in the teaching, so as to evaluate the effectiveness of this visual tool. Reflection on the use of sketching can help teachers perfect their techniques and better integrate this aid into their teaching practices (Al-Sheikh, 2016).

5.3.3 Sketching Techniques

Understanding basic shapes. The foundation of sketching lies in understanding and utilizing basic shapes. These shapes include circles, squares, triangles, and rectangles, serving as building blocks for more complex images. For example, a circle can stand for the sun or a head, whereas a square can be the body of a person or an object like a book. Knowing how to sketch these shapes quickly and accurately is essential for creating clear and recognizable stick figures (see Figure 5.9).

Figure 5.9 Some basic shapes

Using simple lines. Lines are the essence of sketching. They should be simple, straight, and purposeful. Beginners can practice drawing lines with consistent thickness and length to construct uniform figures. Lines can also be used to represent movement or action. For example, by adjusting the angle and direction of the lines, the sketches can be regarded as bending arms or legs. Simple lines can be used to sketch various figures.

Through the basic shapes, various sketches can be drawn, as shown in the following samples. These sketchings can be used in teaching to improve the teaching effectireness and efficiency (see Figure 5.10, Figure 5.11, Figure 5.12, and Figure 5.13).

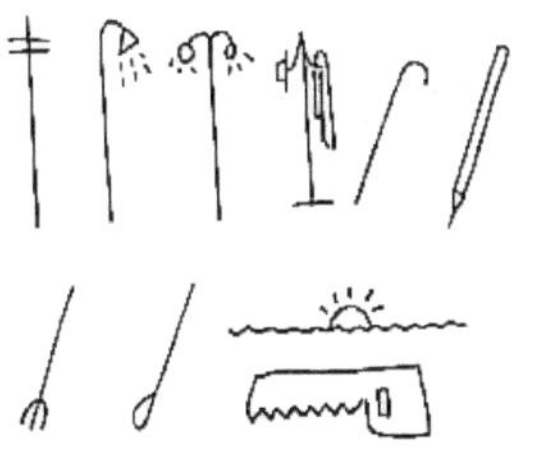

Figure 5.10 Sketching derived from line

Figure 5.11 Sketching derived from angle

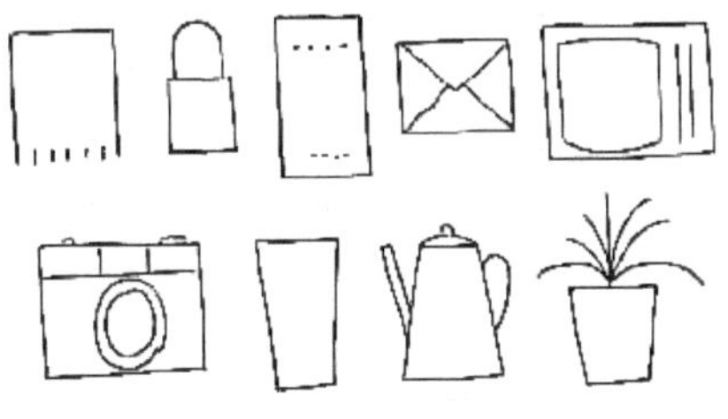

Figure 5.12 Sketching derived from square

Figure 5.13 Sketching derived from circle

Emphasizing proportions. Although sketches are indistinctly simplified, it is still crucial for clarity and recognition by maintaining accurate proportions. Be cautious about the relative sizes of different parts, such as making the head smaller than or the limbs proportional to the body. Proper proportions help avoid confusion and make the sketches easily understandable (see Figure 5.14).

Figure 5.14 Proportion of a person

Adding expressive features. Although sketching drawings are basic, they can still express emotions and dynamics. The position and angle of lines can convey a character's mood or attitude. A downward-curved line might represent sadness, while an upward curve could indicate happiness or excitement. Additionally, facial features like eyes and mouths can be simplified but still convey expressions, such as a smile or surprised eyebrows (see Figure 5.15, Figure 5.16, and Figure 5.17).

Figure 5.15 Showing age and sex

Figure 5.16 Showing emotions

Figure 5.17 Showing emotions & actions

The following are some other sample sketches (see Figure 5.18, Figure 5.19, Figure 5.20 and Figure 5.21):

Figure 5.18 Showing different activities

Figure 5.19 Showing the arrangement of a dinig table

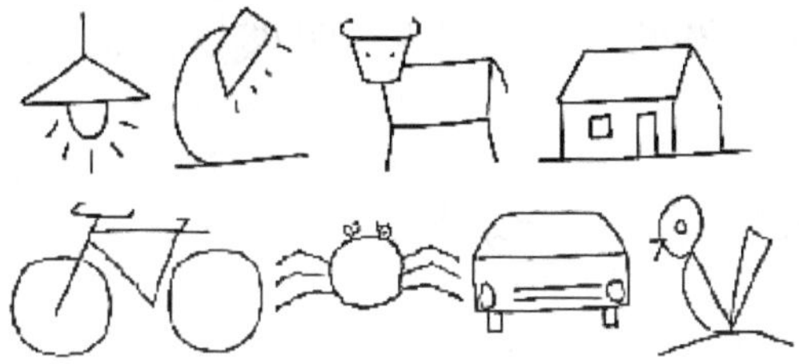

Figure 5.20 Showing everyday life

Figure 5.21 Showing everyday objects

Drawing from life. Practice drawing from real-life objects, scenes, or people to improve observation skills and accuracy. This technique can also help teachers to create more authentic and relatable sketches for their students (Mori, 2014).

5.3.4 Application of Sketching in English Teaching

Pronunciation teaching. Sketching can be used to demonstrate pronunciation principles, especially for phonemes that are difficult to indicate with physical cues. Sketches can visually outline the changes in tongue position and lip shape, helping students quickly grasp the methods and characteristics of pronunciation, thereby improving the accuracy of their pronunciation (see Figure 5.22).

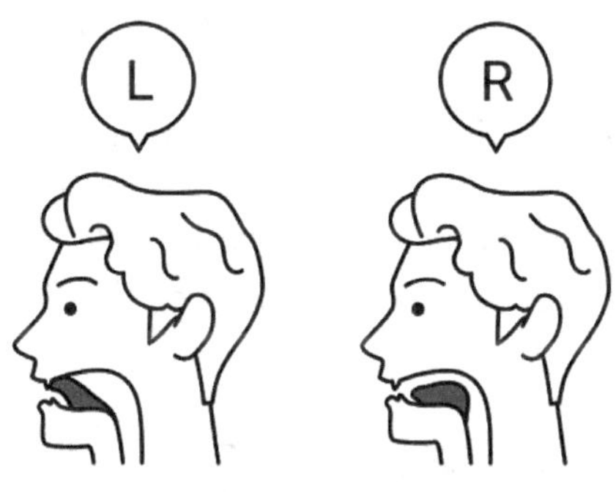

Figure 5.22 Pictures of articulation

Vocabulary teaching. Sketching can be used to illustrate new vocabulary words, especially those related to actions, emotions, or body parts. For instance, when teaching verbs like "run," "jump," or "swim," teachers can draw simple figures engaging in these activities. This visual aid not only helps students understand the meaning of the words but also encourages them to associate the words with real-life scenarios (Nation, 2001).

e.g. (1) Sketching can be used to illustrate action verbs. The following is an example.

T: Look at the figure. What is the man doing?

(Draws a figure running on the board)

Ss: Run!

T: Yes, the verb for this action is "run". Read after me "run"... The man is running.

Ss: Run, run, run. The man is running.

T: Excellent! Now look again, What is this girl doing?

Ss: Swimming!

...

Sketching can be used to illustrate indefinite pronouns, as showing in Figure 5.23.

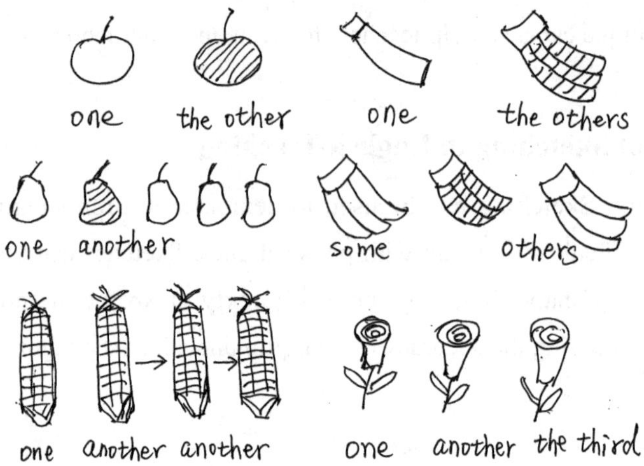

Figure 5.23 Sketching showing indefinite pronouns

Sketching can also be used to illustrate propositional words, making the usage of the words understood easier, such as the words of "above" and "below" in Figure 5.24.

Figure 5.24 Sketching showing propositional words

Sketching can be very useful in teaching pairs of words in opposite meanings, such as "thick" and "thin", "long" and "short" in Figure 5.25.

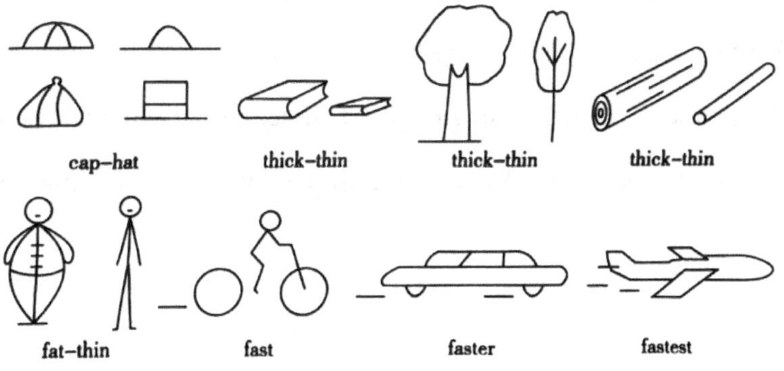

Figure 5.25 Sketching showing a comparison of words

Grammar visualization. Complex grammar concepts can be clarified through the use of sketching. Visual representations can make abstract rules more concrete and easier to understand (Larkin, 2013). The steps are as follows:

- Identify a challenging grammar point to explain.
- Create a sketching to illustrate the concept, such as a timeline for tenses or a figure for sentence structure.
- Use the sketching for explanation, pointing out relevant parts when discussing each element.
- Encourage students to draw their sketches to practice the grammar point.

Storytelling and comprehension. Sketches can be used to facilitate storytelling and comprehension activities. Teachers can create a series of sketches to accompany a story, which can help to visualize the plot and characters (Al-Sheikh, 2016).

The steps are as follows:

- Choose a short story or text that is suitable for the class level.
- Draw a series of sketches that represent key events or scenes from the story.
- Use the sketches to introduce the story, asking students to predict what will happen next.
- After reading the story, have students use the sketches to retell the story in their own words.

Classroom interaction. Sketching can be integrated into interactive games and activities, enhancing a more dynamic and engaging classroom environment.

The steps are as follows:

- Design a sketch-based game such as "look-and-say" or a drawing dictation.
- Prepare a list of words or phrases for students to draw or guess.
- Divide students into groups and explain the rules of the game.
- Encourage students to work together, using English to describe and guess the sketches.

Activity 3 **Draw some sketches with the intended implications in your mind. Ask your partner to "look-and-say".**

Thinking and Doing

A. Discussion questions

1. Is English handwriting important for an English teacher? Why?
2. How to deal with the relationship between blackboard and other media?
3. The following is the board writing of a candidate after finishing his trial lecture. Suppose you are the interview judge of the Teacher Qualification Examination, how will you evaluate his board writing? And why?

   When woutld be a good day?

What did they want to do?

Could they present on time?

How did they suggest another time?

B. Practice

1. Copy paragraphs or discourses about 200 words in your exercise book according to the order of strokes and English writing principles.

2. Draw sketching (single images or a sequence) to illustrate some of the following:

   swimming pool, London, happy, escalator, mouse, exhausted, robbery, whale, planet, overtake.

3. Draw sketching for the following lesson:

   Lucy goes to school early. Lily goes to school earlier. Han Mei goes to school earliest.

C. Exercises for instructional skills

1. About blackboard writing, which of the following is wrong?
   A. Board writing is a very personal matter.
   B. You'd better write things up on the board while students are working on other things.
   C. Be sure that your body is in a slightly sideways position.
   D. You can ask your students to change their handwriting styles.

2. Handwriting may prevent young learners from learning writing in three ways except __________.
   A. these children's written text may be less accessible to others because the legibility of their handwriting is still under development.
   B. young children's handwriting may not influence the teacher's score for them.
   C. young children's writing efforts may be interfered with by other writing processes.
   D. young children's handwriting difficulties may constrain their development as writers.

3. Some studies found that handwriting instruction not only improved young students' handwriting, but it also improved their following writing performance with the exception of __________.
   A. sentence construction skills B. writing output
   C. correct use of words D. writing quality

4. The author suggested several methods to train students' handwriting except __________.
   A. arrangement of some special classes B. write in the air
   C. imitate handwriting on lined paper D. attend the examination

5. Which of the following statements is NOT true?
   A. Handwriting may reflect one's character.

B. You'd better write on the board slightly sideways because it will help you write fast.

C. No matter what kind of board it is, you should write on it with neatness and legibility.

D. Stick people are not detailed pictures.

Checklist

Mark the questions with a check (√) if your answer is yes.

☐ Have I understood the principles of handwriting, board writing and sketching?

☐ Have I known the typical mistakes Chinese learners make when handwriting?

☐ Have I grasped the strategies to integrate board writing into English teaching?

☐ Have I understood the four main types of board writing contents?

☐ Have I grasped the techniques for sketching drawing?

☐ Can I apply sketching drawing effectively to English teaching?

Reflective Journal

Please write down your reflections on what you have/have not learned in this chapter.

◇ The essential skills I need to possess and develop for English teaching:

____

____

____

____

____

◇ Anything I wish to further explore (i.e., puzzles and difficulties):

____

____

____

____

____

References

Al-Sheikh, S. (2016). The use of drawing in the ESL/EFL classroom. *English Language Teaching*, *9*(4), 1–8.

Larkin, M. (2013). Drawing as a means of language learning. *The Language Learning Journal*, *37*(1), 56–69.

Li, Z. S., & Yang, G. Y. (2018). 现代英语教学论 [*Modern English teaching theory*]. Tsinghua University Press.

Meddings, L., & Thornbury, S. (2009). Teaching vocabulary with sketches. *ELT Journal*, *63*(4), 363–372.

Mori, J. (2014). The power of simple drawings in language learning. *TESOL Journal*, *5*(3), 490–505.

Nakata, Y. (2015). The effectiveness of using drawings in teaching English as a foreign language. *The Journal of Education*, *65*(1), 45–58.

Nation, I. S. P. (2001). *Learning vocabulary in another language*. Cambridge University Press.

Chapter 6

Teaching Presence and Instructional Language

Objectives

Upon completion of this chapter, you should be able to:

- Understand the concepts of instructional language and teaching presence
- Grasp the principles and components of instructional language and teaching presence
- Use and integrate different instructional languages and teaching presence under different teaching situations.

Discussion Questions

What are verbal language and nonverbal language? What are their functions in communication? And what are their functions in classroom language teaching?

In classroom teaching, we use sound language to communicate and interact with students, which is called instructional language, or verbal language; there is also a "quiet and silent" language—teaching presence, which literally refers to the general teacher attitudes or postures, also known as body language or non-verbal signals. Teachers rely heavily on both their instructional language and nonverbal signals to convey information, build rapport, and facilitate learning. The successful integration of these two modalities is key to enhancing teacher demeanor and student engagement.

6.1 Teaching Presence

Teacher presence refers to the state presented by the teacher during the teaching process that affects the teaching outcome. It is a comprehensive manifestation of the teacher's facial expression system. Good presence reflects the teacher's personal cultivation, temperament, and overall quality. It is an important aspect of teaching artistry. Teaching posture includes the teacher's appearance, demeanor, look, mood, expression, posture, movement, etc. But in addition to the external image of the teacher (appearance, mannerisms, behaviour, dressing, etc.), it also includes inner thoughts, moral sentiments, cultural accomplishment, etc. reflected in daily behaviour.

6.1.1 The Functions of Teaching Presence

Nonverbal communication plays a crucial role in English teaching, contributing significantly to student engagement, understanding, and the overall learning environment. As Mehrabian (1971) noted, in face-to-face communication, the impact of the message is influenced by verbal content (7%), tone of voice (38%), and nonverbal elements (55%). This underscores the importance of NVC in teaching English, where clear communication is essential.

The way teachers carry themselves sends nonverbal messages that can significantly shape the learning environment and influence student perception (Mehrabian, 1972).

Research suggests that effective teacher posture conveys approachability, confidence, and authority, which are key factors in promoting a positive learning atmosphere (Ambady & Rosenthal, 1993). Studies have shown that when teachers exhibit open and engaging postures, students report feeling more comfortable asking questions and participating in class discussions (Kelly & Gorham, 1988).

Teacher posture not only affects student perception but also has potential effects on learning outcomes. Teachers who use expansive and inclusive gestures tend to have students who perform better academically (Brosnahan et al., 2014). Moreover, a teacher's ability to use posture to convey enthusiasm and passion for the subject matter can make complex concepts more accessible and exciting for students (Gebhard, 2006).

Teaching presence also contributes to a teacher's perceived credibility. Upright postures and purposeful movements convey confidence and competence, enhancing a teacher's authority in the eyes of the students (Tickle-Degnen, 2006). A study by Ambady and Rosenthal (1993) found that teachers with a more confident posture were evaluated more favorably regarding their expertise and trustworthiness.

6.1.2 Components of Good Teaching Presence

1. Attire

Attire plays a significant role in establishing a teacher's professional image. It impacts how students perceive their teacher's credibility and competence (Petrovich & Turbide, 2015). As future English teachers, you should opt for clothing that is clean, appropriate, and reflects a professional attitude. Avoid overly casual or distracting apparel that might diminish your authority in the classroom. Teachers should not wear exotic or unconventional clothing to class, nor should they appear unkempt. Inappropriate accessories should be avoided as excessive adornment can dazzle and distract students. Aim for a balance between approachability and formality to foster respect without creating barriers.

2. Posture

Posture conveys confidence and engagement, which are essential for maintaining student interest (Tickle-Degnen, 2006). An upright posture with squared shoulders indicates alertness and preparedness. Be mindful of your stance; avoid slouching or resting on desks, as these can suggest disinterest or fatigue. Instead, utilize an active stance that allows for natural movement and emphasizes your commitment to instructional delivery.

e.g.: Enter. Upon entering the classroom, walk with your head up and chest out, appearing energetic and alert; stand steady and upright, avoid fidgeting with your hands or shuffling your feet unnecessarily; do not lean on the lectern with your hands, nor put them in your pockets.

3. Gestures

Gestures are powerful tools for enhancing communication and understanding. They can be categorized into four types:

- Indicative gestures: These are used to point out objects or people, helping to focus student attention on specific elements during your explanations.
- Demonstrative gestures: These involve illustrating concepts through manual representations, such as tracing the shape of a graph in the air or modeling the spelling of a word.
- Directive gestures: These are used to guide student behavior, like signaling a student to speak or indicating when to shift activities.
- Iconic gestures: These represent concrete objects or actions and can aid in storytelling or describing scenarios relevant to your lessons.

When using gestures, ensure they are purposeful and complement the verbal message rather than distract from it.

4. Facial expressions

Your facial expressions can convey emotions, enthusiasm, and approachability. Smiles, nods, and eyebrow raises can all encourage student participation and reflect your passion for the subject matter (Mehrabian, 1971). Maintain positive and encouraging expressions to create a welcoming learning environment.

However, also be aware of overdoing facial expressions as they might become distracting or insincere.

5. Eye contact

In order to manage a class successfully, the teacher has to be aware of what students are doing and, where possible, how they are feeling. This means watching and listening just so carefully as teaching. It means being able to move around the class, and getting the level of proximity right. It means making eye contact with students (provided that this is not culturally inappropriate), listening to what they have said, and responding appropriately.

It is almost impossible to help students learn a language in a classroom setting without making contact with them. The exact nature of this contact will vary from teacher to teacher and from class to class.

Effective eye contact includes scanning the room (environmental gaze), focusing on individual students (direct gaze), and using a more diffuse gaze to avoid distractions (indirect gaze) (Argyle, 1988):

- Scanning (Environmental Gaze): Occasionally scan the entire classroom to monitor student engagement and the overall class dynamics.
- Focusing (Direct Gaze): Use direct eye contact when addressing a specific student or group, indicating your attention and inclusion of all in the dialogue.
- Diffusing (Indirect Gaze): When needing to think or avoid distraction, adopt a more general gaze that doesn't single out any student, reducing the potential for discomfort.

6. Spatial distance

The physical space between you and your students can significantly affect the classroom atmosphere. Appropriate distance varies culturally and contextually but strives for a balance that allows for authority while maintaining approachability (Hall, 1959).

Proximity. Teachers should consider how close they want to be to the students they are working with. Some students resent it if the distance between them and the teacher is too small. For others, on the other hand, distance is a sign of coldness. Teachers should be conscious of their proximity and, in assessing their students' reactions to what is happening in the classroom, they should take this into account.

Appropriacy. Deciding how closely you should work with students is a matter of appropriateness. So is the general way in which teachers sit or stand in classrooms. Many teachers create an extremely friendly atmosphere by crouching down when they work with students in pairs. In this way, they are at the same level as their seated students. However, some students find this information worrying. Some teachers are even happy to sit on the floor, and in certain situations this may be appropriate. But in others, it may well lead to a situation where students are put off from concentrating.

All the positions teachers take-sitting on the edge of tables, standing behind a lectern, standing on a raised dais, etc., make strong statements about the kind of person the teacher is. It is important, therefore, to consider what kind of effect such physical behavior has so that we can behave in a way which is appropriate to the students we have and the relationship we wish to create with them. If we want to manage a class effectively, such a relationship is crucial.

7. Movement

Some teachers tend to spend most of their class time in one place at the front of the class, for example, to the side, or in the middle. Others spend a great deal of time walking from side to side, or striding up and down the aisles between the chairs. Although this, again, is to some extent a matter of personal preference, it is worth remembering that motionless teachers can bore students, whilst teachers who are constantly in motion can turn their students into tennis-match spectators, their heads moving from side to side until they become exhausted.

Most successful teachers move around the classroom to some extent. That way they can retain their students' interest (if they are leading an activity) or work more loosely with smaller groups (when they go to help a pair of groups).

How much a teacher moves around in the classroom, then, will depend on his or her personal style, where he or she feels most comfortable for the management of the class, how she or he feels it easiest to manage the classroom effectively, and whether or not he or she wants to work with smaller groups.

8. Voice

Perhaps the teacher's most important instrument is the voice. How we speak and what our voice sounds like have a crucial impact on classes. When considering the use of the voice in the management of teaching there are three issues to think about.

Audibility. Clearly, teachers need to be audible. They must be sure that the students at the back of the class can hear them just as well as those at the front. But audibility cannot be divorced from voice quality: a rasping shout is always unpleasant.

Teachers do not have to shout to be audible. In fact, in most classrooms, there is a danger of the teacher's voice being too loud. Good teachers try to get this balance between audibility and volume just right.

Variety. It is important for teachers to vary the quality of their voices and the volume they speak at depending on the type of lesson and the type of activity. So the kind of voice you use to give instructions or introduce a new activity will be different from the voice which is most appropriate for conversation or an informal exchange of views or information.

In one particular situation, teachers often use very loud voices, and that is when they want students to be quiet or stop doing something. But it is worth pointing out that speaking quietly is often just as effective a way of getting the students' attention when they realize that you are talking. They will want to stop and listen in case you are saying something important or interesting. However, for teachers who rarely raise their voices, the occasional shouted interjection may have an extremely dramatic effect, and this can sometimes be beneficial.

Conservation. Just like opera singers, teachers have to take great care of their voices. It is important that they breathe correctly from the diaphragm so that they don't strain their larynxes. It is important that they vary their voices throughout the day, avoiding shouting wherever possible so that they can conserve their vocal energy. Conserving the voice is one thing teachers will want to take into account when planning a day's or a week's work.

6.1.3 Major Tips for Teaching Presence

Nonverbal messages are very powerful. In language classes, especially, where students may not have all the skills they need to decipher verbal language, their attention is drawn to nonverbal communication. Consider these pointers (see Figure 6.1).

- Your face should reflect optimism, brightness, and warmth.
- Use facial and hand gestures to enhance meanings of words and sentences that might otherwise be unclear.
- Make frequent eye contact with all students in the class.
- Do not "bury yourself" in your notes and plans.
  Do not stand in one place for the whole hour.
- Move around the classroom, but not to the point of distraction.
- Follow the conventional rules of proxemics (distance) and kinesthetics (touching) that apply for the culture(s) of your students.
- Dress appropriately, considering the expectations of your students and the culture in which you are teaching.

Figure 6.1 Considerations of nonverbal languages

Activity 1 Practice classroom English teaching by presenting the following teaching case (Xiao & Li , 2016) within your learning group, learning from each other through assessment and correction.

Teaching case

The first class for grade one of junior high school

T: (Enter the classroom, walk onto the platform, looking around the whole class with smile)

Monitor: 起立！

T: No. (Stretch out both hands and press downward, mentioned for all students to sit down. Then step down from the platform, move toward the monitor, extend both hands with palms up, signaling standing up, and read after) Stand up.

Monitor: Stand up.

T: Stand up.

Monitor: Stand up.

T: (Step onto the platform again. Look around the whole class, gaze at the monitor, stretch out hands and mention for the monitor to speak again)

Monitor: Stand up.

T: (Extend both hands with palms rising up, mentioning for the whole class to stand up. Thereafter, look around the whole class) Sit down, please.

(Stretch out hands with palms pressing down, mentioning for the whole class to sit down. Demonstrate the above activity twice)

T: My name is XXX. (Simultaneously point at him/herself, fetch a chalk, and turn toward the blackboard to write the name "XXX". My name is XXX (Step down the platform with both hands toward a student) What's your name?

S1: Han Meimei.

T: Good. Your name is Han Meimei. Hello, Han Meimei.

(Shake hands with her, and turn to the blackboard to write "Han Meimei" on it. Demonstrate the same process with several other students in the classroom)

6.2 Classroom Instructional Language

Language is a very important tool in teaching. For a language teacher, English is not only the tool for communication, but it is also the content for the teacher to teach. There are some rules for the appropriate use of language.

6.2.1 Overview of Instructional Language

Classroom instructional language refers to the set of verbal and nonverbal communication methods used during teaching activities to convey information, facilitate learning, manage the classroom, and establish interactive relations between teachers and students. This language includes not only the teacher's lecturing, questioning, feedback, and evaluation but also paralinguistic features such as voice modulation, rhythm, and pauses, along with nonverbal elements like facial expressions, body language, blackboard writing, and demonstrations. The classroom instructional language in this book only refers to the verbal language of English.

Generally speaking, instructional language in teaching has the features of accuracy, clarity, and organization, adapted properly to students' cognitive levels and interests. Effective instructional language can motivate students' learning, assist their comprehension and absorption of new knowledge, and enhance critical thinking and interaction in class. Instructional language can also establish a positive classroom environment and promote mutual respect and understanding between teachers and students.

Instructors should be aware of the impact their instructional language has on student learning and try to improve and develop their instructional language skills to meet the evolving educational needs and contexts.

6.2.2 Principles of Effective Instructional Language

As English majors in professional teacher training program, grasping the principles of English instructional language is crucial for future teaching. The following are some key principles:

Teachers should offer scaffolding to students by using instructional language to help students move from their current level of understanding to a higher level, that is to say, teachers use slightly more complex language than that students can produce independently (Vygotsky, 1978).

The language teachers use in instruction should be comprehensible to students, not too difficult nor too simple. Messages should be clear and precise (Krashen, 1985).

The instructional language should attract students' interest and engage active thinking. Teachers can ask more open-ended questions and promote more dialogue (Piaget, 1953).

Prompt and constructive feedback when using clear instructional language helps students understand their strengths and areas for improvement (Hattie & Timperley, 2007).

Teachers should recognize and respect the diverse cultures embodied in different nations. It is crucial for teachers to use inclusive instructional language and avoid cultural biases in their speech (Nieto, 2002).

Teachers should encourage students' autonomous thinking and learning by using instructional language that empowers students, instead of limiting their responses to "yes/no" or single-word answers (Deci & Ryan, 1985).

Teachers may remember the following points when applying the instructional language in English teaching:

Clarity

Ensure that your language is clear by abiding by the following strategies:

- Use simple constructions: Apply short sentences and avoid complex grammatical structures that may cause confusion for students (Chaudron, 1988).
- Explicit explanations: Explain new concepts clearly and explicitly, avoiding ambiguity or vagueness.
- Consistent vocabulary: Use consistent terms during the whole teaching process so that students can familiarize themselves with keywords and phrases.
- Visual aids: Utilize visual aids such as figures, charts, and sketching to make up for your verbal explanations and improve understanding.

Relevance

Make sure to use techniques to relate instructional language to students' real lives and interests, increasing motivation and participation in class.

- Real-world examples: Seek examples from students' daily lives to illustrate abstract concepts.
- Autonomous learning: Use examples and discussions that can represent students' interests whenever possible.
- Current events: Incorporate current issues and events into the lesson to show the applicability of the English language in the real world (Schmidt, 1994).
- Contextualization: Provide contexts for instructional language use by creating real-life situations.

Enthusiasm

Convey excitement and passion through instructional language to show a teacher's infectious enthusiasm, facilitating students' participation and excitement for learning.

- Various tone and pace: Adjust the tone and pace of your speech to emphasize key points and show passion and concern for the subject matter.
- Active listening: Show enthusiasm by actively listening to students' responses, appreciating their contributions, and building on their ideas.
- Positive reinforcement: Employ affirmative language to praise students' effort and progress, enhancing a positive learning atmosphere.
- Share personal stories: Share amusing anecdotes connected with the course to suggest your enthusiasm for the topic, making it more relatable and engaging (Gebhard, 2006).

6.2.3 Categories of Instructional Language

6.2.3.1 Language for classroom management

A successful learning atmosphere is rooted in effective classroom management. The instructional language used in classroom management involves starting and ending class, redirecting off-task behavior, organizing group work, and using nonverbal signals, etc.

- Phrases and expressions for starting and ending class effectively. The language you use at the beginning and end of a class sets the tone for the entire session.

e.g.: Starting the class:

- *Good morning/afternoon, everyone! Today we're going to...*
- *Let's get started with today's lesson. I'm looking forward to seeing...*

- Before we begin, let's review what we learned in our last class...

Ending the Class

- That's all for today. Let's quickly summarize what we've learned.

- Remember to study...

- Keep up the good work, and see you next time!

- Language for redirecting off-task behavior and promoting a positive learning Environment. When students are off-task, it's important to address the behavior while maintaining a positive atmosphere.

e.g.: Redirecting attention

- I see that you're having fun, but let's bring our attention back to the lesson.

- Can we please wrap up the side conversations so no one misses out?

Promoting Positivity

- I appreciate your enthusiasm, but let's channel it into our discussion.

- I understand you're excited, but let's save it for break time.

- Group work requires clear instructions and organized language.

e.g.: Assigning Groups

- I'd like you to form groups of four. Each group will...

- Let's create pairs based on your interest in...

Guiding Group Work

- Your group's task is to...

- Each pair should discuss...

- Nonverbal cues are essential for maintaining classroom control and encouraging participation.

e.g.: Maintaining Control

- A gentle raise of the hand or a silent gaze can signal that it's time to stop talking.

- Moving to the front of the room can capture attention without saying a word.

Encouraging Participation

- Nodding and smiling can encourage shy students to speak up.

- Gesturing towards a student who hasn't spoken in a while can invite them to share their thoughts.

6.2.3.2 Language for instructional delivery

Instructional delivery consists of conveying language rules, concepts, and vocabulary, etc. to students, such as the vocabulary and syntax for illustrating grammar and language concepts, strategies for delivering questions effectively, and language for presenting and practicing new vocabulary.

- Vocabulary and syntax for delivering grammar and language concepts clearly.

e.g.: *- Use metalanguage terms like "subject," "predicate," and "object" to clarify grammatical roles.*

- Use simple sentences to explain complex concepts, gradually building up to more intricate explanations.

- Integrate diagrams and illustrations to make up for verbal explanations and provide a visual reference for students.

- Strategies for delivering questions effectively to test comprehension and stimulate critical thinking.

e.g.: *- Use more open-ended questions that require more than a "yes/no" answer.*

- Start with simpler questions to set comprehension, then move to more challenging ones that improve deeper thinking.

- Allow enough wait time after the question to offer students the opportunity to think before responding.

- Examples of language for presenting and practicing new vocabulary. Introducing new vocabulary requires a deliberate approach to ensure understanding and retention.

e.g.: *- Pronounce new words clearly, emphasizing correct stress and intonation patterns.*

- Explain the meaning of words within contexts, such as through sentences or short dialogues.

- Repeat new vocabulary items as many times as possible during the teaching to enhance memory and understanding.

6.2.3.3 Language for interaction and feedback

In a communicative English teaching setting, interaction and feedback are essential. There are three techniques.

- Techniques for encouraging students' participation by open-ended questions and prompts.

e.g.: *- Use questions that require more than a "yes/no" answer to inspire critical thinking and discussion.*

- Use instructions like "Can you explain further?" or "What do you think about..." to encourage further explanation.

- Give students time to reflect before sharing their ideas to encourage deeper participation.

- Language for giving constructive feedback on students' output to enhance learning and development.

e.g.: *- Address specific points of the student's output to make feedback feasible.*

- Use a positive tone even when pointing out shortcomings for improvement to motivate students' learning.

- Integrate feedback into learning objectives to help students comprehend the goal behind the feedback.

- Examples of language for facilitating peer-to-peer interaction and collaboration. Promoting peer interaction enhances collaborative skills and learning.

e.g.: *- Role assignments: Assign roles such as "discussion leader" or "note-taker" to encourage active participation.*

- Group norms: Establish group norms for interaction to create a respectful and collaborative environment.

- Feedback: Encourage students to provide feedback to each other, fostering a culture of constructive criticism.

6.2.3.4 Language for assessment and evaluation

Assessment and evaluation play vital roles in leaning and teaching. They provide insights into students' understanding, guide teaching decisions, and improve students' growth. The following are some techniques.

- Terms and phrases to evaluate tests and assignments

e.g.: A. Clarifying expectations

- Use clear and concise language to explain test instructions.

- Set the context for assignments by outlining goals or objectives.

B. Consistent terminology

- Remain consistency in terminology in different evaluations.

- Avoid jargon or overly complex language that may cause confusion for students.

C. Feedback-oriented language

- Build feedback within a perspective of growth mindset perspective.

- Use positive language that emphasizes effort and improvement rather than fixed ability.

- Language for providing meaningful feedback during assessments

e.g.: A. Descriptive feedback

- Provide specific, descriptive feedback that addresses strengths and areas for improvement.

- Avoid obscure or general comments that lack clear or feasible steps.

B. Feedback for encouragement

- Integrate motivating words that encourage students' further improving.

- Appreciate effort and achievements, even if the final result is not fully successful.

C. Feedback for learning goals

- Connect feedback with learning objectives and future tasks.

- Help students understand how feedback transform into specific learning steps.

- Strategies for applying language to foster students' self-assessment and reflection

e.g.: A. Questions that foster reflection

- Ask open-ended questions that prompt students to evaluate their work critically.

- Encourage students to reflect on their learning process and not just the outcomes.

B. Self-assessment prompts

- Integrate checklists or rubrics that guide students in assessing their own work.

- *Provide opportunities for students to identify their strengths and areas for growth independently.*

C. Collaborative dialogue

- *Facilitate discussions where students share their reflections and learn from peers.*
- *Create a supportive environment where students feel safe discussing challenges and triumphs.*

6.2.4 Strategies for Using Instructional Language

6.2.4.1 The use of language

Language is a very important tool in teaching. For a language teacher, English is not only the tool for communication, but it is also the content for the teacher to teach. There are some rules for the appropriate use of language.

Successful English teachers use English most of the time in every class, including beginners' classes. Students experience frequently real communicative English, which increases students' exposure to English by means of listening comprehension, and provides them opportunities to speak English, because English is not only the communication medium, but it also offers a scenario for learners to learn the language itself.

When teachers introduce new lessons, they need to provide clear descriptions of the concepts or processes, which determine the success or failure of a lesson. Some research shows that students regard the ability to explain things well as one of the most important qualities of a good teacher.

The following are some guidelines for effective instructions:

- **Prepare:** It is shown that teachers' instructional language is often not so clear to their students as they are to themselves! Therefore, teachers should think for a while about the words they will use, the illustrations they will provide, etc., and even write the instructions out before they enter the classroom.
- **Ensure to draw the class's full attention:** Sometimes students' attention may stray, but if you are explaining something essential, you should try some ways to get their attention back. For example, when teachers give instructions for a group-work task, it is advisable to give the instructions before the teacher divides the class into groups or give out materials, because once they are in groups, students' attention will be naturally directed to each other rather than to the teacher.
- **Present the information more than once:** A repetition or paraphrase of the necessary information may make all the difference. Represent the information in a different way, for example, say it and write it up on the blackboard, give students more than chance to understand what they need to do.
- **Be brief:** People usually have only a limited attention span; So make your explanation as brief and clear as you can. Teachers should think carefully about what to omit and what to include. Therefore, sometimes it is advisable for teachers to use the mother tongue ranter than the lengthy and difficult target-language.

- **Explain with examples:** When giving instructions for an activity, it often helps with a "dry run" , which means the teacher provides an actual demonstration of the activity by himself with the full class or with a volunteer student before inviting students to participate in the task.
- **Get feedback:** When teachers have finished explaining, check with the class that they have understood. Do not just ask: "Do you understand?"; It is better to let them do something that will show their understanding, for instance, to paraphrase in their own words, or provide further demonstrations of their own.

6.2.4.2 Modifying the language

A major section of class time in English teaching is taken up by teachers speaking in class. Along with other activities in class, teachers should spend time giving directions, illustrating tasks or activities, clarifying procedures of activities for students, and checking their understanding of learning.

A large proportion of teachers' total communicative efforts can be occupied with coaxing during the communicative process itself, especially when the students are beginners. Teachers have to engage students' attention, check their understanding of the lesson by continuous checking, clarifying, explaining, defining and appropriate summarizing.

The following teaching case illustrates how a teacher explains a textbook exercise to students and monitors their learning and progress.

T: Have you finished yet? Have you completed the questions at the bottom of the page?

S1: Not yet.

T: (to another student) Where are you up to, Juan? Have you finished yet?

S2: No, not yet.

T: Try to finish up here (points at book).

T: Write your answers on a separate piece of paper, Xu Mingming, don't do it in your book.

T: You work together with Xu Mingming now and check your answers. Do you understand?

S3: OK. Check answers.

T: Yes. Check your answers. You and Xu Mingming check your answers together.

The teacher's repetitive requests and instructions are a typical phenomenon of what happens in English teaching. Repetition is one of the relatively easy and convenient ways to make directions and instructions understandable to students.

Other strategies include (Chaudron,1988) :

- Speaking more slowly: When teachers give instructions to language learners in the classroom, they need to speak more slowly than they would use in other situations.
- Using pauses: When speaking to language learners, especially lower-level students, teachers need to have more pauses and use longer pauses, since the pauses provide students more time to promote their understanding by assimilating what the teacher has said.
- Changing pronunciation: Teachers sometimes need to adopt a clearer articulation or a more standardized style of speech, which contains fewer reductions and contractions than they would use outside of a teaching situation.
- Modifying vocabulary: Teachers often use what they think is a more commonly used word instead of a difficult word. For example, the teacher may ask, "What do you think this photo shows?" instead of "What do you think this photo depicts?" nevertheless, teachers sometimes would unconsciously "complicate" vocabulary rather than simplify it. For example, teachers may say, "What do you think this picture is for?" providing an idiomatic (but not necessarily simpler) replacement for depicts.
- Modifying grammar: English teachers tend to simplify the grammatical structure of sentences in classroom teaching. For instance, some teachers might use fewer subordinate clauses in a classroom situation than in other contexts, or avoid using complex tenses.
- Modifying discourse: Teachers may repeat themselves or answer their own questions in order to make themselves understood, as we saw in the dialogue earlier.

These kinds of modifications in teachers' speech can lead to a special type of discourse which has been referred to as teacher talk. When teachers use teacher talk they are trying to make themselves as easy to understand as possible, and effective teacher talk may provide essential support to facilitate both language comprehension and students' production. Krashen (1985) argues that this is how teachers provide students with "comprehensible input" (input which is finely tuned to the learner's level of comprehension), which he sees as "the essential ingredient for second language acquisition".

However, sometimes teachers may develop a variety of teacher talk which would not sound natural outside of the classroom. The following are examples of teachers using this variety of teacher talk when teaching low-level ESL learners.

In your house, you ... a tub... you (gestures) *wash.* (The teacher is explaining the meaning of "wash".)

I want to speak another person. He not here. What good thing for say now? (The teacher is explaining how to take telephone messages.)

Not other students listen. I no want. Necessary you speak. Maybe I say what is your name. The writing not important. (The teacher is explaining an interview procedure.)

The book...we have... (holds up book) *...book is necessary for class. Right... necessary for school. You have book.* (The teacher is reminding the students to bring their books to class.)

Although these examples may be extreme, they illustrate that in their efforts to provide students with comprehensible input, teachers may sometimes develop a style of speaking that does not reflect natural speech.

Activity 2 **The following is a teaching case involving the teacher's instructional language (Zou Weicheng, 2008). Find out all the instructional language and analyze the function of each instructional language the teacher uses.**

Teaching case

1. Teaching material

John: I need a single room, please.

Receptionist: It's £49 for one night.

John: £49 a night! Sorry, I can't afford that.

Receptionist: Why don' t you try the next door? It's cheaper there.

2. Video clip in the classroom

T: (Putting a picture of hotel on the board) OK. What's this?

Ss: It's a hotel.

T: An expensive hotel?

S1: Maybe.

T: Why do you say so?

S1: It's very big.

T: Are all big hotels expensive?

S1: In England, yes.

S2: Especially in London, big hotels are very expensive.

T: London, all right. This hotel's in London and it's very expensive. (Pause) Now here comes John Drawing a man and writing "Liverpool" on the board). (Pause) Do you think he lives in London?

Ss: No. He lives in Liverpool.

T: Yes. And where is he now?

Ss: London.

T: Right. What else do you know about him?

S4: He doesn't have enough money.

T: Why do you say so?

S4: He has poor clothes.

T: OK. Now he goes to this hotel and he sees a woman behind the desk. (Pause) What do we call her in English?

S5: Receptionist.

T: Yes. (Board writing: receptionist. And at the same speak more slowly.) Receptionist.

Ss: Receptionist.

T: OK. John wants a room for himself. So ... a single or a double room?

S6: A single room.

T: Yes. Then how does he ask?

S7: Excuse me, madam, could I have a single room?

T: That's right and very polite in fact. But let's keep it short.

S8: Single room.

T: Yes, but more polite.

S8: Single room, please.

T: Single or ...?

S8: A single room, please.

T: Good. Now again, please.

S8: A single room, please.

T: (Board writing: A single room, please. And at the same time slow down the speech.) A single room, please.

Ss: A single room, please.

T: Any other ways to ask for a room at a hotel?

S9: Can we say "Have you got a spare room?"

T: (Pause) But do we say that when we ask for a room at a hotel?

S10: No, only in houses when we ask the landlady if we can use a room.

T: Yes. Possibly even in hotels if we want to use a room which isn't a bedroom for something unusual.

S11: A free room?

T: Yes, possibly. But not "Have you got a free room?" Why not?

S12: It means the room doesn't cost any money. It's for free.

T: Yes. What should we say then?

T: What should we say then?

Ss: (Silence)

T: Have you got any rooms free? (Board writing: Have you got any rooms free?

Ss: Have you got any rooms free?

T: Any other ideas?

S13: Have you any vacancies?

T: That's good. Come and write it on the board.

Thinking and Doing

A. Discussion questions

1. Give a rating of 1 (=just right) to 5 (=absolutely terrible) for a teacher you remember well.

   □ Appearance　　□ Audibility

   □ Clarity　　□ General presence in class

   □ Movement in class　　□ Vocal quality

   In the case of a low score, explain your reasons. Now score yourself as you are or are likely to be.

2. Try to complete the following chart with situations/activities which might be appropriate for the behaviour described. If you cannot put anything in the column, explain why not.

Teacher behaviour	Appropriate situations
The teacher shouts.	
The teacher is at the back of the class.	
The teacher is at the front of the class.	
The teacher is sitting on a table round which four students are working.	
The teacher is sitting on the floor.	

3. The following are some instructional classroom languages by a teacher. What is your opinion about the remarks, and what are your suggestions for the teacher?

   "I will give you two minutes."

   "I want you to have a pair work." "I want you to read the passage."

   "Who can answer this question? It is so easy." "You." "Then, you."

B. Practice

1. Obverse a video clip of an excellent teaching model, and evaluate the teacher's behaviour in the video clip according to what you have learned in this section.

2. Try to give a lecture in your group according to the following teaching plan, and help and correct each other.

Teaching plan

Presenting the present continuous tense

T: Look, what am I doing? (play the action of patting the ball and shooting the ball)

Ss: You are playing the basketball.

T: Yes. I am playing basketball. (write down "I am playing basketball" on the blackboard. Now, what am I doing? (play the action of running.)

Ss: You are running.

T: Yes. I am running.(write the whole sentence on the blackboard.)

(Continue to present "I am drinking. I am swimming. I am drawing.")

C. Exercises for instructional skills

1. Which of the following is most effective for a teacher when students do not understand how to do an activity that he/she has described?
   A. Demonstrating how to do it.
   B. Asking students to talk freely.
   C. Encouraging students to share their ideas.
   D. Walking around the classroom and answering questions.

2. If a teacher says "Why don't you have pair work or group work? If you are good enough, please discuss these questions after reading." in a class, he/she __________.
   A. doesn't tell students exactly what to do and how to do
   B. gives a clear instruction
   C. gives a suggestion
   D. shows students how to discuss questions

3. Classroom language can be called in-class language which is the specially used language system by both teachers and students in classroom teaching. Which of the following does not belong to it?
   A. Spoken language　　B. Body language
   C. Spelling language　　D. Written language

4. For better classroom management, what should the teacher do while the students are doing activities?
   A. Participate in a group.
   B. Prepare for the next procedure.
   C. Move around to monitor, prompt students, and provide help.
   D. Stand in front of the class.

5. Which of the following statements about teachers' instructions is NOT true?
   A. Instructions should be simple and clear.
   B. Instructions can be long and complicated for students to follow.
   C. Teachers can use body language to assist students to understand.
   D. Instructions should be kept to a minimum during activities.

Checklist

Mark the questions with a check (√) if your answer is yes.

- □ Have I understood the concept of instructional language and teaching presence?
- □ Have I grasped the functions of verbal and nonverbal language?
- □ Have I grasped the principles and components of instructional language and teaching presence in classroom teaching?
- □ Can I deliver the proper instructional language and behave properly by using proper verbal and nonverbal language in class?

Reflective Journal

Please write down your reflections upon what you have/have not learned in this chapter.

◇ The essential skills related to instructional language as well as verbal and non verbal language I need to possess and develop for English teaching:

____

____

____

____

____

◇ Anything I wish to further explore (i.e., puzzles and difficulties):

____

____

____

____

____

References

Ambady, N., & Rosenthal, R. (1993). Half a minute: Predicting teacher evaluations from thin slices of nonverbal behavior and physical attractiveness. *Journal of Personality and Social Psychology*, *64*(3), 431–441.

Argyle, M. (1988). *Bodily communication*. International University Press.

Chaudron, C. (1988). *Second language classrooms: Research on teaching and learning*. Cambridge University Press.

Deci, E. L., & Ryan, R. M. (1985). *Intrinsic motivation and self-determination in human behavior*. Plenum.

Gebhard, D. (2006). Language, attitude, and the maintenance of learner engagement. *ELT Journal*, *60*(4), 357–366.

Hall, E. T. (1959). The silent language. Retrieved October 10, 2023, from https://monoskop.org/images/5/57/Hall_Edward_T_The_Silent_Language.pdf

Hattie, J., & Timperley, M. (2007). The power of feedback. *Review of Educational Research*, *77*(1), 81–112.

Kelly, S. D., & Gorham, J. C. (1988). Communicative behaviors, teacher immediacy, and student learning. *Communication Education*, *37*(4), 254–268.

Krashen, S. D. (1985). *The input hypothesis: Issues and implications*. Pergamon Press.

Mehrabian, A. (1971). *Silent messages: Implicit communication of emotions and attitudes*. Wadsworth Publishing Company.

Nieto, S. (2002). *Language, culture, and teaching: Critical perspectives for a new century*. Routledge.

Petrovich, C. J., & Turbide, M. (2015). Teacher attire and student perception: Does what a teacher wears matter? *Journal of Educational Psychology*, *43*(2), 243–252.

Piaget, J. (1953). The origins of intelligence in children. W. W. Norton & Company.

Schmidt, R. (1994). *The role of consciousness in second language learning*. University of Hawai'i Press.

Tickle-Degnen, L. (2006). Postural divergence and rapport: Analysis by gender and familiar status. *Journal of Nonverbal Behavior*, *30*(4), 209–224.

Van den Bogert, N., Van Bruggen, J., Kostons, D., & Jochems, W. (2014). First steps into understanding teachers' visual perception of classroom events. *Teaching and Teacher Education*, 37, 208–216.

Vygotsky, L. S. (1978). *Mind in society: The development of higher psychological processes* (M. Cole, V. John-Steiner, S. Scribner, & E. Souberman, Eds.). Harvard University Press.

Xiao, X., & Li, H. P. (2016). 英语教师职业技能训练简明教程（第二版）[*Concise training course for English teachers' professional skills* (2nd ed.)]. Higher Education Press.

Zou, W. C. (2008). 外语教师职业技能发展 [*Developing professional skills of teaching foreign languages*]. Higher Education Press.

Chapter 7

Opening, Presentation, and Practice Skills

Objectives

Upon completion of this chapter, you should be able to:

- Understand the concepts and principles of openings, presentation, and practice
- Grasp some components of openings, presentation, and practice methods
- Integrate the methods of openings, presentation, and practice properly into practical teaching

Discussion Questions

Chinese people often say, "Everything is difficult at the beginning," and also, "A good beginning is half the battle." What do you think are the criteria to have a good start?

Classroom opening, presentation, and practice are crucial steps in teaching. As the saying goes, "a good beginning is half the success." Serving as the starting point of classroom instruction, this phase bears the responsibility of creating a harmonious classroom atmosphere, stimulating students' desire for knowledge, and helping students quickly reach an optimal learning state.

7.1 Classroom Openings

7.1.1 Methods of Classroom Opening

Here are the classroom opening methods, along with a brief description, their function, and examples.

1. Self-introduction method

- Description & function: Teachers introduce themselves at the beginning of a new course or to a new class, helping to establish rapport and trust with students.

e.g.: *"Good morning, everyone. I'm Ms. Johnson, your new science teacher. Outside of school, I enjoy hiking and exploring nature, which ties right into our new topic on ecosystems."*

2. Direct opening

- Description & function: The teacher directly states the learning objectives and what students will cover in the lesson, setting clear expectations.

e.g.: *"Today, we are going to learn about the Water Cycle. Our goals are to understand the process and be able to identify each stage."*

3. Review opening

- Description & function: By reviewing old knowledge related to the new lesson, finding the connection point between old and new knowledge, naturally leading to the new knowledge.

e.g.: *"Last class, we discussed the properties of matter. Today, let's see how these properties affect the way matter changes from one state to another."*

4. Preview opening

- Description & function: Assigning preview tasks for students to complete before class can prepare them for the upcoming lesson and generate questions.

e.g.: *"Last week, I asked you all to preview chapter 3 on 'Energy Transformations.' What were some concepts or ideas that stood out to you?"*

5. Intuitive opening

- Description & function: Using physical objects, models, images, or experiments to give students a direct perception of abstract concepts.

e.g.: *"Look at this model of the solar system. Notice how each planet rotates around the sun. This will help us understand the concepts of revolution and rotation in astronomy."*

6. Storytelling opening

- Description & function: Starting the lesson with a story related to the content can engage students' imagination and interest.

e.g.: *"Imagine you're a pirate looking for hidden treasure. Just like you need coordinates to find the treasure, we need to understand maps and symbols, which we'll learn today in geography."*

7. Performance opening

- Description & function: Using drama, role-play, or other performing arts to introduce new topics and energize the classroom.

e.g.: *"Let's reenact the debate between Alexander Hamilton and Thomas Jefferson on the topic of federalism. This will lead us into discussing the principles of American government."*

8. Situational opening

- Description & function: Creating a relevant context or atmosphere related to the lesson's content to immerse students in the learning experience.

e.g.: *"Imagine yourself as a meteorologist predicting a storm. Let's look at the tools and scientific knowledge you would use, which we're covering in today's physics class."*

9. Example opening

- Description & function: Using real-world examples to connect abstract concepts to students' lives, making learning more relevant.

e.g.: *"Think about a time when you had to make a difficult decision. Today, we'll explore the economic concept of 'opportunity cost' and how it applies to our everyday choices."*

10. Question opening

- Description & function: Posing thought-provoking or intriguing questions to stimulate students' curiosity and start a discussion.

e.g.: *"What if I told you there's a planet like Earth out there? Let's discuss the possibilities of finding extraterrestrial life in today's astronomy class."*

11. News opening

- Description & function: Introducing current events or recent news stories related to the lesson's content to highlight its relevance.

e.g.: *"Did you hear about the recent discovery of a new species in the Amazon rainforest? Today, we'll talk about biodiversity and why every creature matters."*

12. Cliffhanger opening

- Description & Function: Leaving a suspenseful hook from a previous lesson to create intrigue and continuity in learning.

e.g.: *"As we discovered last class, the fate of our character in the story was uncertain. Today, we'll uncover what happens next and relate it to our theme of suspense in literature."*

13. Brainstorming opening

- Description & function: Engaging students in a collaborative thinking process to activate prior knowledge and generate ideas about the topic.

e.g.: *"Before we dive into the history of ancient civilizations, let's brainstorm what we already know about the Egyptians. This will help us build upon that knowledge."*

Each of these methods has its advantages and is most effective when tailored to the specific context and students' needs. But just as an ancient Chinese saying goes: "There is a method to teaching, but no fixed method; the key lies in finding the appropriate method," we should embrace various teaching styles and strategies based on students' needs and the objectives of the lesson. Using a diverse range of introduction methods can keep students engaged and motivated throughout the learning process.

7.1.2 Considerations of Choosing Opening Methods

Selecting the most appropriate method for classroom opening requires considering the different characteristics of students, including age, interests, learning styles, and knowledge backgrounds.

1. Age characteristics

Younger students: Use intuitive and vivid methods such as stories, games, pictures, and videos, as these methods can attract their attention and stimulate interest.

Elder students: Abstract and in-depth methods such as questions, debates, and examples can be used, as they have developed a certain level of abstract thinking ability.

2. Interests

Analyze the interests of students and choose opening methods related to their interests, such as using topics or activities that students are interested in at the beginning of the class.

3. Learning styles

Visual learners: Use visual materials such as pictures, videos, and charts.

Auditory learners: Use auditory materials such as music, stories, and lectures.

Hands-on learners: Use activities that require hands-on operation, such as experiments, role-playing, and games.

4. Knowledge background

Choose the appropriate opening method based on the students' knowledge level. If students are unfamiliar with the topic, a review opening or example opening can be used to establish a foundation. If students have some understanding of the topic, question opening or debate opening can be used to further explore.

5. Attention concentration

If students' attention is easily distracted, interactive methods such as games and experiments can be used to attract their attention.

6. Emotional state

Consider the emotional state of students and use methods that can evoke emotional resonance, such as music opening or story opening.

7. Course content

Choose the opening method based on the nature of the course content. For example, science courses may be more suitable for experimental openings, while literature courses may be more suitable for story openings.

8. Teaching objectives

Clarify the teaching objectives and choose opening methods that can help students achieve these objectives. For example, if the goal is to cultivate students' critical thinking, debate opening can be used.

9. Cultural background

Consider the cultural background of students and choose opening materials related to their culture to enhance resonance and understanding.

10. Classroom atmosphere

Adjust the opening method flexibly according to the classroom atmosphere and the emotional state of students. If the classroom atmosphere is dull, lively games or music can be used to boost spirits.

7.1.3 Relating Opening Activities to Purposes

Lesson beginnings can serve a variety of purposes. According to McGrath, et al., (1992) , specific lesson openings can be used to:

- Help learners relate the content of the new lesson to that of the last or previous lessons (cognitive contribution).
- Assess relevant knowledge (cognitive contribution).
- Establish an appropriate "set" in learners: i.e., prepare them for what is to follow (cognitive or affective contribution).
- Allow "tuning-in" time which may be especially important in situations where learners have come directly from a radically different environment (pragmatic contribution).
- Reduce the disruption caused by late-arriving students (pragmatic contribution).

The purpose of a lesson beginning will determine the kind of activity or strategy the teacher uses to begin the lesson (see Table 7.1).

Table 7.1 Lesson openings—relating activities to purpose

Purposes	Illustrative activities
Ⅰ. to establish an appropriate *Affective Framework*	
1. create a friendly, relaxed atmosphere 2. create a suitable physical environment. 3. focus attention 4. make class enjoyable 5. get everyone involved 6. raise confidence 7. stimulate interest	music, introductions, greetings, joke, chat (personal, topical) get Ss to arrange furniture greetings listening activity, visual stimulus (incl. video) game, lighthearted oral activity game, pairwork activity, go over homework chat (familiar questions, topical issues), controlled activities, review, homework (prepared, plenary choral activity) anything lively or unusual—vary the beginning
Ⅱ. to establish appropriate an *Cognitive Framework*	
1. provide a organizing framework 2. stimulate awareness of need (ling/ cult.) 3. elicit relevant linguistic knowledge 4. elicit relevant experience	make connections with the last lesson, describe activities or objectives for part of/whole lesson, introduce a topic questions (e.g. based on picture), quiz, brainstorming, oral activity questions
Ⅲ. to encourage *Student Responsibility and Independence*	
make Ss aware of learning skills and strategies	consciousness-raising activities (e.g. memorization game), elicitation of Ss' individual strategies
Ⅳ. to fulfill the *Required Institutional Role*	
1. give feedback 2. check on previous learning 3. give value for time/money	go through (previous) homework quiz, game, brainstorm, ask for summary, questions, check homework (This has more to do with how you start—e.g. punctuality and relevance—than what you do)
Ⅴ. to overcome *Pragmatic Difficulty*	
minimize problems of (and for) Ss arriving late	short (e.g. revision) activities, chat

For example, beginning a lesson with a short review provides additional opportunities to learn previously taught material and allows the teacher to provide correction or reteach areas that students are having difficulty with. This can be accomplished by the following activities:

- Asking questions about concepts or skills taught in the previous lesson.
- Giving a short quiz at the beginning of class on material from previous lessons or homework assignments.
- Having students meet in small groups (two to four students per group) to review homework.
- Having students prepare questions about previous lessons or homework. They can ask questions to each other, or the teacher can ask them to the class.

- Having students prepare a written summary of the previous lesson.
- Having students ask the teacher about problems on homework and having the teacher review, re-teach, or provide additional practice.

McGrath et al. (1992) found that lesson openings are used principally "to establish an appropriate affective framework for learning and, to a lesser extent, to establish an appropriate cognitive framework". They also found that learners are sensitive to the contribution of lesson beginnings.

Activity 1 Read the following lesson transcript carefully, and find out what kinds of opening methods the teacher used, how did the teacher make progress in the teaching?

The following is the beginning of a language arts class for ESL students at secondary level. After greeting the students (Ss) and dealing with non-instructional matters, the teacher (T) begins:

T: The other time we were talking about figures of speech. And we have already in the past talked about three kinds of figures of speech. Does anybody remember those three types? Mary?

S: Personification, simile, and metaphor.

T: Good. Let me write those on the board. Now, can anybody tell me what personification is all about again? Juan?

S: Making a non-living thing act like a person.

T: Yes. OK. Good enough. Now what about simile? ... OK, Cecilia?

S: Comparing two things by making use of the words "like" or "as".

T: OK. Good. I'll write that on the board. The other one-metaphor. Paul?

S: It's when we make a comparison between two things, but we compare them without using the words "like" or "as".

T: All right. Good. So, it's more direct than a simile. Now, we had a poem a few weeks ago about personification. Do you remember? Can you recall one line from that poem where a non-living thing acts like a human person?

S: "The moon walks the night."

T: Good. "The moon walks the night." Does the moon have feet to walk?

Ss: No.

T: No. So this is a figure of speech. All right. Now, our lesson today has something to do with metaphor. We already did simile and we just slightly touched on metaphor before. Now we're going to see what they have in common. So, by the way, do you have your songs with you?

T: Last week I told you we were going to share songs and this week it's my turn to share with you a song that I like. And I have chosen a song by Simon and Garfunkel.

(The class then listens to the song "I Am a Rock" and discusses the metaphors in the lyrics.)

____

____

____

____

____

____

____

____

7.2 Presenting New Language Items

In English language teaching, the presentation stage is a critical component where new language items are introduced to the learners. When learners encounter new items they need to know what they mean and how they are used in communication. They also usually need to know how to pronounce them, their grammatical structure, and how they relate to other language items. All these aspects of new items are usually dealt with best by introducing them in a context in which they are normally used. It is important to remember that learners need to be able to do more than just remember and repeat new items; they must be able to use them actively to communicate. It is generally convenient to present the spoken form before the written form. Presentation usually leads immediately into the practice of the new item.

7.2.1 The Aims of Presentation Teaching

Presentations and explanations by teachers comprise one-sixth to one-fourth of all classroom time. The amount of time devoted to presenting and explaining new knowledge increases at the higher grade levels of elementary school, middle school, and high school. Some educators have argued that teachers devote too much time to talking, and over the years considerable effort has gone into creating approaches to teaching aimed at decreasing the amount of teacher talk and making instruction more student-centered. Nonetheless, the presentation of information remains a popular model of teaching, and the amount of time devoted to it has remained relatively stable over time.

The particular view about presentation teaching highlighted here includes not only more formal presentation commonly referred to as lectures, but also the more informal explanations used by teachers in a variety of instructional settings, such as stopping during group discussion to explain a difficult concept or bending down to a student during seatwork to explain an idea that seems to be confusing.

The learner outcomes of presentation teaching shown in Figure 7.1 are rather clear and straightforward: namely, to help students acquire, organize, and retain new knowledge; expand conceptual structures; and develop important habits of listening and thinking. You will discover that although presentation teaching is effective for some purposes, it is not very effective for others. For instance, it does not do a very good job of helping students acquire particular skills, nor does it encourage higher-level thinking. Other approaches described in subsequent sections are better suited to achieve these types of learner outcomes.

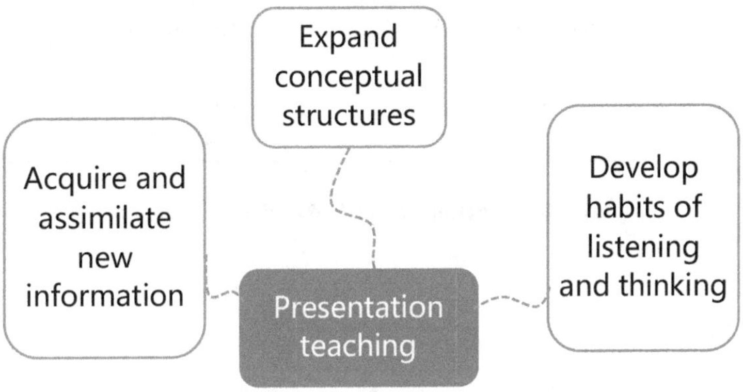

Figure 7.1 Three learner outcomes for presentation teaching

Presentation is mainly teacher-centered and consists of four major phases. The flow proceeds (1) from the teacher's initial attempt to clarify the aims of the lesson and to get students' attention through (2) presentation of an advance organizer and (3) presentation of the new factual and conceptual knowledge to (4) interactions aimed at checking student understanding of the new information and extending and strengthening their thinking skills. When using presentation teaching, teachers strive to structure the learning environment tightly. Except in the final phase, the teacher is an active presenter and expects students to be active listeners. Presentation teaching requires a physical learning environment that is conducive to presenting and listening, including appropriate facilities for the use of multimedia technology.

7.2.2 New Items in an English Language Course

New language items will probably be prominent, even dominant, in your syllabus or coursebook, and learners must learn new grammar and vocabulary in order to make progress in English. However, it is important to remember that learners need to be able to do more than just remember and repeat new items; they must be able to use them actively to communicate.

Not all coursebooks or syllabuses indicate the items to be taught in the same way, but this kind of division is typical of most modern materials. Functions are the communicative things we do with language. New functional items may be indicated only with a description of the function, for example (see Figure 7.2):

BOOK 2 Contents

Unit Topics	**Functions**	**Language**
1 Famous cities	Describing/comparing places	Comparison with adjectives
	Making reservations	
		I'd like to...
		Wh-questions
2 Personal plans arrangements	Making arrangements	Present progressive
	Making excuses	for future
		Let's...
		I'm afraid...

Figure 7.2 Functions described in the coursebook

Functions include:

- Introducing yourself
- Expressing likes and dislikes

Models of language commonly used to carry out the functions may also be given, for example:

- Introductions: *Hello. I'm Michael.*
- Likes/dislikes: *I like cats. I don't like dogs.*

  Mary likes dogs. She doesn't like cats.

New grammatical items may be indicated with grammatical terminology, for example:

Present Continuous Comparisons with adjectives or models of the structures may be given:

- *What's Mary doing? She's swimming.*
- *Glasgow is bigger than Edinburgh. Edinburgh is more famous than Glasgou.*

No matter how new items are indicated, you will almost certainly be dealing with new functions and new grammar. Both types of items, and new vocabulary, are usually connected in a unit or lesson. For example, a lesson may deal with the function "Talking about routine activities". This will probably mean teaching the grammatical structure "The Simple Present Tense" and vocabulary such as "get up", "take a shower", "have breakfast" and "go to school".

7.2.3 What You Need to Know About New Items

There are several aspects of new items that you may need to know about and learners may need to learn. First, it is always necessary to know the meaning of new items; for example, "good night" is equivalent to "goodbye" in the evening or at night. It is also necessary to know about their use in communication; for example, in some languages, the same form is used to say "hello" and "goodbye" at night, but "good night" is used exclusively to say "goodbye", never "hello". In other words, it is a farewell, never a greeting.

It is usually necessary to know how new forms are pronounced and written. For example, in spite of its spelling, "good night" is pronounced /gʊd naɪt/, not /go:d nɪgt/. It is usually useful to understand how compound forms (i.e. forms which contain more than one word) are structured. For example, "good night" is structured the same as "good morning" (*adjective+noun*). It may be useful to know how one form relates to another, for example, the "good morning/afternoon/evening/ night" relationship. It may also be necessary to know about other aspects of grammar. For example, adjectives in English normally precede the noun and have no plural form, so it is "good books" (not "books good" or "goods books").

It is also worth considering what is new for your learners. In a beginners' course for young learners at primary or secondary level, you can assume that virtually all the "new" items in the course will indeed be new for all the learners. However, if you are teaching older false beginners' (learners who are repeating the beginning stages) or intermediate learners of any age, it is probable that some will know or partially know virtually every "new" item in the course.

In the first case, with young beginners, you will probably have to give examples of each item. In the second case, you can interest and motivate the learners more if you elicit—that is, get examples of items from one or more learners and then use them to teach the item to those learners who do not know or remember it.

Activity 2 Anticipate any difficulties your learners might have with the following items because of their native language?

Good afternoon/evening/night

/gʊd a:ftənu:n/ i:vniŋ/ naɪt/

I've got a stomach ache/ cold/ temperature

/aɪv gɒt a stʌmək eɪk/ kəuld/ tempritʃə/

____

____

____

____

7.2.4 Presenting New Functional-Grammatical Items

Teachers should plan how to involve the learners actively in the presentation and practice of new items.

In notes made by a Mexican secondary-school teacher about to teach "stating /asking about occupations", she takes into consideration the following points:

1. Meaning/concept

She plans to present models related to a clearly defined group of occupations—those related to the film industry. This will be in the context of an international film festival reception on television. She will use a collage "television screen" of magazine cutouts of the people and film advertisements, plus excerpts from songs and film music.

2. Use in communication

She plans to organize "conversation" about the people:

A. *Look, that's Denis Rodman!*

B. *What does he do?*

A. *He's a basketball player and an actor.*

B. *Oh yes, of course.*

She will also use a role play with each learner as a famous person at the crowded reception:

A. *Hi. What do you do?*

B. *I'm a composer.*

A. *Oh, you're Bebu Silvetti!*

B. *That's right. What do you do?*

A. *I'm*__________.

3. Structure

She intends to highlight—that is, draw attention to—the use of "a/an" with occupations. No article is used in Spanish and her learners will be tempted to say "He's singer." Although she plans to treat the questions as formulas rather than as examples of the present simple, she still intends to make the "does s/he+do you" change clear.

4. Pronunciation

She plans to deal with specific problems her learners might have. She plans to indicate weak forms and last-word sentence stress:

- What d'y' DO? I'ma SINger.
- What d'ss'e DO? He'sa comPOser.

She also plans to make a general point about word stress. English usually has penultimate syllable stress in words ending -or/-ress/-er, while Spanish has final syllable stress with the corresponding words ending -or/riz, for example:

English: ACtor, ACtress, diRECtor Spanish: acTOR, actRIZ, direcTOR

The written form is not considered in her notes as she plans to teach it in a future lesson.

5. Grammar

She does not plan to explain the auxiliaries "do/does". Teachers often find themselves explaining that in this context these words indicate a question and do not have a dictionary meaning, unlike the main verb "do" ("work at"). This teacher would apparently prefer to avoid such an "explanation" or "discussion" if possible, since it can make an essentially simple formula seem mysteriously illogical and complicated for many learners.

In these notes, she has covered the most important points for presentation, and the beginning of practice. Even if she had decided to use the textbook material, she would still have needed to do some of the same analysis and planning to convert the material into a clear, interesting lesson.

7.2.4.1 Presentation procedures

The following shows an example of how the Present Progressive is presented to a secondary-school class. The teacher has chosen a situation that he hopes will appeal to his 11- and 12-year-old learners, that of astronauts on a spaceship.

Extract 1

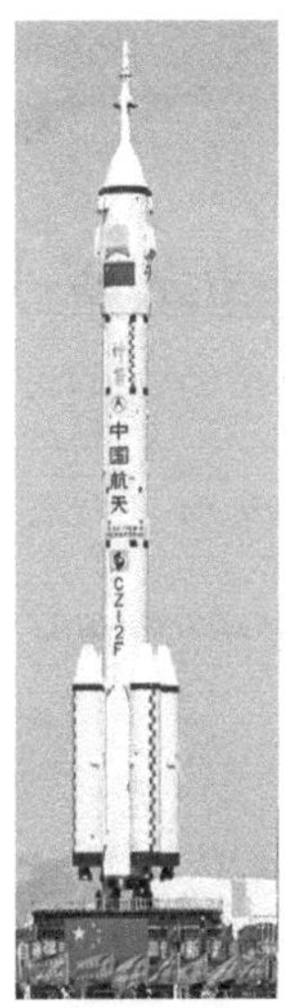

T: Look at this picture. Do you know what it is?

S1: Spaceship.

T: Right, Li Yueyue! It's the Shenzhou-18 crewed spaceship. What do you know about it?

S2: It's Chinese.

S3: Yes, Chinese astronauts. There are three astronauts for Shenzhou-18 crewed spaceship.

T: Who are the three astronauts?

S4: Ye Guangfu, Li Cong, and Li Guangsu.

T: Yes, Chinese astronauts go in it. Very good, Xu Mengmeng. So this is a spaceship and this is a rocket. Listen—rocket, rocket. Everyone.

Ss: Rocket.

T: Good. Listen—spaceship, spaceship.

Ss: Spaceship.

T: Again.

Ss: Spaceship.

T: Good. Now, are all these people astronauts?

S5: No, astronauts and tecni...tecni...

T: Right, Liu Xiaohu. These are technicians. What else is there in the picture? Other things?

S6: There are photographs.

T: Right, Mao Yufei, photographers. A photograph is a picture, a photo. These people are photographers. Are the astronauts in the spaceship?

S7: No. They're out.

T: Right, they're outside the spaceship. Does anyone want to be an astronaut? What are your ambitions—astronaut, space technician, doctor, or engineer?

S8: Astronaut, Mr. Li.

T: You want to be an astronaut?

S8: Yes.

T: And you, Yang Haotian?

Extract 2

T: Now, look at this picture. The rocket and spaceship are going up. They're going up into space. Now the spaceship's separating from the rocket. Now look, this is the earth. And here's the spaceship. The spaceship's orbiting the earth. The spaceship is orbiting the earth. Orbiting. Orbiting. The spaceship is...The spaceship's...The spaceship's orbiting the earth. Listen! The spaceship's orbiting the earth. The spaceship's orbiting the earth. Everyone.

Ss: The spaceship's orbiting the earth.

T: Again.

Ss: The spaceship's orbiting the earth.

T: Good. Yuan Xiaoliu.

S1: The spaceship's orbiting the earth.

T: Good. Hao Feifei.

S2: The spaceship's orbiting the earth.

T: Wonderful. Let's look at the sequence again. Here the rocket and spaceship are going up into space. And here the spaceship's... mm?

S3: Separating from the rocket.

T: Very good! The spaceship's separating from the rocket. And here.

Ss: The shuttle's orbiting the earth.

T: Right! So what about this picture, Hao Yifei?

S4: The rocket and spaceship is... are going up into space.

T: And this picture, He Xiangyu?

Extract 3

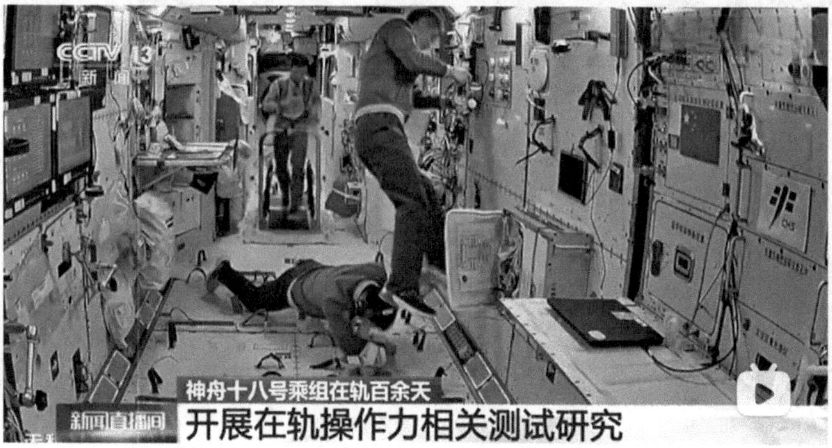

T: Now let's look inside the spaceship. Here we are. There are three men. Who are they?

Ss: Astronauts.

T: Good. They are Chinese astronauts. Who are they? Yes, the man at the back of the spaceship is Ye Guangfu, the commander, another astronaut in the middle is Li Cong, and at the front is Li Guangsu. Now what are they doing?

S1: Test... they test.

T: Yes, they are testing. They are doing an on-orbit manipulation force related test. Listen, manipulation force.

Ss: Manipulation force.

T: Actually at this moment, they are doing exercise. So, what kinds of exercise are they doing? Firstly, how about Ye Guangfu? The astronaut at the very back of the spaceship? Wang Ziqi, please?

S2: Ye Guangfu is running.

T: Good! He is running on a running machine. Can you repeat that, Wang Ziqi?

S: He's running on a running machine.

T: Yes, he's running on a running machine. Everyone.

Ss: He's running on a running machine.

T: Good... he's running on a running machine in the spaceship. And what is the spaceship doing?

S3: It's orbiting the earth.

T: OK! So, Ye Guangfu is running on a running machine. What about the others? Mm, Li Guangsu at the front? Li Cong in the middle? What's Li Guangsu doing? Anyone?

S4: Li Guangsu is do push-up.

T: Pardon, Li Yangyang? Do push-ups?

S5: Er... Li Guangsu's doing push-ups.

T: Very good! What about Li Cong, in the middle? What's he doing? Anyone?

S6: Li Cong's exercising arm strength.

T: That's right! Now listen carefully—Li Cong exercises arm strength a lot, and at the moment he's...

S7: ... exercising arm strength.

T: Li Guangsu does push-ups a lot, and at...

Ss: the moment he's doing push-ups.

T: Ye Guangfu runs on the running machine a lot, and...

Ss: ... and at this moment he's running on the running machine.

If we analyze the three lesson extracts we can see a number of clear stages and techniques. The teacher does not use a rigid method, but he is quite methodical. In each extract he has one major purpose, and he uses specific techniques to achieve his objectives.

In Extract 1, the context or situation for the presentation of the present progressive is established. The teacher tries to involve the students, and manages at times to make this stage fairly conversational, for example, when he asks about Shenzhou-18 crewed spaceship and students' own ambitions. Of course, this conversational element is restricted by the fairly low level and the compulsory nature of this English class. At higher levels and with naturally motivated learners, the conversational element can be developed more.

In Extract 2, the first models of the present progressive are presented. The meaning is clear from the pictures, and the teacher probably also uses gestures, for example, indicating going up, separating, and orbiting with his hands. The grammar is made clear by highlighting the key elements:

T: The spaceship—IS—orbitING—the earth. Orbit-ING...orbiting. The spaceship IS—The spaceship'S... The spaceship's—orbiting the earth.

The pronunciation is taught through getting the students to listen to fairly naturally spoken models, and then imitate them, chorally and individually:

T: Listen—The spaceSHIP's ORBiting the EARTH. The spaceSHIP's ...

Ss :The spaceship's orbiting the earth.

T: ORBiting the EARTH. Everyone.

In Extract 3, the students' understanding of the form and its use is checked. The teacher elicits more examples from the students, using verbs they have already seen with the present simple, to check that they have grasped the "IS verbING" pattern:

S5: Er... Li Guangsu's doing push-up.

T: Very good! What about Li Cong, in the middle? What's he doing? Anyone?

S6: Li Gong's exercising arm strength.

Then the teacher checks the learners' grasp of the distinction between the use of the present simple and the present progressive, emphasizing the moment:

T: That's right! Now listen carefully—Li Cong exercises arm strength a lot, and at the moment he's...

S7: ... exercising arm strength.

T: Li Guangsu does push-ups a lot, and at...

Ss: the moment he's doing push-ups.

T: Ye Guangfu runs on the running machine a lot, and...

Ss: ... and at this moment he's running on the running machine.

This general procedure is represented diagrammatically in Table 7.2.

Table 7.2 The progress of presentation

Establish a context →(Extract 1)	Present key model/s →(Extract 2)	Check understanding →(Extract 3)
Involve the learners in building up a context or situation which makes the meaning and use of the new item as clear as possible, and which also engages the learners' interest and imagination as much as possible.	Give (or elicit from the learners) a clear model of the new item. Make the grammar clear by highlighting the key elements. Get the learners to listen and imitate the normal pronunciation of the model.	Check the learners' grasp of the grammar by eliciting more examples of the new item. Through this elicitation in context, check understanding of meaning and use.

Learners do not learn from presentation alone, or even from presentation followed by practice. This first focus on new language items is only a beginning, and the learners must continually use the language for communication. You will probably have to focus on most basic functional-grammatical items again from time to time, right through to the intermediate level and beyond.

The sequence of steps described above usually provides an effective way of presenting new functional-grammatical items, but it should not be seen as a rigid, mechanical procedure. You are not only teaching English, but also learners, and you need to respond to their human behaviour, often rather unpredictable. You may find, for example, that the learners do not know some of the vocabulary items that you expected them to understand, or that they easily master some aspect of pronunciation with which you expected problems.

Different functional-grammatical items in English also require some flexibility. Some items, for example, are more typical in the written language than in the spoken language. The oral presentation steps given above may then be preceded or substituted by written examples. Other items are grammatically very simple but their meaning and use are complex or subtle, in which case there may be much more emphasis on the context and concept from the beginning and less attention to the structure, for example, "should", contrasted with "must" and "have to".

7.2.4.2 Coursebook material

We have considered how teachers can prepare for and carry out the presentation and early practice of new items with their own ideas and materials. It is good to do this as much as you can since no coursebook writer knows your learners' specific needs and interests, and your own teaching style, as well as you do. However, especially at the beginning of your teaching career, you will probably need to use a lot of the presentation and practice material in your coursebook. Even experienced teachers do not usually have time to prepare everything themselves, and both institutions and learners often demand regular use of the coursebook.

7.2.4.3 The place of writing in the presentation

In the procedure suggested above, the written form would usually be introduced after oral presentation, and probably oral practice. It is usually better to present items orally first and the written form later on, especially at beginner and elementary levels. There are at least two advantages to this.

First, it is easier to get the learners' attention and interest with a context or situation created orally than with a text printed in a book or sentences written on the board. Second, written forms in English can exert a strong distorting influence on learners' pronunciation.

However, there are exceptions to this order of presentation. A reading text may be used to help establish the initial presentation context, especially at higher levels when spelling and pronunciation are no longer a problem. Written texts will be used extensively when the goal of the course is focused principally on reading and/or writing skills.

When the written form is presented, it can be used to clarify and consolidate the oral presentation and practice. This is especially important for those learners who are more visually oriented. If they know from your regular system of teaching that they will soon see the written form, this will reduce any anxiety they may have during oral presentation and practice.

7.2.4.4 From presentation to practice

There is no clear dividing line between presentation and practice. Presentation normally develops into practice, often quite naturally. This can be seen in part of Extract 3 from the lesson we discussed previously:

T: Good... he's running on a running machine in the spaceship. And what is the spaceship doing?

S3: It's orbiting the earth.

T: OK! So, Ye Guangfu is running on a running machine. What about the others? Mm, Li Guangsu at the front? Li Cong in the middle? What's Li Guangsu doing? Anyone?

S4: Li Guangsu is do push-up.

T: Pardon, Li Yangyang? Do push-up?

S5: Er... Li Guangsu's doing push-ups.

T: Very good! What about Li Cong, in the middle? What's he doing? Anyone?

S6: Li Cong's exercising arm strength.

The teacher elicits models the class has already repeated, and then he elicits new models "created" by the learners themselves. This is the beginning of practice. In the early stages of practice, it is often necessary to move backward and forwards between practice and presentation, for example, with question-answer (Q-A combinations. In the lesson we examined above, the teacher handled the Q-A combination: What's __________ doing? He/she/it's __________ ing... in the following stages:

- Presentation of A (Extract 2)→Practice (Extract 2) → Presentation of Q (Extract 3)→ Practice (Extract 3)→Practice of Q-A (Extract 3)

This procedure could also be described in terms of who asks and who answers-the teacher (T) or the learner (L):

TQ—LA→LQ—TA→LQ—LA

While the learners were practising answers (TQ LA in Extract 3 they were listening and responding to the teacher's questions, so they became quite familiar with them.), the teacher simply needs to clarify the interrogative form and function when moving from practice of the answer to presentation of the question, and LQ—TA, then LQ—LA.

7.2.4.5 What happens in an effective presentation?

1. Attention

The students are engaged, directing their concentration toward the teacher and/or the subject matter to be grasped. It's essential to ensure that students are genuinely engaged. It is beneficial if the subject matter is regarded as engaging on its own.

2. Perception

The target material is perceived by students in a clear manner, whether through sight or sound. It often entails reiterating the information to provide additional chances for perception or to enhance retention. It is beneficial to elicit some form of feedback from them, such as through repetition or written exercises.

3. Understanding

The students grasp the significance of the introduced content and recognize how it relates to their prior knowledge (how it integrates into their established understanding of the world, or schema). Consequently, it may be necessary to clarify, create associations with past learning, and provide explanations. Feedback from the students, such as paraphrasing concepts in their own terminology, can offer valuable insights into their level of comprehension.

4. Short-term memory

It is essential for the students to transfer the information to their short-term memory in order to retain it. It's important to note that some individuals tend to retain information more effectively when it is visually presented, while others find it more memorable when linked to physical activities (visual, optimal presentations should ideally engage a variety of sensory experiences, including auditory and kinesthetic elements). After an extensive discussion has occurred,concluding with a concise summary of the central idea is beneficial.

Activity 3 Design a presentation process for students to learn and practice the structure "have sth done", making use of what you have learned in this part.

____

____

____

____

____

____

7.3 Practice

Engagement in practices can essentially be seen as the repetition of specific actions aimed at reinforcing learning and enhancing skills. A natural, instinctive understanding is essential for achieving ease and fluency in both comprehension and expression. This kind of understanding is typically achieved through repetitive practice.

7.3.1 The Function of Practice

According to Anderson (1981), the acquisition of skill through instructional lessons can be characterized as a tripartite progression consisting of verbalization, automatization, and autonomy.

Initially, the target skill can be articulated and illustrated through explanations that are both "verbalized and demonstrated. For instance, in a swimming lesson, the trainer might not only detail but also physically demonstrate the proper techniques for arm and leg movements; In language acquisition, the instructor might clarify the significance of a term or elaborate on grammatical rules, all while contextualizing these elements. It is important to recognize that students may produce verbalizations themselves after initial practice sessions highlighting specific components of the skill that require further attention. This process aligns closely with what has been referred to as "presentation" in earlier discussions.

The instructor then prompts the learners to showcase the specific behaviors, while keeping watch over their execution. Initially, mistakes may occur, necessitating corrections provided through additional explanations or demonstrations; As they continue to focus, students may eventually start performing the actions correctly. During this period, they engage in repeated practice of the skillful behavior, often through exercises provided by the instructor, until they can execute it automatically. At this stage, it can be said that they have made the behavior automatic, and they might forget how it was originally articulated.

Ultimately, students begin to apply the skills they have acquired and seek to enhance their abilities independently through additional practice. They start to increase their execution speed, explore or invent new combinations, and express their individuality; At this point, students become self-directed in their practice. While some refer to this phase as "production", it is misleading since it encompasses both reception and creation, representing a more sophisticated stage of practice as initially outlined in this unit. Students find they require minimal guidance from instructors, viewing them more as allies or catalysts for growth, and are close to achieving a mastery of the skill. A concise representation of this learning process is illustrated in Figure 7.3.

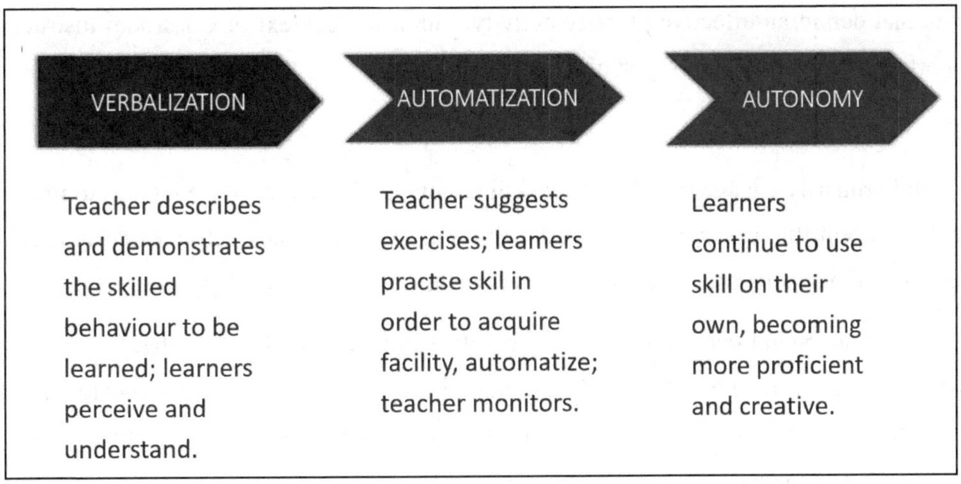

Figure 7.3 Skill learning model

A significant portion of language training aligns with the aforementioned skill-enhancement framework, but some of it does not: even in cases where learners have not consciously articulated or encountered the information, they can still internalize and develop language abilities and knowledge through engaging directly with texts or through communicative exercises. In essence, their learning begins during the stages of becoming automated and developing independence through fluency practice that lacks structure. Nonetheless, this remains a form of practice, which is crucial for effective learning.

Therefore, engaging in practice serves as the means by which individuals solidify and fully comprehend their language abilities and knowledge. Consequently, this aspect can be seen as a crucial phase in the overall learning process; a key responsibility for teachers in the classroom is to design and oversee exercises that facilitate meaningful practice for their students.

7.3.2 Traits of an Effective Practice Session

Regardless of your perspective on whether arranging language practice is the foremost responsibility of teachers in a classroom, it is undeniable that this organization plays a crucial role in facilitating effective language acquisition. Thus, it is important to consider the various elements that enhance the efficiency of classroom activities.

Practice typically occurs through methods referred to as "exercises" or "activities." The latter often denotes a greater degree of participation and initiative from students compared to the former, yet there is considerable overlap between the two concepts: numerous procedures can fit either category. Both exercises and activities may, of course, pertain to various dimensions of language learning; they might aim at reinforcing the comprehension of a specific grammatical element, for instance, enhancing the ability to comprehend spoken language, or developing proficiency in reading and writing, or the acquisition of word knowledge.

Key features that define an effective practice activity within the context of classroom instruction include several important aspects (Kington A., et. al., 2012).

1. Validity

Students should primarily engage in the specific skill or content that the exercise intends to focus on. This is a fundamental concept that is surprisingly overlooked. For instance, many activities designed for speaking have students spending more time listening to the instructor rather than speaking themselves.

It is important to understand that the term "validity" does not necessarily mean that the language must be employed for a direct replication of authentic communication. For instance, pronunciation exercises and vocabulary training can also be considered valid, provided that their primary objective is to practice and enhance the targeted elements.

2. Pre-learning

Students need to possess a solid foundation of the language they are supposed to practice, even if their ability to use or understand it is initially slow and requires careful consideration. Should the learners be tasked with an exercise involving content they have yet to familiarize themselves with, they will likely find themselves either entirely unable to participate or generating ineffective replies. In both scenarios, the exercise will likely prove ineffective in delivering the intended practice; rather, its primary role will serve as a diagnostic tool for the instructor to recognize and address the language skills that students have yet to acquire. Should they manage, albeit with some uncertainty, to deliver correct responses, this provides a solid foundation for engaging in further productive practice of the target language material.

3. Volume

Generally speaking, the greater the involvement students have with the language during the exercise, the greater their exposure to it will be. When the time allocated for the activity is viewed as a capacity holder, it should be maximized with a substantial amount of linguistic interaction. If there are periods where students are not participating in the target language for various reasons (such as being unchallenged at that time, due to the use of their native language, or because they are focused on managing the classroom or handling organizational matters, or due to distractions or off-topic discussions) leads to ineffective time usage regarding the practice activity.

4. The road to success

Overall, effective learning is reinforced by executing tasks correctly. Ongoing errors or inadequate performances can lead to the entrenchment of incorrect habits and a sense of frustration. Thus, it is essential to choose, structure, and implement practice tasks in a manner that increases the likelihood of learners achieving success. When students repeatedly accomplish their tasks, it fosters the development of automaticity regarding the skills being practiced along with promoting the learners' confidence as competent language users and motivating them to pursue additional challenges.

Achieving success does not equate to achieving flawless results! A classroom setting can effectively promote language practice in smaller groups, where errors may happen occasionally; in any case, the majority of responses are satisfactory, allowing for a significant amount of practice. This approach is often more advantageous compared to full-class engagement overseen by the teacher, which might yield completely accurate replies but sacrifice the overall practice volume and limit the active involvement of most students.

5. Heterogeneity

An effective exercise should cater to the varying skill levels present in the classroom, ensuring that most, if not all, participants can engage meaningfully. Presenting an activity that only requires input from a single level of understanding means that many students in the class will miss out on valuable learning opportunities.

Take into account the following component in an exercise focused on the concepts of ability and inability:

Jenny is an infant. Jenny has the ability to ride a bicycle (or she does not).

Individuals who lack assurance in their grasp of how to utilize "can" may choose not to attempt the question at all. Meanwhile, those at a more advanced level, capable of constructing far more intricate and engaging statements using the same structure, find themselves with no chance to do so, resulting in a lack of valuable practice at a suitable level for their abilities.

On the other hand, envision a scenario where the text and task are restructured as follows:

Jenny is an infant. She is able to grasp a toy and show a smile, yet she lacks the ability to ride a bike. What other abilities does Jenny have or not have?

As a result, the activity takes on a varied nature. Support has been offered to those who may struggle, through examples of responses, and all participants have been encouraged to engage at various levels suitable for them. Responses can range from basic statements, such as, "Jenny can drink milk", to more intricate and inventive forms like, "Jenny can't open a bank account." This approach allows a significantly larger number of students to engage and learn effectively.

6. Teacher support

A teacher's primary role, after suggesting an activity and providing precise directions, is to facilitate the students' successful execution. Should an assignment be given, and the teacher remains passive while students struggle with aimless conjectures or exhibit significant uncertainty, they are failing to assist effectively; evaluations and revisions that occur afterward, which provide valuable insights to learners regarding their errors, do not inherently provide opportunities for practice, in terms of aiding in the development of habitual responses. Should, however, you saved them, this enhances their likelihood of achieving success and improves the overall effectiveness of the practice activity. Such support could be provided by allowing ample time for contemplation, by providing guidance through prompting questions and suggestions that simplify the responses, by validating the initial parts of responses, thereby fostering further elaboration, or, in group work. By walking around the classroom to be accessible for queries. This approach allows for this also subtly communicates a distinct understanding of the teacher's role and mindset: the teacher genuinely desires the students to thrive in their studies and is dedicated to facilitating that success.

7. Interest

When the language tasks lack sufficient challenge due to their emphasis on achieving positive outcomes and there is excessive repetition of the intended structures, there is a significant risk that the practice will become monotonous. This monotony can lead not only to discomfort but also to disengagement. It can also result in students becoming disengaged, experiencing diminished enthusiasm, and consequently, achieving less effective learning outcomes.

However, if the thrill of overcoming the problem does not spark interest, it must be grounded in different facets of the endeavor: a captivating subject, the need to convey meaningful information, a game-like "fun" task, attention-catching materials, engage learners emotionally, or stimulate their cognitive abilities. For instance, an exercise designed to encourage students to practice constructing "yes-no" inquiries might simply require them to formulate questions based on brief prompts by converting declarative sentences into interrogative forms; however, this task will elicit more engaged and curious participation if the learners frame their inquiries as part of a meaningful exchange of information, such as deducing the contents of a teacher's bag or identifying a person's job.

7.3.3 The Difference Between Accuracy and Fluency Practice

Practice may emphasize formal accuracy or communicative fluency. In accuracy practice, errors are usually dealt with immediately, but, as much as possible, the teacher helps the learners to correct themselves. In fluency practice, errors are not usually corrected during activities, although the teacher may bring some errors to the learners' attention afterward. It is important to realize that presentation and practice of specific new items is only the beginning of the learning process. A great deal of communicative use, clarification, and remedial work is usually necessary to complete the learning of a language item or system.

The presentation and practice of new language items is a major part of most English language courses, but you should not forget the main goal of English language teaching is to enable learners to use English effectively in real communication. Some kind of context should normally be provided for the new items when you first present them. Presentation usually develops naturally into practice, and the context often means the practice has at least an element of communication.

Presentation and practice have some specific objectives that are not in them- selves communicative. In presentation, we expect learners to grasp how new items are structured and pronounced, as well as what they mean and how they are used in communication. The objectives of practice include enabling learners to recognize, pronounce, and manipulate new language items with some degree of subconscious automaticity. In other words, after practice, we want them to be able to make statements or ask and answer questions without always painfully constructing each sentence word by word.

To promote automaticity, practice usually includes some repetition of new language items. However, organized repetition can be only the very beginning of the learning process. Repetition in the sense of "repeated use in communication" is much more important. Repetition practice of new items often produces very unnatural discourse. Did anyone outside an English language classroom ever have a "conversation" like this?

A: Is there a chair in your bedroom?

B: Yes, there is. Is there a table in your bedroom?

A: No, there isn't. Is there a television in your bedroom?

B: No, there isn't. Is there a mirror in your bedroom?

This practice is more communicative than getting learners to say things like "There's a blackboard in this classroom". The learners are at least exchanging real information about their bedrooms while repeating the structures again and again.

This kind of practice activity could be made even more communicative if each learner had to find someone else with a specific item at home (for example, a computer, a bicycle, or a washing machine), and also some extra information about the item (for example, where it is kept, its age, or its make). This would mean the practice would require the use of more than just one structure or set of structures, for example:

A: Is there a computer in your house?

B: No, there isn't. Is there a washing machine in your house?

A: No, there isn't. Sorry. (A and B look for other people to ask.) Is there a computer in your house?

C: Yes, there is.

A: Ah, good! Where is it?

C : In my father's... er... studio.

A: Um...study. How old is it?

A distinction is often made between accuracy practice and fluency practice. Accuracy practice is intended to establish some correctness in the production of new items immediately after they are presented, or to correct errors later on. Fluency practice is intended to get the learners to use new items in more natural communication. In accuracy practice, learners are usually very aware that they are repeating the new item or items over and over again. They also know that they are expected to avoid errors. However, this does not mean that after accuracy practice they will always produce and use the new items correctly in real conversations. Anyone with experience of learning, using, or teaching a foreign language knows that errors persist. In fluency practice you should try to get the learners' attention off the language and onto the communication of ideas. Repetition, or repeated use, of the new items is important, but it should be naturally combined with other languages in communication. This means there may be more errors in fluency practice than in accuracy practice, but you should not normally interrupt learners to correct errors. Some teachers and learners feel unhappy with this tolerance of errors, but it is simply what will happen when learners use English outside the classroom. Errors in foreign language learning cannot be avoided.

Activity 4 **Analyze which of the four class extracts below are probably intended as accuracy practice and which as fluency practice? Why?**

Extract 1

S1: Have you ever been to Prague?

S2: No I haven't. Have you?

S1: Yes. Its wonderful.

S2: How long did you stayed?

S1: One week.

S 2: The buildings are beautiful, yes?

S1: Yes, and the streets... the river...

S2: Ah. Have you ever been in Rome?

Extract 2

S1: Is the Neon bigger than the Chevy?

S2: Yes, it is. Is the Lexus cheap than...

T: Cheap... ?

S2: Is the Lexus cheaper than the Chevy?

S3: No, it isn't. Is the Lexus faster than the Neon?

S4: Yes, it is. Is prettier the Neon...

T: Is the...

Extract 3

S1: My TV is three years old.

S2: My TV is one hundred years old.

T: Really?

S2: No, but it is very old.

T: Ah, I see! And your TV, Alex?

S3: My TV has two years old.

T: My TV...

S3: ... is two years old.

T: Right. Ana. How old is your TV?

Extract 4

S1: Hello. My name's John Smith.

S2: Pleased to meet you. I'm Mary Swift.

S1: Where are you from, Mary?

S2: Ireland. And you?

S1: I'm from Australia. What you do?

S2: I'm a doctor. What do you do?

S1: Chef. What are you doing in Paris?

S2: I'm visiting a friend. And you?

S1: I'm study French.

Your answer:

____

____

____

____

Thinking and Doing

A. Discussion questions

1. What are the opening methods commonly used in English classroom teaching? Hew to judge whether the the opening is rational and effective?

2. How to move smoothly from presentation to practice?

B. Practice

Practice the following cases of presentation teaching plan.

Case: Teaching plan: Content: Part 1 Step2 Book2 dialogue

1) Please be careful.

2) Don't go too high.

3) I can't reach them.

4) It's dangerous.

5) Don't fall.

T: What's this? (While drawing a tree)

Ss: It's a tree.

T: Yes. It's a tree. It's a tall tree. (Drawing some apples on the tree)

What's on the tree?

Ss: There are some apples on it.

T: (Draw a ladder against the tree) What's this?

Ss: It's a ladder.

T: Yes. It's a ladder. It's a long ladder.

(Draw a girl on the ladder) This is He Jiajia.

What is she going to do?

Ss: She is going to pick the apples.

T: Yes. She is going to pick the apples. The apples are too high. (Draw a boy holding the ladder). This is Jack. He is holding the ladder. Class, look! Tall tree, long ladder. The apples are too high. He Jiajia is too short (or Her hands are too short). She can't reach the apples. She is going higher. Now she is in the tree. (Writing the word "reach" in red chalk) Now, class. What is Jack saying? (Now listen: What is Jack saying?)

Ss: Don't go too high...

T: (Help the Ss say) Please be careful! It's dangerous. Don't fall.(Writing down the underlined part on the blackboard.

C. Exercises for instructional skills

1. When a teacher says "You'd better talk in a more polite way when speaking to the elderly.", he/she is drawing the students' attention to the __________ of language use.

   A. fluency B. complexity C. accuracy D. appropriacy

2. Which of the following is least recommended at the lead-in stage in a reading class?

   A. Activating students' schemata of the topic.

   B. Giving advice on how to use reading strategies.

   C. Sharing background information about the text.

   D. Correcting language mistakes students have made.

3. What is being practised if a teacher asks students to read words like "cot, hot" and "dog, log"?

   A. Spelling and structure. B. Stress and sound.

   C. Minimal pairs. D. Phonetic symbols.

4. Which of the following practices can encourage students to read an article critically?

   A. Evaluating its point of view. B. Finding out the facts.

   C. Finding detailed information. D. Doing translation exercises.

5. Which of the following practices is most likely to encourage students' cooperation in learning?

   A. Doing a project. B. Having a dictation

   C. Taking a test D. Copying a text.

6. All the following activities aim to develop students' oral fluency except__________.

   A. role-playing B. making sentences with given words

   C. retelling a story D. doing an oral report

7. If a teacher asks students to pay attention to the tense when making up dialogues, he/she focuses on __________.

   A. accuracy B. fluency C. appropriacy D. content

8. If a teacher wants to organize retelling exercises in class and every student has a chance to practice, he/she had better direct the students to work at __________.

   A. whole class level B. group level

   C. pair level D. individual level

9. In communicative output activities, the criterion of success is whether the learner gets the message across. _________ is not a consideration unless the lack of it influences the understanding of the message.

A. Accuracy B. Consistency C. Fluency D. Intelligibility

10. Which of the following statements is NOT true?

A. Practice is usually carried out through procedures called "exercises" or "activities".

B. Presentation and practice have specific objectives that are communicative.

C. Sometimes presentation and practice cannot be separated totally.

D. Fluency practice is intended to get the learners to use new items in more natural communication.

Checklist

Mark the questions with a check (√) if your answer is yes.

☐ Have I understood the concepts of principles of opening, presentation, and practice?

☐ Have I grasped the components of opening, presentation, and practice?

☐ Have I known the interrelationship between the opening, presentation, and practice?

☐ Can I integrate the methods and strategies of opening, presentation, and practice into lesson design and teaching practice?

Reflective Journal

Please write down your reflections on what you have / have not learned in this chapter.

◇ The essential skills I need to possess and develop for English teaching:

____

____

____

____

◇ Anything I wish to further explore (i.e., puzzles and difficulties):

____

____

____

____

References

Anderson, J. R. (1981). *Cognitive skills and their acquisition*. Taylor & Francis Group.

Kington, A., Sammons, P., Day, C., Gu, Q. (2012). What makes teachers effective?: Profiles of innovative classroom practice. In C. Day (Ed.), *The Routledge international handbook of teacher and school development*. Routledge.

McGrath, I., Davies, S., & Mulphin, H. (1992). *Lesson beginnings. Edinburgh Working Papers in Applied Linguistics*, 3, 92–108.

Chapter 8

Questioning, Feedback, and Correcting Skills

Objectives

Upon completion of this chapter, you should be able to:

- Understand the concepts of questioning, feedback, and correcting
- Remember the types of questioning, feedback, and correcting
- Integrate the methods of questioning, feedback, and correcting properly into practical teaching.

Discussion Questions

Chinese people often say, "Everything is difficult at the beginning," and also, "A good beginning is half the battle." What do you think are the criteria to have a good start?

Classroom questioning and feedback are essential components of effective teaching. They are crucial for fostering student engagement, promoting critical thinking, and supporting continuous learning.

8.1 Classroom Questioning

Classroom questioning is a crucial aspect of effective teaching and learning. It serves as a bridge between teachers and students, fostering communication, enhancing comprehension, and promoting critical thinking. This guide outlines the principles, techniques, and strategies for effective classroom questioning, along with practical examples and references.

8.1.1 Reasons for Questioning

According to Ur (2000) , the reasons why a teacher asks questions in the classroom teaching may be varied. Look through the following list of reasons rummarized by Ur P. in Figure 8.1, and add any more that you can think of.

- To provide a model for language or thinking.
- To find out something from the learners (facts, ideas, opinions).
- To check or test understanding, knowledge or skill.
- To get learners to be active in their learning.
- To direct attention to the topic being learned.
- To inform the class via the answers of the stronger learners rather than through the teacher's input.
- To provide weaker learners with an opportunity to participate.
- To stimulate thinking (logical, reflective or imaginative); to probe more deeply into issues;
- To get learners to review and practise previously learnt material.
- To encourage self-expressiotn.
- To communicate to learners that the teacher is genuinely interested in what they think.

(Note: Any specific question is likely to involve more than one of these aims; for example, it might review and practice while simultaneously encouraging self-expression.)

Figure 8.1 Reasons for questioning

8.1.2 Types of Classroom Questions

There are many different ways to classify questions, and as researchers have observed it is sometimes difficult to arrive at discrete and directly observable categories. For the purposes of examining the role of questions in the classroom, three kinds of questions are distinguished: procedural, convergent, and divergent (Wilen, W., 2003).

8.1.2.1 Categories of classroom questions by functions

1. Procedural Questions

As opposed to the content of learning, procedural questions are connected with classroom procedures and routines, as well as classroom management. The examples of the following questions show that the teacher is checking whether the assignments have been finished, directions for a task are clear, and students are prepared for a new activity.

- Did everyone bring their homework?

- *Do you all understand what I want you to do? How much more time do you need?*

- *Can you all read what I've written on the blackboard? Did anyone bring a dictionary to class?*

- *Why aren't you doing the assignment?*

2. Convergent questions

Convergent questions encourage similar student responses, or responses which focus on a central theme. These responses are often short answers, such as "yes" or "no" or short statements. They do not usually require students to engage in higher-level thinking in order to come up with a response but often focus on the recall of previously presented information. Language teachers often ask a rapid sequence of convergent questions to help develop aural skills and vocabulary and to encourage whole-class participation before moving on to some other teaching technique. For example, the following questions were used by a teacher in introducing a reading lesson focusing on the effects of computers on everyday life. Before the teacher began the lesson she led students into the topic of the reading by asking the following convergent questions:

- *How many of you have a personal computer in your home? Do you use it every day?*

- *What do you mainly use it for?*

- *What are some other machines that you have in your home? What are the names of some computer companies?*

- *What is the difference between software and hardware?*

3. Divergent questions

Divergent questions are the opposite of convergent questions. They encourage diverse student responses which are not short answers and which require students to engage in higher-level thinking. They encourage students to provide their own information rather than to recall previously presented information. For example, after asking the convergent questions above, the teacher went on to ask divergent questions such as the following:

- *How have computers had an economic impact on society?*

- *How would businesses today function without computers?*

- *Do you think computers have had any negative effects on society?*

- *What are the best ways of promoting the use of computers in education?*

8.1.2.2 Categories of classroom questions by cognitive level

Questions have been classified according to various different criteria, for example:

What kind of thinking they try to elicit (plain recall, for example, analysis, or evaluation);

Whether they are "genuine" or "display" questions (does the teacher really want to know the answer, or is he or she simply checking if the student does?);

Whether they are closed-or open-ended (do they have a single right answer or many?), and many others.

Following are seven categories of questions, mainly based on Bloom' cognitive level, ranging from display questions to referential questions, with typical classroom question words associated with each category (adapted from Kinsella, 1991, and Bloom, 1956) (see Table 8.1).

Table 8.1 Categories of questions

Categories	Functions	Common question words
Knowledge questions	Eliciting factual answers, testing recall and recognition of information	Define. Tell. List. Identify. Describe. Select. Name. Point out. Reproduce. Who? What? Where? When? Answer "yes" or " no".
Comprehension questions	Interpreting, extrapolating	State in your own words. Explain. Define. Locate.
Application questions	Applying information heard or read to new situations.	Demonstrate how. Use the data to solve. Illustrate how. Show how. Apply. Construct. Explain. What is used for? What would result? What would happen?
Inference questions	Forming conclusions that are not directly stated in instructional materials.	How? Why? What did mean? By what does believe? What conclusions can you draw from?
Analysis questions	Breaking down into parts, relating parts to the whole	Distinguish. Diagram. Chart. Plan. Deduce. Arrange. Separate. Outline. Classify. Contrast. Compare. Differentiate. Categorize. What is the relationship between? What is the function of? What motive? What conclusions? What is the main idea?
Synthesis questions	Combining elements into a new pattern	Compose. Build. Combine. Estimate. Invent. Choose. Hypothesize. Solve. Design. Develop. What if? How would you test? What would you have done in this situation? What would happen if? How can you improve? How else would you?
Evaluation question	Making a judgment of good and bad, right or wrong, according to some set of criteria, and stating why	Evaluate. Rate. Defend. Dispute. Judge. Decide which. Select, Grade. Verify. Choose why. Which is best? Which is more important? Which do you think is more appropriate?

All of these types of questions have their place in the interactive classroom.

Even those that are more on the display end of the continuum are very useful in eliciting both content and language from students. Usually, the higher the proficiency level you teach the more you can venture into the upper, referential end of the continuum. One interesting study of high intermediate pre-university ESL students (Brock, 1986) found that teachers who incorporated more referential questions into their classes stimulated student responses that were longer and more grammatically complex. Make sure, then, that you challenge your students sufficiently but without overwhelming them.

8.1.3 Common Considerations for Using Questioning

In view of the importance of questioning as a teaching strategy, the skill with which teachers use questions has received a considerable amount of attention in teacher education. Among the issues that have been identified are the following.

8.1.3.1 Teachers' preference for question types

It has often been observed that teachers tend to ask more convergent than divergent questions. These questions serve to facilitate the recall of information rather than to generate student ideas and classroom communication. Since convergent questions require short answers, they may likewise provide limited opportunities for students to produce and practice the target language. Long and Sato (1983) compared the number of "display questions" (questions that teachers know the answer to and which are designed to elicit or display particular structures) and "referential questions" (questions that teachers do not know the answers to) in naturalistic classroom discourse. They found that in naturalistic discourse referential questions are more frequent than display questions, whereas display questions are much more frequent in whole-class teaching in ESL classrooms.

8.1.3.2 Student participation

In many classrooms, students have few opportunities to ask questions on their own, although they may be given the opportunity to answer questions. Even when teachers give students opportunities to ask and answer questions, they may address their questions to only a few of the students in the class-those lying within their action zone. Jackson and Lahaderne (1967) found that some students are twenty-five times more likely to be called on to speak in a class than others. In language classrooms, where students may be of different levels of ability, the fact that some students have much more difficulty answering questions than others may lead the teacher to call on only those students in the class who can be relied upon to answer the question in order to maintain the momentum of the class. This reinforces the teacher's tendency to direct questions to only certain students in the class.

8.1.3.3 Wait-time

An important dimension of a teacher's questioning skills is wait-time, that is, the length of time the teacher waits after asking the question before calling on a student to answer it, rephrasing the question, directing the question to another student, or giving the answer. Teachers often use a very short wait-time (e.g., one second)., which is rarely sufficient to enable students to respond. When wait-time is increased to three to five seconds, the amount of student participation as well as the quality of that participation often increases.

8.1.4 Effective Questioning

There are a few basic principles that would seem to characterize effective questions within the conventional IRF structure, defining 'effective questions' in terms of the desired response. As language teachers, our motive in questioning is usually to get our students to engage with the language material actively through speech; so an effective questioning technique is one that elicits fairly prompt, motivated, relevant and full responses. If, on the other hand, our questions result in long silences, or are answered by only the strongest students, or obviously bore the class, or consistently elicit only very brief or unsuccessful answers, then there is probably something wrong.

Some useful criteria for effective questioning for language teachers are suggested in Figure 8.2.

1. **Clarity:** Do the learners immediately grasp not only what the question means, but also what kind of an answer is required?
2. **Learning value:** Does the question stimulate thinking and responses that will contribute to further learning of the target material? Or is it irrelevant, unhelpful or merely time-filling?
3. **Interest:** Do learners find the question interesting, challenging, stimulating?
4. **Availability:** Can most of the members of the class try to answer it? Or only the more advanced, confident, and knowledgeable? (Note that the mere addition of a few seconds' wait-time before accepting a response can make the question available to a significantly larger number of learners.)
5. **Extension:** Does the question invite and encourage extended and/or varied answers?
6. **Teacher reaction:** Are the learners sure that their responses will be related to with respect, that they will not be put down or ridiculed if they say something inappropriate?

Figure 8.2 Criteria for effective questioning

Activity 1 **Look at the following four exchanges, which are loosely based on events observed in classrooms. Identify what the purpose of the teacher is in questioning, and comment on the way he or she went about it, perhaps applying the criteria suggested above?**

Exchange 1

T: Now today we are going to discuss circuses. Have you ever been to a circus?

Ss: (immediately) Yes, yes.

T: Yes. Where you see clowns, horses elephants, and acrobats...

Exchange 2

T: Yesterday we learned various words that express feelings. Can you tell me what does "relief" mean? (pause)

Well, when might you feel relief? (pause)

Can you remember a time when you felt relief? Yes, Maria?

S1: When my friend was late, I thought he wasn't coming and then he came.

T: Good. Fran?

S2: I thought I would fail the exam, and then in the end, I passed.

T: Good. Now, "fear"?

Exchange 3

T: Right, what was the story about? Can anyone tell me? Claire?

S: Man.

T: Yes, a man. What did this man do? Can you tell me anything about him?

S: He... married.

Exchange 4

T: Here's a picture, with lots of things going on. Tell me some of them. For example: the policeman is talking to the driver, perhaps he's telling him where to go. What else?

S1: The little girl is buying an ice-cream.

S2: There's a woman, old woman, in the middle, she's crossing the road.

S3: A man... sitting... on a chair...

T: OK, a man is sitting on a chair, there in the corner. What else?

Your comments on the above exchange:

Extract 1:____

____

____

____

____

____

____

Extract 2: ____

____

____

____

____

____

____

Extract 3: ____

____

____

____

____

____

____

Extract 4: ____

____

____

____

____

____

8.2 Giving Feedback

Classroom feedback is the immediate and ongoing communication process within the classroom setting, where teachers convey information to students (and vice versa) about the progress, comprehension, or participation in learning activities. This process helps to clarify concepts, address misconceptions, motivate learners, and ultimately guide both teachers and students towards achieving educational goals more effectively. It encompasses both verbal and nonverbal communication, as well as formative and summative assessments, aimed at fostering a dynamic and responsive learning environment.

Some examples of feedback in language teaching are as follows:

- the words "Yes, right!", said to a learner who has answered a question;
- a grade of 70% on an exam;
- a raised eyebrow in response to a mistake in grammar;
- comments written in the margin of an essay.

8.2.1 Principles of Effective Classroom Feedback

1. Timeliness

Feedback should be provided promptly after the relevant learning activity. This ensures that students can quickly correct mistakes and reinforce correct understanding. For example, during a speaking activity, teachers should not interrupt students unless absolutely necessary. Instead, feedback can be given after the student has finished speaking.

2. Specificity

Feedback should be specific and focused on the specific learning objectives. Avoid vague comments like "good" or "not good." Instead, provide concrete examples and explanations to help students understand what they did well and what needs improvement. Specific feedback enables students to understand their strengths and weaknesses clearly. For instance, saying "You did well, but you should pay more attention to your pronunciation" is more effective than simply saying "Good job."

3. Positivity and encouragement

Feedback should be delivered in a positive and encouraging manner. Avoid negative criticism that may discourage students. Instead, emphasize their strengths and offer constructive suggestions for improvement. Teachers should use expressions like "I'm sure you can do this" and "You did well, but you can do better next time" to motivate students and eliminate their fear of making mistakes.

4. Interactivity

Feedback should involve two-way communication between teachers and students. Encourage students to ask questions and express their opinions. This promotes active learning and engagement. Two-way communication is crucial for effective feedback. Teachers should ask open-ended questions and encourage students to reflect on their learning.

8.2.2 Strategies for Feedback

Use multiple forms of feedback: Incorporate both verbal and nonverbal forms of feedback. Verbal feedback includes specific comments and questions, while nonverbal feedback includes gestures, facial expressions, and body language.

Focus on process rather than just results: Feedback should not only focus on final outcome but also on learning process. Acknowledge students' efforts and strategies used to achieve their results. Emphasizing the learning process encourages students to reflect on their strategies and improve their future performance.

Encourage self- and peer-assessment: Promote self-assessment and peer-assessment to help students develop critical thinking and self-reflection skills. This also encourages collaboration and mutual support among students. Self- and peer-assessment can help students develop a deeper understanding of their strengths and weaknesses.

Use technology and multimedia: Leverage technology and multimedia tools to enhance feedback. For example, use recording devices to capture students' speaking and provide audio feedback. Multimedia tools can provide a more engaging and interactive feedback experience for students.

8.2.3 Feedback Presentation in Classroom Teaching

8.2.3.1 Feedback on content

Different forms of feedback can be used to reflect the content in teaching.

Suggesting a correct answer. For example, the teacher says: "Good," "Yes, that's right," or "Fine."

Indicating incorrect answers. For example, the teacher says: "No, that's not quite right," or "Mmm."

Showing praise. For example, the teacher compliments a student by saying: "Yes, an excellent answer."

Modifying an answer. The teacher replies to some unclear or incomplete answers by providing more information or rephrasing the answer. For example:

T: Does anyone know the capital of the United States?

S: Washington.

T: Yes, Washington, D.C. That's located on the east coast.

Repeating an answer. The teacher repeats the answer given by the student as an affirmation.

Summarizing. The teacher summarizes what the student has said.

Criticizing. The teacher criticizes the student's response. For example:

T: Raymond, can you point out the topic sentence in this paragraph?

S: The first sentence.

T: How can it be the first sentence? Remember, I said the first sentence is not always the topic sentence in every paragraph. Look again!

8.2.3.2 Feedback on form

In language classroom teaching, feedback is often directed toward the accuracy of student's responses. A lot of possibilities are involved in error feedback. These include decisions about:

- whether the student's errors should be corrected,
- which kinds of student's errors should be corrected,
- how student's errors should be corrected (Hendrickson, 1978).

Both students and teachers have different preferences for error correction. Nunan (1988) reports that adult learners in Australia regarded error correction as very important, while their teachers did not value it as highly. Similar findings have been found elsewhere by Chaudron (1988). He finds that are most likely to correct content errors, followed by vocabulary errors, and errors of grammar or pronunciation (Chaudron 1988).

In language teaching, how learner errors should be corrected has been a focus of considerable discussion (Harmer, 1991; Omaggio, 1986). Feedback on form can be accomplished in different ways, such as:

- Asking the student to repeat what he or she said.
- Pointing out the error and asking the student to self-correct.
- Commenting on an error and explaining why it is wrong, without having the student repeat the correct form.
- Asking another student to correct the error.
- Using a gesture to indicate that an error has been made.

The following example illustrates the different kinds of feedback teachers give during classroom interaction. The teacher is questioning students about when they began their studies.

T: When did you start? (nominates by gesture)

S4: I start in the research on the eleventh of January.

T: When did you arrive? You arrived on the eleventh of January, did you?

You must have started the next day, did you?

S2: The eleventh of January.

S5: No, we start at thirteenth.

T: On the thirteenth of January. When did you start the research? (nominates by gesture)

S1: I start at research on the thirteenth of January.

T: On the thirteenth of January.

S1: Yes.

T: Again.

S1: I start at the research on the thirteenth of January.

T: Eulyces (pause) I started.

S2: I stotted .

T: Started.

S1: Start.

S2: I...( ) (aside to S1 in Spanish) I start on the research on the fourteen of January.

T: I.

S2: Fourteenth January.

T: I started at research on the thirteenth of January. All right Eulyces: on the thirteenth of January ...

S2: On the the...

T: Thirteenth.

S2: On the fourteenth of January.

T: Of January.

S2: Of January.

T: On the thirteenth of January.

S2: On fourteenth of January.

T: All together... on the thirteenth SSS On the thirteenth of January.

T: All right. I started at the research (gestures for choral response) .

Ss: I started at the research on the thirteenth of January.

T: Good. Good. Were you at university before?

(*Allwright, 1984*)

In this example, the teacher gives feedback for correcting both the form and the content of the student's response. At the very beginning of the dialogue, the teacher neglects the grammatical errors but picks up the factual error relating to the date. After the students figure out the correct date the teacher provides a model of the correct phrase. In the next utterance, the student makes an error in verb tense form. The teacher neglects this error, confirms the correct date, and then asks the student to repeat. The verb tense error occurs again and the teacher calls on a different student. The student hesitates and the teacher models the beginning of the sentence with the correct verb tense. The student makes an error in pronunciation, which the teacher corrects by modeling the correct form. However, the student, after consulting another student in Spanish, repeats another student's error rather than using the form provided by the teacher. The teacher remodels the sentence, seems to realize S2's difficulties, and then re-models the final phrase. At the end of the extract, the teacher transfers the error treatment to the whole class through choral repetition.

Teachers often provide imprecise feedback on student errors. They tend only to repeat the correct language form rather than indicating to the student where the error occurred and why it was wrong. Teachers may also be inconsistent in whom they correct and which errors they correct. For example, they may correct errors made by some students but not by others, and they may sometimes correct an error of tense but at other times ignore it. Therefore, teachers should implement a more consistent way of error correction so as to avoid confusion among students.

The need for feedback on errors can also be lessened by reducing the student error rate during practice activities. The following are some suggestions as to how this can be accomplished:

- Break down the instruction into smaller steps. Give the students instruction and practice to mastery each step before proceeding to the next step.
- Provide the students with very explicit demonstrations of the skills whenever possible.
- Intersperse the demonstration with questions in order to maintain students' attention and to check for student understanding.
- Provide the students with teacher-monitored practice prior to seat-work activity so that the teacher can correct errors before they become part of the students' repertoire.
- With especially confusing material, provide pre-corrections by advising the students about particularly confusing areas.
- Provide sufficient independent practice—both in length and number of exercises—to enable students to master skills to the point of over-learning (with additional exercises for the slower students).
- Re-teach the material when necessary.

Activity 2 **The following are teachers' classroom teaching segments. Please analyze the two teachers' ways of feedback. How to improve the second teacher's feedback in Segment 2?**

Segment 1:

T: Turn to page 21, and tell me your answer to question 1 "Can the driver see the bus in the picture?"

S1: Yes, he can.

T: Yes, he can? Do you really think so? In the first paragraph, there is a sentence: "On one side the mountain rises steeply; on the other side there is a sheer drop. It's a bend". What does it mean?

S1: No, he can't, as there is a bend on the road.

T: Quite right.

Segment 2:

T: Why is the marathon the last Olympic event?

S2: I don't know.

T: Did you listen to me carefully?

S2: ...

T: You can sit down.

Your answer:

____

____

____

____

____

____

8.3 Correcting

Correcting refers to the method for teachers to correct students' misuse of the English language such as pronunciation, spelling, vocabulary, grammar, discourse, etc., in the activities of practicing listening, speaking, reading, and writing. It can help students cultivate good language learning habits and improve their oral and written language skills.

8.3.1 The Relationship Between Feedback and Error Correction

Feedback and error correction are closely linked and mutually reinforcing in the teaching process. On the one hand, feedback provides the necessary information and basis for error correction; on the other hand, error correction is the direct manifestation and deepening of feedback results. Specifically:

Feedback is the prerequisite for error correction: Without feedback, students cannot understand their learning status and where their errors lie, making it impossible for them to conduct targeted error correction.

Error correction is the extension of feedback: Feedback points out students' errors and deficiencies, while error correction involves an in-depth analysis and rectification process aimed at these errors and deficiencies. Error correction is not merely a simple negation of errors but also an in-depth analysis of their causes and an active exploration of correct methods.

Feedback and error correction reinforce each other: Through the continuous cycle of feedback and error correction, students can gradually improve their learning abilities and levels. At the same time, teachers can continuously adjust their teaching strategies and methods based on the results of feedback and error correction to meet students' learning needs and development levels.

8.3.2 Aims for Correction

Students might be wary of making a mistake and thus don't often volunteer answers to the teacher's questions. Mistakes are a "bad thing"—not really to be encouraged—evidence that they have not been working properly, or are lazy or a little bit stupid.

Yet in most things, humans largely learn by trial and error, experimenting to see what works and what does not. And if fear of getting it wrong prevents you from doing something in the first place, then you are very unlikely to move forward or learn anything at all.

Many teachers nowadays regard student errors as evidence that progress is being made. Errors often show us that a student is experimenting with language, trying out ideas, taking risks, attempting to communicate, and making progress. Analyzing what errors have been made clarifies exactly where the student has reached and helps set the syllabus for future language work. In dealing with errors, teachers have looked for correction techniques that, rather than simply giving students the answer on a plate, help them to make their connections. This may raise their awareness about the language they are using.

What you tell me, I forget; what I discover for myself, I remember. To summarize, our aims when correcting might include:

- building confidence;
- raising awareness;

- acknowledging achievement and progress;
- helping students to become more accurate in their use of language.

8.3.3 Techniques for Correction

Sometimes language can be grammatically correct but completely inappropriate in the context in which it is used. Errors can also be made in intonation and rhythm; in fact wrong intonation seems to cause more unintended offence to native speakers than almost any other kind of error. So five teacher decisions should be made when working with (oral) errors in class:

- What kind of error has been made (Grammatical? Pronunciation?)?
- Whether to deal with it (Is it useful or correct it?)?
- When to deal with it (Now? End of activity? Later?)?
- Who will correct (Teacher? Student self-correction? Other students?)?
- Which technique to use to indicate that an error has occurred or to enable correction?

1. What to correct

In teaching, error correction is a crucial aspect that aids students in identifying and rectifying mistakes made during the learning process, thereby facilitating the mastery of knowledge and enhancement of skills. Regarding "what to correct," we can delve into the following aspects:

Linguistic accuracy

Grammatical Errors: Including improper usage of tense, voice, subject-verb agreement, articles, prepositions, and subordinate clause connectors.

Spelling Errors: Misspelled words directly impact the communication of information, necessitating special attention to the spelling rules of common words.

Punctuation: The correct use of punctuation, such as commas, periods, question marks, and quotation marks, is vital for conveying the intended meaning of sentences.

Content accuracy

Factual Errors: Ensuring that the information or data presented by students is accurate and avoiding the dissemination of misinformation.

Logical Errors: Examining the coherence of the logical chain in students' arguments and verifying that the evidence supports the thesis.

Clarity of expression

Sentence Structure: Encouraging students to employ clear and concise sentence structures to articulate complex ideas.

Word Choice: Guiding students to select appropriate vocabulary based on context, avoiding inappropriate or overly obscure words.

Coherence: Ensuring smooth transitions between paragraphs and sentences for a fluid overall expression.

Cultural sensitivity

Cultural Customs: When teaching foreign languages or cross-cultural communication, paying attention to and correcting potential cultural misunderstandings or offensive expressions.

Value Differences: Guiding students to understand and respect the value differences across different cultural backgrounds, preventing unintentional offenses in their expressions.

2. Whether to correct

An important consideration is the aim of the activity. Is it to improve learners' accurate use of English? If this is the case, then immediate correction is much more appropriate than in an activity where fluency is the objective (and interruptions and corrections might get in the way of the work).

There are other factors to take into account when deciding if a correction should be made:

- Will it help or hinder learning?
- Am I correcting something they haven't learned yet?

  (If so there doesn't seem much point.)
- How will the student take the correction?
- What is my intention in correcting?

3. When to correct

immediately;	after a few minutes;	at the end of the activity;
later in the lesson;	at the end of the lesson;	in the next lesson;
later in the course;	never.	

The options include:

If the objective is accuracy, then immediate correction is more likely to be useful; if the aim is fluency, then immediate correction is less appropriate and any correction will probably come after the activity has finished or later (see Table 8.2).

Table 8.2 Objectives determing correction time

Main objectives of the speaking activity	When to correct
accuracy	immediately (or later or not at all)
Fluency	later (or not at all)

Since fluency is about effective communication without much hesitation, interrupting an activity in order to correct a student could kill the activity. You should not interrupt activities too often. Do so only when many learners are making the same basic error, or when errors interfere with communication. Instead, while the students are working, you can monitor the activity, listen in discreetly, and note common errors. After the activity has finished, teachers can write sentences with significant errors on the board-without saying who made the errors, get the students to, discuss, identify, and correct them, or use this list of errors to set an exercise, plan the next lesson, etc.

4. Who corrects

In classroom teaching and learning, who can be the main subjects for the correction?

Figure 8.3 shows the different correcting subjects.

Figure 8.3 Who corrects?

5. How to correct

This question concerns techniques to indicate that an error has been made or to give or invite correction. There are different ways and techniques for correcting errors, such as direct teacher correction, indirect teacher correction, self-correction, peer correction, whole class correction, etc. The following are some specific ways:

- Tell them (e.g. *There's an error in that sentence*).
- Facial expression: surprise; frown; raised eyebrows; interest.
- Gesture combined with facial expression (e.g. *worried look and hand out—stretched to "hold" the sentence—you won't let the class move on until they deal with the sentence you are holding*).
- Finger correction (hold on to the "error" finger, e.g the third word.).
- Repeat sentence up to error (e.g. *They looked for a*...?).
- Echo sentence with changed intonation or stress (e.g. *You go to a disco yesterday? or He wanted to eat a kitchen*?)

This is a use of echo with a clear purpose.

- Ask a question (e.g. *Was this last week*?).
- Ask a one-word question (e.g. *Tense? Past?*).
- Draw a time line on the board.
- Draw spaces or boxes on the board to show the number of words in a sentence. Indicate which word is the problem.
- Write the problem sentence on the board for discussion.
- Exploit the humor in the error

  (e.g. *Student: The doctor gave her a recipe. Teacher: So she made a nice cake? Student: Oh not the right word?*

  Another student: Prescription.)

This technique is often more amusing for the teacher than for the students!

- Use the phonemic chart to point at an incorrect phoneme.
- Teacher reformulation (i.e. tell them the correction). Sometimes this may be the quickest, most appropriate, most useful way of helping.
- Encourage student self-correction or student-student correction

The following two steps can be used:

- Indicate an error has been made. You may also indicate what kind of error it is, where in a sentence the error is, etc.

- Invite correction or help the student towards a correction.

The "chain" is one important student-student correction technique: If student A makes an error, the teacher elicits a correction from student B. If she also fails to get it right then he gets another student C to help her. This is where the chain comes in: C corrects B, and only when B has got the idea, does B then correct A. A then gives the correct answer back to the teacher. The effect of this is to involve many people in thinking about the problem and finding a solution; done effectively, the errors and their corrections can be passed around the class like a ball of string unwinding, tying together a network of enquiry and support (see Figure 8.4).

Figure 8.4 How to correct

8.3.4 Correction Sequence

Self-correction

Teachers do not themselves correct the learners' errors—they help the learners to self-correct. The trick is to first give learners the opportunity, encourage them to identify some errors, get them used to self-correcting, helping as necessary because if it is an error, the student himself/herself will be able to correct it. If the student cannot self-correct, it means there is a lack of competence and the teacher can help with the correction or may ask other students to help correct it.

Peer-correction

If a learner cannot self-correct, teachers should invite other learners to make the correction. Peer correction should be handled sensitively: for example, do not always call on the same "good" learners to correct the same "weak" ones.

Whole classroom correction

Sometimes, the whole class can be invited to correct as well. For example, you can select the main error types. Write four or five on the blackboard. Put students in pairs for a few minutes to discuss and correct the errors. Then the whole class can do the correction together. The focus can be the choice of vocabulary, use of grammar, or pronunciation. With higher-level learners you can also focus on appropriate context, e.g. *"Was the expression polite enough?" "Was it too formal?"*

Indirect teacher correction

If no other learner can make the correction, the teacher should make the correction yourself. Indirect techniques include "repeating the problem sentence with an emphasis on the problem in a rising tone", "asking a question to invite the student to say it again with a hint of a problem", "a simple repetition of a correct sentence as a model", and "using facial expression or gesture to indicate a problem", etc.

Direct teacher correction

Direct error correction means that the teacher directly points out the students' errors, which might plunge them into some awkward situations.

As a general rule, indirect teacher correction is encouraged rather than direct teacher correction to avoid damaging students' self-esteem and confidence.

In sum, when teachers decide to intervene to correct errors, the recommended self→peer→teacher correction sequence is fulfilled. But the following two considerations should be given much attention.

- Speaking and making errors in a foreign language with the rest of the class looking and listening makes most learners nervous. Teachers should consider the learners' sensitivities as well as the language teaching objectives.
- If self- and peer-correction fail, and teachers eventually have to make the correction themselves, it may mean something went wrong in the earlier stages of the lesson, and some aspects of the presentation may need to be repeated.

Activity 3 **Read the following examples of learner errors and decide on an efficient way of indicating what is wrong or correcting it. Practice with your partner.**

a. I am boring with this lesson!

b. I enjoy to swim.

c. He brokened the car.

d. I go to the party last Saturday.

e. I'd like some informations about the plane times.

Write down the teaching steps for one or two of the examples.

____

____

____

____

____

____

Thinking and Doing

A. Questions for discussion

1. What are the main types of questions? Generally speaking, What is the proper proportion of the questions distributed in the classroom teaching?
2. What is the relationship between feedback and correction? Discuss within your group by giving some examples.
3. What methods can teachers use to provide feedback on student's error?

B. Practice

Match the errors in the following list with their descriptions.

Errors	Descriptions
1. He like this school.	a. pronunciation (/ɪ/ vs /iː/)
2. Where you did go yesterday?	b. pronunciation (/ʃ/ vs /ʧ/)
3. Give me one butter bread!	c. grammar (wrong tense)
4. I eat chocolate every day.	d. lexis (incorrect collocation)
5. After three years, they made a divorce.	e. grammar (verb-noun agreement)
6. I am here since Tuesday.	f. grammar (word order)
7. I'm going to heat you.	g. lexis (incorrect word, and rude!)

Answers 1._____ 2._____ 3._____ 4._____ 5. _____ 6. _____ 7. _____

C. Exercises for instructional skills

1. What type of questions is more likely to motivate learners to talk more and get new information?

A. Yes-no question.　　B. Closed question.

C. Referential question.　　D. Display question.

2. When a teacher says "What do you mean by that?", he/she is asking the students for __________.
   A. repetition B. suggestion C. introduction D. clarification

3. Which of the following is a display question?
   A. What part of speech is "immense"?
   B. How would you comment on this report?
   C. Why do you think Hemingway is a good writer?
   D. What do you think of the characters in this novel?

4. Which of the following is a referential question?
   A. Where was Yang Liwei born?
   B. Who is the first Chinese astronaut?
   C. Why do you think Yang Liwei is a great astronaut?
   D. When did Yang Liwei begin his historic space travel?

5. The most suitable question type to check students' comprehension and develop their critical thinking is __________.
   A. rhetorical questions B. referential questions
   C. closed questions D. display questions

6. Which of the following types of questions can least elicit students' ideas?
   A. Display questions. B. Divergent questions.
   C. Open questions. D. Evaluation questions.

7. Which of the following is a referential question used by a teacher in class?
   A. Who is the laureate of Nobel Prize for Literature in 2019?
   B. Where did the 2008 Olympic Games take place?
   C. What's the highest mountain in the world?
   D. How can we become good learners?

8. Which of the following is a closed question?
   A. What are the advantages of jogging?
   B. Why do you think *Jane Eyre* is a good novel?
   C. What are the elements of success?
   D. Where is the capital of China?

9. When the teacher asks questions, which should be expected?
   A. Questions that require students to compare, evaluate, or infer should be encouraged.
   B. Questions should be balanced among different types.
   C. Questions should be focused on those who can answer them.

D. Questions should be closely related to the suggested class lesson plan.

10. Which of the following is NOT a procedural question?
   A. Do you all understand what I want you to do?
   B. Do you understand this word?
   C. Have you finished your homework?
   D. Do you always bring a note-book when you come to class?

Checklist

Mark the questions with a check (√) if your answer is yes.

☐ Have I understood the principles of questioning, feedback, and correcting?

☐ Have I remembered the different types of questioning, feedback, and correcting?

☐ Have I grasped the strategies to integrate the questioning, feedback, and correcting strategies into English teaching?

Reflective Journal

Please write down your reflections on what you have/have not learned in this chapter.

◇ The essential skills I need to possess and develop for English teaching:

____

____

____

____

____

◇ Anything I wish to further explore (i.e., puzzles and difficulties):

____

____

____

____

____

References

Allwright, R. L. (1984). The importance of interaction in classroom language learning. *Applied Linguistics*, 5, 156–171.

Bloom, B. S. (1956). Taxonomy of educational objectives: The classification of educational goals. *Handbook I: Cognitive domain. Longman.*

Brock, C. A. (1986). The effects of referential questions on ESL classroom discourse. *TESOL Quarterly*, *20*(1), 47–59. https://doi.org/10.2307/3586430

Chaudron, C. (1988). *Second language classrooms: Research on teaching and learning*. Cambridge University Press.

Harmer, J. (1991). *The practice of English language teaching*. Longman.

Hendrickson, J. M. (1978). Error correction in foreign language teaching: Recent theory, research, and practice. *Modern Language Journal*, *62*(2), 129–138. https://doi.org/10.1111/j.1540-4781.1978.tb00653.x

Jackson, P. W., & Lahaderne, J. (1967). Patterns of teacher-student interaction in the classroom. *Journal of Educational Psychology*, *68*(5), 572–579. https://doi.org/10.1037/h0024780

Kinsella, K. (1991). *Understanding and empowering diverse learners in ESL classrooms*. Heinle & Heinle.

Long, M. H., & Sato, C. J. (1983). Classroom foreigner talk discourse: Forms and functions of teachers' questions. In H. W. Seliger & M. H. Long (Eds.), *Classroom-oriented research in second language acquisition* (pp. 268–285). Newbury House.

Nunan, D. (1988). *The teacher's role in the communicative classroom*. Cambridge University Press.

Omaggio, A. C. (1986). *Teaching language in context*. Heinle & Heinle.

Ur, P. (2000). *A course in language teaching: Practice and theory*. Foreign Language Teaching and Research Press.

Wilen, W. (2003). *Questioning in second language classrooms*. Heinle & Heinle.

Chapter 9

Closure, Review, and Homework Design Skills

Objectives

Upon completion of this chapter, you should be able to:

- Understand the concepts and principles of closure, review and homework design
- Remember the strategies of closure, review and homework design.
- Integrate the methods of closure, review and homework design into practical teaching.

Discussion Questions

Do you think the closing, review, and homework are important for English teaching? If yes, in what way?

If you are asked to write a lesson plan, what will you consider to plan the closing, review, and homework?

In the realm of English instruction, effectively closing a course, reviewing the material, and designing homework assignments are crucial pedagogical strategies that contribute to the success of both the teaching process and student learning outcomes. This chapter will touch upon these three elements, offering a summary of best practices and their significance in English language education.

9.1 Closure

9.1.1 Purposes of Closure

Understanding the purposes of course closure is fundamental. According to Marzano and Pickering (2013), closing a course allows for:

- Consolidation of learning: Reinforce key topics and skills covered throughout the course.
- Reflection: Encourage students to reflect on their learning processes and outcomes.
- Assessment: Evaluate students' mastery of the course objectives.
- Feedback: Provide students with constructive feedback to support future learning endeavors.

9.1.2 Methods of Closure

1. Summarizing closure

Teachers can guide students to use accurate, concise language or diagrams to summarize the language knowledge and skills discussed in class, summarizing and revealing the connections between various parts of knowledge, and reinforcing the key points of language knowledge.

For example, after learning the reading article "The student who asked questions" from the *Compulsory Module 4 of the High School English Curriculum* by FLTRP, teachers can ask students to fill in the following table to summarize the main points and structure of the lesson.

e.g.: *T: Complete the table below with information about the text.*

Name	
Born (where)	
His childhood	
His experiments in crop breeding	
His contributions to our country	

2. Game-based closure

Game-based learning is an excellent way to engage students and reinforce learning material. Incorporating a game can make the conclusion memorable and effective. This method is particularly suitable for reviewing vocabulary, grammar, or conversational English. The following is an example of a game-based closure (see Table 9.1).

Table 9.1 Example of game-based closure

Process	Description
Direction	Today we've explored several English idioms, and I think you've all shown great progress. To wrap up, let's play a fun game that will help us review these idioms.
Setting	Idiom Relay
Preparation	Students sit in a circle. The teacher starts by giving the first student an idiom card.
Rules	The student must use the idiom correctly in a sentence relevant to the classroom or lesson context before passing the card to the next student.
Timing	Each student has 30 seconds to come up with a sentence. If they fail to do so, they must perform a small task or gesture (e.g., sing a line from a song, give a high-five to everyone, etc.)
Conclusion	The game continues until each student has had a chance to use three idioms. The teacher concludes by highlighting the correct usages and providing positive feedback.
Outcome	This game encourages students to engage with the language material in a low-pressure, competitive environment. It also helps them memorize the idioms and understand their contextual use better. Additionally, it promotes teamwork and rapid thinking, which are beneficial skills for future educators.

3. Rhymes-and-songs closure

Using rhymes and songs is an effective pedagogical tool that can make the conclusion of an English lesson both enjoyable and educational. This approach is especially useful for reinforcing vocabulary, grammar structures, or cultural themes. Look at the following example of a rhymes-and-songs closure (see Table 9.2).

Table 9.2 Example of rhymes-and-songs closure

Process	Description
Direction	Today we've learned about different activities we do in a day. To wrap up our lesson, let's create a catchy tune together that will help us remember our new vocabulary.
Setting	Daily Grind Rhyme
Brainstorming	The teacher invites students to suggest words related to daily routines, such as 'alarm clock', 'breakfast', 'work', 'exercise', etc.
Verse construction	The teacher helps students form these words into a sentence structure that fits the rhythm, for example: Alarm clock ringing, it's morning again, I yawn and stretch, then breakfast I'll grab, off to work, I hasten, with a quick step and a clatter, after work, exercise, I love to sweat and matter.
Melody and rhythm	The teacher either creates or uses a simple melody that students can easily follow, making sure the rhythm matches the lyrics.
Practice	Students practice reciting the verse in unison, clapping out the rhythm to imprint the pattern.
Performance	Once confident, the students sing the song together, perhaps even adding a chorus or a bridge with the teacher's guidance.
Outcome	This song becomes a memorable way to encapsulate the lesson while also providing a fun learning experience. Students are more likely to retain the vocabulary and structures associated with daily routines by setting them to music. Additionally, this activity encourages creativity, collaboration, and confidence in using English.

4. Competition closure

Incorporating a competitive element at the end of an English lesson can create a dynamic and exciting environment that reinforces learning. This method is particularly suitable for reviewing grammar, vocabulary, or language skills. The following is an example (see Table 9.3).

Table 9.3 Example of competition closure

Process	Description
Direction	Today we've covered some challenging English spellings, and I'm impressed with how well you've done. To wrap up, let's have a friendly competition to see who has mastered these words.
Setting	Spelling Bee Showdown
Preparation	The teacher prepares a list of spelling words that were covered during the class, each word on an individual card.
Gameplay	Students are divided into two or more teams. Each team takes turns selecting a representative to compete in the spelling challenge.
Rules	The representative comes to the front and draws a card. They must correctly spell the word aloud within 30 seconds. If correct, their team earns a point. If incorrect, the opposing team can steal the point by correctly spelling the word.
Scoring	One point is awarded for each correctly spelled word. The team with the most points at the end wins.
Conclusion	The game continues until all representatives have had a chance to spell or until time runs out. The teacher concludes by highlighting the correct spellings, providing feedback, and celebrating the winners.
Outcome	This competition encourages students to engage with the language material in a high-pressure, yet fun environment. It also helps them practice accurate spelling and pronunciation, enhancing their memory of the words. The competitive aspect adds excitement and motivates students to perform better.

5. Incentive-based closure

An incentive-based conclusion to an English lesson can be a powerful motivator, encouraging students to consolidate their learning and apply it creatively. This method is well-suited for reinforcing key concepts, enhancing speaking skills, or promoting writing abilities. Look at the follow example (see Table 9.4).

Table 9.4 Example of incentive-based closure

Process	Description
Direction	Today we've delved into the art of persuasive writing, and I've seen some compelling arguments emerge. To conclude our lesson, let's put those skills to the test with a fun challenge.
Setting	Persuade the Judges
Challenge setup	The teacher announces a competition where students will write a short persuasive paragraph on a given topic within a set time limit.
Preparation	Students are given 10 minutes to prepare their arguments, and they are allowed to use reference materials such as dictionaries or thesauruses.

Continued

Process	Description
Gameplay	Each student presents their paragraph to the class, who will act as judges, scoring the presentations based on clarity, cogency, and use of language.
Incentives	The top three presenters will receive small rewards such as extra credit, a book, or the chance to lead a future class activity.
Scoring	Judging criteria are displayed on the board, including creativity, organization, and the use of rhetorical devices.
Conclusion	the teacher leads a debriefing session, discussing the strengths and areas for improvement in each argument. The winners are announced, and their strengths are highlighted as learning opportunities for the entire class.
Outcome	This incentive-based activity encourages students to utilize the persuasive writing techniques they have learned and to showcase their understanding in a pressure situation. The rewards offer a concrete motivation for participating and striving to excel, fostering a competitive yet supportive learning environment.

6. Bookend closure

Bookending a lesson involves echoing the initial activity or concept at the conclusion of the class, creating a sense of unity and reinforcing the main teaching points. This technique is excellent for enhancing memory retention and providing a clear structure to the learning process. The following is an example (see Table 9.5).

Table 9.5 Example of bookending closure

Process	Description
Direction	We began today's class by listening to a classic tale. Now, we will conclude by crafting our own stories, drawing inspiration from that very first story.
Setting	Story Circle
Initial activity reminder	At the start of the class, the teacher read a classic piece of English literature to set the stage for discussing storytelling elements.
Discussion and analysis	Students discussed the story's plot, characters, setting, and theme, and related it to storytelling techniques they have learned.
Creative application	Towards the end of the class, students are challenged to create their own short stories that incorporate the themes or motifs from the original piece.
Story sharing	Each student presents their story to the class, either by reading it aloud or through a creative presentation method.
Echo to the start	After each presentation, the teacher connects the student's story back to the initial piece read at the beginning, highlighting how elements were used or reimagined.
Conclusion	The teacher summarizes by pointing out the development from the initial story to the students' creations, emphasizing how they have internalized and built upon the storytelling concepts covered during the session.
Outcome	This bookend approach reinforces the lesson by showing practical applications of theoretical concepts learned. It also provides students with a creative outlet to express their understanding and encourages critical thinking about literary elements in storytelling.

7. Sequence closure

The sequential conclusion method involves connecting the main content of the current lesson with the knowledge from previous lessons in a logical sequence, or systematically integrating the entire teaching process of the lesson to provide students with an overall impression. It is generally presented in the form of visualized graphics or charts, which are easy to understand and conducive to helping students memorize the content learned. For example, after finishing learning about family members, ask students to draw a Family Tree to understand the relationships between family members, grasp the knowledge structure between characters, and have a better memory of the new words from this "concept map" (see Figure 9.1, from Chen Hua, 2018).

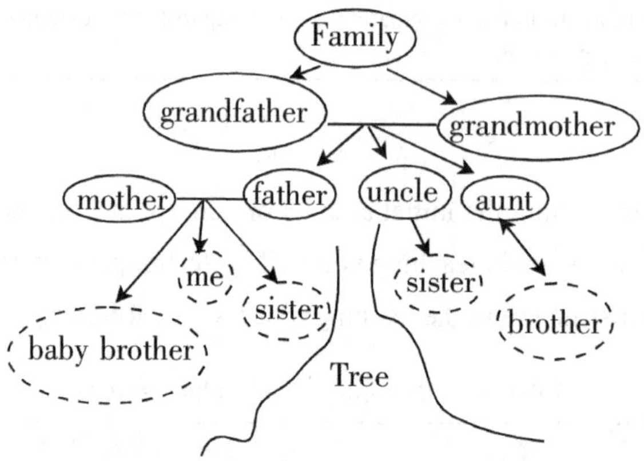

Figure 9.1 Family tree

8. Comparison closure

Comparisons can deepen understanding. This method of concluding a classroom lesson involves making targeted comparisons of the knowledge learned with other previously acquired knowledge in terms of content, structure, language, etc., at the end of the class. It seeks differences among similarities and similarities among differences, thereby enhancing the understanding of the knowledge point. Teachers can use methods such as listing, questioning, summarizing, and diagramming to guide students to compare new linguistic items with existing ones, analyze their essential characteristics and relationship, identify similarities and differences, and understand the knowledge learned more accurately and profoundly. For example, when explaining the usage of non-finite forms, at the end of the classroom teaching, a table can be used to compare the functions of the three types of non-finite forms, allowing students to grasp them clearly at a glance (see Table 9.6).

Table 9.6 The three non-infinite forms

Form	Subject	Predicate	Object	Predicative	Adverbial	Object Complement
V-ing	√		√	√	√	√
V-ed				√	√	√
Infinitive (to + V)	√		√	√	√	√

9. Group discussion closure

Concluding a lesson with a group discussion allows students to synthesize their learning, exchange perspectives, and apply their knowledge in a collaborative context. This case study outlines how to conclude a lesson on environmental sustainability using the group discussion method. Read through the following example (see Table 9.7).

Table 9.7 Example of group discussion closure

Process	Description
Direction	We've explored various aspects of environmental sustainability today. Now, let's finalize our learning through a group discussion.
Setting	Sustainable Solutions
Review	Quickly revisit key concepts such as sustainable development, ecological footprint, and renewable resources.
Formation	Divide the class into small groups, ensuring diversity in each group to foster a richer discussion.
Discussion prompt	Each group is presented with a scenario or problem related to environmental sustainability, such as urban planning, reducing plastic waste, or promoting renewable energy. They are tasked to discuss and propose sustainable solutions.
Group work	Students engage in discussions within their groups, using their course materials and personal experiences to formulate creative and practical solutions.
Presentations	Representatives from each group present their proposed solutions to the class, explaining the feasibility and potential impact of their ideas.
Peer feedback	After each presentation, other groups provide feedback, asking questions or suggesting improvements, leading to further discussion.
Teacher summary	The teacher summarizes by highlighting the importance of collective action in addressing environmental issues and appreciating the innovative thinking displayed by the students.
Call to action	The lesson concludes with a call to action, encouraging students to implement sustainable practices in their daily lives and advocating for policy changes that support environmental sustainability.
Outcome	This group discussion method at the conclusion of the lesson enables students to demonstrate their understanding, critically evaluate real-world issues, and collaborate to find sustainable solutions. It also emphasizes the relevance of environmental education to global challenges and encourages active citizenship.

10. Suspense closure

Suspense is a driving force behind students' desire for knowledge. Creating suspense involves establishing contradictions between the concepts students have already formed, their life experiences with certain issues, and more precise explanations or statements about these concepts or issues. For example, a teacher skillfully uses the content of the reading passage "The Cat that Vanished" from the *High School English Elective Sequential Course 6 Module 2* Reading and Vocabulary Section by SEFC to inspire students to imagine the reasons behind the cat's disappearance during the concluding part of the lesson.

e.g.: *T: Where has the cat gone?*

S1: I think she can hide herself under a tree.

S2: I believe she can hide in a cranny in the stone wall.

S3: I think she hides in something in the air in front of her, and something quite invisible to Will.

S4: I think...

T: Why do you think so? Write down your reasons in 100 words after class.

After class, students transform the assignment given by the teacher into an intrinsic writing need, fostering a habit of active thinking after class and maintaining the continuity of students' interest in learning English.

11. Practice-oriented closure

Practice-oriented closure refers to the process where teachers, based on the content covered and actual teaching situations, focus on key points, difficulties, and essentials to design and organize exercises for students. These exercises aim to deepen students' understanding, mastery, and application of the knowledge presented in the lesson. Practices may include oral activities such as role-playing, group discussions, retelling, knowledge competitions, or games. Alternatively, they can be written exercises like dictation, completing dialogues, reading, writing, and quizzes to reinforce the learned material. For example, after teaching the third lesson of Module 3 from the *High School English Compulsory Course 1* by SEFC, which includes Listening, Pronunciation, Everyday English, Tasks, and Writing sections, teachers can assign students to engage in pair dialogues under the theme "Show Your Response." e.g.: *T: One of you is a superstar, and the other is an interviewer. You're having a talk on CCTV. Try to use expressions you've learned to show your response or attitude towards the other person.*

12. Chart-based closure

Teachers can use diagrams or tables to systematically summarize and organize the knowledge structure and inherent connections of the content discussed, making the framework clear, highlighting key points, and ensuring everything is easily understandable at a glance.

Below is a case example of a chart-based closing for a unit on "Wildlife and Conservation" within a middle school English language course. This unit is designed to teach students how to discuss animals, their habitats, and the importance of conservation (see Table 9.8).

Table 9.8 A Chart-based closing case

Vocabulary	Grammar focus	Reading comprehension	Speaking activity	Writing task	Cultural insights
elephant rhino habitat endangered conservationist	adjectives comparatives superlatives	The Last Elephant (Excerpt)	descriptive animal presentations	argumentative essay on wildlife protection	successful conservation projects
tiger coral reef deforestation biodiversity	past simple past continuous	The Disappearing Coral (Excerpt)	debate on deforestation	A letter to the editor about local ecosystems	profiles of conservation heroes
penguin pollution ecosystem refuge	future simple future continuous	Penguins in Peril (Excerpt)	role-play as conservationists	A proposal for a school conservation club	documentary viewing on climate change impact

Unit: Wildlife and Conservation

Case description: In this unit conclusion activity, students review the key vocabulary, grammar, reading materials, speaking activities, writing tasks, and cultural insights related to wildlife and conservation. The chart provides a visual summary of the unit's content, allowing students to quickly reference and recall the main points.

Demonstration activity: To engage students in the conclusion process, the instructor can lead a "Conservation Fair" activity where students create displays or posters for each topic they've covered. Each display should include:

- A list of key vocabulary words.
- A summary of the grammar points with examples.
- A brief description of the reading comprehension task.
- A visual or written summary of the speaking activity.
- A sample of the writing task or an outline for the writing task.
- A fact sheet or infographic on the cultural insights discussed.

Objective: The objective of this activity is to reinforce of this activity is to reinforce the unit through a creative and collaborative project. It also encourages students to think critically about wildlife conservation and how language is used to discuss these issues.

After the activity, students are asked to reflect on the following prompt:

- Which animal or ecosystem did you find most interesting and why?

- How have you improved your language skills through this unit?
- What actions can you take to help with wildlife conservation?

This reflection allows students to consolidate their learning and consider the real-world implications of the topics covered.

9.1.3 Strategies for Effective Lesson Closure

To achieve the purposes outlined above, pre-service teachers can employ the following strategies:

Review and summarization: Use the last class to revisit major themes and summarize the course content. Create an overview that connects different lessons and highlights critical ideas (Hattie, 2012).

Synthesis activities: Design activities that require students to integrate knowledge from various parts of the course. This could be in the form of projects, presentations, or debates.

Formative assessments: Conduct one final formative assessment to gauge students' comprehension and application of the course material. This can include quizzes, short answer questions, or reflection journals.

Student reflections: Encourage students to write reflections on their learning experience, addressing what they have learned, what was challenging, and how they have grown.

Feedback sessions: Allocate time for individual feedback sessions where students can receive personalised comments on their performance and ways to improve.

Learning celebration: Lead students to celebrate their learning achievements through some interesting ways. This can create a positive and lasting impression of the lesson.

9.1.4 Steps for Lesson Closure

The following steps will show you the main lesson closure process.

- Prepare beforehand: Determine the activities and assessments in class well in advance to ensure smooth execution.
- Integrate lesson objectives: Integrate all closing activities with the lesson objectives to guarantee relevancy.
- Give directions clearly: Provide the students with the purpose and format of the closure activities to prepare them adequately.
- Conduct the plan: Implement the planned activities and assessments while maintaining a supportive and engaging environment.
- Review and reflect: Review the outcomes with students and encourage final reflections on their learning experiences.

- Follow-up actions: Discuss what can be done next steps after class, such as further learning opportunities or additional resources to deepen their understanding.

Activity 1 Read the following closure of a teaching case, and explain how the teaching conducts the closing process.

Teaching case:

T: In this lesson, we are learning three sentence patterns to report a request, a command or a suggestion. What are they?

Ss: Ask sb. to do/not to do sth...; tell sb. to do/not to do sth...; advise sb. to do/not to do...

T: Now let's see how well you have learned the three sentence patterns. Please turn to Page 80 and look at the three pictures.

Ss:...

T: Look at Picture 1. Who are in the picture?

Ss: A customer and a shop assistant.

T: Do you use "ask" or "tell"?

Ss: Ask.

T: So we will say "The customer asked the shop assistant ...". Mingming, please!

S1: The customer asked the shop assistant to show her that coat.

T: Good. Let's do this one by one. Xiaohua, it's your turn.

S2: The customer asked the shop assistant to fetch an umbrella for her.

...

Your answer:

____

____

____

____

____

9.2 Review and Remedial Work

"Review and remedial work" in teaching typically refers to two related but distinct teaching activities.

Review is a segment of the teaching process aimed at helping students revisit and consolidate what has been learned. There are various ways of reviews, such as discussions, exercises, tests, project work, or the use of visual aids such as slides and videos. The purpose of review is to strengthen students' understanding and memory of the material, ensuring they can retain the knowledge learned over the long term.

Remedial work refers to additional teaching measures taken in response to specific difficulties or deficiencies students encounter in the previous learning. When students' performance in a particular subject or skill does not meet the expected level, teachers may design remedial activities to help them bridge these gaps. Remedial work may consists of additional exercises, one-on-one tutoring, the use of different teaching methods or materials, and the provision of more support and resources.

In teaching, "review and remedial work" may be combined in the same teaching segment. For example, during a review class, when a teacher identifies that some students have an insufficient understanding of specific concepts, he/she will provide targeted remedial activities. This combined approach helps ensure that all students can keep up with the lesson and receive additional support when needed.

9.2.1 The Need for Review and Remedial Work

Why review and remedial work should be an integral part of teaching English? This relates both to the nature of the language learning process and the lack of sufficient use of the language in most classroom courses.

In most language courses there is far too little time for the intensive use of the language necessary for permanent learning, use similar to that of children acquiring their L1 or immigrants an L2. For this reason, most teachers and learners consider some review work necessary to reactivate, consolidate, and clarify previously presented language items. And most coursebooks include review units.

Also, errors are an integral part of language learning. They are not just evidence of failure to learn. Anyone who remembers how they learnt a foreign language is aware of how long it took them to eliminate certain elementary errors from their speaking and writing. Even advanced learners who are quite fluent usually have a number of fossilized errors in their English, for example "He said me" instead of "He told me", and leaving off the final "s" in the third person singular of the Present Tense. We have heard competent teachers of English, all with a level well above Cambridge First Certificate or 500 points in TOEFL, make this kind of error. Teachers are also human, simply learners who are further along the same road that their pupils are travelling. This should enable them to understand their pupils' situation very well.

All learners need an enormous amount of use of the language which includes listening to English and thinking in English as well as speaking it to acquire its forms and functions. In situations where opportunities to use the language and receive feedback outside the classroom are limited, review and remedial work in the classroom become vital.

In spite of general agreement about the need for review and remedial work, teachers have different attitudes towards them, and so do learners. For some, review and remedial work are an unattractive or depressing part of language teaching and learning. They are associated with failure to learn properly, and often done just in preparation for tests. Teachers with this attitude may make review and remedial work seem like a constant, frustrating, and sometimes exasperating battle against the learners' dullness and laziness. Some teachers just repeat again and again the same explanations and practice that produced little success previously.

However, other teachers consider review and remedial work an essential part of language teaching and learning, an integral part of the programme. They believe that repeated explanations and practice seldom produce better results the second or third time they are used than they did the first time. What is needed, they believe, is new work on old language. These teachers see review and remedial work as an interesting challenge, requiring ingenuity and creativity. The second view is more appropriate.

9.2.2 Principles for Review and Remedial Work

What are the implications for the review and remedial work of these ideas concerning the language learning process? Remember the following principles.

Use varied, and appropriate activities: Do not just repeat grammatical explanations and drills. Use a variety of review and remedial activities appropriate for the level and age of the learners. Include work with listening and reading texts, and activities where the main focus is on communication.

Get learner output, and provide feedback: Use some activities requiring output from the learners, including a good deal of free production in communication. Provide appropriate feedback on output. Remember that some of this feedback may come from other learners or from the learner who produced the output.

Work with natural, mixed language: Do some review and remedial work with mixed grammar, not always focusing on a single structure or area of grammar.

Be patient and positive: Never show frustration or exasperation, even when the learners get very basic things wrong or cannot remember them. But try to establish clear and realistic objectives, and involve the learners in achieving these.

Make review and remedial work enjoyable and satisfying: Try to make review and remedial work as interesting and challenging as any other work in the course, taking into account learner motivation and differences. Show your pleasure at their successes. Promote learner autonomy as much as possible, for example, with self-correction, and pair and group-work.

9.2.3 Review Activities

Review and remedial work should be a regular part of English teaching. Activities should depend on the level and age of the learners, the language points you are dealing with, and the time available.

The ideas that follow are just some examples of grammar and vocabulary review activities.

1. Recall

Ask the learners to remember what types and uses of sentences they have encountered in the course in the last week or month. In pairs or groups, get them to write examples, naming the forms and uses if they can, for example, "Past Simple", "Comparative", or "Conditional". Then elicit examples from different pairs or groups, write them on the board, and get the learners to decide whether the examples are correct or not.

2. Structure recognition

Prepare about eight sentences, half of them illustrating one structure, and the other half a different structure. For example, you could contrast the simple past and present perfect tenses:

1) *They went to France for their holiday.*

2) *She has taken French classes for two years now.*

3) *He has read several books about French cuisine this year.*

4) *They stayed in an old castle on the Loire.*

5) *They ate the most delicious food.*

6) *They have decorated their living room with posters of the castle and the Loire.*

Then, tell the students to decide in pairs which sentences belong to one group, and which to the other. Discuss the reasons for their decisions, that is, the key features or rules they noticed.

In the example, numbers 1, 4, 5 are simple past, and numbers 2, 3, and 6 are present perfect. The simple past has a single verb in the affirmative, sometimes regular (for example, "stayed") and sometimes irregular (for example, "went", and "ate"). The present perfect has the auxiliary verb have plus the past participle, sometimes regular (for example, decorated., sometimes irregular like the past (for example, "read"), and sometimes irregular and different from the past (for example, "taken").

You can mix more than two, different structures, for example, first, second, and third conditionals.

3. Underlining examples

Get students to read a text and underline all the examples of one or more structures under review. Then, in pairs, get them to check which sentences they have underlined and discuss how they recognized the structures, and how they function. Then check with the whole class.

4. Unscrambling items

Mix up the sentences of two or three texts (best on a prepared handout, not laboriously written up on the board. Then get learners in pairs to write out the texts separately. Here is an example:

1) *One morning, David got up much earlier than usual.*

2) *Jim always gets up at exactly six-fifteen.*

3) *He had a quick shower and left the house without having breakfast.*

4) *Sam has travelled more than anyone else in his class.*

5) *When he got to the university, he went straight to the library.*

6) *He likes to take things in a calm, organized way.*

7) *He has been to Disneyland in the west, and Corfu in the east.*

8) *He hates to be in a hurry.*

9) *He wanted to see Mary, the librarian.*

10) *He has hopes of being an airline pilot-a very punctual and reliable one.*

11) *However, he has never visited a single museum in his own city.*

12) *Unfortunately, she didn't go to work that day.*

In this example, one text is simple past (sentences 1, 3, 5, 9, and 12); one is simple present (sentences 2, 6, 8, and 10), and one is present perfect (sentences 4, 7, and 11). Students should discover this for themselves. The meaning of the sentences will help them.

5. Grammar summary tables

Another useful review task that is easy to organize, is the completion of grammar summary tables. These can be adapted from coursebook grammar tables, for example:

What	________		you	do?
	________		she	
	________		they	
I	________	________	student.	
She	________	________	architect.	
They	________		carpenters.	

Completing a grammar task like this is usually much better for students than being shown a grammar table or being told the rules once again by you. It is more interesting and memorable for them, and therefore more effective.

6. Guided compositions

Get the learners in pairs or groups to write a story or text on the basis of key words, for example:

John-Mary-neighbors-gardens-cat-pond-fish-bones-piranhas-wall

This set of key words should produce plenty of examples of the past simple. Pictures can also be used.

Figure 9.2 Hanzhong City in the 70s

Figure 9.3 Hanzhong City today

This pair of pictures should produce plenty of examples of comparatives.

If students are working in groups, the compositions can be written with marker pens on large sheets of paper. These can be put on the wall so that the other groups can read them. The students can then comment on any changes they consider necessary. Some writing platforms can be used so that each group can upload their compositions on the platform to discuss and comment on.

7. Whispers

"Whispers" is a sentence grammar game. Organize the learners into teams on lines of chairs from the back of the room to the front. The learners at the back of each line come to the front and memorize a sentence that you show them written on a card. The sentences you use can be of recently studied structures or basic structures that learners are having difficulty remembering. They then run back to their place and whisper the sentence to the learner in front of them, who whispers it to the learner in front, and so on. Finally, the learner at the front of the line writes the sentence on the board, which has been divided into sections for each team.

Wait until all the teams have finished, noting the order in which they finished. Then check the sentences with the class. The first team with the sentence correct, or the best approximation to the correct sentence wins. You can play several rounds with different sentences and different structures. The sentences can even build up into a very short story or text so that the growing context helps the learners understand later sentences and the whole activity becomes more communicative.

8. Integrated skills sessions

Whole review lessons can be planned as integrated skills sessions, moving, for example, from reading to discussion to listening to role play and finally to writing.

The whole session can require the use of one structure, for example, simple past. Or you can move from one structure to another, for example, beginning with reading and discussion about two alternative holiday resorts (comparative forms), then moving to the presentation of holiday plans (going to future), reports after imaginary holidays (simple past), and so on. Periodically, you can focus the learners' attention on the structures being practised.

Of course, this kind of session is possible only if you have sufficient time, as well as a collaborative group. You also need time and creativity to prepare such a session yourself. However, some coursebooks have review lessons designed in this way, and you may be able to adapt them easily to your specific situation.

9.2.4 Remedial Work

Remedial work on persistent problems should be done as needed, not on a regular basis like review work. It should be based on your evaluation of learners' problems and identification of specific errors and mistakes. This evaluation is best done by constantly monitoring the learners' performance and noting recurrent errors and mistakes, especially those that occur in fluency work. Remember, the fact that learners can produce certain grammatical structures in accuracy practice or written exercises does not mean that they can do so in more communicative activities.

It is worth mentioning here that a distinction is generally made between errors, mistakes, and slips. Errors are incorrect forms or uses that occur because the learner simply does not know what the appropriate form or use is. He or she needs to become aware or be informed of what is right and wrong. Mistakes are incorrect forms or uses that occur in spite of the learner knowing the appropriate form or use. The learner needs to notice mistakes more, and convert conscious knowledge into automatic or unconsciously produced performance. Slips are just like slips of the tongue of native speakers. They are of little or no significance.

Remedial work should focus on recurrent or persistent mistakes. It should also pay attention to errors that indicate important gaps in the learners' English or persistent misconceptions about English. Persistently used incorrect forms are generally referred to as fossilized errors. In fact they may be "fossilized errors" (the learner thinks they are correct) or "fossilized mistakes" (the learner actually knows the correct form and can self-correct).

In remedial work you need to distinguish between general problems and those of individual learners. General problems require attention in class, but individual problems are often best handled after class and through individualized homework. One of the best general principles in remedial work is never to do for learners what they can do for themselves. Learners must notice mistakes or errors, and discover for themselves what is wrong and right if they are really going to overcome their problems. Here are some ideas for remedial work:

9.2.4.1 Noticing and correcting mistakes

Select some of the most common and significant mistakes your learners make. Write on the board sentences the learners themselves have produced in oral or written work containing these mistakes. Include one or two perfectly correct sentences, also produced by the learners. Keep all the sentences anonymous. Ask the learners, working in pairs, to identify the sentences with mistakes, decide what exactly is wrong, and correct them. Then check with the whole class and discuss the mistakes and the rules.

Similar noticing and correcting can be done with specially prepared texts in which you introduce some typical mistakes.

Another strategy is to establish "the mistake of the week" on Monday. It should be a significant mistake that most learners sometimes make and that many learners make frequently. Every time someone makes that particular mistake, the other learners should raise their hands. Note who raises their hand first and congratulate them. Of course, the learner who makes the mistake can raise his or her own hand-we often notice our mistakes the moment we have made them.

9.2.4.2 Drilling

The repetition of the same structure does not have to be mechanical and boring, and it can be a useful remedial technique. It is useful because some mistakes seem to be the result of strong habits, and to break a bad habit we need to replace it with a good one. You can make drilling fun by using songs, verses, and rap-like chanting. You will need to select, adapt, or create material to do this. You can also make it like a game: for remedial drilling of the Past negative, you say "We went to England" and every learner has to say what they didn't do or what didn't happen there, without repeating a sentence, for example:

S1: I didn't see the Queen.

S2: It didn't rain.

S3: I didn't play soccer.

If the learners run out of ideas, you can change to another country. You can even make it a competition, with learners from two teams alternating. The team that produces the last sentence wins.

9.2.4.3 Mental drilling

Drilling does not have to be out loud. Learners can do it silently, in their heads. Suggest to learners who repeatedly say, for example, "must to+verb" instead of "must+verb" that they repeat in their heads when they have a spare moment: "I must do my homework"; "I must telephone Elisa"; "I must...". This can be done on the bus, driving, or walking. In the next class, you could ask them for some examples of what they "must do".

9.2.4.4 Auction

Show the students a poster with six to eight carefully selected sentences on it, about half of which are correct and half incorrect. Tell them not to discuss or say anything about the sentences. Explain that you will auction the sentences (like an auction of paintings or antiques). Each student (or pair of students) starts with $300 capital, and can bid $100, $200, or $300 for the sentences they think are correct. For example:

> *T: Right. Look at Sentence A-a beautiful sentence. Who would like to start with $ 100? Anybody?*
>
> *S1: $300!*
>
> *T: Ah, you're really convinced it's a good sentence. Right, so Sentence A goes to Omar for $300. Well, that's all your money, Omar. Now, any bids for Sentence B, another beauty?*
>
> *S2: $100!*
>
> *T: Good, $100 from Rebecca. Any advance on $100? No...? OK, going... going... gone to Rebecca for $100, a real bargain. Now...*

When you have finished the auction, get the students to discuss in groups which sentences were in fact correct and which were not. Then check with the whole class.

9.2.4.5 Personalized remedial work

Individual differences tend to increase as learners progress. At beginner level most learners' problems are very similar. At higher levels, learners' strengths and weaknesses usually become more differentiated, sometimes resulting in very heterogeneous classes. They are no longer all close to the pedagogical syllabus, but at different stages of their own "natural syllabuses".

Learners should be encouraged to take as much responsibility as possible for their own learning, and especially for remedial work. You can help, suggesting, for example, "mental drilling", extra exercises for homework, or the rewriting of marked compositions, but they themselves must do the work. If you have self-access facilities in your institution, you can direct learners to appropriate activities there.

Written composition work is one of the best opportunities for you to attend to the learners' more individual needs. Your feedback on written compositions can include:

- Comments that show you understand the process they are going through- their successes as well as their problems.
- A coding system for errors, like the one on page 99, that helps them notice and correct their own mistakes.
- Comments and exercises on areas of language where they make repeated mistakes or errors. For example, if a learner repeatedly produces sentences like " I want that my children succeed in life", you could write:

I want you to avoid a mistake you often make. For that reason, I would like you to complete the following exercise:

1) The policeman wanted ______________________________. (the driver, stop)

2) She would like ______________________________. (her children, speak English)

3) They asked ______________________________. (John, wait outside)

4) He told ______________________________. (me, sit down)

5) I prefer ______________________________. (you, correct your own mistakes)

In the final analysis, most language teaching needs to be personalized in some way. But you can only assist the learners. The actual learning has to be done by the learners themselves, in their own heads. Eventually, every learner must take responsibility for his or her own language learning, although of course, they need all the help you can give them. Paradoxically, that often means not helping them too much.

Activity 2 **Design a lesson plan for an English class that incorporates both review and remedial work. Your plan should include:**

- The objectives of the lesson
- Activities that will achieve these objectives
- The materials you will use (e.g., visual aids, exercises, tests, etc.)
- How you will evaluate students' understanding and progress

____

____

____

____

____

9.3 Homework Design

Homework is an essential component of the learning process, particularly in language education. It not only reinforces classroom instruction but also promotes independent learning and self-reflection.

9.3.1 Categories of Homework

English homework can be categorized into several types based on their nature. According to the nature of the assignment, it can be divided into operational exercises, revision exercises, and application exercises. Based on the time it takes to complete, it can be classified into classroom assignments and extracurricular assignments. As for forms, it consists of oral assignments, written assignments, and listening assignments. Here in this chapter, the assignment mainly refers to extracurricular assignments.

1. Oral assignments

• Forms

Recitations: Reciting and memorizing texts, dialogues, or poems.

Role-plays: Practicing conversations with partners or groups according to given scenarios.

Presentations: Presenting information or personal views before the whole class.

Discussions: Engaging in oral debates or discussions on specific topics.

• Functions

Improves pronunciation, fluency, and speaking confidence.

Enhances communication skills and interaction skills among students.

Encourages independent preparation and critical thinking.

• How to check outcomes

Teacher observation on students' performance in class demonstrations or role-plays.

Peer evaluation through pair work or group feedback sessions.

Audio recordings submitted for teacher review.

• Example

Assignment: Prepare a 2-minute presentation on your favorite book, including a brief summary and your personal reflections.

Assessment: Students present in front of the class, and the teacher provides feedback on pronunciation, fluency, and content organization. Peers can also share their thoughts during a subsequent discussion.

2. Written assignments

• Forms

Essays: Writing short or extended essays on different topics.

Short answer questions: Answering questions from textbooks or in-class discussions.

Grammar and vocabulary exercises: Finishing exercises to practice language structures and vocabulary.

Creative writing: Writing stories, poems, or descriptive paragraphs.

• Functions

Strengthening writing skills, such as grammar, vocabulary, and structure skills.

Providing chances for critical analysis and personal expression.

Developing students' ability to organize and present ideas.

• How to check outcomes

Teacher grading and writing feedback on grammar, structure, and content.

Peer assessment to encourage collaboration and provide different perspectives.

Self-assessment using checklists or rubrics.

• Example

Assignment: Write a 120-word essay comparing and contrasting two films.

Assessment: The teacher evaluates grammar, vocabulary use, coherence of the essay, and the quality of analysis. Students participate in peer assessment, sharing their essays with peers and providing constructive feedback.

3. Listening assignments

• Forms

Listening understanding exercises: Listening to recordings and answering questions.

Podcast or TED Talk analysis: Listening to and giving a summary of the content of the podcast or TED Talk.

Dictation: Listening to a passage or paragraph and writing down what is heard.

- **Functions**

Improving listening skills, such as comprehension and note-taking.

Expanding vocabulary and some idiomatic expressions.

Enhancing listening attention and retention of spoken language.

- **How to check outcomes**

Quizzes or multiple-choice questions based on the listening material.

Oral reports or written summaries of the material.

Teacher observation during dictation activities.

- **Example**

Assignment: Listen to a 10-minute TED Talk and write a 120-word summary of the main points.

Assessment: The teacher evaluates the summary for accuracy, clarity, and comprehension of the talk's main ideas. Students can present their summaries orally in class, and the teacher provides feedback on their listening comprehension and speaking skills.

9.3.2 Integrating Technology into English Assignments

Integrating technology into English homework assignments can make learning more interactive, accessible, and fun. You may use the following strategies:

Online quizzes and games: Platforms like “作业帮” “猿题库” help you to create quizzes for students to complete. This tests students' knowledge and also makes learning more enjoyable.

Digital storytelling: Help students to tell stories by making videos or animations. Platforms like “口语嘟嘟” “流利说英语”, are user-friendly, and enable students to make their own short, animated videos.

Interactive worksheets and exercises: Use tools like Google Docs to create interactive worksheets that students can complete online. You can embed quizzes, polls, and collaborative tasks within the document.

Audio and video recordings: Ask students to give a reading presentation or record reading a text aloud of their own. This can be done by a smartphone app and help improve students' speaking and listening skills.

Virtual reality (VR) and augmented reality (AR): While more advanced, VR and AR are more advanced tools which can provide immersive practice for language learning. For example, students can virtually visit English-speaking countries and explore cultural aspects in an interactive way.

Online language learning platforms: Websites like FluentU offer various videos and interactive quizzes that can be assigned as homework to conduct classroom learning.

Collaborative projects: Project management tools like Trello or Google Classroom can assign collaborative projects where students can work together on research or group presentations.

Formative assessment tools: Some digital tools can be used to provide immediate feedback, such as automated grading systems for multiple-choice quizzes or language analysis tools for written assignments.

Mobile apps: Some educational apps are designed for language learning that can be assigned as homework. These apps often include gamified lessons, flashcards, and pronunciation practice.

When integrating technology, it is important to make sure that the tool is accessible and consider your students' digital literacy, so that all students can participate effectively. Furthermore, try to give clear instructions and guidelines for using the technology. Be sure that the technology you choose aligns with your teaching objectives and is age-appropriate for your students. Also, consider the time cost required for each assignment to avoid overwhelming your students.

9.3.3 Methods of Marking Written Assignments

The following are some useful methods for marking written assignments.

1. Traditional paper marking

Teachers read students' paper-based assignments, give marks, provide comments, point out errors, and offer suggestions.

- Advantages: Intuitive and easy to understand; students can immediately see their work and carry out corresponding modifications.
- Disadvantages: Low efficiency, requiring a large amount of time, especially when dealing with a large number of students. Additionally, paper-based assignments are prone to damage or loss.

2. Electronic marking

With technological advancements, many schools have adopted electronic marking systems. These systems help teachers to mark students' assignments online and provide immediate feedback.

- Advantages: High efficiency, saving time; convenient for archiving and retrieving; easy for statistical analysis and student data analysis.
- Disadvantages: Requires access to electronic devices; students may need certain technical skills.

3. Peer marking

Peer marking means students marking their peers' assignments. This kind of marking not only improves students' critical thinking skills but also strengthen their collaborative spirit.

- Advantages: Promotes communication and cooperation among students; fosters critical thinking and evaluation abilities in students.
- Disadvantages: Requires teacher supervision and guidance; some students may feel uncomfortable criticizing others.

4. Self-assessment

The teacher encourages students to assess and reflect on their own assignments, aiming to improve their self-correction abilities.

- Advantages: Fosters independent learning abilities; helps students establish habits of self-evaluation.
- Disadvantages: Requires high levels of self-discipline and self-reflection; some students may lack objectivity.

5. Hybrid marking

The method of hybrid marking means integrating the advantages of various marking techniques depending on the situation and applying different strategies flexibly. For example, for students with basic skills, traditional paper marking is used; for advanced students, electronic marking or peer review methods are employed.

- Advantages: high flexibility, meet the needs of different students; effectively utilizes the strengths of various methods to enhance teaching outcomes.
- Disadvantages: Requires teachers to possess strong teaching design and organizational skills; implementation may be complex.

Activity 3 Utilize opportunities like teaching internships (probation), educational workshops, and after-school tutoring to grade a student's assignment and conduct a review and commentary.

Thinking and Doing

A. Discussion questions

What are the methods to review a text effectively? How to attract students' attention to the review work?

B. Practice

Read the following classroom teaching segment carefully and answer the questions.

T: Good job, everyone. Today, we've come to the end of an enlightening journey through our English text about Anna and her experience in Greenleaf Valley. Let's review the key points of the story before moving on to your homework.

S1: Yes, Ms. Smith. The story takes place in Greenleaf Valley, which is known for its beautiful landscapes and clear blue rivers.

T: Excellent! And what unusual event did Anna discover one morning by the river?

S2: She noticed a strange discoloration on the water's surface and saw a group of strangers near the riverbank acting in a methodical way.

T: Very good. Can anyone tell me who these strangers were and why they were there?

S3: They were scientists led by Dr. Carter. They were studying the ecosystem but found signs of disruption, possibly caused by humans.

T: That's correct. Now, how did Anna feel about this situation?

S4: She was concerned and worried because she loves the valley and knows every plant and creature there. She was afraid that something might be endangering them.

T: Exactly. And what did Anna decide to do about it?

S5: She joined the scientists to help uncover the truth behind the pollution in the river.

T: Right. After working together, what significant discovery did they make?

S6: They found a clandestine factory upstream that was leaking pollutants into the river.

T: Well done. And how did the community respond to this discovery?

S7: They exposed the factory's secret operations and worked to ensure that Greenleaf Valley would remain untainted for future generations.

T: Wonderful summary, everyone! You've all grasped the essential points of the story. For your homework, I'd like you to write a short essay discussing the importance of community involvement in environmental conservation. Think about how the collaboration between Anna, the scientists, and the town's people made a difference. Use specific examples from the text to support your arguments. Have your essays ready for discussion in our next class. Class dismissed!

1. What is your opinion about the assignments designed in this case?

2. Taking this topic as an example, how would you design the homework assignment?

3. Taking this topic as an example, how would you conduct the closure stage?

C. Exercises for instructional skills

1. What activity are students engaged in when they read each other's writing, provide feedback and make suggestions for revision before their teacher grades them?

A. Discussing. B. Brainstorming.

C. Peer reviewing. D. Draft reviewing.

2. What is a teacher trying to do when he/she asks students to describe what they know about policemen before reading a story about them?

A. To review a passage. B. To make a comment.

C. To provide a title. D. To build a schema.

3. Which of the following grammar activities is the most communicative?

A. Ask students to identify and correct mistakes in the sentences.

B. Ask students to tell the differences between two pictures in groups.

C. Ask students to make sentences with the given words.

D. Ask students to finish the translation exercises.

4. Which of the following statements is NOT true?

A. The review and remedial work can reactivate new language items.

B. The review and remedial can help students correct their errors in learning.

C. The review and remedial work are unattractive parts of language teaching and learning.

D. The review and remedial work can make up for the limited time for practice during the process of teaching and learning.

5. Which of the following statements about "remedial work" is NOT correct?

A. Remedial work is based on the feedback of students' learning.

B. Teachers should distinguish among students' errors, mistakes, and slips when doing remedial work.

C. Teachers should distinguish between typical problems and individual problems.

D. Remedial work is the same as review work in that they both help solve persistent problems.

Checklist

Mark the questions with a check (√) if your answer is yes.

☐ Have I understood the concepts of closure, review, and homework design?

☐ Have I understood the principles of closure, review, and homework?

☐ Have I grasped the methods to have effective closure, review and deliver proper homework in English teaching?

☐ Can I use different ways to correct students' homework?

Reflective Journal

Please write down your reflections on what you have/have not learned in this chapter.

◇ The essential skills I need to possess and develop for English teaching:

____

____

____

____

____

____

◇ Anything I wish to further explore (i.e., puzzles and difficulties):

____

____

____

____

____

____

References

Chen, H. (2018). 概念图：让英语学习从"串联"走向"并联"：以高年级英语教学为例 [*Concept map: Making English learning from "series" to "parallel"—Taking senior English teaching as an example*]. *Primary School Teaching Research*, *16*(16), 84–87.

Hattie, J. (2012). *Visible learning for teachers: Maximizing impact on learning*. Routledge.

Marzano, R. J., & Pickering, D. J. (2013). *Classroom instruction that works: Research-based strategies for increasing student achievement*. Association for Supervision and Curriculum Development.

Part Ⅳ

Teacher Development and Research Skills

The teacher must first reflect on themselves before teaching others.

—Zhu Xi

Zhu Xi (1130–1200) was a renowned Chinese philosopher, educator, and scholar of the Song Dynasty, widely regarded as one of the most influential figures in Neo-Confucianism. He synthesized Confucian thought with elements of Daoism and Buddhism, creating a comprehensive philosophical system that dominated East Asian intellectual life for centuries. Zhu Xi emphasized self-cultivation, moral integrity, and the importance of education. His commentaries on the Four Books became the foundation of the Chinese civil service examination system for over 600 years.

We who are teachers must engage in learning every day and undergo continuous re-education. Only then can we experience the joy of teaching without the bitterness.

—Tao Xingzhi

Tao Xingzhi was a renowned Chinese educator, philosopher, and reformer, born in 1891 and passed away in 1946. He is celebrated for his innovative education philosophy and significant contributions to the modern education system in China. One of Tao's core principles was "teaching by doing," which encouraged hands-on learning and the application of knowledge to real-world situations. He opposed rote memorization and the strict hierarchy of traditional classroom settings, instead promoting an educational environment where students could explore, question, and engage with their learning.

Chapter 10

Classroom Management Skills

Objectives

Upon completion of this chapter, you should be able to:

- Understand the concepts of classroom management.
- Grasp the principles of classroom management.
- Analyse the physical environment of the classroom.
- Grasp the strategies of teaching a large class.
- Understand teachers' proper behaviors in classroom management.

Discussion Questions

Do you think teaching is an art or a science? Why do you think so?

How would you handle a situation where a student needs to use the restroom during class, in a way that is both considerate and does not interfere with learning?

Is teaching an art or a science? Are teachers born or made? Is the relationship between learning and teaching a matter of artistry or a matter of predictability? Such inquiries often circulate in the thoughts of educators, framed not as exclusive alternatives but rather as integrated reflections. It is generally acknowledged that instruction embodies both artistic flair and scientific methodology; an inherent skill set works in harmony with acquired pedagogical techniques. Despite meticulously curated lesson frameworks, an elusive essence remains intrinsic to the learning experience. Yet, how do these two domains seamlessly integrate in practical application? In what ways do the artistic and scientific elements intertwine within the methodologies and strategies employed by ESL instructors?

A significant part of the solution to these inquiries pertains to the concept of managing the classroom effectively, which includes a variety of elements, such as the physical setup of the classroom, approaches to instruction, and even the engaging concept of classroom dynamics. By gaining insights into different aspects of effective classroom management, one can undertake significant measures to enhance their effectiveness as a language educator. Subsequently, as you enhance a number of those recognizable, clearly noticeable abilities, you gain access to the abstract nuances, art, poetics, to the unseen flashes of vitality that ignite the passion for knowledge.

10.1 Fundamental Guidelines for Managing the Classroom

To start, it is important to examine some core principles of managing a classroom that are relevant across different educational settings. Reflect on the following essential aspects of effective classroom governance.

Establish clear teacher and student roles. It is crucial to delineate distinct roles for both instructors and students. Classrooms that prioritize learner engagement and interaction are effective when the expectations of the teacher's role and the significance of student involvement in a structured lesson are communicated. Research indicates that, overall, students are more inclined towards structured guidance from teachers rather than "permissive" approaches that may lead to disorder.

Define clear and specific aims and objectives. When learners understand the main objectives behind lessons and the associated tasks, they are likely to cultivate a stronger internal drive for achievement.

Maintain adaptability. As discussed in Chapter 2, thorough lesson planning is essential, yet as Scrivener (2020) pointed out, unforeseen circumstances can disrupt even the best-laid plans. Therefore, while it is beneficial to prepare for a lesson, one must remain open to modifying and adjusting the initial strategies when necessary.

Provide students with opportunities to select from various activities and exercises. While the activities and tasks you design play a crucial role in guiding learners toward achieving their goals, providing them with a selection of choices enhances their engagement and enthusiasm.

Show a genuine concern for each of your students. Educators often handle a large number of students each day, yet recognizing each student as a distinct individual deserving of attention significantly enhances the educational experience. Casual chats, positive feedback on achievements, and an understanding of each student's circumstances can all enhance the cohesiveness of the classroom community.

Ensure fairness towards every student. While it might be tempting to have certain students whom you prefer, it is crucial to provide every learner with equal love and focus. Failing to do so may lead to conflict and feelings of resentment.

Demonstrate genuine excitement and maintain an optimistic demeanor. Your passion for classroom interactions is likely to inspire a similar positive attitude in your pupils. It's discouraging to see educators whose gestures, tone, and expressions suggest a lack of interest. The essential task is to captivate your learners, with you taking the lead in fostering that interest.

Engage learners who exhibit a wide range of capabilities, both above and below average. A significant difficulty in education lies in effectively engaging all learners, who vary widely in their skills, understanding, and levels of enthusiasm. Achieving this objective can be facilitated through a diverse range of activities, thoughtful grouping of students, personalized support, and meetings outside of class time.

While the core principles of managing a classroom are not exclusive to language instruction, the specific expectations that arise in interactive learning environments do pose difficulties for educators. It's significantly more straightforward to adopt a fully teacher-centered approach and maintain total authority than to allow students to share that authority.

Activity 1 **Write down some specific examples in the following table to show "teacher guidance and control" approaches and "permissive" approaches in classroom management.**

Teacher guidance and control approach	Permissive approach

10.2 The Physical Environment of the Classroom

The physical environment of the classroom plays a crucial role in facilitating effective learning. The setup of the classroom can significantly influence interactions among students and between students and instructors. Arranging the desks, incorporating various learning tools, and providing an inviting atmosphere can enhance engagement and communication. These aspects are particularly pertinent in language instruction, where active participation and collaboration are essential for success.

10.2.1 Visual Perceptions, Auditory Experiences, and Overall Well-being

Although it might seem insignificant at first glance, the choices made in utilizing various innovative approaches to language instruction greatly influence students as they interact with their classroom environment through their visual, auditory, and emotional experiences. Should you possess the ability to influence the following aspects, it would be beneficial to invest your efforts in doing so (see Figure 10.1).

- Maintain a classroom that is neat, clean, and orderly in appearance.
- Erase chalkboards (whiteboards) before each class period.
- Arrange chairs are appropriately.
- If the room has bulletin boards and you have the freedom to use them, take advantage of visual stimuli to interest students.
- As much as possible, keep the classroom free from external noises (machinery outside, street noise, hallway voices, etc.).
- If possible, see to it that acoustics within your classroom are optimal.
- Ensure efficient operation of heating/cooling systems (if applicable).

Figure 10.1 What you can do to control the physical classroom

It is acknowledged that certain aspects mentioned may be beyond your influence. In certain classrooms located in tropical regions, the absence of air conditioning can make conditions uncomfortable; the hard concrete walls amplify every sound, making it nearly impossible to hear one another, while the incessant noise of construction outside adds to the chaos! However, if these conditions are manageable, it is essential to seize the chance to create an environment in the classroom that prioritizes physical comfort.

10.2.2 Seating Arrangements

Imagine stepping into a classroom where the flexible desks are arranged in neat, upright columns that face the front wall, rather than in traditional rows. It may appear quite organized, wouldn't it? Incorrect. If there is no risk of losing your teaching position, be sure to rearrange the seating arrangement right away! Learners should function as part of a collaborative unit, allowing them to engage with one another and communicate (in English!), and should not be treated as if they have just entered a strict military formation.

In classrooms equipped with flexible desk-chair arrangements, it may be beneficial to explore formations such as semi-circles, U-shapes, or concentric circles. For smaller classes, a single circular formation can also be effective, allowing students to engage more dynamically rather than having them all directly facing the instructor. If the setting consists of tables accommodating two to four pupils each, configurations that maximize peer-to-peer interaction should be prioritized. Careful planning of how students will undertake pair and small group activities can help minimize disruption and maintain focus.

Is it your responsibility to decide who sits beside each other? Usually, students are likely to develop their seating preferences and form comfortable arrangements without intervention. Only consider adjusting this setup if there is a specific objective to create a different blend of participants. In some ESL contexts, in settings where learners have diverse linguistic backgrounds, practicing English becomes easier when learners with the same native tongue are not placed next to one another. Additionally, if some students nearby are causing interruptions, it might be beneficial to reposition certain individuals strategically. When forming small groups, it might be beneficial to have a specific strategy in place.

10.2.3 Visual Aids and Equipment

Will you be utilizing the blackboard, the whiteboard, or the projector? Ensure that they function effectively and enhance auditory support. It is important to maintain organization and clarity on the board, frequently erasing where necessary. A disorganized and unclear blackboard can be quite frustrating for students. Visual tools such as real objects should not be displayed unless they are actively being utilized; as this could lead to a loss of focus for the students.

Currently, many educational programs operate under the assumption that necessary devices are either integrated into the learning environment or easily accessible via portable units. When utilizing electrical devices, such as a laptop, projector, or audio/video equipment, it is crucial to ensure that certain factors are managed effectively (see Figure 10.2).

It is quite astonishing how frequently instructional plans derail due to seemingly insignificant practicalities related to equipment usage.

- Check that the room's electrical outlets are within reach of the cord provided, or, if not, that an extension cord is on your equipment list.
- Make sure the equipment fits comfortably in the room.
- Confirm that everyone can see (and/or hear) the visual/auditory stimulus.
- Leave enough time before and after class to get the equipment and return it to its proper place.
- Try out equipment ahead of time to ascertain that it actually works.
- Familiarize yourself with how to operate it.
- There is an extra light bulb or battery or whatever else you'll need if a routine replacement is in order.

Figure 10.2 Guidelines for ascertaining functioning equipment

Activity 2 **Sketch two classroom seating arrangement types and explain their advantages and disadvantages.**

Type	Brief description	Advantages	Disadvantages
Type 1			
Type 2			

10.3 Strategies for Teaching in Challenging Conditions

The term "challenging situations" encompasses a variety of managerial issues that vary greatly in nature. This suggests that no educational environment is flawless. There will always be organizations, individuals, and situations that are less than ideal to confront. How these challenges are navigated is a key element influencing one's career achievements.

10.3.1 Managing Large Groups of Students

How might one respond to such a circumstance? In an ideal scenario, a language lesson should include no more than twelve to fifteen learners (LoCastro, 2012). Classes should strike a balance that allows for sufficient variety and engagement among students, while also ensuring that each individual has ample opportunities to engage and receive personalized guidance. Regrettably, due to meager funding for education worldwide, many language classes tend to be notably larger. It is not unusual for class sizes to range from 50 to 75 students in various parts of the world. Although it is important to continuously remind school officials, who may mistakenly think that language acquisition occurs primarily through memorization, about the limited effectiveness of groups larger than 25 or 30 students, one might still need to face the situation of managing a sizable class for the time being.

There are certain challenges associated with large classes (Shamim, 2016):

- Students exhibit a wide range of skills and competencies.
- You often depend on instructional sessions, multimedia resources, and various presentations delivered to the entire class.

- A significant portion of collaborative efforts might go without supervision, and it may be necessary to select group "reports" at random.
- The level of individualized attention provided to each student by teachers is significantly reduced.
- The chances for students to address the entire class are diminished.
- The feedback provided by instructors on the written assignments of students is somewhat restricted.

There exist several approaches to address these issues. Please take into account the following considerations that may pertain to one or more of the aforementioned issues:

- It is essential to ensure that every learner feels valued and recognized as individuals rather than merely as a statistic; this can be accomplished by familiarizing oneself with their names and actively incorporating them into interactions. In the initial sessions, the use of name tags or placards at desks can help reinforce this personal connection.
- Encourage students to engage in as much interactive work as feasible, starting with numerous activities aimed at helping them familiarize themselves with each other. This approach ensures that they do not feel isolated or anonymous within the group but rather become part of a cohesive community.
- Enhance opportunities for students to practice English through the effective implementation of pair and small group activities. When forming groups, it is important to take into account the differences in students' language proficiency.
- Increase the frequency of activities focused on listening comprehension by incorporating various formats such as audio recordings, videos, and direct instruction. It is important for learners to grasp the type of feedback that is anticipated. Engaging in focused listening exercises enables students to acquire language skills that are beneficial in their reading, speaking, and writing endeavors.
- Whenever suitable, incorporate evaluation, feedback, and peer-review in written assignments.
- Provide pupils with a variety of activities beyond classroom learning, establishing a baseline for all while also offering more demanding options for those with advanced abilities.
- Avoid gathering assignments from every student simultaneously; distribute the collection over a planned schedule to reduce your burden and ensure that students receive their graded assignments more promptly.
- Create small "learning hubs" within the classroom that allow students to engage in personalized tasks.
- Facilitate informal discussion circles and collaborative study sessions.

10.3.2 Teaching Different Levels of Students Within a Single Classroom

Students in a single classroom often demonstrate a diverse spectrum of skill levels, particularly in larger groups; however, even smaller classes frequently comprise learners who, in your assessment, may not be suitable for uniform placement. Regardless of the situation, the challenge lies in meeting the needs of advanced learners without causing frustration for those who are less experienced, while simultaneously ensuring that the intermediate group is making steady progress towards their objectives. It is insufficient to focus solely on the middle group and assume that the other students will benefit. Often, the diversity of skill levels among students in a classroom stems from placement policies and financial constraints set by the institution, making it challenging to adjust the level of all students, particularly those at the extremes. What strategies can one employ to address this situation? Here are a few recommendations worth exploring:

Generalizing proficiency levels can lead to inaccuracies. Many educators mistakenly categorize learners as either “strong” or “weak.” Given the intricate nature of language skills, it can be challenging to assess whether a student’s output stems from natural talent, skill level, an inherent gift, or simply the investment of time and effort.

Customize the methods you employ. Whenever possible, assess the unique talents and skills of each student in the classroom, enabling the adaptation of teaching methods to suit their individual requirements. By utilizing diagnostic assessments and keeping a daily check on learners, educators can effectively determine particular linguistic targets and guide students towards achieving those goals.

Provide alternatives. By allowing learners the freedom to choose between various individual methods (both written tasks and activities outside class) tailored to their specific needs and obstacles, there is potential to engage a broader spectrum of students. It is important to communicate to all students that they each face their own set of challenges and aspirations, and that any perceived advantage one may have over another is likely a result of prior learning experiences, exposure, and personal drive.

Utilize digital tools. Utilize the various resources offered by the Internet. Individuals at all skill levels stand to gain from online exercises for review and practice, which are frequently recommended in educational resources and textbooks.

Aim at the center. Assess the intricacy of the instructional language utilized by the classroom teacher (such as directions, clarifications, and presentations).suitable for the average skill level among students in the classroom.

Vary group work tasks. Change group task Collaborative activities create avenues for addressing issues related to varying skill levels. It is possible to group students with diverse abilities together for a task tailored to their varied skills, while in other instances, it may be more effective to assemble students who share similar proficiency levels. Each of these situations has its own set of benefits and drawbacks.

10.3.3 Classroom Discipline

Numerous studies and practical guidance have addressed the topic of maintaining order in classrooms. Even in a situation where every student is industrious, self-driven, engaged, committed, and intellectually capable, one can still encounter what may be classified as issues with discipline! While this section will not serve as a comprehensive guide to discipline, it will provide several tips for consideration and allow for application in various contexts.

Authority. Embrace the confidence that comes with holding a leadership role.

Fairness. Attaining the admiration of students requires treating each individual with consistent impartiality.

Guidelines for behavior. Clearly outline the expected conduct of students during lessons, which Harmer (2015) refers to as a "behavioral framework." He proposed that when these guidelines are created through a collaborative process with the students, rather than imposed as authoritative decrees, they tend to be more influential and accepted.

Expectations. Highlight the significance of norms related to taking turns, honoring fellow classmates, actively listening, policies regarding attendance (including lateness and absence), as well as responsibilities beyond class hours.

Firmness. Approach variations from these standards with a balance of firmness and compassion.

Ensuring the respect of students. In cases where it becomes necessary to issue a verbal warning, reprimand, or other disciplinary measures, prioritize maintaining the student's respect, regardless of your own feelings of frustration or the specifics of any agreed-upon guidelines.

Proper conduct. It is advisable to attempt to address behavioral issues with students privately rather than interrupting class time—consider speaking with a student after the lesson to express your concerns while allowing them a chance to respond, ensuring that class sessions remain focused and productive.

Identifying the root cause of issues. When dealing with behavioral challenges, it's important to discover the underlying factors instead of merely addressing the observable effects (for instance, if a learner appears disengaged in class, it may result from insufficient rest due to working a night job; in such cases, recommending a different work schedule or an alternate timing for the English lesson could be beneficial).

Institutional assistance. In situations where ongoing behavioral issues cannot be addressed satisfactorily, it is advisable to seek guidance from the counselor or administrator at your institution.

Activity 3 **Write down at least five methods to remember students' names quickly in teaching large classes.**

____

____

____

____

____

____

10.4 Teachers' Roles and Styles

In these final sections on classroom management, we turn a little more centrally to the affective or emotional side of being and becoming a good teacher.

10.4.1 Teachers' Roles

The role is a visual representation of functions and also a generalized refinement of capabilities. Through roles, we can understand the functions that teachers should perform in a smart environment and clarify the abilities and qualities that teachers should possess.

10.4.1.1 A new examination of teachers' roles in the AI era

After experiencing three industrial revolutions, humanity is currently in the era of the Fourth Industrial Revolution, characterized by artificial intelligence, robotics technology, quantum information technology, virtual reality, and is also known as the intelligent era.

As for the relationship between AI era and modern education, the AI era encompasses four types of logic (Zhang X. G., 2024): First, as a background, education is situated within the macro-background of the AI era; second, as a guarantee, the technological conditions and achievements of the AI era provide the foundation for the conduct of education; third, as a means, by studying how machines learn in AI, we can better understand how humans learn; fourth, as content, education promotes the development of AI. Currently, countries around the world are deploying AI strategies, focusing on the guarantee logic and content logic of intelligence, both of which are essentially technological rationality. But on the other hand, more focus should be placed on its value rationality-the means logic, to explore how the intelligent era can better facilitate the realization of educational goals, as well as the a background logic, to put forward corresponding requirements for educational development.

Zhang X. G. (2024) states, in the era of intelligent development, the purpose of education requires teachers to embody a three-dimensional role encompassing cognition, relationship, and motion. Regarding educational development, the mainstream academic approach divides it into four stages based on the four industrial revolutions, from Education 1.0 to Education 4.0. According to the varying demands of the times, these four stages differ in their views on education, teachers, students, and teaching methodologies. The focus has shifted from solely concentrating on students' academic performance to emphasizing holistic development, and from passive reception learning to cooperative discussion-based learning. Therefore, teachers have also transformed from being the dominant authority in the classroom to co-learners, guides, and caregivers for students. Despite changes in the times, the essence of education has remained unchanged: education always promotes human development and is concerned with nurturing growth. On one hand, as natural beings with biological attributes, humans require sound physical and mental development; cognition and emotion are indispensable. On the other hand, as social beings with social attributes, humans need to develop within social relationships. Thus, human development is inseparable from the three dimensions of cognition, relationship, and emotion. With the progression of time, the characteristics of education reflected in these three dimensions have evolved. Table 10.1 summarizes the characteristics of different eras of educational development in terms of cognition, relationship, and emotion.

Table 10.1 Three-Dimensional Characteristics of Education from 1.0 to 4.0

Stage	Feature		
	Cognition	Relationship	Emotion
First Industrial Revolution (Education 1.0)	Knowledge Memorization	Person-to-Person (Teacher Authority)	Face-to-Face Communication
Second Industrial Revolution (Education 2.0)	Knowledge Acquisition and Memorization	Person-to-Person (Teacher Centered)	Face-to-Face Communication
Third Industrial Revolution (Education 3.0)	Knowledge Construction	Person-to-Person (Student Centered)	Face-to-Face Communication
Fourth Industrial Revolution/ Intelligent Era (Education 4.0)	Critical Thinking Creative Thinking	Person-to-Person (Student Centered) Person-to-Machine	Face-to-Face Communication (Weakened) Screen Communication (Strengthened)

10.4.1.2 Teachers' roles under smart education

The Horizon Report (Becker A., 2016) has been prompting us to rethink the role of teachers in a technological environment, pointing out that the teacher's role will transform from being an instructor to guides and coaches. Characterizing teachers through roles has become an important international method for defining and describing teacher competencies (Zhu Z. T., Wei F., 2018). For example, the AMEE Guide (2000) believes that teachers play twelve different roles, including curriculum planner, organizer, evaluator, student assessor, mentor, and learning facilitator; ISTE (2016) summarizes the teacher's role in "National Educational Technology Standards for Teachers" as a learner, leader, citizen, collaborator, designer, promoter, and analyst. Although these role breakdowns and descriptions are conclusions drawn under different research contexts and practical needs, they all reveal how the powerful tide of digital technology shapes and interprets the role of teachers in a digital environment. Differentiation and specialization have become an "inevitability" (Zhu Z. T., Wei F., 2017) to achieve the goal of supporting education to realize differentiated and personalized development.

In the context of smart education, teachers are tasked with nurturing students who possess high-level thinking qualities, adeptness at solving complex problems, outstanding innovation abilities, and strong social adaptability. Teachers should embody advanced concepts of intelligent education, prioritize the development of students' cognitive skills, possess excellent data literacy, and have exceptional lifelong learning capabilities. They should act as disseminators of intelligent educational concepts, builders of intelligent environments, practitioners of intelligent teaching methods, and participants in intelligent assessments. In essence, they are key embodiments of educational intelligence (Zhu Z. T., Wei F., 2018) (see Table 10.2).

Table 10.2 Teachers' roles under smart education

Role	Function	Work Scope
Learning Designer	Design a learning environment, resources, and content to support students' comprehensive and full development.	Target design, question design, content design, tool design, environmental creation, etc.
Learning Guide	Provide advice and guidance on learning, motivation for learning, and improve learning ability during the learning process.	Learning style assessment, planning and guidance of learning skills, motivation and maintenance of motivation, etc.
Teaching Evaluator	Design evaluation programs, evaluate teaching and learning, and be responsible for monitoring the quality of teaching.	Diagnostic evaluation, summative evaluation, formative evaluation, reflective evaluation, etc.
Activity Organizer	Responsible for planning, and hosting various activities that are beneficial to students' physical and mental health and comprehensive development, and responsible for shaping educational culture.	Activity plan design, activity flow planning, organization and evaluation of activities, campus cultural atmosphere construction, etc.

10.4.2 Teachers' Teaching Styles

The teaching style of a teacher means the manner when teachers deliver instruction and interact with students. It involves various factors such as their approach to lesson planning, classroom management, communication skills, and assessment methods. A teacher's teaching style can significantly impact student engagement, motivation, and overall learning outcomes. Different teachers may have distinct teaching styles that resonate with different types of learners.

10.4.2.1 Teachers' teaching style continua

The approach adopted by educators during instruction is a crucial factor in the enhancement of their professional skills. This instructional approach often aligns closely with the individual characteristics of the instructors, which can significantly differ from one person to another. It is important for educators to reflect on the various instructional methods outlined below, keeping in mind that each method exists along a spectrum of alternatives (see Figure 10.3).

shy	←——→	gregarious
formal	←——→	informal
reserved	←——→	open, transparent
understated	←——→	dramatic
rational	←——→	emotional
steady	←——→	variety of moods
serious	←——→	humorous
restrictive	←——→	permissive

Figure 10.3 Teaching style continua

On what part of these scales do you find yourself? Is it deemed essential to favor one extreme to be a successful educator? How might one articulate their position as being between the extremes of a spectrum? Reflect on the various teaching approaches one might consider adjusting to enhance their effectiveness in the classroom.

Outstanding educators can be found at various points along these teaching style spectrums. As one becomes more at ease with their role as an instructor, it is essential to ensure that their teaching approach aligns seamlessly with their authentic self and the way they feel most comfortable expressing themselves in the classroom; Therefore, it is important to understand how to leverage the advantages inherent in your approach to teaching. Generally, it is not advisable to conform to a typecast that does not align with your most effective persona within the classroom.

10.4.2.2 Societal norms

In cultures prevalent in the West, teaching approaches and roles often prioritize a style that is non-directive and avoids authoritarianism, as illustrated in the right-hand column of the list below. A significant factor influencing the success of role-playing and stylistic approaches lies in the cultural context of the teaching environment and/or the backgrounds of the learners involved.

Table 10.3 several cultural norms regarding the roles and behaviors associated with educators, learners, and educational institutions (based on Hofstede's work from 1986).

Table 10.3 Contrasting cultural norms of teacher and student roles

Traditional authoritative teaching social norms	Modern student-centered teaching social norms
Teachers are expected to have all the answers.	Teachers are allowed to say "I don't know."
Teachers are expected to suppress emotions (and so are students).	Teachers are allowed to express emotions (and so are students).
Teachers interpret intellectual disagreement as personal disloyalty.	Teachers interpret intellectual disagreement as a stimulating exercise.
Teachers reward students for accuracy in problem solving.	Teachers reward students for innovative approaches to problem solving.
Students admire brilliance in teachers.	Students admire friendliness in teachers.
Students should speak in class only when called on by the teacher.	Students are encouraged to volunteer their thoughts.
Teachers should never lose face; to do so loses the respect of students.	Teachers can admit when they are wrong and still maintain students' respect.
Students expect the teacher to show them "the way."	Teachers expect students to find their own way through self-discovery.

Wherever you find yourself teaching, the above forces will come into play as you attempt to be an effective teacher. If a particular approach resonates more with your identity than another, it is vital to approach the establishment of connections with students and colleagues with care, particularly if their backgrounds differ from yours. Being attuned to how others perceive your actions is important, but it's equally crucial to act in a way that you believe will foster progress in perspectives. Being open to adjusting your idealized self-image to some degree can be beneficial, particularly at the onset of a teaching role. Charging in with excessive zeal can lead to distancing oneself from coworkers and ultimately could result in job loss within a few months. It is important to hold firm to your beliefs about effective teaching, it is beneficial to take a measured approach in gradually achieving your aspirations. Considering that there could be valuable insights to gain from their experiences!

Activity 4 Complete the following two simplified versions of assessment scales to test your personality and teaching style.

Here is a simplified version of a Teacher Teaching Style Assessment Scale, which includes a series of questions designed to evaluate the style and characteristics of teachers in the teaching process. This assessment scale is for reference only; for professional evaluation, please consult relevant professionals.

1. Personality Assessment Scale

Instructions: Please select the option that best matches your situation based on your understanding of yourself. Each question has five options, ranging from "Strongly Disagree" to "Strongly Agree."

Items	Strongly disagree	Disagree	Neutral	Agree	Strongly agree
1. I enjoy giving speeches or performing in front of a crowd.					
2. I tend to rely on logic and facts when making decisions.					
3. I often feel anxious or worried.					
4. I like to try new things and take risks.					
5. I am very sensitive to the feelings and needs of others.					
6. I prefer to stick to plans and do not like sudden changes.					
7. I am often the center of attention at parties or social events.					
8. I feel comfortable expressing my emotions.					
9. I tend to avoid conflicts and seek harmony					
10. I have high standards for both myself and others.					

Scoring Method:

- "Strongly Disagree" scores 1 point

- "Disagree" scores 2 points

- "Neutral" scores 3 points

- "Agree" scores 4 points

- "Strongly Agree" scores 5 points

Total Score Calculation:

Add up the scores of all questions to get the total score.

Result Analysis:

- Total score of 10–20: You may be an introverted, cautious, and emotionally stable person.

- Total score of 21–40: You may have a balanced personality, with traits of both extroversion and introversion.

- Total score of 41-50: You may be an extroverted, open, and emotionally expressive person.

2. Teacher Teaching Style Assessment Scale

Instructions: Please select the option that best fits your situation based on your teaching practice. Each question has five options, ranging from "Never" to "Always."

Items	Strongly disagree	Disagree	Neutral	Agree	Strongly agree
1. I often use discussions and group work in the classroom.					
2. I tend to use traditional lecture methods to impart knowledge.					
3. I encourage students to ask questions and participate in classroom discussions.					
4. I frequently use multimedia and information technology in teaching.					
5. I value individual differences among students and try to adjust my teaching methods to meet the needs of different students.					
6. I focus on developing students' critical thinking skills in the classroom.					
7. I often organize extracurricular activities to support classroom teaching.					
8. When assessing students, I pay more attention to the process rather than just the outcome.					
9. I tend to use standardized tests to evaluate students' learning outcomes.					
10. I often give students positive feedback and encouragement.					

Scoring Method:

- "Never" scores 1 point

- "Rarely" scores 2 points

- "Sometimes" scores 3 points

- "Often" scores 4 points

- "Always" scores 5 points

Total Score Calculation:

Add up the scores of all questions to get the total score.

Result Analysis:

- Total score of 10–20: You may lean more towards a traditional, teacher-centered teaching style.

- Total score of 21–40: You may combine traditional and modern teaching methods in your teaching, with a certain degree of flexibility.

- Total score of 41–50: You are likely a student-centered teacher, focusing on student participation and individual differences.

10.5 Creating a Positive Classroom Climate

The roles you play and the styles that you develop will merge to give you some tools for creating a classroom climate that is positive, stimulating, and energizing.

10.5.1 Establish Rapport

Developing a positive classroom atmosphere hinges on the somewhat elusive yet critical idea of rapport. This rapport refers to the connection or relationship forged with students; it is a bond grounded in mutual trust and respect, paving the way for students to feel capable, competent, and inventive. What strategies can be employed to cultivate such a relationship? To foster such a connection, it is essential to consider some guiding principles that can enhance the bond between educators and learners.

- show interest in each student as a person;
- give feedback on each person's progress;
- openly solicit students' ideas and feelings;
- value and respect what students think and say;
- laugh with them and not at them;
- work with them as a team, and not against them;
- Develop a genuine sense of vicarious joy when they learn something or otherwise succeed.

10.5.2 Balance Praise and Criticism

Establishing a rapport involves carefully managing the interplay between commendation and critique. Below are several recommendations for delivering effective acknowledgments when compared to unproductive ones (inspired by Brophy, 1981) (see Table 10.4).

Table 10.4 Effective praise versus ineffective praise

Effective praise	Ineffective praise
shows genuine pleasure and concern	is impersonal, mechanical, and "robotic"
shows verbal and nonverbal variety	shows bland uniformity
specifies the particulars of an accomplishment, so students know exactly what was performed well	is restricted to global comments, so students are not sure what was performed well
is offered in recognition of noteworthy effort on difficult tasks	is offered equally strongly for easy and difficult tasks
attributes success to effort, implying that similar success can be expected in the future	attributes success to ability, luck, or other external factors
fosters intrinsic motivation to continue to pursue goals	fosters extrinsic motivation to perform only to receive more praise
is delivered without disrupting the communicative flow of ongoing interaction	disrupts the communicative flow of ongoing interaction

An excess of either force diminishes its impact and effectiveness. Sincere acknowledgment, when given in a suitable manner, allows learners to embrace feedback and apply it constructively.

10.5.3 Power Generation

How do we define the concept of "energy" within a classroom setting? In certain respects, it can be likened to a dynamic force that emerges within a classroom, possibly detectable only through an intuitive understanding developed through teaching experience. This energy is often what comes to mind when one reflects after a class, exclaiming, "Wow! This is a great lesson! One might exclaim, "What a remarkable group of learners!" The vigor present in a classroom is a manifestation of multiple intellects entwined in a continuous loop of discussing, reflecting, and creating. This dynamism serves as a catalyst for innovation, ignited by student interactions. Such enthusiasm encourages learners to immerse themselves more deeply in their endeavors (Wright, 2005). Whether they are in class or not, both students and educators carry this inspiration with them, returning the next day ready to engage once more.

What methods can one employ to generate this kind of enthusiasm? Energy can be generated not only through grand gestures or showmanship, sharp humor, or profound insights. There are times when a tranquil, composed educator can spark energy within the classroom. At other moments, the collective focus of students engaged in seemingly ordinary assignments can create a powerful energy. Our experience in teaching suggests that fostering interaction and teamwork is vital for building that energy—participation from students, whether in large groups or pairs, often serves as a crucial element.

You hold an essential role in this process. Since learners primarily turn to you for direction and support, it is your responsibility to ignite their creative energies. Regardless of how you achieve this, it is done through thorough preparedness, assurance in your teaching skills, a sincere belief in your students' learning potential, and a true enthusiasm for your profession.

The realms of teaching, encompassing both artistic and scientific elements, often intersect with the challenges of managing a classroom. On one side, effectively sustaining the pace, energy, and rhythm during lessons calls for the creative touch of spontaneous decisions made at the moment. With a classroom full of unique individuals, each having their own distinct needs, emotions, and drives, it becomes nearly impossible to foresee all the reactions and contributions they might present.

Conversely, the insights you possess are shaped by the wisdom and effective practices of predecessors, offering a framework of strategies for successful management. By integrating proven strategies with one's instinct, an individual can approach the unpredictable nature of the classroom with both assurance and inventiveness.

Activity 5 **Observe an English class (live or via video), analyze how the teacher gives praise or criticism to students during the teaching process, what kind of language is used, how the students respond, and the effectiveness of the approach.**

Topic:	Lesson type:

Thinking and Doing

A. Discussion Questions

1. Consider the list of solutions to problems encountered in large classes. Are the solutions practical? Do they apply to actual circumstances that you or your classmate may be familiar with? What are some further measures that can be taken to maximize student opportunities for practice in large classes?

2. Can you think of other "challenging conditions" of teaching? Describe them. How would you deal with them?

B. Practice

Suppose you are the English teacher for Class 1 of the first year in a middle school. You are going to declare the disciplinary requirements to the students at the beginning of the first meeting with the students. Write the details of the requirements, following the example.

1. Being late: Please arrive on time for class. If you are late, kindly report to the teacher and explain the reason for your tardiness. ______________________________

____

____

____

____

____

____

C. Exercises for instructional skills

1. What role does he/she play when a teacher explains the purpose of a task, the steps to do it, and its time limit?

   A. An organizer. B. An observer. C. An evaluator. D. A prompter.

2. When the teacher attempts to elicit more information from the students by saying "And?" "Good. Anything else?", etc., he/she is playing the role of ________.

   A. prompter B. participant C. manager D. consultant

3. In which of the following situations is the teacher playing the role of an assessor?

   A. Give feedback to correct mistakes.

   B. Offer help to students who are in need of language.

   C. Organize students to do activities by giving instructions.

   D. Walk around to see how each student performs in group work.

4. Before students start the task, the teacher divides students into groups of four and explains how the task is carried out. What role does he/she play?

   A. An assessor. B. An organizer. C. A prompter. D. A researcher.

5. During the activity, the teacher participates in groups and works with students. What role does he/she play?

   A. A researcher. B. A resource-provider.

   C. A facilitator. D. A participant.

6. What role does the teacher play when he/she guides students on how to conduct autonomous learning?

   A. An instructor. B. A controller.

   B. C. A facilitator. D. An assessor.

7. If a teacher intends to maintain discipline in the class, what instruction would he/she give to the students?

   A. Close your books. B. Listen to the tape.

   C. Raise your hands. D. Be quiet, please.

8. Which of the following is the most advantageous relationship mode between teachers and students?

   A. The managerial mode. B. The arbitrary mode.

   C. The democratic mode. D. The permissive mode.

9. Which of the following activities is the most suitable for group work?

   A. The guessing game. B. The story telling.

   C. The information gap activity. D. The drama performance.

10. Which of the following statements is NOT correct?

A. "Rapport" is a kind of relationship that can help students' capability, competence, and creativity.

B. Students are given equally strong praise whenever they finish a difficult task or an easy one.

C. Teachers may have different roles based on different cultures.

D. Even if all of the students work hard, and are active, dedicated, and intelligent, there still exists the "discipline" problem.

Checklist

Mark the questions with a check (√) if your answer is yes.

☐ Have I understood the concepts of classroom management?

☐ Have I understand the principles of classroom management?

☐ Have I grasped the strategies to control and management a large class?

☐ Have I understood what a positive classroom environment look like?

☐ Can I analyze my own personality and teaching styles?

Reflective Journal

Please write down your reflections on what you have/have not learned in this chapter.

◇ The essential skills I need to possess and develop for English teaching:

____

____

____

____

____

◇ Anything I wish to further explore (i.e., puzzles and difficulties):

____

____

____

____

____

References

Becker, A., Freeman, A., Giesinger Hall, C., Cummins, M., & Yuhnke, B. (2016). *NMC Horizon Report: 2016 K–12 Edition*. The New Media Consortium.

Brophy, J. (1981). Teacher praise: A functional analysis. *Review of Educational Research*, 51(1), 5–32.

Crosby, R. M. H. (2000). AMEE Guide No 20: The good teacher is more than a lecturer—The twelve roles of the teacher. *Medical Teacher*, 22(4), 334–347. https://doi.org/10.1080/014215900409429

Harmer, J. (2015). *The practice of English language teaching* (5th ed.). Pearson Education.

Hofstede, G. (1986). Cultural differences in teaching and learning. *International Journal of Intercultural Relations*, 10, 301–320.

International Society for Technology in Education. (2016). *ISTE standards for educators*. http://www.iste.org/standards/standards/for-students

LoCastro, V. (2012). *Pragmatics for language educators: A sociolinguistic perspective*. Oxford University Press.

Scrivener, J. (2020). *Learning teaching: The guide to English language teaching*. Foreign Language Teaching and Research Press.

Shamim, F. (2016). Teaching large classes in difficult circumstances. *In The Routledge handbook of English language teaching*. Routledge.

Wright, T. (2005). *Classroom management in language education*. Palgrave Macmillan. https://doi.org/10.1057/9780230514188

Zhu, Z. T., & Wei, F. (2017). 面向智慧教育的教师发展创新路径 [Innovative pathways for teacher development in the context of smart education]. *Journal of Chinese Education*, (9), 21–28.

Zhu, Z. T., & Wei, F. (2018). 教育信息化 2.0: 智能教育启程，智慧教育领航 [Education Informatization 2.0: Embarking on smart education, navigating with intelligent education]. *Journal of Educational Technology Research*, 39(9), 5–16.

Chapter 11

Observation, Assessment, and Reflection Skills

Objectives

Upon completion of this chapter, you should be able to:

- Understand the concepts and principles of observation, assessment, and reflection.
- Grasp different types of observation, evaluation, and reflection. Learn to apply observation, assessment, and reflection methods to English teaching and research.
- Improve and enhance professional development.

Discussion Questions

Why do you think a test is needed after you finish learning a course? What kinds of tests can you think of ? What is the difference between a test and an evaluation?

11.1 Classroom Observation

Classroom observation refers to a systematic and purposeful research method where researchers or educators utilize their senses and relevant auxiliary tools (such as observation sheets, audio, and video recording devices) to collect data directly or indirectly from classroom settings (Wang & Li, 2014). The development of classroom observation technology has gone through three stages: live observation, video recording observation, and information technology-supported observation (Yu et al., 2024) . It involves recording, analyzing, and researching the operational status of classroom activities, with the ultimate goal of enhancing student learning outcomes and promoting teacher development.

11.1.1 Five Types of Observation Under Different Purposes

In a general sense, the act of observation can be categorized into five distinct types, each defined by the specific objectives of those who initiate them.

Training. Training is a component of a development program designed to help facilitators assess your existing skill level and identify areas for improvement. Typically, observations during training sessions are carried out according to an external framework, meaning participants are evaluated in relation to achieving predetermined objectives within a specific curriculum.

Development. The notion of "development" differs significantly from the idea of training, as it implies that your personal objectives take precedence over formal course requirements or guidance from an instructor. In an observation focused on development, you would generally determine the specific aspects on which you would most like to receive input.

Evaluation. Evaluation is conducted to measure both your performance and teaching methods against established standards of excellence, suitability, and other relevant factors. This evaluation can form part of an educational program, possibly resulting in grades or levels, or it might involve an assessment from external entities, such as a national accreditation body.

Data collection. In some cases, educators, schools, or others may wish to conduct an objective examination of certain elements within the classroom environment (for example, "analyzing how participation differs between male and female students" or "types of questions posed by teachers"). These evaluations often rely on quantitative investigation methods (such as determining the frequency, extent, etc. of various activities). Typically, these observations are made by peers instead of trainers or individuals within the school administration.

Peer observation. It is when a coworker attends your class (or a section of it) to observe your teaching. The purpose is for both individuals to gain insights. It is not anticipated that your coworker will provide feedback typical of a trainer; however, this situation can lead to an engaging exchange of ideas, discussions on various pedagogical approaches, and comparisons of perspectives, among other things.

Considering the educational topics and aims specified in this tutorial, the observation being conducted here aligns with the fifth category, which is peer observation. The intention behind this approach is to promote collaborative teaching research and shared learning experiences, particularly focusing on the professional growth of teachers themselves.

11.1.2 Three Stages of Classroom Observation

The process of implementing classroom observation can be divided into three stages: before observation, during observation, and post observation.

11.1.2.1 Pre-observation

Prior to entering the classroom, it is crucial to plan the observation thoroughly. This includes:

- **Setting objectives:** Clearly define the purpose of the observation, such as evaluating a particular instructional strategy, assessing student engagement, or observing classroom management.
- **Selecting focus areas:** Identify the specific aspects of teaching and learning you intend to observe (e.g., teacher-student interaction, use of language, and instructional materials).
- **Preparing tools:** Choose or create appropriate observation tools, such as checklists, rating scales, or field note templates.

Obtaining permission: Seek the permission of the teacher and, if necessary, the school administration to conduct the observation.

11.1.2.2 During observation

1. Observation techniques

During the observation, employ a combination of techniques to capture a holistic view of the classroom dynamics:

- **Attentive engagement:** Observe the expressions utilized by educators and learners meticulously, assessing their clarity, suitability, and overall impact.
- **Thorough documentation:** Take notes in a structured manner, capturing specific instances, timestamps, and your spontaneous thoughts.
- **Recording of video or audio:** With the approval of those involved, utilize technology to capture the session for future evaluation and reflection.
- **Engaging in participant observation:** In various environments, it is beneficial to immerse oneself in educational activities to attain a more comprehensive grasp of the situation (Cui et al., 2007).

2. Focus areas

Direct attention to crucial aspects pertinent to the teaching of the English language, including:

- **Language evaluation:** Assess the precision, coherence, and sophistication of the language utilized by both instructors and learners.

- **Teaching approaches:** Evaluate the success of various instructional techniques, such as tailoring instruction to meet diverse needs, providing structured support, and incorporating real-world resources.
- **Participation observations:** Assess the levels of involvement, enthusiasm, and emotional reactions that students demonstrate towards classroom activities.
- **Classroom supervision:** Evaluate the educator's effectiveness in fostering a secure, structured, and welcoming educational setting.

11.1.2.3 After observation

Evaluating and contemplating following the observation.

• Methods and tools for compiling observation data

Transcription and annotation: The observation notes should be reformatted into a structured layout, like a transcript, which facilitates effective annotation and emphasis on significant interactions and moments.

Employing digital solutions for managing data: Make use of digital resources such as spreadsheets, databases, or qualitative analysis applications to systematically code, organize, and access observational information in an effective manner.

Thematic exploration: Create classification frameworks to organize observational data into distinct themes or categories, facilitating analysis and linking visible practices to overarching educational trends.

• Recognizing the strengths and difficulties in teaching and learning

Assessment based on solid evidence: Identify strengths and weaknesses by relying on tangible observations, and utilize particular instances to substantiate your findings.

A comparative evaluation: Assess various groups, educators, or instructional strategies to identify which methods are most impactful and where enhancements might be beneficial.

Reflection on student outcomes: Assessing student results involves a thorough examination of their work, behaviors, and responses in order to gauge the effectiveness of teaching methods on their educational progress.

• Making connections between theoretical insights, observations, and individual teaching approaches.

Theoretical framework basis: Correlate the observed actions with educational theories and models to comprehend their relevance in practical situations.

Connection to personal philosophy: Consider how this experience relates to one's own educational beliefs and reflect on whether it supports or challenges those principles, while also contemplating its potential impact on future instructional strategies.

Strategic modification: Utilize insights from theory to adjust or refine teaching approaches with the aim of boosting student involvement and educational results.

- **Participating in meaningful dialogue and providing constructive criticism**

Collaborative inquiry: Engaging in collective inquiry involves collaborating with colleagues and mentors to share insights, which serve as a foundation for joint reflection and the creation of strategies.

Feedback sessions: Participate in organized meetings aimed at both providing and receiving evaluations, where insights are shared in an encouraging and developmental setting.

11.1.3 Utilization of Insights from Classroom Observations

Integrating observed practices into one's own teaching

Targeted implementation: Certain observed approaches may not be appropriate for every educational setting. Carefully select strategies or approaches that correspond with one's teaching style and the specific needs of students, making sure they are appropriate for the learning environment.

Trial and reflection: Experiment with various methods in your lessons by implementing chosen approaches on a trial basis, then refine these techniques using insights and results from student experiences to identify the most effective ones.

Jointly engaging: Discuss with colleagues the strategies you have implemented based on your observations, sharing specific instances along with an analysis of the potential advantages and obstacles you have faced.

Tailoring approaches to suit various groups of learners

Customized teaching methods: Adapt the identified strategies to meet the varied requirements of students, incorporating approaches such as differentiated tasks, adaptable group configurations, and diverse methods of presenting information.

Awareness of cultural differences: When applying innovative techniques, it is important to take into account the various cultural heritages of the students, guaranteeing that the approaches remain inclusive and honor the diversity within the learner community.

Feedback loop: Establish a mechanism that encourages learners to share their insights regarding the newly implemented methods, enabling ongoing adaptation and enhancement of teaching techniques to maximize both engagement and educational outcomes.

Reflecting on the impact of observed techniques on language learning

Language acquisition evaluation metrics: Implement specific evaluation criteria related to language learning, such as fluency, precision, and intricacy, to assess how effectively the observed methods contribute to the linguistic progress of students.

Conducting an extended evaluation: Utilize the methods over a prolonged timeframe, monitoring learners' achievements through diverse assessments to evaluate the enduring effects on their language abilities.

Linguistic diversity: Examine how the identified strategies facilitate the development of various linguistic abilities (including listening, speaking, reading, and writing) and modify these approaches to enhance comprehensive language proficiency.

Creating an environment of prioritizing ongoing professional growth

Professional learning communities: Engage in or establish collaborative learning networks for educators aimed at exchanging insights from classroom observations and jointly investigating effective instructional strategies.

Mentorship and coaching: Participating in mentorship schemes or pursuing coaching opportunities can enhance one's ability to reflect on and utilize insights gained through observations, while also obtaining personalized advice that aligns with professional development goals.

Promoting reflective practice: Foster activities such as collaborative lesson study groups, workshops focused on self-evaluation, or programs for observing peers, which would strengthen an environment of ongoing professional development and enhancement for teachers.

11.1.4 Ethical Considerations in Classroom Observation

Throughout the observation process, adhere to ethical guidelines (Zhang, 2012).

- Respect privacy: Ensure that all observations and recordings are kept confidential.
- Informed consent: Obtain the informed consent of all parties involved.
- Minimizing disruption: Ensure that your presence and activities do not disrupt the learning environment.
- Fairness and impartiality: Maintain an unbiased and non-judgmental attitude.

11.1.5 Avoiding Observer Biases in Classroom Observation

Classroom observation is widely used in educational settings to assess teacher performance, identify areas for improvement, and promote professional development. However, the presence of observer biases can limit the effectiveness of this practice.

11.1.5.1 Types of observer biases

Confirmation bias

Confirmation bias occurs when observers seek, interpret, and remember information that confirms their preconceptions while giving disproportionately less consideration to alternative possibilities (Nickerson, 1998). For example, an observer who believes a teacher is ineffective may only notice instances that support this belief, ignoring evidence to the contrary.

Halo effect

The halo effect is a type of cognitive bias where an observer's overall impression of a person influences their judgment about that person's specific traits (Thorndike, 1920). In classroom observation, this may lead to an observer overestimating the effectiveness of a teacher based on a single strong lesson or underestimating a teacher with a single weak lesson.

Observer expectancy effect

The observer expectancy effect occurs when the observer's expectations about a situation or person influence their behavior, leading to a self-fulfilling prophecy (Rosenthal & Jacobson, 1968). For instance, if an observer expects a teacher to be unengaging, their demeanor and feedback may inadvertently discourage the teacher, affecting the observation results.

Selective attention

Selective attention bias arises when observers focus on specific aspects of a classroom and neglect others, potentially leading to an incomplete evaluation (Brophy & Good, 1986). For example, an observer might concentrate on teacher-student interaction while ignoring student engagement or the classroom environment.

11.1.5.2 Strategies to avoid observer biases

Training and awareness

Observers should receive training on various biases and their potential impact on classroom observations. Increased awareness can help observers recognize and mitigate their biases.

Use of checklists and rubrics

Utilizing checklists and rubrics can help observers remain focused and objective during an observation. These tools ensure that all relevant aspects of the lesson are considered, reducing the likelihood of selective attention.

Multiple observations

Conducting multiple observations can provide a more comprehensive view of a teacher's performance and help counteract the influence of any single observation bias (Ginsberg & Daniels, 2014).

Peer observation and feedback

Peer observation and feedback can offer alternative perspectives and reduce the likelihood of observer biases (Goldberg & Theune, 2012). Colleagues may notice different aspects of a lesson and provide balanced feedback.

11.1.6 Classroom Observation Framework

There are many factors involved in a classroom, and it is necessary to have a concise and scientific observation framework as a specific "handle" or "support" for observation; otherwise, the observation will fall into randomness and disorder. Shen and Cui (2008) points out that the classroom is constructed mainly by four elements, namely student learning, teacher instruction, curriculum traits, and classroom culture. Through deconstructing the four elements of classroom teaching, a four-dimension classroom observation framework is constructed, which is called LICC Classroom Observation Framework (L stands for learning, I for instruction, C for curriculum and culture) (Cui, 2012) (see Figure 11.1). Compared with other observation frameworks, the LICC observation framework is more systematic (Lin & Yu , 2016)

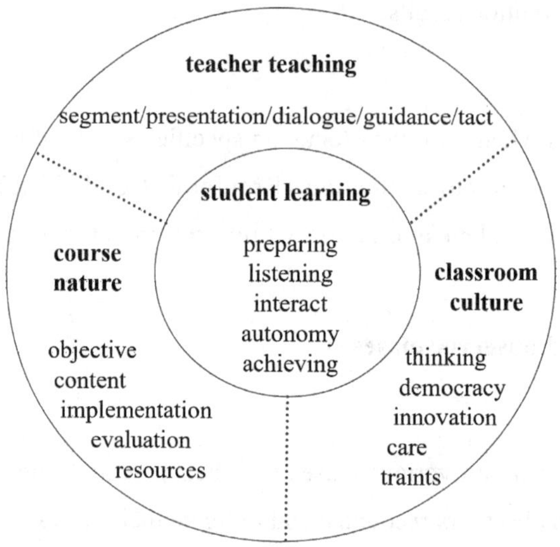

Figure 11.1 LICC Classroom Observation Framework

The following are the observation points of the four-dimension framework (Wang & Li, 2014).

11.1.6.1 Student learning observation points

1. Preparation

- What did the students prepare before class? How did they prepare?
- How well were they prepared? How many students made preparations?
- What are the preparation habits of high-achieving and struggling students?

2. Listening

- How many students can listen to the teacher's lecture? For how long can they listen?
- How many students can listen to their classmates' speeches?

- While listening, what auxiliary behaviors do students have (taking notes / consulting / responding)? How many are there?

3. Interaction

- What types of interactions are there? Does the student interaction help achieve the goal?
- How many people, time, subjects, processes, and quality are involved in asking/answering questions?
- How many people, time, subjects, processes, and quality are involved in group discussions?
- How many people, time, subjects, processes, and quality are involved in classroom activities (individual/group)?
- What are the interaction habits of students? What emotional behaviors have emerged?

4. Autonomy

- How much time do students have for self-directed learning? How many students are involved? What is the participation level of struggling students?
- What forms of self-directed learning do students engage in (inquiry/note-taking/reading/thinking)? How many students are involved in each?
- Is the students' self-directed learning organized? Do students engage in self-directed inquiry activities? How are both high-achieving and struggling students doing?
- What is the quality of students' self-directed learning?

5. Achievement

- Are students clear about the learning objectives of this lesson?
- What evidence is there that the set objectives have been achieved (opinions/homework/expression/board work/demonstration)? How many students have achieved them?
- What objectives have been generated in this lesson? How effective were they?

11.1.6.2 Observation points for teacher instruction

1. Segments

- What segments are composed of? Are they centered around the teaching objectives? Are these segments aimed at all students? How is the time allocated among different segments, behaviors, and content?

2. Presentation

- How is the explanation given? Is the explanation effective (clear, structured, relevant to the topic, concise, speaking rate, volume, rhythm)?

- How is the blackboard writing presented? Does it provide help for student learning?
- How is the media presented? Is it appropriate? Is it effective?
- How are actions (such as experiments, movements, and creations) presented? Are they standardized? Are they effective?

3. Dialogue

- What are the targets, frequency, types, structure, cognitive difficulty, and waiting time for questions? Are they effective?
- How is the teacher's response method and content? What are the auxiliary methods? Are they effective?
- What topics are there? How are the topics related to the learning objectives?

4. Guidance

- How is student self-learning guided (reading/assignments)? Is it effective?
- How is student collaborative learning guided (discussions, activities, assignments)? Is it effective? (In the design of student collaboration segments, teachers should also be well-prepared, with clear objectives)
- How is student inquiry learning guided (experiments, project research, assignments)? Is it effective?

5. Tact

- What adjustments are made to the teaching design? Why? What is the effect?
- How are unexpected events from students or situations handled? What is the effect?
- What nonverbal behaviors (facial expressions, movements, body language) are demonstrated? What is the effect?
- What are the characteristic classroom behaviors (language, teaching demeanor, knowledge, skills, ideas)?

11.1.6.3 Observation points for course traits

1. Objectives

- What are the preset learning objectives? Are the expressions of learning objectives standardized and clear?
- Are the objectives preset based on what (curriculum standards, students, teaching materials)? Are they suitable for the students in this class? Are new learning objectives generated in the classroom? Are they reasonable?

2. Content

- How is the teaching material handled (added, deleted, combined, established, replaced)? Is it reasonable?

- What content is generated in the classroom? How is it handled?
- Does it highlight the characteristics, ideas, core skills, and logical relationships of this subject?
- Is the capacity suitable for the students in this class? How to meet the needs of different students?

3. Implementation

- What methods are preset (lecture, discussion, activities, inquiry, interaction)? How well do they fit with the learning objectives? Do they reflect the characteristics of this subject? Is there attention to guidance on learning methods?
- What kind of situation is created? Is it effective?

4. Evaluation

- What are the main evaluation methods used to detect learning objectives? Are they effective? (After setting teaching objectives, there must be assessments that match the objectives, which is the summative evaluation of this lesson.)
- Does it pay attention to obtaining relevant evaluation information during the teaching process (responses, homework, expressions)? How is the obtained evaluation information utilized (explanation, feedback, suggestions for improvement)? (You can observe and study the teacher's evaluative language in the classroom.)

5. Resources

- What resources are preset (teachers and students, texts, physical objects and models, experiments, multimedia)?
- Does the utilization of preset resources contribute to the achievement of learning objectives?
- What resources are generated (mistakes, responses, homework, works)? What is their relationship with the achievement of learning objectives?

11.1.6.4 Classroom culture observation points

1. Thinking

- Does the learning objective focus on higher-order cognitive skills (explanation, problem-solving, transfer, synthesis, evaluation)?
- Is teaching driven by questions? What is the relationship between the question chain and the students' cognitive level and knowledge structure?
- How is independent thinking guided in students?

- How are errors in students' thinking treated or handled? How many students are thinking, for how long, and at what level? What is the classroom atmosphere like?

2. Democracy

- What is the nature of classroom discourse (quantity, time, targets, phrasing, interruptions)?
- How many students participate in teaching activities, and for how long? What is the classroom atmosphere like?
- How are teacher-student behaviors (situational settings, opportunities to answer, seating arrangements)?
- What are the relationships among students like?

3. Innovation

- What is novel in teaching design, situation creation, and resource utilization?
- Does the teaching design and classroom atmosphere help students express their creative ideas? How are they handled?
- What goals and resources are generated in the classroom? How does the teacher handle them?

4. Care

- Are learning objectives aimed at all students? Does it pay attention to the needs of different students? Are the learning needs of special students (with learning difficulties, disabilities, illnesses) addressed?
- Are seating arrangements appropriate?
- What is the nature of classroom discourse (quantity, time, targets, phrasing, interruptions) and behaviors (opportunities to answer, seating arrangements)?

5. Traits

- What strengths of the teacher are reflected in this class (language style, behavioral characteristics, thinking quality)?
- Is there any distinctive feature in the overall design of the class (segment arrangement, textbook handling, introduction, teaching strategies, learning guidance, dialogue)?
- How do students evaluate the teaching characteristics of this teacher?

11.1.7 Examples of Classroom Observation Scales for English Teaching

Classroom observation scales are essential tools for evaluating teaching effectiveness and providing feedback to improve instruction. You need to design observation scales according to different purposes and create a template for your observation scale. The following examples of classroom observation scales derive from a research made by Gan L (2018), The purpose of which is to investigate the problems in English listening teaching and learning, especially the effectiveness of teaching design and classroom questioning in English listening teaching through classroom observation. It finds that listening classroom observation has a promotional effect on English listening instruction, and it positively impacts teachers' English teaching behaviors and professional development.

11.1.7.1 Listening classroom observation scale—teaching design

This observation scale focuses on the topic of "English listening teaching design". It covers five dimensions: teaching objectives, content, implementation, evaluation, and the use of resources (see Figure 11.2).

Date___________ Topic__________ Teacher__________ Observer__________			
Dimension	**Observation points**	**Observation statistics**	**Evaluation reflection**
Objectives	① What are the preset learning objectives? Are they appropriate for the students' level? ② Are there any new learning objectives formed in class? Is it reasonable?		
Content	① How is the listening material handled (combined/replaced/increased/decreased)? Is it reasonable? ② What contents have been generated during the listening teaching process? How to deal with them? ③ Is the difficulty and content of the listening materials suitable for this class? How to meet the needs of different students? ④ How to use listening audio materials? Does it interpret the listening text?		
Implementation	① What are the preset teaching methods? What is the suitability of the learning objective? ② Does it focus on guiding listening strategies? ③ What kind of situation has been created? Is it effective?		
Evaluation	① What are the main assessment methods used to check the learning objectives? Is it effective? ② How to utilize relevant evaluation information obtained during the listening teaching process (answers/homework/emotions)?		
Resources	① What resources were preset (teachers/textbooks/multimedia, etc.)? ② What resources have been generated (mistakes/answers/homework/products)? What is the relationship between these resources and the achievement of learning objectives? ③ What extra-curricular listening resources did you recommend to students?		

Figure 11.2 Classroom observation scale for teachers' teaching design

11.1.7.2 Listening classroom observation scale—effective questioning

The following observation scale focuses on how teachers promote questions in listening teaching (see Figure 11.3).

<table>
<tr><td colspan="20">Teacher__________ Observer__________ Date__________</td></tr>
<tr><td colspan="20">Observation Dimension: Student Learning—Receptive / Interactive / Achieved
Research Question: Effectiveness of Teacher's Questions</td></tr>
<tr><td rowspan="3">Serial No.</td><td rowspan="3">Teacher Question (Original Words)</td><td rowspan="3">Pause Time</td><td colspan="4" rowspan="2">Student response mode</td><td colspan="4" rowspan="2">Teacher response mode</td><td colspan="4" rowspan="2">Motivational methods</td><td colspan="5">The nature of the question itself</td></tr>
<tr><td colspan="2">Direction</td><td colspan="3">Level</td></tr>
<tr><td>no answer</td><td>collective response</td><td>designated response</td><td>independent free response</td><td>discussion report</td><td>no handling</td><td>interruption or proxy answer</td><td>organization and refinement</td><td>follow-up questions</td><td>none</td><td>general language</td><td>specific advantages</td><td>clarity</td><td>ambiguity</td><td>memorization</td><td>comprehensive analysis</td><td>evaluation</td></tr>
<tr><td>1</td><td></td><td></td><td></td><td></td><td></td><td></td><td></td><td></td><td></td><td></td><td></td><td></td><td></td><td></td><td></td><td></td><td></td><td></td><td></td></tr>
<tr><td>2</td><td></td><td></td><td></td><td></td><td></td><td></td><td></td><td></td><td></td><td></td><td></td><td></td><td></td><td></td><td></td><td></td><td></td><td></td><td></td></tr>
<tr><td>3</td><td></td><td></td><td></td><td></td><td></td><td></td><td></td><td></td><td></td><td></td><td></td><td></td><td></td><td></td><td></td><td></td><td></td><td></td><td></td></tr>
<tr><td colspan="2">Frequency</td><td></td><td></td><td></td><td></td><td></td><td></td><td></td><td></td><td></td><td></td><td></td><td></td><td></td><td></td><td></td><td></td><td></td><td></td></tr>
<tr><td colspan="2">Statistic data</td><td></td><td></td><td></td><td></td><td></td><td></td><td></td><td></td><td></td><td></td><td></td><td></td><td></td><td></td><td></td><td></td><td></td><td></td></tr>
<tr><td colspan="2">Analysis</td><td colspan="18"></td></tr>
</table>

Figure 11.3 Classroom observation scale for teacher questioning

11.1.7.3 Listening classroom observation scale—listening strategies training

The following observation scale mainly focuses on strategy training, observing whether teachers follow the concept and principle of strategy training, and training students' listening strategies at the pre-listening, while-listening, and post-listening stages (see Figure 11.4).

<table>
<tr><td colspan="4">Instructor: ________ Class: ________ Time: ________ Recorder: __________</td></tr>
<tr><td colspan="4">Observation Dimension: Guidance and Training of Listening Strategies for Students by the Teacher
Research Question: Does the teacher pay attention to the training of listening skills and strategies? Which aspects are involved in the training? How does the teacher conduct listening strategy training in the classroom?</td></tr>
<tr><th>Stages</th><th>Listening strategy</th><th>How teachers guide</th><th>How students participate</th></tr>
<tr><td rowspan="7">Pre-listening</td><td>Motivation</td><td></td><td></td></tr>
<tr><td>Interest</td><td></td><td></td></tr>
<tr><td>Planing: Establishing listening goals</td><td></td><td></td></tr>
<tr><td>Pre-organization:</td><td></td><td></td></tr>
<tr><td>Conducting preparatory exercises</td><td></td><td></td></tr>
<tr><td>Association/Prediction:</td><td></td><td></td></tr>
<tr><td>Activating related knowledge of the topic and making predictions</td><td></td><td></td></tr>
<tr><td rowspan="9">During Listening</td><td>Selective attention</td><td></td><td></td></tr>
<tr><td>Self-monitoring</td><td></td><td></td></tr>
<tr><td>Note-taking</td><td></td><td></td></tr>
<tr><td>Memory</td><td></td><td></td></tr>
<tr><td>Reasoning</td><td></td><td></td></tr>
<tr><td>Restructuring</td><td></td><td></td></tr>
<tr><td>Imagery: Forming a visual impression of the information obtained in the mind</td><td></td><td></td></tr>
<tr><td>Transfer</td><td></td><td></td></tr>
<tr><td>Reducing anxiety</td><td></td><td></td></tr>
<tr><td rowspan="3">Post-Listening</td><td>Summarizing and evaluating</td><td></td><td></td></tr>
<tr><td>Collaborative learning</td><td></td><td></td></tr>
<tr><td>Seeking explanations or clarifications</td><td></td><td></td></tr>
</table>

Figure 11.4 Classroom observation scale for listening strategy training

11.1.7.4 Listening classroom observation scale—students' learning activities

This observation scale mainly focuses on classroom activities. The specific observation details of students' performances in the listening class can be their level of concentration during listening, note-taking habits, participation in classroom exercises, involvement in group discussions, etc. (see Figure 11.5).

<table>
<tr><td colspan="4">Topic __________ Unit __________ Class __________ Student No. __________
Teacher ______________ Observer ______________ Date __________</td></tr>
<tr><th>Activity content</th><th>Time</th><th>Classification description of students' behavior in activities</th><th>Activity evaluation</th></tr>
<tr><td>Problem introduction</td><td></td><td></td><td></td></tr>
<tr><td>Listening content prediction</td><td></td><td></td><td></td></tr>
<tr><td>Listening to the materials</td><td></td><td></td><td></td></tr>
<tr><td>Group discussion</td><td></td><td></td><td></td></tr>
<tr><td>Individual statements</td><td></td><td></td><td></td></tr>
<tr><td>...</td><td></td><td></td><td></td></tr>
<tr><td>Analysis and suggestions</td><td colspan="3"></td></tr>
</table>

Figure 11.5 Classroom observation scale for students' performance

Activity 1 Design a classroom observation scale according to what you have learned in this section, focusing on one observation point in classroom teaching.

____

____

____

____

____

____

____

____

____

____

11.2 Teaching Assessment

Assessment plays a pivotal role in the teaching and learning process. It not only evaluates student knowledge and skills but also informs instructional strategies and promotes student engagement. This section aims to empower teachers with the knowledge and skills necessary to effectively incorporate assessments into their teaching practice.

11.2.1 Definition of Assessment

When assessment in teaching is talked about, it is inevitable to mention another word: evaluation, even appraisal. A distinction is sometimes made between assessment (of learner performance), and evaluation (of innovation or change in, for example, school organization or a course syllabus). Evaluation and assessment are related terms in education and are often used interchangeably, but they do have distinct meanings and purposes. Assessments are used to measure and evaluate student learning, skills, and knowledge. They provide a snapshot of student performance at a specific point in time. Assessments can be formative (ongoing and used to inform instruction) or summative (evaluating learning at the end of a unit or course). Evaluation is a broader process that goes beyond the measurement of student learning. It involves the systematic analysis of teaching and learning activities to determine their effectiveness, quality, and impact. Evaluations can be used to inform decision-making, guide program improvements, and ensure that educational goals are being met.

Under the purpose of teacher professional development in this textbook, the term assessment is used to refer to teachers' performance to know and use some strategies to judge students' learning outcomes.

11.2.2 Definition of Teacher Assessment Literacy

According to Stiggings R. J.(1991), the creator of the term "assessment literacy", assessment literacy refers to individuals' ability to understand fundamental assessment concepts and procedures, which are believed to influence educational decisions. Assessment literacy includes understanding the connection between assessment and learning, the principles of assessment (such as reliability and validity), assessment techniques and methods, assessment criteria, policies, as well as the purposes and processes of feedback. Latter on, discussion on teachers' assessment literacy is increasingly on the rise. For example, Zheng D. H. (2010) believes that assessment literacy refers to the professional expertise that teachers should possess for engaging in academic assessment. It emphasizes teachers' academic assessment of students rather than all assessment-related matters related to teachers' work, such as teacher evaluation, school evaluation, and program evaluation. Yang G. H. (2011) defines it as "the knowledge, skills, abilities, and related concepts that teachers possess about assessment, especially at the classroom level."

11.2.3 Components of Teacher Assessment Literacy

According to Yang G. H. (2011), teacher assessment literacy contains four dimensions and twelve performance aspects (see Table 11.1).

Table 11.1 The four-dimensional teacher assessment literacy

Dimension	Manifestation Perspective	Behavioral example
Understanding assessment	Beliefs evaluation	Belief in assessment as a form of student research and teaching research; aiming to promote learning, and improve teaching methods; classroom-level assessments are primary channels for assessing students' learning; clear goals and student participation in evaluation processes.
	Awareness evaluation	Understanding internal vs. external evaluation relationships; demonstrating active engagement and stable psychological disposition towards evaluation practices; willingness to collaborate on practical evaluation and research.
	Knowledge evaluation	Recognizing the value and function of educational evaluation; understanding various types of evaluations and their conditions; familiarity with common evaluation methods and tools; comprehension of basic concepts and principles related to evaluation theories; differentiation between measurement and evaluation; application of commonly used evaluation theories in classroom settings.
Utilizing assessment	Selection method	Matching evaluation methods with objectives: diagnostic evaluation (pre-learning diagnosis), formative evaluation (issues identified during class), summative evaluation (post-class outcome assessment); matching evaluation forms with objectives: paper-and-pencil tests (knowledge acquisition), performance tasks (skills demonstration), project-based assessments (application).
	Evaluation developmental	Individual or group improvement/development of evaluation methods and tools. For example, moving towards professionalized classroom observation models—"LICC model".
	Implementation	Developing an evaluation plan: clarifying course standards against expected learning outcomes, converting course objectives into specific evaluation criteria, operationalizing these criteria through observable behaviors; defining content scope for evaluation; selecting evaluators, creating detailed rubrics, designing and refining test questions; appropriately training evaluators and conducting evaluations; scientifically interpreting results.
Managing assessment	Determination grade	Grading systems, combining absolute grading with relative grading; academic achievement evaluation: considering individual abilities, progress, and effort levels to provide objective, fair, comprehensive assessments of students' learning and development.
	Utilization results	Applying evaluation results to enhance individual learning, drive teacher improvements, guide school curriculum development, inform educational policy decisions, and support educational research.
	Communication results	Communicating evaluation findings to students, parents, society, and educational institutions, using appropriate language to express the significance, scope, and recommendations of the evaluation results. Emphasizing strengths while addressing areas needing improvement.

Continued

Dimension	Manifestation Perspective	Behavioral example
Evaluating evaluation	Ethical considerations	Identifying and correcting unethical or illegal behavior in evaluation methodology and information use. For instance, ensuring fairness in evaluation methods for each student, legality of methods that do not infringe upon others' rights, privacy protection in data collection and processing, ethical interpretation, and communication of results.
	Reflection	Reflecting on inappropriate methods and tools encountered in practice. For example, evaluating the diversity of evaluation methods, alignment of methods and tools with objectives, teaching, and learning; appropriateness of method/tool selection based on evaluator and object characteristics.
	Improvement	Comprehensive reflection on the entire evaluation process, timely adjustments, and refinement of evaluation actions. Such as concretizing evaluation objectives, optimizing evaluation plans, developing more suitable methods and tools, improving result interpretation and utilization.

11.2.3.1 Understanding assessment

Before assessment activities, you should first understand "assessment". It mainly includes:

Possess a firm and correct belief in assessment. Clearly understand the interactive relationship between "goals–teaching–learning–assessment"; fully recognize that the focus of assessment must shift from "assessment of learning" to "assessment for learning".

Enhance the awareness of actively carrying out assessment activities. Awareness precedes action. Assessment consciousness is the emotional orientation, emotional experience, and stable psychological tendency that teachers exhibit towards assessment, and it is a prerequisite for evaluation practice.

Possess the relevant knowledge for conducting assessment activities. To effectively carry out assess practices, one must possess the corresponding assessment knowledge, which is the knowledge foundation for solving the issue of teachers "wanting to do but not knowing how" in assessment practice, and it is also the prerequisite for understanding evaluation.

Knowledge of assessment/evaluation

1. Types of evaluation

There are several types of evaluations commonly used in educational settings.

- Diagnostic evaluation: This form of evaluation takes place at the outset of instruction to assess the existing knowledge of students and their preparedness for learning.
- Formative evaluation: Implemented throughout the educational journey, these evaluative practices deliver continuous insights to both participants and educators, enabling them to refine their methods and tactics as needed.

- Summative evaluation: Conducted at the conclusion of a designated timeframe or module, the final assessment evaluates the overall performance and ascertains if the intended learning goals have been achieved.
- Criterion-referenced evaluation: Evaluates personal achievements in relation to established criteria, enabling straightforward comparisons among various individuals or groups.
- Norm-referenced evaluation: This approach assesses individuals by comparing their performance against that of their peers in a specific group, frequently employing standardized tests or assessments.
- Self-evaluation: educators assess their teaching effectiveness through introspection and evaluation, pinpointing their skills and areas needing enhancement for growth.
- Peer evaluation: Educators assess and review each other's instructional methods, offering valuable insights and recommendations for enhancement.
- Student evaluation: Pupils assess the instructional techniques of their educators, how content is shared, the organization of the classroom, and various other factors, providing insights into their educational experiences and the level of satisfaction derived from the course.

2. Principles of assessment

- Long-term persistence: When conducting a summative evaluation of students, in addition to focusing on a key achievement, attention should also be paid to examining the students' daily learning situations. The students' long-term learning performance should be considered as an important basis for assessing their academic level.
- Comprehensive principle: Students' academic progress is an overall process that involves complex changes in their knowledge, emotions, intentions, and actions. Therefore, it is necessary to adopt various methods to comprehensively examine students' learning performance.
- Simplicity and practicality: Evaluation is a complex system, but its complexity should be manifested in the development process. The tools, scales, and exams developed should be easy to operate.
- Prudence and fairness: Summative evaluation is a significant academic assessment with important social significance, and it cannot be carried out lightly. It must be handled with the utmost care, striving for accuracy, objectivity, and comprehensiveness (Niu, 2018).

11.2.3.2 Utilizing assessment

In the process of carrying out evaluation tasks, it is essential to be skilled in choosing and utilizing various evaluation techniques and instruments.

Selecting assessment methods and tools. Various assessment types serve distinct purposes and offer unique advantages. Various assessment objectives necessitate the use of distinct methods and tools for evaluation. Instructors ought to possess proficiency in selecting evaluation techniques that align with the needs of making instructional choices.

Create tools and methods for assessment. Beyond merely identifying available assessment methods and tools, it is essential for educators to be skilled in creating evaluation strategies that align with the requirements of instructional choices.

Implement assessments scientifically and skillfully. This applies to both standardized external tools and those that are custom-designed. Educators should be equipped to design evaluation strategies and specify assessment criteria that align with the evaluation's intended goals effectively and adeptly utilize various assessment methods. Conduct an evaluation. Points allocation and then interpret the assessment findings with a scientific approach. A teacher's assessment literacy is indicated by their ability to demonstrate scientific proficiency and skillfulness in evaluating assessments.

Examples of formative assessment tools

Formative evaluation is an ongoing assessment that is integrated into the learning process. Its primary purpose is to help teachers understand students' learning information in a timely manner and provide personalized teaching feedback to students. This enables teachers to adjust and improve the next teaching segment, thereby promoting student learning and enhancing teaching effectiveness. In terms of formative evaluation, there are five commonly used evaluation methods: evaluative tests, evaluation scales, classroom observations, learning logs, and growth portfolios (Lu, 2009). The following formative assessment scales are derived from Wang Jianping's research and teaching practice (Wang & Huang, 2023). Three specific cases are presented to show formative assessment scales in different stages of picture book reading instruction.

• **Case one: Evaluation of reading and recitation task**

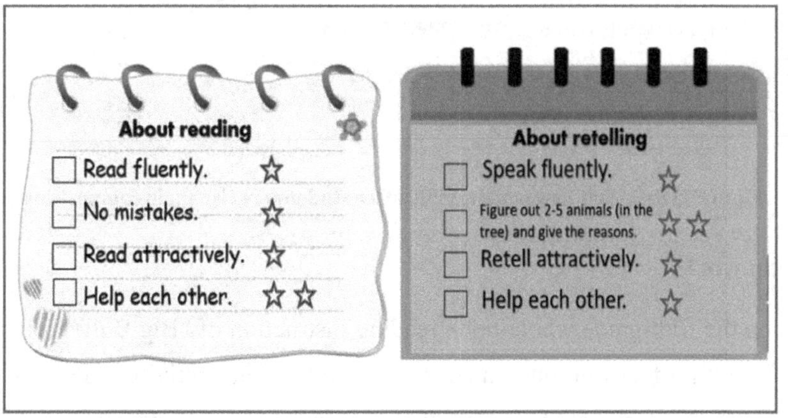

Figure 11.6 Reading and recitation evaluation scale

Activity 2 **This scale evaluates students' following three skills and quality: ____________________, ____________________, and ____________________.**

- **Case two: Evaluation of post-reading paraphrastic tasks**

Figure 11.7 Evaluation criteria

Figure 11.8 A self-assessment form by students

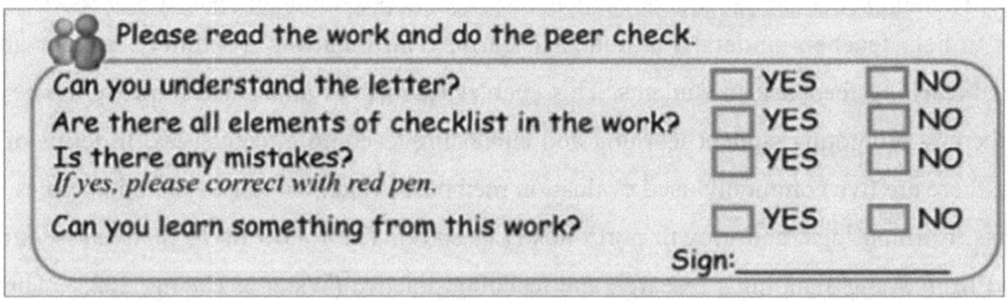

Figure 11.9 Peer evaluation scale

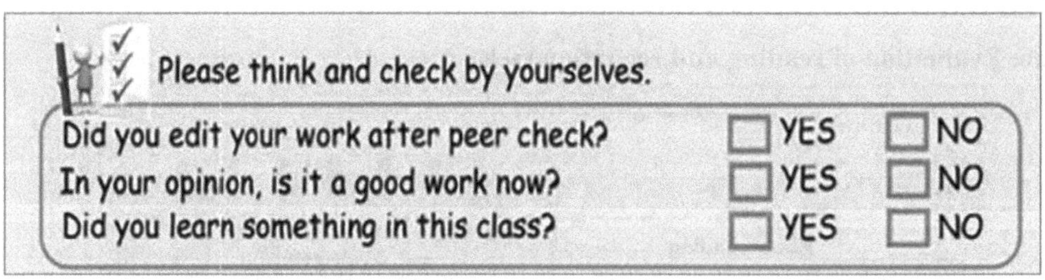

Figure 11.10 Self-assessment scale after students revise their compositions

Activity 3 **Group work**

Case two is based on the fifth-grade whole-book reading instruction of "Big Bull" from "Multidimensional Reading" (Grade 5), with a focus on integrated reading and writing activities. The instruction consists of two class periods: in the first, the reading activity is primary, where students grasp the general meaning of the picture book through self-reading, organize detailed information, and at the same time, the teacher guides students to pay close attention to the consequences brought about by the bull's improper behavior. In the second class period, the main activity is a paraphrastic task, which involves helping the bull write an apology letter. Please reconstruct a more complete teaching design according to the pre-writing, writing, and post-writing stages, using the above evaluation standards and assessment scales.

____

____

____

____

____

____

____

- **Case three: Evaluation of a whole-book reading learning task**

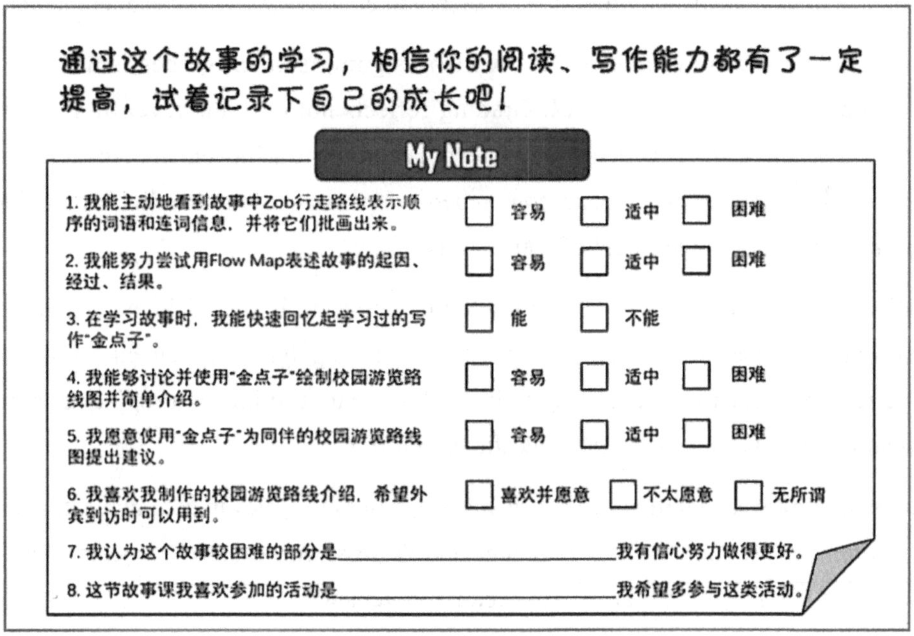

通过这个故事的学习，相信你的阅读、写作能力都有了一定提高，试着记录下自己的成长吧！

My Note

1. 我能主动地看到故事中Zob行走路线表示顺序的词语和连词信息，并将它们批画出来。	□ 容易	□ 适中	□ 困难
2. 我能努力尝试用Flow Map表述故事的起因、经过、结果。	□ 容易	□ 适中	□ 困难
3. 在学习故事时，我能快速回忆起学习过的写作"金点子"。	□ 能	□ 不能	
4. 我能够讨论并使用"金点子"绘制校园游览路线图并简单介绍。	□ 容易	□ 适中	□ 困难
5. 我愿意使用"金点子"为同伴的校园游览路线图提出建议。	□ 容易	□ 适中	□ 困难
6. 我喜欢我制作的校园游览路线介绍，希望外宾到访时可以用到。	□ 喜欢并愿意	□ 不太愿意	□ 无所谓

7. 我认为这个故事较困难的部分是____________________我有信心努力做得更好。

8. 这节故事课我喜欢参加的活动是____________________我希望多参与这类活动。

Figure 11.11 Self-assessment scale for whole-book reading

Activity 4 **Case three is based on the whole-book reading instruction of "Are You Lost, Zob?," a story-based picture book. The learning task for this lesson is to create a campus tour map by imitating the language used in the picture book. Please evaluate this assessment scale from the learning objective, assessment content, language use in the assessment items, etc.**

____

____

____

____

____

____

____

11.2.3.3 Managing assessment

During the conduct of evaluation activities, it is necessary to effectively manage evaluation behaviors.

Grading and academic achievement assessment. Assigning student grades is an important aspect of teachers' professional practice activities. Grading reflects not only the level of students' academic achievement but also the level at which teachers evaluate student achievement. Academic achievement assessment is based on grading and takes a comprehensive consideration of individual student's learning abilities, learning progress, and the extent of their efforts.

The application of assessment results. The essence of assessment is very rich and not limited to narrow rankings, screening, and selection. Teachers should be adept at applying assessment results to educational decisions and research, such as promoting individual student learning, improving teaching methods, developing school curricula, and advancing educational reforms.

The communication of assessment results. The value of assessment lies in communication and feedback; evaluation that promotes learning requires communicating assessment results to students while emphasizing the strengths of their learning and the areas that need improvement.

11.2.2.4 Evaluate assessment

After the evaluation activity is concluded, promptly evaluate and reflect on the assessment activity.

Identify unethical and illegal behaviors in the application of evaluation methods and information. Effective assessment requires fairness and reasonableness towards each student, and the maintenance of each student's legal rights and dignity.

Reflect on inappropriate methods and tools in evaluation practice. For different assessment purposes, content, subjects, and objects of assessment, a detailed analysis and reflection on the appropriateness of assessment methods and tools should be conducted.

Improve assessment behaviors based on assessment reflection. Through comprehensive reflection on the assessment process, timely improvement or refinement of assessment behaviors is both a cyclical process of the interactive relationship between "goals–teaching–learning–assessment" and an effective way to enhance teachers' evaluation literacy.

Activity 5 The two students from different classes in the same grade expressed the same idea in their essays: "I want to be a clown in a circus when I grow up." The comment from the teacher of Class A was, "You lack ambition and are truly unpromising," while the comment from the teacher of Class B was, "May you bring laughter to the whole world." Please evaluate the comments made by these two teachers.

____

____

____

____

____

____

____

11.3 Teaching Reflection

Teaching is an art that requires constant reflection to ensure that both teachers and students are continually improving. In the context of instructing students in English, it is essential to grasp the subtle distinctions of the language, the influence of cultural backgrounds, and the ways to engage learners effectively. Engaging in reflective practices enables teachers to evaluate their instructional strategies, determine their impact, and implement necessary changes to improve educational results.

11.3.1 Understanding Teaching Reflection

Teaching reflection has become an essential aspect of modern education, promoting professional growth, refining instructional methods, and enhancing learners' outcomes. This document is designed to offer an all-encompassing model for educators to partake in reflective practices, utilizing insights from a range of academic sources while incorporating modern viewpoints.

Definition

Teaching reflection entails a thorough evaluation of one's instructional methods, beliefs, and results, aimed at pinpointing necessary enhancements and guiding future practices (Gibbs, 1988). This practice plays an essential role in ongoing professional development, fostering a greater sense of self-awareness and encouraging educators to adopt a more reflective approach to their work.

Benefits of teaching reflection

- **Career advancement:** Engaging in reflective practices allows educators to recognize their competencies and areas needing enhancement, thereby directing their efforts toward personal development. This process fosters ongoing education and skill advancement through the promotion of introspection and improvement in one's professional journey (Korthagen, 2014).
- **Enhanced teaching practices:** By engaging in thoughtful evaluation, educators can assess their instructional techniques and make necessary modifications. This results in teaching strategies that are more efficient and tailored to meet the varied needs of learners.
- **Improved student learning:** By reflecting on student feedback and performance, teachers can make informed decisions about instructional changes that enhance student engagement, motivation, and academic achievement.
- **Promotion of ethical and emotional awareness:** Reflection helps teachers understand their beliefs, values, and emotions related to teaching. It promotes empathy, emotional intelligence, and ethical considerations in the classroom.

Teaching reflection holds a crucial place in the competency-based curriculum, as it allows teachers to assess and enhance their skills that may not be easily measurable through conventional means (Hong, 2022). It fosters good doctor-patient (or teacher-student) relationships, promotes professional identity, and encourages deep learning.

11.3.2 Steps to Engage in Teaching Reflection

Establish a reflective mindset. Begin by cultivating a mindset that values reflection as an integral part of teaching and learning. Recognize that reflection is not a one-time event but a continuous process that permeates all aspects of teaching (Rolfe et al., 2001).

Identify a focus area. Select a specific teaching event, lesson, or interaction to reflect upon. This could be a challenging situation, a successful outcome, or an area where you feel you could improve (Seymour & Watt, 2015).

Gather data. Obtain information from various sources, such as student feedback, classroom observations, teaching journals, and peer evaluations. Ensure that the data is comprehensive and representative of one's teaching practices (Guo et al., 2014).

Analyze the experience. Analyze the experience by Utilizing a structured reflection model, such as Gibbs' Reflective Cycle (Gibbs, 1988). This contains describing the event, exploring feelings and thoughts, evaluating the implications, and formulating an action plan. For example, describing what happened during the teaching event, asking "How you feel about the event", evaluating "What was the outcome?" "What worked well?" "What could have been improved?", analyzing the underlying causes or assumptions that influenced the event, and giving a conclusion of what have learned, and what to improve in future teaching.

Formulate an action plan

Based on your analysis, develop a concrete action plan outlining specific steps you will take to address the identified areas for improvement. Ensure that the plan is realistic, achievable, and aligned with your professional goals.

Implement and monitor

Put your action plan into practice and monitor its effectiveness. Regularly reflect on your progress and adjust the plan as needed to ensure continuous improvement.

Share and collaborate

Share your reflections with colleagues, mentors, or peers to gain diverse perspectives and insights. Collaborative reflection can enhance the depth and quality of your reflections and foster a supportive professional community (Daniel et al., 2013).

11.3.3 Models and Tools for Teaching Reflection

Several models and tools can facilitate the teaching reflection process, including:

11.3.3.1 Gibb's reflective cycle

Gibb's reflective cycle (Gibbs, 1988) is a widely used model that guides teachers through the stages of description, feelings, evaluation, analysis, and conclusion (see Figure 11.12).

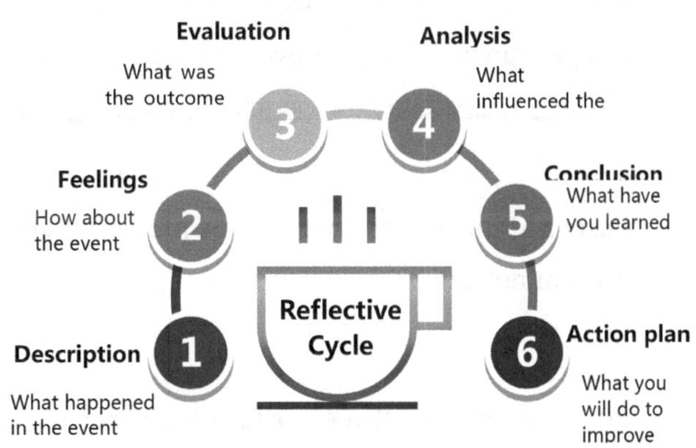

Figure 11.12 Gibb's Reflective Cycle (Gibbs, 1988)

The figure starts from the top with “Description” and then transitions in a clockwise direction to the next stage until it reaches the bottom with “Action Plan”. Each stage is part of the reflective process, helping individuals or teams gain a deeper understanding of the events they experienced and learn and grow from them.

11.3.3.2 Reflection Rubric

Reflection rubric (Wald, et al., 2024) can be used to describe levels of reflection, such as habitual action, thoughtful action, and critical reflection, to assess the depth and quality of reflections (see Figure 11.13).

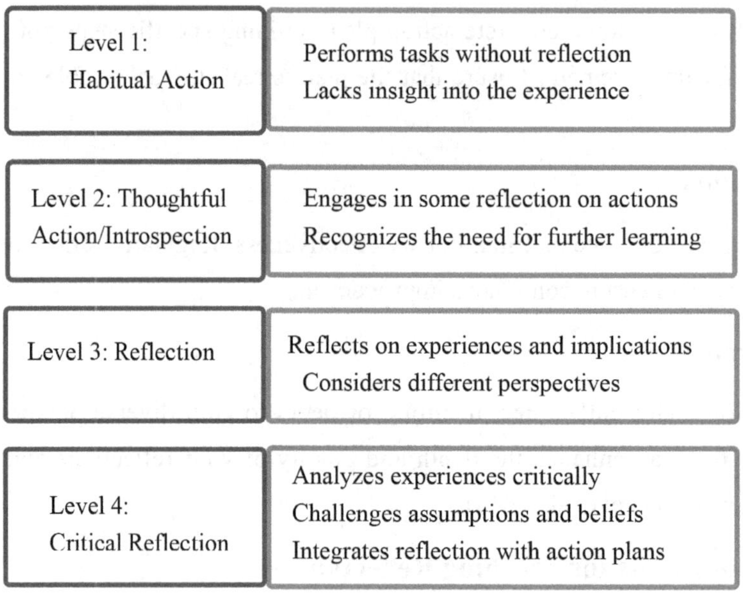

Figure 11.13 REFLECT Rubric (Wald, et al., 2024)

The figure starts from the bottom with “Level 1: Habitual Action,” representing the initial stage of reflection where individuals perform tasks without reflecting. This is followed by “Level 2: Thoughtful Action/Introspection,” where individuals begin to think and introspect about their behavior. “Level 3: Reflection” represents deeper reflection, where individuals not only reflect on their experiences but also consider different perspectives and their implications. Finally, “Level 4: Critical Reflection” is the highest level of reflection, where individuals critically analyze their experiences, challenge assumptions and beliefs, and integrate them into action plans.

This Reflect rubric can help teachers and students understand the different levels of reflection and encourage them to strive towards deeper levels of reflection.

11.3.3.3 Flash cards

Flash cards (Seymour & Watt, 2015) are prompts that encourage teachers to actively look out for neglected needs and reflect on their teaching practices (see Figure 11.14).

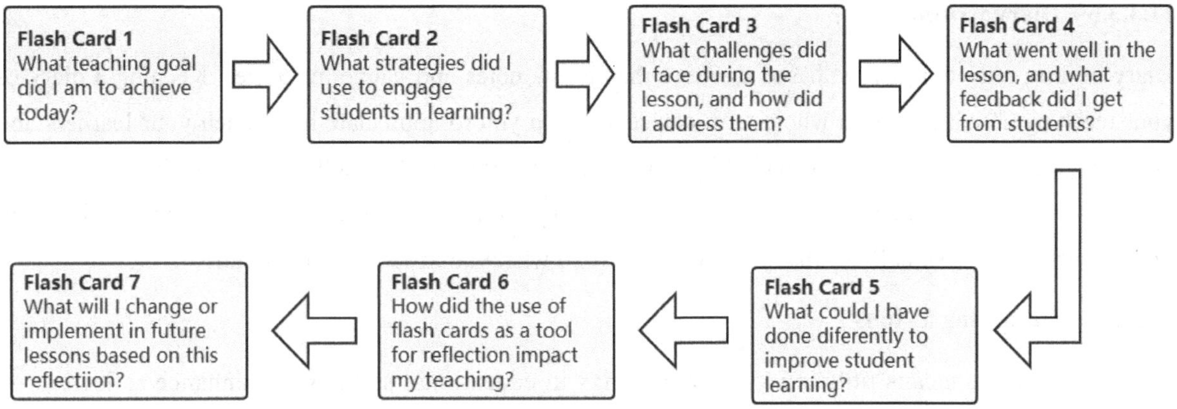

Figure 11.14 Flash cards sequence (Seymour & Watt, 2015)

This sequence of flash cards guides a teacher through a structured reflection process, encouraging them to consider their teaching goals, strategies, challenges, successes, and areas for improvement. It also prompts them to think about the effectiveness of the reflection tool itself (the flash cards) and to plan for future lessons based on their insights. This kind of reflective practice can lead to continuous professional development and enhanced teaching effectiveness.

11.3.3.4 Pendleton's Model

Pendleton's Model (Pendleton et al., 2013) is a structured approach to asking and answering questions about teaching experiences to stimulate reflection. Pendleton's Model is an educational feedback model used in medical education, which can also be applied to teaching reflection. This model typically includes the following steps: prepare, present, discuss, summarize, and plan (see Figure 11.15).

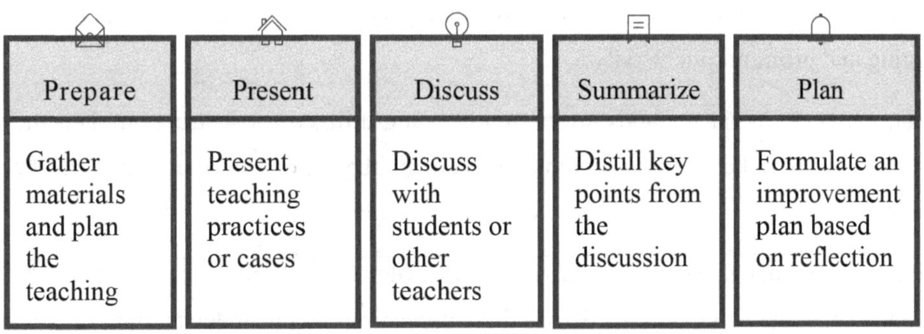

Figure 11.15 Pendleton's Model (Pendleton et al., 2013)

This figure starts at the top with "Prepare," indicating the beginning of the reflection process, and then transitions to the next step in a clockwise direction, ending with "Plan" at the bottom. Each step is part of the teaching reflection process, helping teachers to think systematically and improve their teaching practices.

11.3.3.5 Diary writing

Diary writing reflection can be based on more than a few notes and vague memories. Keeping a diary of your teaching activities over a whole term can really help you to appreciate how much your learners and you yourself have progressed,and why. If you find that the story you are telling in your diary is not very positive, this can motivate you to make changes and explore new options. In this way, you can begin to know yourself professionally—what you are good at and what you need to work on more.

11.3.3.6 Recording lessons

Recording lessons means utilizing video recordings in educational settings can enhance reflection on teaching practices, offering a concrete means to review one's instructional methods and facilitating an impartial evaluation of actions taken in the classroom. Below is a detailed approach to implementing video as a reflective practice in teaching.

Identify a particular instructional event: Focus on a distinct lesson or segment of a lesson for your analysis. This may involve a particularly difficult or successful tasks, or a point where one identified a possible area for enhancement.

Capture the lesson: It is important to film the entire session, documenting the instructor's activities along with the students' interactions. This documentation will offer a detailed understanding of the educational dynamics at play.

Examine the footage: View the recording multiple times, taking breaks to evaluate particular segments. Take into account the following elements:

- Instructor engagement: Are you actively involved and attentive to the learners? Do you implement questioning strategies effectively? Are you fostering an environment in your classroom that is welcoming and promotes inclusivity?
- Teaching methods: What methods are currently being utilized for instruction? Did they work? Is it necessary to modify the teaching methods in order to align them more closely with the needs of the students?
- Participation of students: Are they involved and contributing actively during the lesson? Do they seem to grasp the concepts being presented? Are there indications of misunderstanding or lack of interest?
- Evaluation: In what manner is student comprehension being measured? Is the evaluation process oriented towards ongoing improvements or intended to evaluate overall outcomes? Do you offer feedback that is timely and helpful?

Consider and evaluate: Reflect on what aspects were successful and identify areas that require enhancement based on your insights. Take a moment to contemplate the following inquiries:

Which methods proved to be successful? What do you believe contributed to their success? Which methods proved to be less effective in my approach? What reasons might explain their diminished effectiveness? What strategies can be implemented to enhance teaching effectiveness? What strategies can be implemented to enhance the support provided to students?

Engage in dialogue: Exchange your insights with fellow educators or advisors. Engaging in conversations about one's insights and evaluations can lead to meaningful revelations, fostering innovative approaches to teaching.

Formulate a strategy for ongoing enhancement: Drawing on your insights, create an approach aimed at fostering future growth. Explore ways to integrate innovative tactics or methods into your instructional practices to better facilitate student learning.

11.3.4 Four Categories of Educational Reflection

Self-reflection: Analyzing one's own teaching methods and experiences. This involves assessing the effectiveness of one's teaching methods, pinpointing opportunities for enhancement, and formulating new tactics based on personal observations.

Peer reflection: A cooperative process where fellow educators assess teaching approaches and offer insights. It creates a nurturing atmosphere in which educators can exchange ideas, draw insights from the experiences of their peers, and obtain valuable feedback for improvement.

Situational reflection: Considering particular educational experiences like delivered lessons, interactions with students, or evaluation activities. It allows educators to evaluate how certain methods work effectively in different scenarios.

Theoretical reflection: Analyzing wider educational concepts and principles that govern teaching methodologies. This entails a thorough assessment of current theories, examining their relevance or lack thereof in various teaching contexts.

Student reflection: Students are an excellent source of feedback on your teaching: arguably the best. Their information is based on a whole series of lessons rather than on isolated examples, and they usually have a fairly clear idea of how well they are learning and why. Moreover, they appreciate being consulted, usually make serious efforts to give helpful feedback; and the process tends to enhance rather than damage teacher-student relationships.

Applications to students should be phrased so as to direct their appraisal towards themselves as well as to you, and towards positive suggestions rather than negative criticisms. A structured questionnaire is one possibility (see Figure 11.16).

Name______________________ Class________________________

1. On the whole I feel I am learning very well/fairly well/don't know/not very well/badly
2. I find the lessons interesting/moderately interesting /boring
3. Things I would like to do MORE in our course:
   pronunciation practice/vocabulary/grammar/listening/speaking/reading/writing/literature/homework/group or pair work/individual work
   Other (say what):
4. Things I would like to do LESS in our course:
   pronunciation practice/vocabulary/grammar/listening/speaking/reading/writing/literature/homework/group or pair work/individual work
   Other (say what):
5. In order to get the most out of the course, I need to try to...
6. In order to make the course better, my suggestions to my teacher are...
7. Anything else:

(Ur, 1996)

Figure 11.16 A questionnaire of teaching reflection from students

11.3.5 Practical Strategies for Teaching Reflection

Establish a routine for reflection: Integrate regular reflection sessions into your daily routine or schedule specific times for reflection activities throughout the school year (Hatton & Smith, 1995). Encourage teachers to maintain a reflective journal where they document their thoughts, feelings, and observations about their teaching practices.

Use different models for reflection: Incorporate various reflection models such as Gibb's reflection cycle (experience, feeling, analysis, conclusion), The 4F model (Feelings, Findings, Future actions), or The Onion model (multiple layers of reflection) to facilitate different perspectives on teaching practices.

Facilitate avenues for educators' advancement: Motivate teachers to engage in workshops, seminars, or digital courses that focus on reflective practices and their professional development. Create an environment where educators can engage in collaborative efforts, allowing them to exchange their experiences and gain valuable insights from one another.

Incorporate digital tools: Adopt various digital resources such as interactive storytelling, video documentation of classroom exchanges, or web-based forums to support reflective practice beyond conventional environments. These resources offer a visual representation of instructional methods that can be examined and critiqued during reflective meetings.

Foster a culture of open communication: Establish an environment that supports educators in voicing their worries, difficulties, and achievements without apprehension of being judged or criticized. Promote a culture of open communication by holding regular team gatherings or individual conversations, allowing educators to exchange valuable insights regarding each other's instructional methods.

Emphasize moral implications: Foster a sense of ethical responsibility by contemplating topics surrounding diversity, inclusion, fairness, and societal equity within the educational environment. Teachers should reflect on the implications of their instructional methods on various student populations, ensuring they implement changes necessary to uphold fairness and equity in their educational approaches.

Incorporate evaluation into the process of reflection: Implement formative evaluation methods such as quizzes, feedback forms, or observational checklists to collect insights from students regarding their experiences in the classroom. Such feedback serves as crucial information for evaluating teaching methods and implementing necessary adjustments in response to learner input.

Provide opportunities for professional development: Encourage teachers to participate in workshops, seminars, or online courses related to teaching reflection and professional growth. Foster a culture of collaboration among teachers where they can share their experiences and learn from others' insights.

Utilize technology tools: Embrace technological tools such as digital storytelling, video recordings of classroom interactions, or online discussion forums to facilitate reflective practices outside traditional settings. These tools provide visual evidence of teaching practices for further analysis and evaluation during reflection sessions.

Encourage open dialogue: Create a supportive environment where teachers feel comfortable sharing their concerns, challenges, and successes without fear of judgment or criticism. Encourage open dialogue through regular team meetings or one-on-one discussions where teachers can provide constructive feedback on each other's teaching practice.

Focus on ethical considerations: Promote ethical awareness by reflecting on issues related to diversity, inclusion, equity, and social justice in the classroom. Encourage teachers to consider how their teaching practices impact different groups of students and make necessary adjustments for fairness and justice in education.

Integrate assessment into reflection: Use formative assessment techniques such as quizzes, surveys, or observation checklists to gather feedback from students regarding their learning experiences in the classroom. This information can be valuable input for reflecting on instructional strategies and making necessary improvements based on student responses.

11.3.6 Lifelong Learning

In Chapter 1, Chapter 8, and other chapters, teacher qualities or teacher characteristics are mentioned by numerous experienced, seasoned teachers with their lists of attributes, and they all differ in a variety of ways. Now, take a look at another list of successful language-teaching characteristics, a synthesis of several unpublished sources, and they are especially for language teachers. You may wish to use this list as a self-check to earmark some areas for continued professional growth, to prioritize those areas, and to articulate some specific goals to pursue.

The items on all lists make a substantive list of challenges for your professional growth. However, they are not prescriptions! The key to healthy teacher development is to take a reflective approach, which "requires that teachers have the opportunities to observe, evaluate, and reflect systematically on their classroom practices in order to promote understanding and self-awareness and to make changes when necessary" (McDonough, 2006). So, treat such lists as suggestions, possibilities, and perhaps mental prods to stimulate some further growth (see Figure 11.17).

Background Knowledge

1. Understands organizational, pragmatic, and sociocultural systems of the English language.
2. Comprehensively grasps basic principles of language learning and teaching.
3. Has fluent competence in speaking, writing, listening to, and reading English.
4. Knows through experience what it is like to learn a foreign language.
5. Understands the close connection between language and culture.
6. Keeps up with the field through regular reading, collaboration with others, and conference/workshop attendance.

Pedagogical Skills

1. Has a comprehensive, informed approach to language teaching.
2. Efficiently designs and executes lesson plans.
3. Understands and appropriately uses a variety of techniques.
4. Monitors lessons as they unfold and makes effective mid-lesson alterations.
5. Effectively perceives students' linguistic and personal needs, along with their various styles, preferences, strengths, and weaknesses.
6. Gives optimal feedback to students.
7. Stimulates interaction, cooperation, and teamwork in the classroom.
8. Uses appropriate principles of classroom management.
9. Uses effective, clear presentation skills.
10. Creatively adapts textbook material and other audio, visual, and technological aids.
11. Innovatively creates brand-new materials when needed.
12. Uses authentic, washback-giving techniques to assess students.

Interpersonal Skills

1. Is aware of cross-cultural differences and is sensitive to students' cultural traditions.
2. Enjoys people; shows enthusiasm, warmth, rapport, and appropriate humor.
3. Values the opinions and abilities of students.
4. Is patient in working with students of lesser ability.
5. Offers challenges to students of exceptionally high ability.
6. Cooperates harmoniously and candidly with colleagues, including seeking opportunities to share thoughts, ideas, and techniques.

Personal Qualities
1. Is well organized, conscientious in meeting commitments, and dependable.
2. Is flexible when things go awry.
3. Engages in regular self-reflection on teaching practices and strives to learn from those reflective processes.
4. Maintains an inquisitive mind in trying out new ways of teaching.
5. Sets short-term and long-term goals for continued professional growth.
6. Maintains and exemplifies high ethical and moral standards.

Figure 11.17 Characteristics of a successful language teacher

Activity 3 If you are asked to write a diary to reflect your teaching, what would you consider to write in the diary? Please design an outline for your diary.

____

____

____

____

____

____

____

Thinking and Doing

A. Discussion Questions

1. What is your understanding of observation, evaluation, and reflection? Please explain them from "what", "why", and "how".

2. Talk about your understanding of reflection and how to improve reflection behavior from the perspective of enhancing reflection awareness.

B. Practice

Observe one of your teachers' classroom teaching and note down the important process. Try to write a feedback report about the teacher's classroom teaching behavior so as to help the teacher to improve his/her teaching.

C. Exercises for instructional skills

1. Which of the following about "observation" is NOT correct?
   A. It is a teaching-training course.
   B. It is unnecessary to have a reflection after observation.
   C. It is a part of in-service teacher support.
   D. Both the observer and the being observed need to have some agreements for the observation.

2. Which of the following about "evaluation" is correct?
   A. Evaluation mainly refers to the test and assessment of learners.
   B. Assessment, evaluation, and appraisal refer to the same thing.
   C. Learner evaluation is more important than teacher evaluation.
   D. When evaluating, an observer may focus on the testing, the course design, and the course implementation.

3. If a teacher wants to check how much students have learned at the end of a term, he/she would give them a(an) __________.
   A. diagnostic test　　B. placement test
   C. proficiency test　　D. achievement test

4. Supplementing, deleting, simplifying and reordering are often used in __________.
   A. adapting teaching materials　　B. delivering teaching materials
   C. evaluating teaching materials　　D. presenting teaching materials

5. Constant reflection comes from __________.
   A. learning teaching
   B. feedback from your colleagues and students
   C. feedback from you
   D. feedback from your diary

Checklist

Mark the questions with a check (√) if your answer is yes.

☐ Have I understood the concepts and principles of observation, assessment, and reflection?

☐ Have I grasped the different kinds of evaluations in teaching?

☐ Have I known the different types of observation, assessment, and reflection?

☐ Have I known the main contents of teacher assessment literacy for a modern teacher?

☐ Can I use the observation, assessment, and reflection strategies properly in English teaching and research?

Reflective Journal

Please write down your reflections on what you have/have not learned in this chapter.

◇ The essential skills I need to possess and develop for English teaching:

____

____

____

____

____

◇ Anything I wish to further explore (i.e., puzzles and difficulties):

____

____

____

____

____

References

Brophy, J. E., & Good, T. L. (1986). Teacher-student relationships: Causes and consequences. In M. C. Wittrock (Ed.), *Handbook of research on teaching* (3rd ed., pp. 317–329). Macmillan.

Cui, Y. H. (2012). 论课堂观察 LICC 范式：一种专业的听评课 [On the LICC paradigm of classroom observation: A professional approach to lesson observation and evaluation]. *Educational Research*, (5), 79–83.

Cui, Y. H., Shen, Y., Zhou, W. Y., et al. (2007). 课堂观察 20 问答 [20 questions and answers on classroom observation]. *Contemporary Educational Science*, (24), 6–16.

Daniel, G., Auhl, G., & Hastings, W. (2013). Collaborative feedback and reflection for professional growth: Preparing first-year pre-service teachers for participation in the community of practice. *Asia-Pacific Journal of Teacher Education*, *41*(2), 159–171. https://doi.org/10.1080/1359866X.2013.777025

Gan, L. (2018). 中学英语听力教学的课堂观察 [Classroom observation of English listening teaching in middle schools]. *English Learning*, (3), 15–20.

Gibbs, G. (1988). *Learning by doing: A guide to teaching and learning methods*. Further Education Unit, Oxford Brookes University.

Ginsberg, M. B., & Daniels, D. H. (2014). The impact of multiple observations on teacher evaluation. In A. J. Artzt (Ed.), *Teacher evaluation policies: The role of multiple observations* (pp. 45–67). Teachers College Press.

Goldberg, M., & Theune, M. (2012). The power of peer observation to improve teaching. *The Teaching Professor*, *26*(7), 1–4.

Guo, J. J., Li, M., & Wang, J. Y. (2014). 解析教学反思：成分、过程、策略、方法 [The analysis on teaching reflection: Component, process, strategy, method]. *Teacher Education Research*, *26*(4), 29–34.

Hatton, N., & Smith, D. (1995). Reflection in teacher education: Towards definition and implementation. *Teaching and Teacher Education*, *11*(1), 33–49.

Hong, M. (2022). 高师生教学反思能力培养的实验研究 [Experimental research on cultivating the reflective teaching ability of pre-service teachers in normal universities]. *Advances in Psychology*, *12*(8), 2692–2699.

Korthagen, F. A. J. (2014). Promoting core reflection in teacher education: Deepening professional growth. *In International teacher education: Promising pedagogies* (Part A) (pp. 73–89). Emerald Group Publishing. https://doi.org/10.1108/S1479-368720140000022007

Li, X., & Yu, S. Z. (2016). 中小学四类观评课模式比较 [Comparison of four types of observation and evaluation models for primary and secondary school lessons]. *Educational Science Research*, (7), 10–13.

Lu, Z. W. (2009). 英语教学论 [*English language teaching methodology*]. East China Normal University Press.

McDonough, K. (2006). Action research and the professional development of graduate teaching assistants. *The Modern Language Journal*, *90*(1), 33–47.

Nickerson, R. S. (1998). Confirmation bias: A ubiquitous phenomenon in many guises. *Review of General Psychology*, *2*(2), 175–220. https://doi.org/10.1037/1089-2680.2.2.175

Niu, R. X. (2018). 教学评价研究 40 年回顾、反思与展望 [A review, reflection, and prospect of 40 years of research on teaching evaluation]. *Curriculum, Teaching Material, and Method*, *38*(11), 60–66.

Pendleton, D., Scofield, T., Tate, P., et al. (1984). *The consultation: An approach to learning and teaching*. Oxford University Press.

Rolfe, G., Freshwater, D., & Jasper, M. (2001). *Critical reflection in nursing and the helping professions: A user's guide*. Palgrave Macmillan.

Rosenthal, R., & Jacobson, L. (1968). *Pygmalion in the classroom: Teacher expectation and pupils' intellectual development*. Holt, Rinehart & Winston.

Seymour, P., & Watt, M. (2015). The professional competencies toolkit: Teaching reflection with flash cards. *Medical Education*, *49*(5), 518.

Shen, Y., & Gui, Y. H. (2008). 课堂观察：走向专业的听评课 [*Classroom observation: Moving towards professional lesson observation and evaluation*]. East China Normal University Press.

Stiggins, R. J. (1991). Assessment literacy. *Phi Delta Kappan*, *72*(7), 534–539.

Thorndike, E. L. (1920). A constant error in psychological ratings. *Journal of Applied Psychology*, 4, 25–29.

Ur, P. (1996). *A course in language teaching: Practice and theory*. Cambridge University Press.

Wald, H. S., Borkan, J. M., Taylor, J. S., et al. (2012). Fostering and evaluating reflective capacity in medical education: Developing the REFLECT rubric for assessing reflective writing. *Academic Medicine*, *87*(1), 41–50. https://doi.org/10.1097/ACM.0b013e31823b55fa

Wang, J. P., & Huang, Y. (2023). 形成性评价量表在英语绘本阅读教学中的设计与应用 [Design and application of formative assessment scales in English picture book reading instruction]. *English Learning*, (5), 27–31.

Wang, J., & Li, Z. L. (2014). *Classroom observation and analysis techniques* [课堂观察与分析技术]. Gansu Education Press.

Yang, G. H. (2011). 教师评价素养的内涵及框架 [The connotation and framework of teachers' assessment literacy]. *Educational Science Research*, (4), 17–19.

Yu, X. H., Peng, Y., & Hu, T. Y. (2024). 数字化课堂观察与反馈：现状、评述与实现路径 [Digital classroom observation and feedback: Current status, review, and implementation pathways]. *Open Education Research*, *30*(3), 98–108.

Zhang, X. W. (2012). 课堂观察中的伦理初探 [A preliminary exploration of ethics in classroom observation]. *Modern Primary and Secondary Education*, (5), 24–27.

Zheng, D. H. (2010). 教师评价素养的内容框架探析 [An exploration of the content framework for teachers' assessment literacy]. *Educational Science Research*, (10), 34–38.